Namibia
The Last Colony

Namibia
The Last Colony

Edited by Reginald H. Green, Kimmo Kiljunen, Marja-Liisa Kiljunen

Longman

Longman Group Limited
Longman House
Burnt Mill, Harlow, Essex
U.K.

First published 1981

British Library Cataloguing in Publication Data

Namibia.
I. Namibia — History
I. Green, Reginald H II. Kiljunen, Kimmo
III. Kiljunen, Marja-Liisa
968′.8 DT711 80-40465
ISBN 0-582-59734-X
ISBN 0-582-59735-8 Pbk

ISBN 0 582 59735 8 (paper)
59734 X (cased)

Printed in Great Britain by
Butler & Tanner Ltd, Frome and London

Contents

List of Maps

To the people of Namibia and to the success of their struggle for liberation

Notes on contributors

Editors

Reginald Herbold Green, Professorial Fellow, the Institute of Development Studies, University of Sussex; a consultant to the United Nations Institute for Namibia and to SWAPO.

Kimmo Kiljunen, Research Fellow, Labour Institute for Economic Research, Helsinki; 1975–80 at the Institute of Development Studies, University of Sussex.

Marja-Liisa Kiljunen, Research Officer, the Institute of Development Studies, University of Helsinki; 1977–80, Research Officer, the Institute of Development Studies, University of Sussex.

Contributors

Robert Chambers, Fellow, the Institute of Development Studies, University of Sussex.

Justin Ellis, official of the Christian Centre in Windhoek, deported from Namibia in December 1978.

Duncan Innes, Research Fellow, University of Warwick.

Constantine Vaitsos, Professor of Political Economy, University of Athens and Professorial Fellow, the Institute of Development Studies, University of Sussex; a consultant to the Centre on Transnational Corporations.

Rauha Voipio, Head of the Mission School of the Finnish Missionary Society; a lecturer in the Teachers Training College of the Evangelical Lutheran Church of South West Africa, 1947–74.

Preface

Namibia has always been of central concern to Namibians. It has also been of some interest to South Africans. Beyond that, until quite recently, only specialists – ranging from mining companies to missionaries – have seen it as of importance. As a result there is a lack of general literature on Namibia. The quest for information – even for Namibians and specialists – is made very difficult by the colonial regime's quite understandable desire to keep much of Namibian reality secret and to issue statistics and other data which 'prove' its assertions.

This book seeks to present a serious treatment of Namibia – accessible to the general reader but also of use to the specialist and to the Namibian reader. It has evolved from earlier work by the co-editors over several years in several countries. Earlier versions of some of the present chapters appeared in a Finnish volume edited by Kimmo and Marja-Liisa Kiljunen following their 1978 visit to Namibia (*Namibia-Viimeinen Siirtomaa*, Tammi, Helsinki, 1980). Initial work on the statistical section was done by Reginald Green while participating in the 1977 United Nations Institute for Namibia's project on personpower development for an independent Namibia.

The collection of data and the refinement of ideas has been helped by many individuals, Namibians and others. To list all of them would be rather lengthy – and for some now in Namibia unsafe – but the editors wish to make clear their debt and appreciation. We are also grateful to those who helped in the physical preparation of the volume: Lyn Shaw with the technical editing; Francine Spencer, Janice Hingley, Wendy Taylor, Janice Cosham with the typing and retyping of successive drafts; Tarja Wilson and Raili Watkins with translation; Risto Kari in drawing the maps. A special debt is due to Richard Moorsom whose copious and detailed comments were of great value in pointing out errors and in final editing.

The volume was prepared at the Institute of Development Studies at the University of Sussex. Without its generous provision of time, space, secretarial support and a stimulating, supportive atmosphere it would certainly not have been completed. The Scandinavian Institute of African Studies financed the Kiljunens' trip to Namibia and, together with SIDA, made a vital financial contribution to the preparation of the volume.

RHG, KK, MLK
Brighton
January, 1980

1 Unto what end? The crisis of colonialism in Namibia

REGINALD H. GREEN AND KIMMO KILJUNEN

We possess South-West Africa once and for all; it is German territory and must be preserved as such.[1]

– Chancellor von Caprivi, 1893

The future of South West Africa is inextricably tied to that of South Africa. Nothing except war can alter this association between South West Africa and South Africa.[2]

– Prime Minister Smuts, 1947

In the present phase, armed struggle has become the main form of SWAPO's resistance to South Africa's racist, oppressive and exploitative occupation of Namibia.[3]

– SWAPO, 1976

The people of the Territory will have to get independence sooner or later. This political momentum has been set in motion.[4]

– Foreign Minister Botha, 1979

It must be borne in mind that the Namibian people are shedding blood to liberate each and every inch of the Namibian soil, thus each and every inch of the Namibian land must and will belong to the Namibian people.[5]

– S. Nujoma, SWAPO President, 1979

The web of violence

These quotations sum up the continuity and change of Namibia's colonial history over the past century. Violence has been at its core. First, there was the violence of the German conquest, of the attempted Nama–Damara–Herero war of liberation, and of the German reconquest which culminated in genocide. Second, there was the violence of the South African expedition which drove the Germans out, of South African suppression of risings, and of the final conquest of the north. Third, there is the violence of the police, who in 1959 shot down the protestors at the Windhoek Old Location, and who continue to detain and torture. Fourth, there is the violence of the national liberation movement. Fifth, there is the violence of the South African forces ravaging Namibia and striking into Zambia and Angola.

Such a summary understates the pervasiveness of violence. Much is less overt, less immediately apparent. There is the theft of land which has made the African people unable to subsist in their 'reserves' and left only one choice, to work or to starve. There is the contract labour system which breaks up families and makes possible wages below family subsistence because dependents are left in the 'reserves'. There is the systematic seizure, by force, by law and by administrative devices, of most of the usable land, virtually all of the water and all of the mineral and fishing rights.

There is another tier of violence which is designed to justify the first two tiers: the systematic legislation and enforcement of the old Boer tradition of the Transvaal Republic of no equality of black and white, in state or church, life or death, now or forever. This is based on an ideology of inequality which implies the denial of the dignity of the Namibian, the worth of Namibian cultures, and the possibility of Namibian development, as opposed to European development of and in South West Africa.

Colonialism in general and in Namibia

Violence characterizes colonialism in general, not just in Namibia, bearing out, in part, Frantz Fanon's conclusion:

> Colonialism is not a thinking machine, nor a body endowed with reasoning faculties. It is violence in its natural state and it will only yield when confronted with greater violence.[6]

In Namibia violence has been and remains greater than in most African colonies, comparable to that in French Algeria which gave rise to Fanon's comments. The third tier of violence, the ideological attempt to legitimize inequality, is also a general one to some extent.

> Colonial administration, because it is total and tends to oversimplify, very soon manages to disrupt in spectacular fashion the cultural life of a conquered people. This cultural obliteration is made possible by the negation of natural reality, by new legal relations, introduced by the occupying power, by the banishment of the 'natives' and their customs to out-lying districts, by colonial society, by expropriation.[7]

However, the systematic denial of worth to the colonized, combined with the construction of absolute barriers against his becoming one with the colonizers, is virtually unique to South Africa and Namibia. Even in Algeria the destruction was not so complete and an Algerian could aspire to be a second-rank Frenchman.

There are several reasons why the situation in Namibia is different. The first is lateness; while it was Germany's first colony, it was one of the last colonies to be seized. Today, Namibia is the last major colony. Germany and South Africa, as latecomers to the colonial sweepstakes, were in general hastier and more brutal, and South Africa, as the last colonial power with a will to hold, is necessarily more committed to using force to do so.

The second reason is that Namibia has been a settler colony. The thoroughness of land theft, the tenacity of settlers in holding on, the exclusion of colonized people, have tended to be emphasized in settler colonies. One could cite Kenya vis-à-vis Ghana, Algeria vis-à-vis Tunisia, Angola and Mozambique vis-à-vis Nigeria and Madagascar.

The third reason is that Namibia is economically and strategically important to South Africa. Namibia is, given its natural resources, an exceptionally rich country. The remittances from and the exports to Namibia add up to a significant share of the Republic's investible surplus and foreign exchange earnings. Moreover South Africa's strategic vulnerability – dictated by geography – in respect to her colony has been much greater than was typical in more conventional colonial relations. Namibia gives direct access to the Atlantic in the west and stands as a buffer area against hostile black Africa in the north.

The fourth is a psychological reason. The admission that a sophisticated economy and a population including a large European community, which had long been a virtual province of South Africa, could become an independent black African state challenges the psychological security and the worldview of South Africa and its white tribes in a way utterly different from the challenge that the independence of India posed to the United Kingdom and the British.

The fifth point is that South African racism is unique. No parallel system based on a coherent, internalized, operationalized ideology existed in any other colonial territory. To accept the independence of Namibia as a unitary, black state would not merely involve admitting the inapplicability of that ideology to Namibia but would also deal a savage blow to its moral, logical and practical justification in South Africa itself.

The sixth reason is that South Africa is not a true capitalist core economy; its ability to hold remittance and trade gains in a neo-colonial relationship is suspect. Until the late 1960s this was a very strong point; today it may be less so. Geographic and historical links suggest that, if a neo-colonial settlement were to be achieved, a South African Customs Union and Rand Monetary Zone membership might continue as well as the technical assistance needed to ensure that economic choices, tender documents, purchasing policy and construction contracts still went South Africa's way. (Botswana and Swaziland have not found it in the least easy to loosen dependency links.) However, South Africa may not perceive fully its present stronger position in neo-colonial economic terms, so this point may remain of some real significance.

The seventh point involves the interplay of the preceding six. The violence of the liberation/repression struggle of the past fifteen years makes a safe, neo-colonial or amicable, post-colonial solution very hard to envisage or articulate, much less to negotiate or implement. The totality of the political economy of theft and of statutorily enforced racism means that there is no dependable middle class to serve as compradores or junior partners to head a neo-colony. Equally they have created a South African, and especially settler, worldview which makes negotiation with Africans who do not believe Europeans to be superior almost impossible. The opposite side of the process is equally stark. No Namibian nationalist trusts the word or deed of South Africa, and what appear to be narrow gaps or only marginally different counter proposals in tentative negotiations are read by Namibians in terms of a history of violence, theft, deceit and rejection of their humanity.

Finally the war, while it has made South Africa more willing to concede something, has equally rapidly radicalized the Namibian liberation movement. The 'safeguards' for settler ranches of trade with South Africa for 'reserved seats' or company mining concessions that would have been accepted readily in 1964 are no longer open to consideration in 1979. The torture, the massacres and the detentions have had much to do with that change, as have the abortive attempts by South Africa to create a credible, junior-partner African 'leadership' for a neo-colonial settlement. The impact on the approach and sophistication of the liberation movement in socio-economic and political and economic analysis has been marked.

From mandate to illegally occupied territory

In 1915 South African troops occupied German South West Africa. South Africa's desire to annex at once was frustrated, but in 1920 the League of Nations awarded the mandate over the territory to the British Crown, to be administered by South Africa. When the League of Nations was superseded by the United Nations after the Second World War the mandate system was modified into trusteeship. South Africa, however, refused to enter into a trusteeship agreement.

This act, together with South Africa's refusal to regard the United Nations as the successor to the League even in respect to the reporting obligations of the mandate, started an international juridical and political controversy. This culminated in 1966 in the United Nations General Assembly resolution (carried by a large majority) to terminate South Africa's mandate over Namibia and to make the territory the direct responsibility of the United Nations. This position was confirmed by the United Nations Security Council in 1969. In 1971 the International Court of Justice advised, in an almost unanimous decision, that the termination of the mandate by the General Assembly was valid. The decision, which has been accepted by all but two United Nations members (South Africa and the United Kingdom), held that, from the date of the mandate's termination, South Africa was in illegal occupation. Further, it held that South Africa, as an illegal occupier, had no right to carry out economic transactions, e.g. mining contracts, fishing conventions, as if it were a lawful administrator, and that United Nations member states were bound not to give cognisance to such actions. It also ruled that the United Nations had the right to create new structures for the administration of Namibia as a trust territory.

The legal and legislative victories were one thing; enforcing them has proved quite another. The United Nations Council for Namibia is, given the ruling of the International Court of Justice, the *de jure* governing authority for Namibia. However, *de facto* power remains with the South African occupation forces and administration. While at least some governments, such as the United States government, have advised their companies that they accept the International Court of Justice rul-

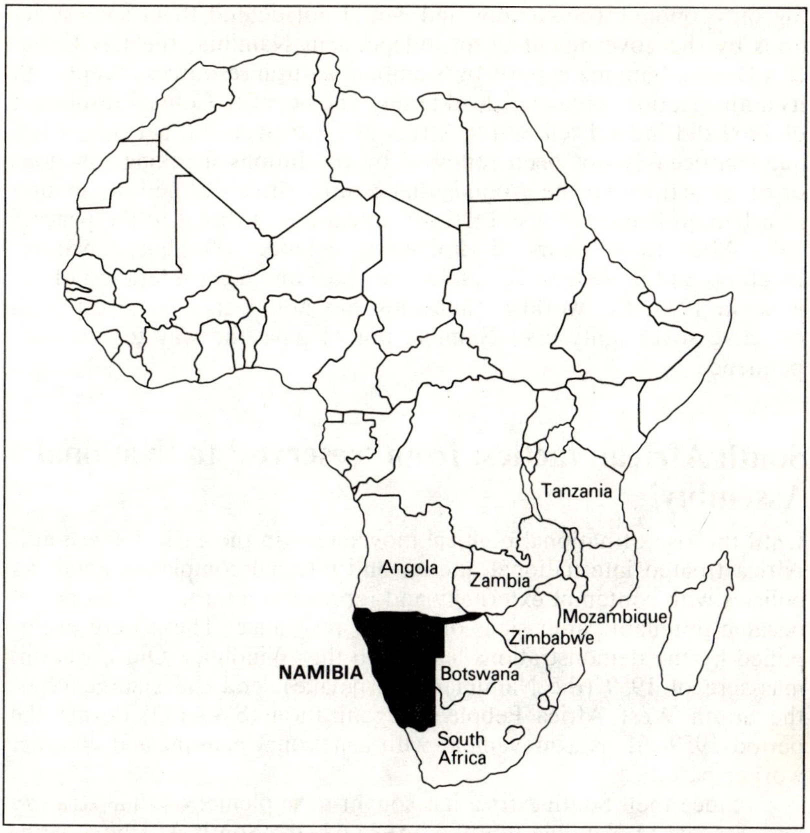

Map 1.1 Namibia and her neighbours

ing on economic transactions and would not defend them against actions by the government of an independent Namibia, the UN Council's Decree banning exports of Namibian natural resources except with its authorization remains a dead letter. The Security Council resolution of 1969 did indeed tell South Africa to hand over and get out; it has quite noticeably not been followed by resolutions invoking sanctions or other actions on the grounds that South Africa's armed occupation of a United Nations Trust Territory constitutes a threat to the peace.

After thirty years of diplomatic debate, 900 United Nations meetings and more than 70 resolutions since initial consideration of the issue in 1947, the world organization has not been able to establish effective sovereignty over Namibia nor to pave the way for its independence.

South African tactics: from 'reserves' to 'National Assembly'

Until the rise of national political movements in the early 1960s South Africa treated international queries and internal complaints about its policies with contempt externally and repression internally. This policy became untenable after signs of greater resistance. These were exemplified by the demonstrations leading to the 'Windhoek Old Location' massacre of 1959 (the Namibian Sharpeville), and the emergence of the South West Africa People's Organization (SWAPO) during the period 1959–61 as a movement with a national peasant and contract worker base.

Since then South Africa has sought to implement a dual strategy with respect to Namibia. On the one hand, the South African government has appeared to be seriously prepared to find an internationally acceptable solution, keeping the door open for negotiations with the United Nations or major Western powers. An image has been sustained of something really taking place or talks reaching a real breakthrough. Simultaneously South Africa has implemented successive plans inside Namibia designed to continue repression or to restabilize on new lines while maintaining the content of old policy.

This dual strategy had been put into effect earlier, although in a less marked form. South Africa treated United Nations Trusteeship Council efforts to assert some authority over it as a mandatory or trust power as a judicial dispute over whether the United Nations was the legal successor to the old League of Nations and whether the mandatory provisions of the League were transferable to the United Nations. Simultaneously, it moved at home to regularize and formalize the *de facto* integration of 'South West' as a virtual fifth province by reducing the formal powers of its Territorial Assembly and creating seats in the Capetown parliament for the settlers.

The first time that South Africa was ostensibly prepared to take into consideration mounting international pressure for Namibia's independence was in 1961–62. Certainly the Odendaal Commission prepared a plan for Namibia's socio-economic and future administrative structure. Odendaal, however, proposed a strategy of 'Homeland' development according to which different ethnic 'nations' within Namibia were gradually to be given independence, while 'white' South West Africa was to be integrated more closely into the Republic. It was in fact a prototype for 'Bantustan' projects in the Republic.

The aim was to maximize ethnic differentiation and diffusion of political power. South Africa hoped, and probably actually believed, that tribal rule in the 'Homelands' would break up nationally based movements; 'Homelands' would allow the Africans to be classed as 'foreigners' in the white 'Homeland' and in the longer term forestall any pressures to remove it from South Africa, and would prevent any moves towards black majority rule. In the short run it defied international opinion, and between 1964 and 1966 implementation was suspended to avoid prejudicing the Republic's position in the first international Court of Justice case.

The policy of 'Homeland' balkanization led to increasing international and internal criticism. The national liberation struggle led by SWAPO achieved a broad and effective mobilization. Its first ventures into armed struggle were unsuccessful but the resulting trial of its leaders and the sentencing of several, including Toivo ja Toivo to Robben Island, did not break it either internally or externally. Both contract worker unrest and church criticism continued to mount. It became obvious that Odendaal was not working domestically; nor was it any more successful internationally with the 1966 UN General Assembly, 1969 Security Council and 1971 International Court of Justice decisions.

New moves toward achieving Namibia's independence began in 1972 when the United Nations Secretary General, Dr Kurt Waldheim, and his special representative, Alfred Escher, were empowered to initiate talks with South Africa. These made little progress and were terminated by the United Nations General Assembly in 1973, but at the same time SWAPO was recognized as the 'authentic representative of the Namibian people'.[8]

South Africa viewed it as desirable to make some marginal concessions and to recognize Namibia's territorial integrity while at the same time minimizing the possibility of African political control at territorial level. South Africa hoped to be able to create the appearance of change as a means to meet the pressures resulting from the 1971 ICJ decision, the 1971–73 Security Council Resolutions, and the collapse in 1974 of the Portuguese colonial empire. The first step in this direction was the creation of a Prime Minister's 'Advisory Council' in 1973, drawn from representatives of all the ethnic groups and assigned 'overall responsibility for the territory as a whole'. The establishment of a multi-racial Advisory Council was presented as a concrete result of talks with United Nations representatives. However, its composition was on a strictly ethnic and arbitrary basis, with none of the African political parties represented. Further, by its character, it was a discussion group. The main aim was once again to obstruct the national liberation effort and to deflect international pressure.

Within Namibia polarization continued. The nationwide general strike in 1971–72 was not only about details; it represented a rejection of 'contract' which the workers perceived as central to what one of their leaders called 'a system that sells people'. A similar evolution was taking place within the churches; from criticism of details, church leaders were moving to open challenges to the legitimacy of the system. In a territory which is nominally 90% Christian and with a high proportion of active church members this meant that both mass mobilization channels – the contract labour system and the churches – were openly hostile to the continuation of the colonial system.

South Africa apparently agreed with Engels on the role of religion in

> the early stage of every [political] movement . . . as ascetic austerity of morals . . . opposes the ruling classes with the principle of spartan equality on the one hand, and is, on the other, a necessary transitional stage without which the lowest stratum of society can never set itself into motion.[9]

Deportations of senior clergy, eventually to include three successive Anglican bishops, began and the printing works of the largest church (the Evangelical Lutheran Ovambo–Kavango Church) was fire-bombed.

The strike was broken by use of the work-or-starve weapon. Few real changes were made in the contract system. At the same time, the South African government attempted to keep alive negotiations with the United Nations and also launched a policy of *détente* with black African countries, which for a time met with some success.

After the revolution in Portugal in 1974, Angola and Mozambique achieved independence in 1975. This radically changed the conditions for the national liberation struggle in southern Africa, a point not missed by the white minority regimes in South Africa and Rhodesia who recognized that it was necessary to make some concessions in order to prevent more radical changes. In Rhodesia the government began to move towards formal majority rule; in South Africa perceptions were somewhat different. The South African government noted that the colonial war of 1960–74 had resulted in the collapse of the Portuguese government at the hands of the colonial army high command; similarly, the French army of Algeria, frustrated by a war it could not win, had overthrown the Fourth Republic and installed de Gaulle.

While this interpretation required the avoidance of an interminable war in Namibia, it left open two alternatives for immediate action. The first, apparently backed by the Bureau of State Security (BOSS), then headed by General Van den Bergh, was to speed up a neo-colonial settlement for Namibia which would create a safe buffer state (another Malawi or Lesotho). The second, backed by the Defence Minister Pieter Botha, was to create the buffer state in Angola by installing a friendly government there.

In Angola in 1975 UNITA and FNLA were losing the civil war to the MPLA (the dominant liberation movement and subsequent government). Their external governmental, covert and mercenary resources were inadequate. In desperation, UNITA requested training arms and personnel from South Africa, thus opening the way for Botha's strategy to be put into effect with – so he claimed – US approval. South African columns, thinly disguised as mercenaries, struck deep into Angola and for a time put the survival of the MPLA government in jeopardy. However, two things went wrong for South Africa. The United States Congress refused to finance or countenance continued American armed involvement in the Angola war, and reinforcements for the MPLA troops arrived from Cuba and defeated the South African columns in preliminary encounters.

South Africa withdrew, first to the border area, then to Namibia. While raids were to continue, the effort to install an Angolan buffer state to protect 'South West' was in ruins. Further, the resultant pattern of relations with Angola prevented implementation of the Portuguese–South African water and power scheme on the Kunene. (While the Ruacana Falls power house is in Namibia, the key water control works are at Calueque in Angola.)

The attempt to reach *détente* with black African countries was wrecked by the Angolan adventure, and West African states which had been interested declined further secret talks. The front line states viewed South Africa's action in Angola as only too clear an answer as to whether South Africa could be used to put pressure on the Rhodesian rebels. The United Nations Security Council condemned South Africa's intervention in Angola and sharpened its demand for immediate South African withdrawal from Namibia and transference of power to the people of Namibia with United Nations assistance.[10]

The armed liberation struggle continued to expand. For the first time the South African government admitted publicly that SWAPO's activities were causing military insecurity, and launched a nationwide 'anti-terrorist' campaign. As repression was intensified, preparations were also started for an internal political settlement to lead eventually to 'South West's' independence under European management so as to avert the emergence of Namibia. In 1975 the South West African National Party invited representatives from all ethnic groups to constitutional talks at Turnhalle in Windhoek to discuss the political future of Namibia. For the first time in Namibian colonial history representatives of the black majority were to be present at negotiations concerning their country's future. An attempt was to be made to create a Namibian political class, or rather a series of sub-classes, as ethnic differentiation was to be reinforced, to whom it would be safe to entrust the appearance of power in an independent Namibia.

The Turnhalle Declaration stated that within three years, that is by the end of 1978, Namibia was to move to independence from South Africa, as a single state, with the participation of all population groups in the new government. The constitution envisaged three tiers of government, local, ethnic (or 'Homeland', though the concept was ethnic, not strictly territorial), and confederal. Most powers directly affecting individuals (education, housing, personal income tax) were to be at the second level. At the confederal level, both the assembly and the cabinet (with one member per ethnic group) were to be subject to consensus of all ethnic groups. Superficially, this appeared to give African groups some leverage over matters such as company tax and mining legislation. However, the power at the centre was related to a *status quo* which was satisfactory to the Europeans. For them, any government that could do no more than continue within the existing framework of laws and procedures posed no problems. Further, until independence, extensive and vaguely defined powers remained with the State President in Pretoria.

The Turnhalle formula left the *status quo* substantially unchanged, implementing the ethnic sub-states system. Even so, the South West African National Party split, with a majority unwilling to go as far as the Turnhalle proposals. The new Republican Party of Dirk Mudge became South Africa's chosen vehicle, but most settlers stayed with the National Party.

The constitutional talks were formally dissolved in 1977, following an initiative by five Western members of the Security Council (United Kingdom, United States, France, Federal Republic of Germany and Canada) aimed at achieving a peaceful, internationally acceptable solution for Namibian independence. The Administrator-General, Justice Steyn, was appointed by the South African government to supervise Namibia's transition to independence until a Constituent Assembly was elected. The participants in the Turnhalle Conference formed a coalition of ethnic parties, the Democratic Turnhalle Alliance (DTA), led by the Republican Party. The DTA received massive official backing, probably including 'Muldergate' funds, to buy the two leading Windhoek newspapers, *The Windhoek Advertiser* and *Die Allgemeine Zeitung.*

Marginal reforms were made in apartheid legislation over 1978–79. The Pass Laws were modified and the Immorality Proclamation and Prohibition of Mixed Marriages law revoked. Africans gained the right, for the first time, to own freehold property in ethnic subdivisions within black urban areas. Some hotels, restaurants and swimming pools were opened to individuals of all races.

At the same time South Africa was engaged in acquiring control over Namibia's second city and only major port. Walvis Bay had been British and then South African before 1915; it had been administered as an integral part of Namibia. The German port of Swakopmund had been abandoned and Walvis Bay transformed from a sleepy village into the centre of Namibia's maritime trade and fishing. Its formal return to Cape Province administration on 1 September 1977 was transparently a device to increase leverage over an independent Namibia.

In the spring of 1978, the South African government accepted, or appeared to accept, the revised proposal of the Western Contact Group for an internationally acceptable transition to independence, with free elections under United Nations supervision for the election of a Namibian Constituent Assembly. However, at the same time new emergency powers were given to the Administrator-General and a wave of detentions of SWAPO officials and supporters took place. Finally, the Ascension Day massacre occurred in Angola when the South African Army and Air Force struck Namibian refugee camps, especially the main centre for students who had been sent for further training at Kassinga.

In spite of these events, and apparently much to the surprise of the South African government, SWAPO agreed to proceed with the Western proposals. The United Nations Special Representative for

Namibia, Martti Ahtisaari, was sent to Namibia to make a preliminary survey. He was met by some 20 000 SWAPO supporters. His report to the Security Council proposed a peace-keeping force of 7 500 troops, a civilian team of about 1 200 officials, and 360 police. Independence elections were to be held seven months after United Nations acceptance of these proposals.

At this point, after decades of insisting that independence was unthinkable and a decade and a half of studied delay, South Africa suddenly saw an urgent need to grant independence to Namibia. It would not agree with the proposed extension of the time table to independence in order to allow a six-month campaign period before elections. Prime Minister Vorster announced the South African government's rejection of the compromise proposals and the intention unilaterally to call an election without further delay. General elections were organized in Namibia from 4 to 8 December 1978. The DTA was declared the winner, securing 41 out of the 50 seats in the so-called Constituent Assembly set up at the end of December. However, the elections were boycotted not only by SWAPO, but by the parties within the Namibia National Front. They, like the churches, condemned them as rigged and called for elections supervised by the United Nations.

The methods used to force the African majority to the polls must be viewed in the context of registration and polling taking place under conditions of martial law. There is extensive evidence of large-scale irregularities, threats and intimidation by South African authorities and by political parties (notably the DTA) taking part in the elections.[11]

Five parties contested the elections, the DTA, Aktur (the ethnic party front led by the old National Party, no longer a branch of the South African National Party), the Herstigte Nasionale Party (HNP) (the Namibian branch of the South African HNP, a right-wing splinter from the National Party), and two rather obscure fringe groups. Despite the DTA's majority in total votes counted, it was clear that Aktur and HNP had captured a majority (possibly up to two-thirds) of white votes.

From a South African point of view the internal results were unsatisfactory. Strikes increased in number and in bitterness, and in some the South Africans believed they saw the influence of the SWAPO-linked Namibian National Union of Workers. The churches continued toward overt support of the armed struggle which they now declared to be a matter for the individual church member's or the pastor's conscience, while forthrightly condemning the continued South African presence. SWAPO continued to organize internally and to build up units to go underground (as it was forced to do in mid-1979). The People's Liberation Army of Namibia (PLAN) stepped up its campaign, establishing semi-liberated zones and striking further south. White farmers began to call the rich Otavi–Tsumeb–Grootfontein area north of Windhoek 'the triangle of terror'. By 1980 it came to be called 'the triangle of death'. South African losses had risen to perhaps 10 to 15 a week. A major air base was raided and very badly damaged by SWAPO and the Ruacana Falls Dam headquarters mortared and its power-line blown up. Major-General Geldenhuys admitted his troops could not protect farmers from guerrilla attacks. The scenario is strongly reminiscent of Zimbabwe in 1977 or 1978.

During spring 1979, the South African government rejected a new initiative by the Western Contact Group, but promised to leave the door open for further contact. The elected Constituent Assembly was transformed into a so-called National Assembly with legislative power. The first issues to be considered by the new legislative body were proposals to ban SWAPO formally, a bill to establish a fund to assist 'terrorist' victims, a bill to remove race bars in the purchase of land, and a bill for identity documents 'enabling the security forces to establish the identity of a suspect without any doubt', that is, a restoration of the Pass Law which had been abolished in 1977.[12]

The South African army and police force in Namibia were reinforced, military operations there intensified, and in addition, renewed South African ground and air attacks were made into southern Angola.[13] Martial law was extended to the central and northern parts of the country, including the capital, Windhoek, affecting 80% of Namibia's population. In the north, a curfew was declared prohibiting all movement between sunset and sunrise. Up to 2 400 people were arrested in June 1979 in Windhoek's black township of Katutura and arrests in other towns were reported.[14] This could be regarded as the period of the most severe political repression in the sixty years of South African colonialism in Namibia. Ironically, it was occurring 'when Namibia [was] in a transition to independence'.[15]

The South African strategy has been to appear to cooperate with international negotiations while simultaneously attempting to consolidate its hold over Namibia. Each major crackdown on SWAPO has been timed to coincide with some fresh development in South Africa's longstanding strategy. This pattern continued through 1980. South Africa continued to find 'new' issues to raise despite purportedly 'accepting' the United Nations' (basically 'contact group') proposals. These included inviting UNITA, DTA and NNF to talks. The fairly evident aim was to gain time. These tactics were paralleled by increasingly savage raids into Angola and continued arrests and detentions of SWAPO members in Namibia.

In May 1978, South Africa responded positively to Western proposals, but when SWAPO was about to give its response, the Ascension Day massacre occurred. In October 1978, when the Foreign Ministers of five Western powers were having talks with the South African government in Pretoria and Windhoek, a church coach hit a mine (almost certainly not a SWAPO mine) in Ovamboland, killing sixteen people. On the eve of the December elections there were two bomb blasts in Windhoek and the whole of SWAPO's internal leadership was arrested. In March 1979, during international negotiations, there was a series of South African attacks into Angola. Finally, while working out an internal settlement by establishing a National Assembly, the South African government carried out mass arrests and clamped down on SWAPO's activities inside Namibia.[16]

The purpose of these tactical juxtapositions was twofold. First, attacks and detentions afforded a breathing space for South African

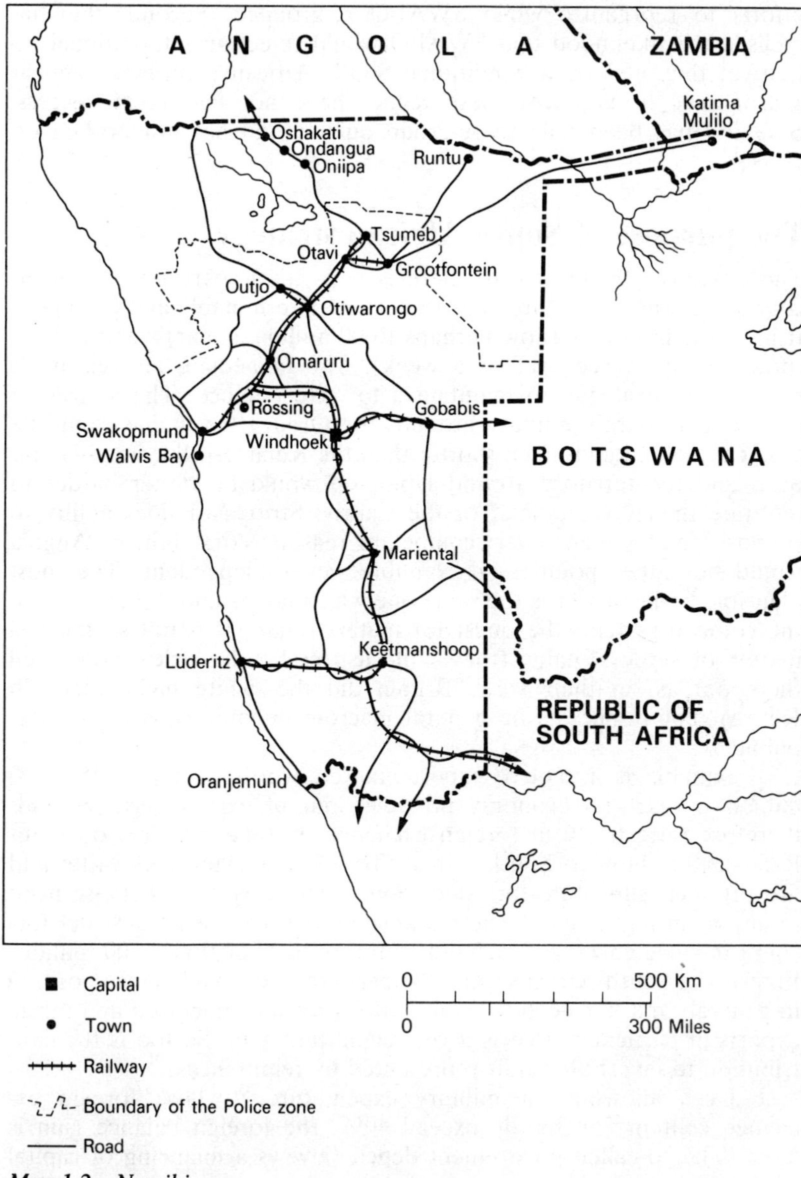

Map 1.2 Namibia

efforts to reorganize while SWAPO re-grouped. Second, they increased the likelihood that SWAPO would reject an international initiative, thus making a conditional South African acceptance appear reasonable. In practice, these tactics have not had great success. SWAPO has been able to re-group quickly and has not broken off talks.[17]

The purpose of South African strategy

The obvious question to ask here is why South Africa is willing to continue a war which threatens to become interminable and to impose rising costs in money (now perhaps R600 million a year)[18] and in lives (now perhaps three or four a week). The immediate answer might seem to be strategic, to maintain a forward defence. This is true in part, but on purely military grounds the Orange River line would be easier to defend and much shorter than the Kunene–Okavango–Zambezi, and the territory around Upington would be rather harder to infiltrate than Ovamboland or the Caprivi Strip. Nor does ability to support UNITA seem a very compelling reason as destabilizing Angola would be rather pointless if Namibia were independent. The most plausible basic answer is the same one which lay behind the creation of the colonial system: the quest for material gain. It is not so much a matter of settlers' gains (they half suspect South Africa would sell them out as, in their view, Britain did the 'white highlanders' in Kenya), but rather of the general macro-economic gains to the Republic.

Namibia is a captive export market, worth perhaps R450–500 million a year. Its economy provides, out of export earnings and, therefore, effectively in foreign exchange, income transfers of about R250–300 million to South Africa. To a lesser extent, its cattle and fish products substitute for goods South Africa would otherwise need to import at higher cost. These and some lesser items suggest net foreign exchange earnings (excluding military cost) of R600–700 million. In terms of South Africa's rather beleaguered external balance position in general, and her need to gain markets for manufactured and maize exports in particular, that is a very significant sum. So too is the contribution to investible funds represented by remittances.[19]

Even allowing for military expenditure,[20] whose foreign exchange content can hardly exceed 40%, the foreign balance gain is large. The so-called government deficit (always a financing of capital investment greater than surplus on recurrent account, not a true recurrent subsidy) has virtually vanished with the explosion in diamond prices, of which about 60% go straight to the South African state treasury.[21] Seen from Pretoria, Namibia still pays. To preserve that profit was and is the key purpose of the manoeuvres. The problem has been, and remains, to find a tactical solution with a good chance of preserving the colonial profit, a chance of territorial stability and at least a modicum of international acceptability.

This is not to argue that colonial profit is the only motive. Security, as noted, is another. The maintenance – for complex political, economic and security reasons – of a sphere of dominance and the avoidance of a psychological defeat (blow to confidence at home) are not insignificant. However, solutions maintaining profit would, almost by definition, maintain dominance (e.g. the 'Constellation' scheme) and be presentable domestically as major triumphs, not defeats. To that extent, the operative motives are both complementary and hard to separate.

Odendaal was excellent in relation to colonial profit as it changed nothing. However, it failed to offer enough incentive to enough Africans to serve any domestic stabilization purpose; continued contract labour and a few South African-appointed functionaries and Bantu Development Corporation-aided traders in the 'Homelands' was hardly an alluring package. Internationally there was amazement that South Africa should suppose that what it had proposed could be viewed as independence for Namibia.

Turnhalle, at least its DTA version, was almost as well designed to preserve profit. Somewhat higher company tax, some progress on African wages, a rather more lavish 'Homeland'-based political class could have been financed out of the surplus from resumed growth. However, domestically, it was almost as severe a disappointment to its authors as Odendaal. Genuine support for DTA is minute and manifestly cannot deliver stability or security. Internationally, Turnhalle came a decade too late: in 1963 it might have been saleable; in 1977 it was viewed as a failure to face reality, even by the Western Contact Group.

The DTA election–Constituent Assembly–National Assembly gambit makes it slightly more difficult to hold on to economic gains. It has offered a few more handouts, some more access for Africans, but domestically its reception has been more disappointing than that of its predecessors. Black support remains elusive and alarm within the settler majority has created visible cleavages in the white front. Internationally, the results have been counterproductive: even the Contact Group views these steps as in bad faith given the previous negotiations with them and the United Nations Secretary-General.

A unilateral declaration of independence cum 'internal settlement' on the Smith-Muzorewa model of 1979 presumably would still meet the profit preservation test although it might entail more sacrifices of settler land and small businesses. There is no reason to suppose it could attract much African support; the moderate coloured and black parties which boycotted the election denounce such proposals. Internationally, there would be no real chance of recognition: Namibia is not Rhodesia, the army to preserve a 'UDI' Namibia would have to be the South African, and this would be a rather too naked fraud to be sold abroad.[22]

The approach calling for a United Nations-supervised election has different drawbacks. If held, this would presumably lead to a universally recognized Namibian state, and unless the election results were very indecisive, a government with substantial backing would emerge. But BOSS has long warned that SWAPO would get 60% of the votes in a free election, a view shared by Afrikaners in Namibia. The optimists see 45% SWAPO, 40% NNF, 15% DTA/Aktur/HNP, which is no better. The stable, internationally recognized Namibia would set out to cut remittances and imports from the Republic of South Africa as a matter of policy. Equally it would be a most unlikely recruit for the 'Constellation' and even SABC (South African Broadcasting Corporation) would be hard-pressed to explain how the emergence of a SWAPO government represented a 'victory for the Republic'

Economic blockage

The colonial economy is still generating profit, but it is no longer growing.[23] Confidence is a thing of the past and unlikely to reappear until a solution is achieved. Despite its desperate efforts to protect the basic mechanisms of the colonial economy, the credibility of the South African regime has rapidly deteriorated among the European population, with large firms contemplating significant withdrawal of investments. The Great Trek to the Republic has not yet started – albeit a few outriders have already gone ahead – but capital is disappearing.

The Namibian economy is experiencing 15% inflation and zero per cent growth. Private fixed investment, including mineral prospecting and development, has gone into a sharp decline. Not a single revenue-producing building has been erected in Windhoek's central business district since 1973 and not a single private white residence has been built in the capital for four years. White businessmen based in Namibia are investing heavily in property, but in the Cape Province, not in Namibia.

Farm prices are falling. North of Otjiwarongo, in the prime cattle-ranching regions, land prices fell about 20% in 1979, despite intensified army actions against SWAPO guerrilla forces. The white farmers have threatened to sell, ship or kill all their cattle if it is necessary for them to leave, and already tonnes of antelope meat have been smuggled out of the Nature Reserves.[24]

Cattle ranching, like fishing, faces problems greater than the overall political economic uncertainty. Costs have risen, prices controlled by South Africa have not, and the key South African quota has been cut. Only in mid-1979 was action begun to raise local slaughtering capacity to allow higher exports to other markets.[25] Fish resources, especially pilchard, have been wrecked by over-fishing and 1979 will have been the third consecutive disastrous year. Owners of fishing boats may not wait for an independence settlement before leaving Walvis for Table Bay.

In 1978 the Namibian railway depot was transferred from Windhoek to Upington on the South African side. Thus, the entire railway machinery can quickly be moved out of the country. This, like the Walvis Bay transfer, was almost certainly a tactical move to increase leverage over an independent Namibia, but its misreading as 'cut and run' contingency planning has done nothing for business confidence.

On the face of it mining is less affected.[26] Present operations continue and, if the 1979 rise in copper prices is sustained, Otjihase, which was closed at the end of 1977, may be re-commissioned. General Mining continues development of the pilot plant and uranium mine at Langer Heinrich, albeit in slow motion. Uranium prospecting and proving has not ceased. Soekor, which in 1977 claimed it had found a huge natural gas deposit off the Namibian coast, has acquired a new rig, increased its budget, and seems to be planning to prove its find, although its 1977 condition that the political situation should 'stabilize itself' has hardly been met.[27]

But the appearance is something of an illusion. No new mines are being developed (even the half-complete Langer Heinrich mine is unlikely to be brought to full-scale completion). The 250 000 tonne cement project is on ice. Prospecting and especially proving is declining. Natural gas, particularly important as it may contain extractable oil, might be an exception. South Africa's vulnerability to oil sanctions makes liquid hydrocarbon potential of strategic importance.

The one partial exception to lack of confidence, Anglo American, is illuminating. To Anglo, Consolidated Diamond Mines is critical both for profits and for maintaining the sellers' cartel in gem diamonds (the latter an interest it shares with Botswana, Angola, Tanzania and the USSR). Anglo has reached agreements, which it feels are tolerable, with Zambia, Botswana, Tanzania and Angola. The one future event it really fears is a prolonged war. This is not to say it would not prefer a neo-colonial or moderate solution, nor that it urgently wants a settlement. It has given a technical high school to the Ovamboland 'government' and is to build an office block in Windhoek, which will almost certainly not be commercially viable. Its relatively high wages and decent labour relations (e.g. refusing to force workers to vote, unofficially recognizing a workers' committee), even though they have not averted at least one strike, means that its operations at Oranjemund in the extreme south remain fairly free from strife. It is continuing to invest in prospecting, proving and development; it views the training of African artisans and foremen and the building of family houses for them as good investments; its office-block venture is evidently aimed at quelling panic.

However, while Anglo may be correct in believing it can have a future in almost any future Namibia, few other investors share that view. The settlers, especially the ranchers, face a very different set of problems, as do the mines developed since the revocation of the mandate in 1966. Spending five years re-building the fishing industry or bringing in a new mine, let alone sinking one's life savings in a commercial or residential building, look wildly unsound to the individual, small company or purely South African-based firm.

The future: five scenarios

Predicting the short-term course of the Namibian liberation struggle in detail is likely to prove stale, flat and unprofitable. Basically there are five conceivable scenarios.

1 War *à l'outrance* – to the Orange River

In this scenario SWAPO would literally battle South Africa's occupation forces south to the border. Assuming no outside intervention at multi-division level (a reasonable assumption[28] despite South African scare stories about 1 000 East Germans, a derisory number for the purpose), that war could well last out the century. It would leave a shattered country with nothing to lose by supporting immediate guerrilla incursions in force into South Africa. Much earlier it would turn colonial Namibia into a liability after ranchers fled and most mines ceased to be operational (only Oranjemund might be kept going to the last minute). The real question to arise is, however, not so much related to military or even economic matters for Namibia, but to what would happen meanwhile in the Republic.

2 War *à l'outrance* – the fall of Pretoria

This presumably is South Africa's nightmare: the war in Namibia drags on and it becomes clear at home that it cannot be won. Fleeing settlers spread despondency; military costs lead to tax increases which spark discontent. More seriously, the system of sending national-service conscripts to die in what is admitted to be a foreign land is challenged, draft evasion spreads, emigration increases. South Africa's African community watches the war in Namibia and draws its own conclusion; urban guerrilla warfare and infiltration from the north (ironically through the Kruger National Park) increase, as does systematic sabotage on the Rand and in the key coal/oil conversion plants. The question here is why South Africa would allow itself to be trapped in this scenario as it could always cut its losses and fall back with a negotiated withdrawal. The 1980 strikes and riots in the Republic had they all been at the same time would already have over-extended its police/military forces outside Namibia.

3 UDI – the settler state

This is not a real scenario; there is no settler army. A unilateral declaration of independence without the South African military would last at most a few weeks before the People's Liberation Army of Namibia reached the Orange River.[29]

Therefore, this scenario – though perhaps it will be attempted – collapses back to one of the others unless and until a 25 000-man white settler army, willing to die for DTA, and with substantial training and some combat experience, exists. It is already too late for that condition to be met, if it ever could have been.

Further, the Rhodesian trajectory has demonstrated the international unacceptability of what has been termed 'a white government with a black face'. There is no black ally in sight for DTA with even the inadequate degree of credibility that characterised Bishop Muzorewa. That too would render an attempted 'UDI' an unconvincing exercise doomed either to speedy collapse or rapid retreat to South African-ruled status. South Africa was stunned by the 1980 Zimbabwe elections. It apparently actually expected a Muzorewa plurality. Since those elections it has continued moves toward creating a pseudo-independent 'SWA/Namibia' but in a leisurely fashion and potentially to demand conference-table places for DTA and NNF and/or to threaten 'UDI' more than from actual commitment to implementing it.

4 The free and fair election – enter UNTAG

This is of course SWAPO's preferred solution: it does not wish to see Namibians die or their country desolated. It is also the Western Contact Group's preferred solution: to close an avenue for 'Soviet penetration', to safeguard access to raw materials and markets, to buy time to see whether South Africa can be coaxed, cajoled or coerced into reform at home.

South Africa, at least to date, could ill afford to alienate the Western powers as this might lead to a Security Council resolution enforcing oil and finance (bank loan) sanctions. The question here is why this scenario has not already happened. The answer is that South Africa will accept it only when it sees no other alternative, or when it sees serious sanctions as the immediate price of continued refusal. The willingness of Western powers to negotiate interminably to make concessions to South African objections, and to use negotiations as an excuse for not implementing sanctions is rapidly eroding whatever confidence SWAPO might once have had in the Contact Group's willingness to force through a settlement guaranteeing free and fair elections.

5 Another Aden – cut and run

At the end of 1967 a British civil servant, in the last helicopter to leave, dropped the master keys to the government buildings at Aden into the hands of his Adeni successor as Secretary to the Treasury. The war to hold South Yemen had become unwinnable, talks for a compromise had failed, the British forces were pulled out under a *de facto* cease-fire, and a tacit bargain had been made that their exit would not be impeded nor their businessmen harassed if things were left in reasonable running order. While a literal repetition in Namibia is hardly likely, a scenario on these lines is not totally implausible. SWAPO would certainly negotiate (or participate in a tacitly agreed) cease-fire to evacuate so long as a scorched-earth policy was not followed. If the war situation worsened, the settlers became both more frightened and more intractable, and the election option looked certain to return a SWAPO government anyhow, then South Africa might come to see this sequence as the last available option.

These scenarios are based on a decisive break having taken place in the previous continuity of the colonial history of Namibia; South Africa has lost the initiative and cannot regain it. It can fend off early political or military débâcle; what it cannot do is restore or even stabilize the situation. It is possible to debate when the decisive break occurred: the 'Windhoek Old Location' massacre; the founding of SWAPO; the independence of Angola; the establishment of SWAPO operational areas in the north; the 1978–79 PLAN breakthrough into the main cattle and base-metal mining zone from Tsumeb/Grootfontein to Windhoek. Perhaps the timing is unimportant now; the point is that the break has occurred.[30]

In practice, the last two scenarios appear the least unlikely, although it is possible that an abortive exploration of the third (UDI) might be made. Namibia is likely to be independent by 1985, largely as a result of PLAN raising the cost and lowering the profit of South

Africa's hanging on, but not by a literal driving of the South African armies back across the Orange.

Namibia – the colonial present and the future

This volume is not a detailed examination of scenarios for the transition to independence. Rather it seeks to explore the nature of the colonial present and the possible transformations in the post-colonial future. Following a brief survey of 'The land and its people', two chapters, 'The colonial economy' and 'South African capital and Namibia', analyze the history, dynamics, structure and present realities of the colonial economy. Two further chapters, 'The white man's burden: Africans under apartheid' and 'Contract work through Ovambo eyes', detail and document the nature of compulsory racism and of one of its key components, the contract labour system, as they affect Namibians. 'The church in mobilization for national liberation' and 'National resistance and the liberation struggle', explore the origins, evolution, dynamics and present nature of the two dominant Namibian social institutions, the churches and SWAPO. An interview with SWAPO President Nujoma and a chapter on 'The ideology of national liberation' link the sections on the course of the liberation struggle and the future of post-colonial Namibia. The possibilities for, problems of, and constraints on change in post-colonial Namibia are analyzed in 'The political economy of liberation', 'Transnational corporations in the future of Namibia' and 'Agrarian change'. A set of social and economic statistical tables, constructed to fill the absence of usable (or indeed available) official statistics, and a select bibliography, conclude the volume.

Notes

1 Cited in H. Bley, *South-West Africa Under German Rule*, Heinemann, London, 1971, p. 3.

2 Union of South Africa, *House of Assembly Debates*, 1964, Col. 5557, Government Printer, Pretoria.

3 *Political Programme of the South West Africa People's Organisation*, Lusaka, 1976.

4 *Windhoek Advertiser*, 8 June 1979.

5 See below, Chapter 9

6 Frantz Fanon, *The Wretched of the Earth*, Macgibbon and Kee, London, 1965, p. 48.

7 *Ibid.*, p. 190.

8 For a more detailed presentation see J. H. P. Serfontein, *Namibia*? Fokus-Suid, Randburg, 1976, pp. 245–249. For a detailed 1975–1978 chronology see Foreign and Commonwealth Office, *Namibia (South West Africa) Independence Proposals: Background and Chronology*, London, 1979.

9 'The Peasant War In Germany' in Marx and Engels, *Selected Works*, Progress Publishers, Moscow, Vol. II, p. 97.

10 United Nations, Security Council Resolution 385 (1976).

11 See J. Ellis, *Elections in Namibia*? British Council of Churches/Catholic Institute of International Relations, London, 1979; G. and S. Cronje, *The Workers of Namibia*, Defence and Aid, London, 1979, Appendix B.

12 *Windhoek Observer* and *Windhoek Advertiser*, June, July and August 1979 issues.

13 *Focus*, no. 23, July–August 1979.

14 *Financial Times*, 27 June 1979 and *Windhoek Observer*, 20 June 1979.

15 See *Windhoek Advertiser*, 8 June 1979.

16 *Windhoek Observer*, 23 June 1979.

17 By August 1979 South Africa was rather hard put to think up plausible reasons why a *cordon sanitaire* on both sides of the Angolan border, patrolled by United Nations troops was not an acceptable guarantee against a SWAPO invasion during a United Nations-supervised election run-up; *ibid.*, 25 August 1979.

18 See *Africa Contemporary Record*, 1978–79, 'Namibia', Africana, London, 1979.

19 *Ibid.*

20 Some of which would be transferred to operations within the Republic, not saved.

21 See Table 32. *The Financial Mail* has what may be somewhat lower revenue estimates in 'SWA Economy – On Ice', 17 August 1979, but even they would show a very large recurrent account surplus. They may also not be lower as it is unclear whether they cover Territorial as well as Republic of South Africa, South West Africa Account revenue.

22 This does not stop inspired rumours about it, for example, Administrator-General Viljoen reported in *Windhoek Observer* 25 August 1979, 'UDI Inevitable – But When?' *To the Point*, May 1979; 'The Mirage Fades', *Financial Mail*, 25 May 1979. In addition, calls for a national SWA Defence Force have begun – see *Observer*, 15 September 1979.

23 *Financial Mail*, 25 May, 17 August 1979.

24 *Ibid.* and *Windhoek Advertiser*, February 1978.

25 *Windhoek Observer*, 11 and 18 August, 1 September 1979.

26 *Financial Mail*, 25 May and 17 August 1979.

27 *Rand Daily Mail*, 27 January 1977; *Windhoek Advertiser*, 5 July 1979.

28 Both cases of substantial Cuban/Soviet combat forces (Angola, Ethiopia) have special characteristics. A new, credible, radical government seeking to consolidate its authority faced a threat to its existence from foreign (South African, Somali) troops. When these conditions have not been met, either the radical African state has not sought non-African combat forces (e.g. Mozambique) or the Soviet Union, even when it had previously invested in the regime, has declined support (e.g. Idi Amin Dada's Uganda regime). Liberation movements have consistently sought foreign bayonets and foreign trainers for using them, but none to date has sought or received foreign hands to hold them.

29 Arming UNITA mercenaries, homeguards, African army units would not help. Most colonial wars were indeed won by armies with many colonial

subjects fighting for their masters – one of the German monuments to the dead of the 1904–07 war states 'Here Rest The Faithful Bantu Soldiers of the Kaiser' – but colonial levies did not fight without the presence of their 'masters'. 'Vietnamisation' is a misleading parallel to draw in order to demonstrate the effectiveness of a DTA 'black army'; the South Vietnamese state did have substantial classes backing it, notably a large professional military class with over a decade of experience. Nor is Rhodesia a good parallel. Rhodesia had a territorially-based army from 1923, while the proto-'SWA Army' has less than three years' history and is still very much an integral part of the South African Defence Force. PLAN in 1980, by contrast, is much more formidable than the Zimbabwean liberation movement's fighting forces were in 1965 – or even at the beginning of the 1970s.

30 The reality of the break is recognized by the settler community and the South Africans. A senior Afrikaner journalist, transferred from the *Citizen* (the centrepiece of the Secret Operations to buy hearts and minds that led to 'Muldergate') to the *Advertiser* (a DTA mouthpiece), has set out the 'problem' (from a settler/RSA angle), quite frankly and lucidly. (See Leon Kok, 'The Vital Importance of Northern SWA', *Windhoek Advertiser*, 29 June 1979.) Unless the north can be pacified the economy will stagnate. Further, only development in the north – not possible without pacification – can avert rapidly rising African unemployment. If the white economy erodes and black unemployment rises, the conditions will exist for PLAN to move south and to launch urban-based operations. But the writer sees no way of pacifying the north by action based in Namibia; present efforts can contain and delay but not reverse or avert. The parallel drawn is Zimbabwe.

An alternative is proposed: the permanent South African occupation of Southern Angola and/or the installation of a UNITA government in Luanda. However, this is settler wishful thinking as South Africa is not about to engage in such febrile adventurism. UNITA as the force behind an insurgency on the southern plateau is viable; as a tool to seize Luanda it is inconceivable. Cubans defeated South African columns before and in a frontal assault on Luanda probably would again, quite apart from the terrifying (from a South African viewpoint) risk of escalation and the fury with which the Western countries would react to this type of reckless escalation. The annexation of southern Angola would pose the same escalation problems and is a step on a well-known road to ruin, the need to create an infinite series of buffer zones to protect buffer states or border areas. Prime Minister Botha is not a rash adventurist and he knows from bitter experience that the 'forward' strategy is not viable. He knows that the initiative in Namibia is lost and cannot be regained except by a successful disengagement; his problem is how to disengage without party, electoral or economic disaster.

2 The land and its people

MARJA-LIISA KILJUNEN

Geography[1]

Situated in the south-west corner of Africa, Namibia[2] covers an area of 824 269 square kilometres,[3] almost four times the size of the United Kingdom. It is sparsely populated and nearly half of it is desert. It shares long borders with Angola in the north and Botswana in the east, it touches Zambia and Zimbabwe at the extreme east of the Caprivi Strip, and is bounded by the Republic of South Africa in the south. The western and most of the northern and the southern boundaries follow major geographic features, the Atlantic Ocean, the Kunene, Okavango and Zambezi river systems, and the Orange River. The eastern boundary does not follow any natural geographical features.

Topographically the country is divided into three distinct areas: the Namib Desert, the Central Plateau and the Kalahari Desert (see Map 2.1). Natural conditions vary greatly from one part of the country to another, according to soil, vegetation or annual rainfall.

The Namib Desert, one of the oldest deserts in the world, stretches along the South Atlantic coast from the Angolan to the South African border. Its width varies from 80 to 130 kilometres. The desert covers about one-sixth of the total area of the country and is almost totally uninhabitable. The southern half has hardly any vegetation and between Swakopmund and Lüderitz, sand dunes of up to 300 metres in height are to be found. The northern part is also barren, apart from a few desert species such as the long-rooted *Welwitschia mirabilis*, the hollow-branched kokerboom and low thorny bushes. In the north the sand sometimes shifts to reveal part of shipwrecked vessels, hence the name 'Skeleton Coast'.

The desert contains enormous riches despite its barrenness. Since 1908 the large quantities of diamonds extracted have made Namibia one of the world's largest producers of gem diamonds. The southern half of the Namib Desert has been divided into two enclosed diamond zones, which are under strict control. Diamonds are found not only in coastal dunes but also in the sand at the bottom of the sea. The central portion of the desert, stretching to the mountainous area north west of Swakopmund, has recently become equally valuable with the discovery of uranium, first near Rössing Mountain, and later on several other sites, most notably Langer Heinrich.

The coast also contains rich salt-fields, and the cold Benguela stream brings fish to the Namibian coast which, it is claimed, has the best fishing waters in the world. The fish attract birds which produce guano, an excellent natural fertilizer, which is found in layers up to

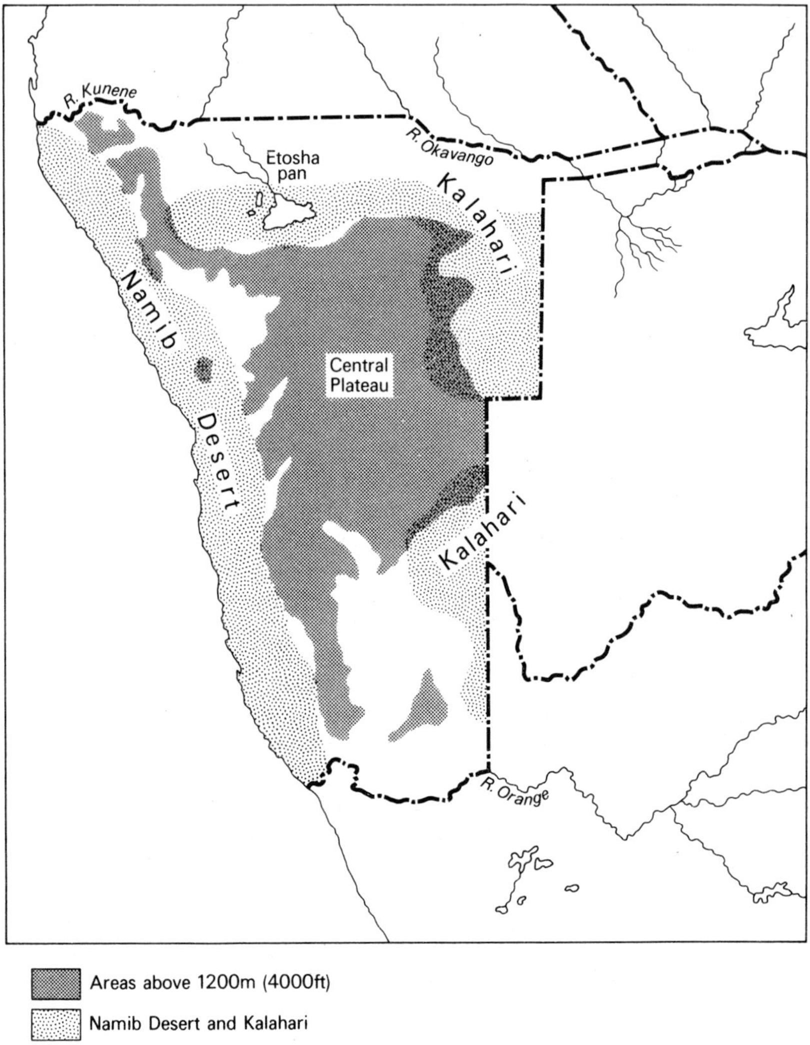
R. Kunene
Etosha pan
R. Okavango
Kalahari
Namib
Desert
Central Plateau
Kalahari
R. Orange
Areas above 1200m (4000ft)
Namib Desert and Kalahari

several metres deep in off-shore islands and bird-platforms. It was birds, whales and seals which first encouraged European exploitation of the area, when sealing and guano-collecting were begun on the offshore islands, and whaling from a base near Lüderitz.

The Central Plateau, a savannah and bush area which rises 1 000 to 2 000 metres above sea level, encompasses over half the total area of Namibia. Its mountain ranges contain substantial mineral deposits of copper, lead, zinc, tin, vanadium, sulphur, cadmium, wolfram, silver, lithium, iron, germanium and uranium, as well as a wide array of semi-precious stones. The northern part of the plateau is well suited to cattle-grazing; the arid southern part provides excellent pasture land for the valuable Karakul sheep. Together with the capital Windhoek, the coastal towns, the plateau farming town of Grootfontein and the mining town of Tsumeb are the main centres of European population.

The Kalahari Desert, into which the plateau merges to the east, is flat with a few trees, bushes and grasses. The scanty rainfall and sandy surface make it largely unsuitable for cultivation. The Kalahari sand surface is in places intermixed with hardveldt of the plateaus. It extends as far north as Okavango and Ovamboland, where rainfall and seasonal watercourse flows are adequate for crop cultivation. Karakul sheep are raised in the southern part of the desert. The extreme eastern portion forms the lifeless, shifting sands of the Omaheke.

Apart from the oshana (temporary watercourse) and Okavango Valley country of the north, the Zambezi system areas of the Caprivi, and a few patches on the Central Plateau, Namibia is not suitable for natural water-fed cultivation. In some cases this is purely due to the low rainfall, in others to the nature of the sand and rock surface. Rainfall varies greatly from district to district and from year to year, from the tropical showers of the Caprivi Strip to the nearly rainless areas of the Namib Desert (see Map 2.1). Namibia has experienced several prolonged droughts, which have proved disastrous to man, beast and vegetation. In most parts of the country rain falls as torrential thunderstorms, causing substantial erosion, and very little surface water is left due to rapid run-off and evaporation.

The rainy season occurs during the summer months, October to April. It lasts over five months in the Caprivi Strip, two to four months in the northern and central areas, and less than one month in the south and the Namib Desert. During these months innumerable shallow watercourses in the north (oshanas), as well as larger rivers are full of water. Two of the larger rivers, the Swakop and Kuiseb, are quite substantial, the former at times reaching the sea at Swakopmund, and the latter almost reaching the coast at Walvis Bay. However, only the four frontier rivers are perennial.

Because permanent surface water is so scarce and flowing water is seasonal and uncertain from year to year, it has been necessary to rely on ground water and storage dams. In most parts of the country ground water runs so deep that boreholes, which range from 20 to 30 metres up to 200 to 300 metres in depth, have been the only means of getting water. The South African government initiated the Kunene project in the Namibian/Angolan border area, which includes plans for a network of irrigation canals to reach as far as the central ranching country near Okahandja as well as to supply mines and towns. Other sources of water include springs in some areas, and, to a limited extent, water obtained from the sea by an evaporation process.

The potentially arable land in the north and north east (Ovamboland, Okavango and Caprivi), in the northern parts of the Central Plateau (Grootfontein, Otjiwarongo and Okahandja), in the Kalahari Desert (Gobabis), and in the southern zone (Keetmanshoop and Mariental), is fairly extensive if sufficient irrigation is provided. However, because of overpopulation and overgrazing, the ground has eroded in many areas, especially the north, and the soil, even in most potentially arable areas, is of only moderate to poor quality, lacking adequate humus and with too much salt and phosphate or too much sand.

It is difficult to consider Namibia in purely geographical terms. Certainly natural conditions in general are extremely harsh, with inadequate water being the major constraint. However, ecological and environmental conditions vary greatly from area to area and reflect more than simple physical and climatic conditions. A clear pattern can be seen: conditions are worst in the African areas, where little has been done to prevent the natural environment from deteriorating or to improve the physical environment; they are best in areas held by Europeans. Thus the main irrigation experiments have been under Hardap Dam near Mariental in the south, not in the Oshana or Okavango water system areas of the north.

Population

According to South African estimates, the population of Namibia was 960 000 in 1977 (of which less than 12% were whites). However, this figure has been challenged as too low. SWAPO's estimate for 1970 was at least double the South African figure of 762 184 and the latest United Nations Institute for Namibia estimate of population in 1977 was 1 250 000.

It is difficult to organize an accurate census in a territory like Namibia given the lack of rural population registers, the lack of cooperation over being counted which seems to typify colonial subjects, and the dubious legality of the status of many urban residents which leads them to avoid being counted. Most colonial censuses in Africa have underestimated actual population figures by at least 25%; it would seem reasonable to suppose that the Namibian figures are subject to a similar degree of inaccuracy.

The unreliability of the results of the censuses of 1960 and 1970 is evident from Table 2.1.[4] Several annual average changes are too high. Growth rates such as 5.9% or 6.9% (or even 3.9% and 4.4%) are impossible given that there has not been black immigration except for Angolan immigrant workers. On the other hand, decreases of the order of 3.4% or 0.6% are highly unlikely given the absence of full-scale war, natural disasters or large-scale emigration. The 1960 census is clearly not an adequate estimate; there is no *a priori* reason to suppose the 1970 one to be much better.[5]

TABLE 2.1 Population in 1960, 1970 and 1974

	1960	1970	Annual average change 1960–70	1974	
Africans					
	(000)	(000)	%	(000)	(%)
Ovambo	239	353	3.9	396	46.5
Damara	44	66	4.1	75	8.8
Herero	35	51	3.7	56	6.6
Kavango	28	50	5.9	56	6.6
East Caprivians	16	26	4.9	29	3.4
San ('bushmen')	12	23	6.9	26	3.0
Kaokolanders	9	7	−3.4	7	0.8
Tswana	10	4	. .	5	0.6
Others	. .	15	6.9	15	1.8
	394	594	4.4	665	78.1
'Coloureds'					
Nama	35	33	−0.6	37	4.3
'Coloureds'	13	29	8.2	32	3.8
Rehoboth Basters	11	17	3.9	19	2.2
	59	78	2.8	88	10.3
Whites					
Afrikaner	. .	62	. .	68	7.9
German	. .	20	. .	21	2.5
English	. .	7	. .	8	1.0
Others	. .	2	. .	2	0.2
	73	91	2.2	99	11.6
Total	526	762	3.7	852	100

Sources: Republic of South Africa, Department of Foreign Affairs, *South West Africa Survey*, Pretoria, 1967 and 1974.

Namibian population density is very low, about 1.5 persons per square kilometre. Vast areas are practically uninhabited. The highest densities are found in the northern agricultural areas (especially in Ovamboland), in the agricultural and mining zone extending from Grootfontein to Windhoek and Rehoboth in the Central Plateau, and in the Rössing–Swakopmund–Walvis Bay coastal area with its mining, port and fishing communities.[6]

The distribution of population has been determined to a large extent by the institutionalized racial discrimination (and 'ethnical' categorization) imposed by South Africa. Half of the country has been allocated to 'White' ranches and towns. This includes 90% of the usable land in the Police Zone (that part of central and southern Namibia defined by the line the Germans drew around the area they had sub-divided and administered). The African population is subject to residence control; a majority lives in 'Homelands' north of the Police Zone, many others live in 'reserves' within the Police Zone. Since most of the 'reserves' cannot sustain their populations and since the white economy depends on black labour, there is substantial migrant and permanent African residence in 'White' areas and separate 'Black' and 'Coloured' urban townships.

The population of Namibia is not homogeneous but characterized by complex historical, national, clan and cultural differences, which does not of course justify the type of racial and ethnic policy that South Africa pursues. From an anthropological viewpoint, and to a degree from a historical viewpoint as well, the four broad groupings are Khoisan, Negroid, 'Coloured' and European. The first includes Namibia's earliest known inhabitants, the San, subsequently called 'bushmen' by the colonialists. They comprise four different groups, the Khung, the Heikum, the Naron and the Mbarakwengo. Each has its own click language. The Khoisan group also includes the Nama, the 'Hottentots' of colonial literature, of which there were, historically, numerous nations or clans.

The Negroid group comprises several tribes or nations, the Ovambo, the Kavango and the Herero, all speaking Bantu languages; the Damara, not of the Bantu linguistic groups; the 'tribes' living in the Caprivi Strip who are clans of Zambian and Angolan peoples; the Tswana who are closely related to the Tswana living in Botswana; and the Himba of the Kaokoland who are a sub-group of the Herero people.

The Ovambo nation comprises seven tribes, the Kuanjama, Ndonga, Kuambi, Ngandjera, Mbalantu, Kualuthi and Nkolonkati. Their languages are closely related and three (the Ndonga, Kuanjama and Kuambi) have written languages. The Kavango group is historically an offshoot of the Ovambo, formed of five Ovambo tribes (the Kuangali, Mbunza, Sambju, Keiriku and Mbukushu) who settled by the river Kavango to the east of the main group of the Ovambo.

The population in eastern Caprivi is composed of several tribes, for example, the Masubia and the Mafue, both related to tribes in Zambia. The residents of Kaokoland include Himba (a Herero clan separated from the rest of the Herero nation), Nama, Damara and San, who have either moved or been expelled to the barren, rock country of north-western Namibia. The Herero belong to the Bantu linguistic group and are divided into several tribes. The origins of the Damara (or berg–dama) have not been tráced. They now speak a Nama language acquired during several centuries under Nama rule. They are variously asserted to be the longest resident nation of the Negroid group or to have accompanied the Nama from the Cape.

The 'Coloured' group includes the Rehoboth people (or 'Basters'), a community of Boers' and Namas' descendants who moved from the Cape Colony in the late nineteenth century. Many identify themselves with the Afrikaner group, whose language they speak. The 'Cape Coloured' are also descendants of Boers, Khoisans and Negroids and are largely post-Second World War immigrants from the Cape Province.

The European group is predominantly Afrikaner (Boer) and German with a smaller British component. Some German residents migrated during the 1874–1915 colonial period, but the majority are post-Second World War immigrants, and half are West German citizens. The Afrikaners began entering the country on a large scale in 1915 and, while a number are settlers, many are expatriates whose territorial base continues to be the Republic. The British are for the most part South African English, with some expatriate technicians and managers from the United Kingdom. Each group tends to speak its own language within the community and all three are official territorial languages; but the *lingua franca* is Afrikaans, the language of the dominant group.

Notes

1 Standard sources covering these aspects in more detail include The Odendaal Report, Chapter 1 (*Report of the Commission of Enquiry into South West African Affairs 1962–1963*, Government Printer, Pretoria, 1964), and J. H. Wellington, *Southern Africa – A Geographic Study* (2 vols), Cambridge, 1955.

2 Until quite recently Namibia was generally known as South West Africa, as named by the Swedish explorer C. J. Andersson in the 1840s. SWAPO started calling the country Namibia after the Namib Desert as early as the 1950s. (*Namib* in the Nama language means 'shield', suggesting the protection it gives against the perils of the sea and those who come across it.) In 1968 the United Nations General Assembly officially called the country Namibia, a name which was banned in South Africa until 1977.

3 This includes Walvis Bay (1 124 km^2) and offshore 'seal' islands. South Africa claims that these are part of the Republic because they were annexed by Britain in 1868 before the Germans colonized the rest of the South West African territory. The territory was transferred to the Cape Colony in 1884. From 1915 until 1977 it was administered by South Africa as an integral part of South West Africa.

4 This table is, for practical reasons, based on the official South African classification of the population into 'native nations' for the purpose of 'divide and rule', and does not imply any recognition of its validity. The classification system does not objectively reflect the ethnically distinct groups and has, in some cases, given rise to inter-group differences not based on historical fact. An example of this is the repetition of the myth of Ovambo-Herero conflict. In fact there was little pre-colonial contact between the two, but systematic South African attempts to separate them have subsequently created antagonism.

5 South Africa has used the low estimate population data to minimize the importance of the Namibian problem. Equally its education, health and food supply data for Africans look better with a low rather than a high population estimate.

6 See further Ruth First, *South West Africa*, Penguin African Library, London, 1963, pp. 27–48; Heinrich Vedder, *South West Africa in Early Times*, Oxford University Press, and C. H.C. Hahn, H. Vedder and L. Fourie, *The Native Tribes of South West Africa*, Frank Cass & Co., London, 1966.

3 The colonial economy: structures of growth and exploitation

REGINALD H. GREEN AND KIMMO KILJUNEN

We made South West. Why should we give it to you?
–Settler Proprietor to
Namibian Employee

We are outcasts in our own country . . .
We ask . . .
A dwelling place of our own.
– Chief Hosea Kutako

The last colonial economy

The penetration and restructuring of Namibia's territorial economies can be traced back to initial European mercantile entry over a century ago. In particular, it includes the merchant–missionary–market mechanisms which eroded the self-sufficiency, the socio-political structures and ultimately the economic viability of the pre-colonial African states[1] and the military–settler–mercantilist mechanisms of the German colonial period.[2] However, this chapter concentrates on the present colonial territorial economic and political economic structures which, in their present form, are largely the product of the last three decades. Until after the Second World War Namibia was a very peripheral South African colony with a few subsidized settlers, a little fishing, a tiny mining sector – a very small captive market or source of foreign exchange. At that time the 'proprietors' (Consolidated Diamond Mines, via De Beers, part of the Anglo American group) of its largest known asset, the diamond deposits, were mainly interested in preventing their full-scale exploitation by someone else.[3]

Over the three decades 1945–75 Namibia, as a territory, was developed by South Africa as a full-scale, high-output colony. In a world in which neo-colonialism and dependent development had already become the dominant strategies of the centre vis-à-vis the periphery, Namibia became the last colony, the last application of *mise en valeur* territorial development as a significant contribution to the economy of the metropole.

Colonial economies have varied with the particular historical context, local possibilities, and metropolitan political and economic needs which brought them into being. The 'plantations' of New England were unlike the pure 'plantation economies' of the Caribbean in the eighteenth century; the Indian Empire evolved in significant ways between 1750 and 1925; French colonial political economy diverged from Dutch or Belgian or British. However, historically they have had a number of common characteristics. Namibia under South African rule (over the 1920–1966 mandatory period) and occupation (since the revocation of the mandate) is a classic illustration of the colonial economy, indeed one so stark and skeletal it almost seems a parody or caricature of itself.

Namibia demonstrates with brutal clarity the contradictions, as well as the achievements, of a 'successful' (to its operators) colonial economic policy: rapid growth of certain sectors and destruction of social or economic patterns hindering (or believed to hinder) that growth; major imports of knowledge, technology, funds, personnel and goods and, at best, minimal progress economically, socially or politically for the colonized people; high levels of productivity for export and inability to meet the most basic domestic needs; integration into the metropolitan economy on its terms and disintegration of the territorial economy; radical alterations of economic pace and structure in response to external forces and radical inability to respond to domestic requirements.

Three special factors have influenced Namibia's colonial economy. First, its metropole, the Republic of South Africa, is a semi-dependent rather than a central industrial economy and therefore has been more singlemindedly concerned with net foreign exchange earnings from 'its' colony than a more structurally advanced colonial power might have been. Second, the particular, interaction of capitalist economic development and statutorily enforced racism which characterizes South Africa, and therefore Namibia, is, while not unique (*vide* the slave colonies of the Americas), not fully typical of colonial economy exploitation or exclusion of indigenous peoples. Third, unlike most other southern African economies, Namibia as a territory has not been a labour reserve; its colonial economy is territorial with its labour reserve/migrant system internal to the colony, not linked with the metropole.

Main characteristics of the colonial economy

It is convenient to list a number of the characteristics of the colonial economy in Namibia before examining its interactions and sectors in greater detail:[4]

- economic growth in response to external initiatives and contexts (the Republic of South Africa and global);
- domination of directly productive sectors by exports;
- service sectors primarily oriented to support of export/import sectors;
- concentration of exports and therefore production on a limited number of natural resource-based products;
- processing limited to the degree necessary to prepare raw materials for export;
- consumption and production heavily dependent on imports because of almost total absence of integrated territorial production pattern;
- external trade primarily through or to metropolitan power (Republic of South Africa);
- substantial export surplus with 'rest of world' and deficit with colonial power within substantial visible trade surplus;

- a sharp divergence between domestic (territorial) and national (retained) product because of substantial interest, dividend, profit and expatriate salary remittances;
- monetary and customs union with colonial power;
- foreign ownership of means of production (via forcible acquisition from the indigenous population in the case of natural resources);
- extremely unequal distribution of assets and of income on 'dual economy' lines including a radically greater European/African income disparity than that for South Africa itself;
- integration of the colonized peoples into the colonial economy as a cheap labour input;
- manipulation of the remnant 'subsistence' economy both to extract wage labour and to hold the necessary wage below family subsistence cost;
- implantation of a substantial expatriate and a not insignificant settler community to operate the 'modern' economy and of a substantial metropolitan run 'security' force to protect it;
- a fragile economy in respect to ecology, resource base, technological requirements, dependence on externally-based personnel, vulnerability to external economic shocks;
- a massive ratio of gross productive unit surplus to territorial product and to labour remuneration without any parallel expansion of public services, beyond the colonial production/personnel sectors, or of domestically financed fixed investment;
- apparent dependence on external investment because of expatriation of private and public sector surpluses;
- domination of production, trade, transport and finance, including settler production and commerce, by large-scale, external (Republic of South Africa and global) private and public sector enterprises.
- deliberate, often detailed, colonial and metropolitan state economic intervention to sustain and reproduce these characteristics;
- economic contradictions of a secondary nature among the colonial economy sub-sectors and between them and the metropolitan power;
- major economic contradictions between the colonial economy and the indigenous workers/peasants taking the form of politico-military conflict leading to both fiscal and security erosion of the colonial economy and more particularly of its capacity for sustained expanded reproduction.

The dual economy and the unity of exploitation

The Namibian territorial economy has been led and dominated by a rapidly growing, technologically modern, relatively high productivity European export and export support sector. However, the residual African sector accounts for almost half of the labour force and up to three-quarters of the population while generating only 2% of territorial product. It is now an enforced parody of a traditional sector and is unable to, or prevented from, providing physical subsistence to its members so that 'residual' is the only plausible adjective.

In part the division is geographic. Towns (or at least urban centres and amenity residential areas), mines, ranches, game parks, railways and communications, power and water, coastal waters (i.e. fishing) and ports are European. The residual areas are semi-desert margins, one 'Coloured' community (Rehoboth), created as a buffer zone during European penetration, and the northern and north-eastern frontier districts, remote from the ranching–mining–coastal complexes and beyond the old German-defined Police Zone. When a 'European' resource is in a 'residual' zone, e.g. the Kunene River with its power and irrigation potential, it becomes an enclave (e.g. Ruacana Falls dam) or is transported to the European zone (e.g. the proposed use of Kunene water for mines, towns and central European farms).

The dual nature of the economy and the apparent physical separation of its two segments does not mean that they evolved separately or that they are unrelated. Quite the contrary is true. Primitive accumulation to build the European economy meant theft from the African population – of sovereignty to give colonial control, of land to give room for ranchers and miners, of life (especially in the German wars which gave the world the word 'genocide'), of more land to force the Africans to seek jobs in the European sector, of freedom to organize to prevent political or economic mobilization for change. The creation of the European economy required the destruction of the traditional African economy and society and its reduction to the grotesque parody which is the residual economy, and the deformed society it carries with it.[5] The foundations of the modern Namibian economy were indeed laid by the Teutonic folk theme of blood and iron – African blood shed by European iron – and today the theme is played again by the South African occupation forces in their attempt to sustain and reproduce that economy.

TABLE 3.1 Distribution of Economically Active Population in 1977 (000)

	African	**'Coloured'**	**White**	**Total**	
				(000)	**(%)**
Residual sector	230	10	–	240	46
Migrant labour force	98	12	–	110	21
Commercial agriculture	15	3	7	25	5
Urban sector	90	23	30	143	28
Total	433	48	37	518	100

Source: Derived from *Manpower Estimates and Development Implications for Namibia*, UNIN, 1977. For further details, see Annex Table 4.

The occupational pattern shown in Table 3.1 is striking evidence of the interlocked dualism of the economy. Almost 50% of the economically active (and two-thirds of the people) are nominally in the so-called subsistence sector. However, the share of gross domestic product (GDP) derived from that sector is 2% on normal calculations (Table 3.2) and not over 4% on an adjusted price basis.[6] The productivity is so low that this residual sector cannot provide subsistence. It can only subsi-

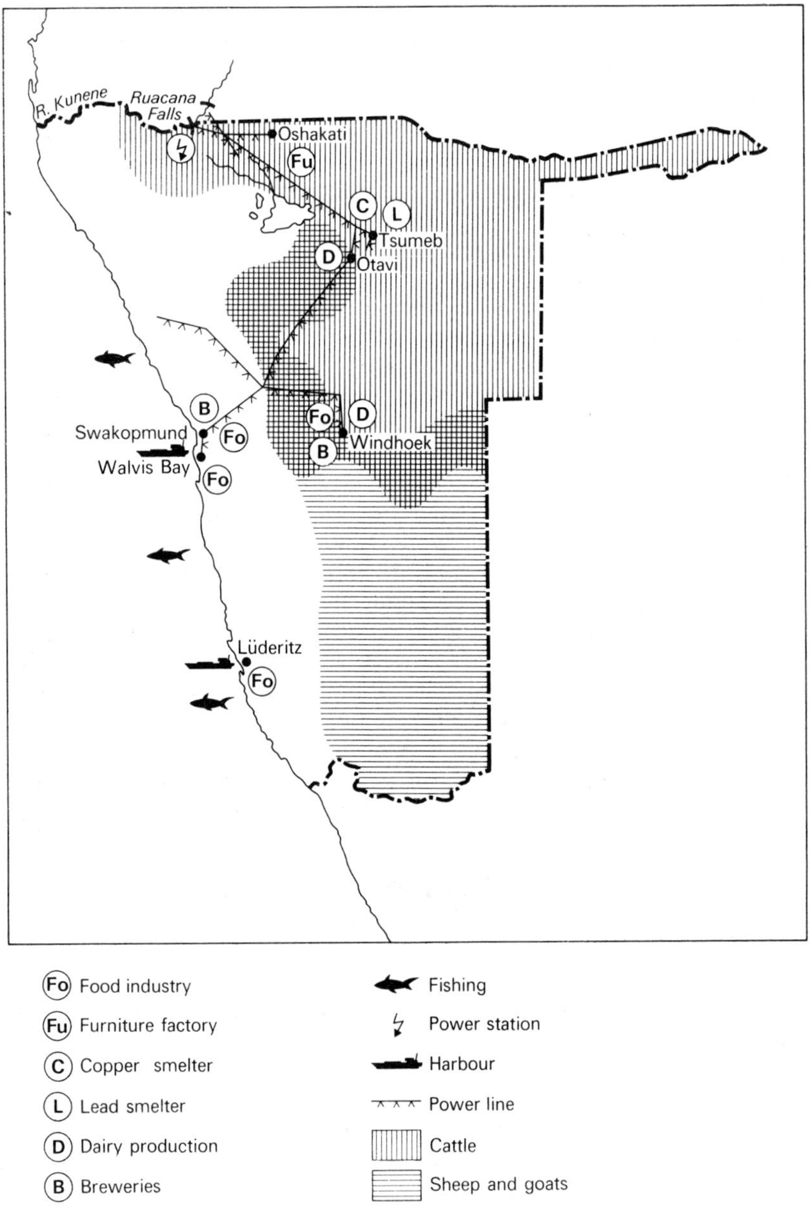

Map 3.1 Namibia's economy

dize the European sector by providing part subsistence and a dumping ground for dependents of workers who can then be housed in prison-like compounds or farm shacks and paid wages less than those necessary for family subsistence.

It is true that migrant contract labour probably was only 100–110 000 out of 275 000 European sector African and 'coloured' employees, but it set the wage pattern. Another 50–75 000 employees are domestic workers and perhaps 25 000 seasonal farm and fishery employees who are paid far below minimum family subsistence levels, i.e. they must have another wage-employee in the household, scrape out some subsistence income, or have an urban informal sector partial livelihood.

Apartheid, pass laws and contract were certainly designed to separate, but they were not aimed at 'separate development'. On the contrary, the state apparatus was used to integrate the African worker into European development in a particular way. The dual economy was, and is, characterized by unity of exploitation in the normal as well as the technical sense of the term.[7]

Natural resources: a fragile bonanza

Territorially Namibia is very well endowed with natural resources which have been exploited to levels yielding $1 250–$1 500 (Table 3.2) *per capita* territorial output. Abject poverty in Namibia is the result of policy and distribution, not of any absolute lack of resources or their exploitation.

Namibia ranks virtually co-equal with Zaire and Zambia as the second largest African producer of non-petroleum mineral products.[8] Rössing is one of the world's largest uranium oxide (yellow cake) complexes at 5 000 tonnes rated capacity. Langer Heinrich will be an equally major producer, and well-identified prospects exist for perhaps 10 000 further tonnes on at least three sites. Uranium oxide is worth $40 per pound and a boom is expected in the mid-1980s.[9]

A sixth of the world's gem diamonds are produced in Namibia by Consolidated Diamond Mines (a major member of the De Beers/Charter Consolidated/Johnies/Anglo American Group). Present output of about 1.8–2.0 million carats is sustainable for fifteen years on known reserves. Major exploration and prospecting within the 70- to 100-kilometre 'diamond zone' continues with a view to extending the Oranjemund mining (actually sand collection and sorting) operation's life.

In respect to base metals – copper, lead, zinc, tin, etc. – Namibia is not a major producer in world terms. However, the copper–lead–zinc output comes to 200 000 tonnes a year, which places Namibia fourth in Africa, and Tsumeb (part of the AMAX group) is a major base-metal mining and smelting unit.

Mineral prospects are by no means fully exploited, *vide* uranium, or even fully known. Additional viable copper, lead, zinc, as well as uranium deposits are virtually certain. Coal and iron are more problematic in economic terms, and petroleum, offshore and in the northern Etosha Pan (an interior river delta), is questionable. However, in 1980 development of the small Etosha Pan reserves was begun by the

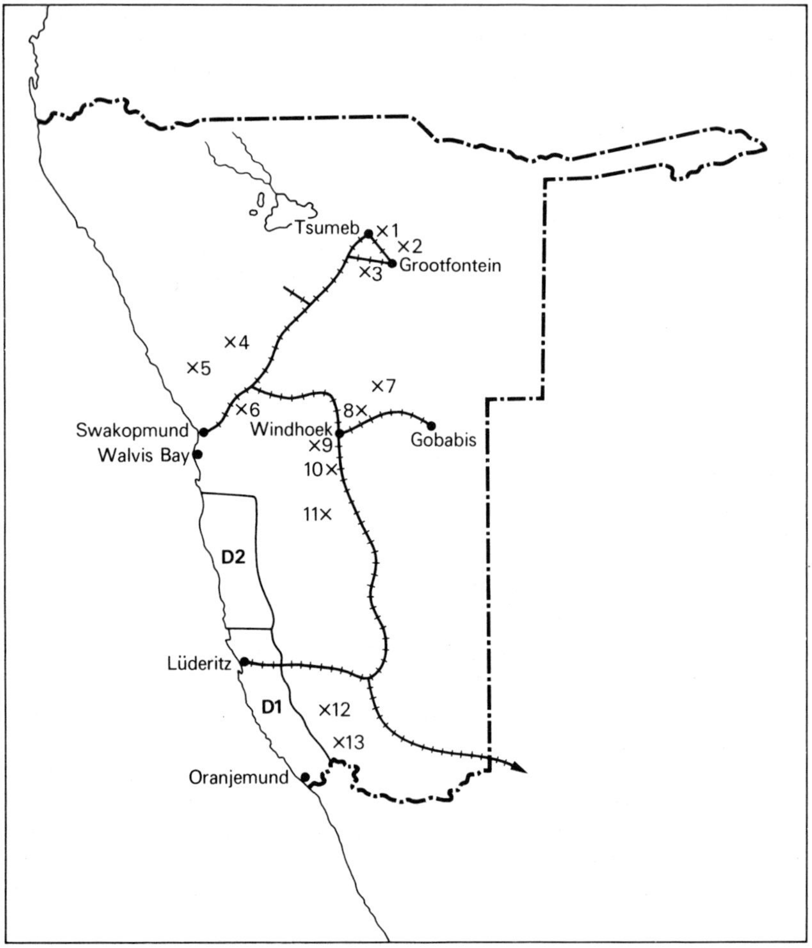

1 Tsumeb
2 Berg Aukas
3 Kombat
4 Uis
5 Brandberg
6 Rössing
7 Onganja
8 Otjihase
9 Matchless
10 Oamites
11 Klein Aukas
12 Rosh Pinah
13 Loreley

D1 Diamond area 1
D2 Diamond area 2

Map 3.2 Namibia's mines

United States oil company which controls Falconbridge Nickel and through it Oamites. International pressures, uncertainties and security 'problems' have limited exploration for a decade, although initial surveys suggested promising formations and minimal finds of gas, and perhaps oil, were located. A natural gas-field was located in 1977 but its size is a matter of conjecture.

Namibia's inshore coastal waters have yielded catches approaching 1 000 000 tonnes (mainly pilchard for tinning and anchovy for fish-oil and fish-meal), and offshore waters within the potential 322-km economic zone limit up to 1 000 000 tonnes (largely hake). However, those levels are not sustainable and the reckless overfishing (by South African and South West African settlers inshore and foreign vessels offshore, mainly from USSR, Spain, Cuba and Bulgaria) has created a crisis situation in which medium-term catch limits of perhaps 250 000 and 400 000 tonnes are urgently needed if this resource is not to be permanently destroyed.[10]

Agricultural potential is more problematic: without irrigation only the extreme north and north east and some small pockets elsewhere are suitable for crops. However, the ranching potential is high and exploited: 90 000 tonnes of beef (80% in the form of 400 000 head of live cattle exports) and 3 000 000 Karakul ('Persian Lamb') pelts (50% of world production). Indeed, the potential may be more than fully exploited as desertification is a threat in the southern Karakul and the residual African 'Homeland' grazing areas.

Paradoxically, while most of Namibia is desert or semi-desert it has substantial irrigation potential because it is bordered by two major rivers, the Kunene in the north, and the Orange in the south, and crossed by another, the Okavango in the north. To date this potential is almost unexploited except for the Ruacana Falls hydroplant, but the research and experimental groundwork for developing European irrigated agriculture in central Namibia and a twenty-five-year water plan to serve the overall European economy was carried out in the early 1970s with Ruacana (and associated pumping and irrigation works) seen as the first step.[11]

The colonial economy of Namibia is built on selective natural resource exploitation for export. About 90% of domestic production of goods is for export – 100% for minerals, 99% for fish, 100% for Karakul, 90% for cattle. The economy is fragile: vulnerable to the misuse of renewable resources, which has occurred in respect of fishing and ranching; vulnerable to fluctuations in the world economy which have badly affected copper since 1974, forcing the closure of a major mine; vulnerable to the explosive tensions created by a unity of exploitation and a dual economic and social system.

Agricultural and fishing production

Agriculture and fishing contribute one-sixth to GDP but account for three-fifths of the economically active population. Of this, commercial agriculture accounts for about 12% of GDP and 11% of employment (including self-employment). It is virtually confined to about 6 500 European ranching units specializing in cattle and Karakul sheep pro-

TABLE 3.2 Namibian Gross Domestic Product in 1977 (R000 000)

Sector			%	
Agriculture	157		13.9	
Subsistence		20		1.9
Commercial		137		12.0
Forestry	2		0.2	
Fishing	41		3.5	
Mining	375		33.2	
Primary sector	575		50.7	
Manufacturing	85		7.5	
Food processing		50		4.4
Other large-scale		25		2.2
Small-scale		10		0.9
Construction	60		5.3	
Electricity/water	15		1.3	
Secondary sector	160		14.1	
Transport/communication	60		5.3	
Trade	110		9.7	
Accommodation	25		2.2	
Financial services	85		7.5	
General government	70		6.2	
Social and personal services	50		4.4	
Tertiary sector	400		35.2	
Gross Domestic Product	1 135		100.0	

Source: Derived from Annex Table 15.

duction. A limited number of 'Coloured' and a handful of African commercial ranches exist and a limited number of European farms with dairy, horticultural and/or grain production. However, 90% of sheep and 70% of cattle are European-owned [12] and in all agricultural products other than beef Namibia is a net importer – 50% for grain, perhaps 25% for dairy products, 90% for other foodstuffs.

African agricultural production for household or local market consumption is under 1% of GDP and a seventh of total agricultural production at standard valuation (perhaps twice as much valued at consumer prices). Its 46% share in occupations, as noted earlier, is deceptive as very few African households can subsist on their own production. This is not simply a matter of lack of land or water, although in the centre and south those facts alone would prevent the 'reserves' from providing even subsistence incomes to all of the households for which they are actually or nominally 'home'. Indeed the African land in the north and north east comprises much of what is potentially the best land for crops and mixed farming in Namibia.

However, while extension services, credit, marketing, farm planning backed by long-term finance, subsidies and veterinary services are available intensively and efficiently for European farmers, they are notable for their near absence for African and 'Coloured' farmers. The exceptions demonstrate the nature of the general rule. Vaccination

TABLE 3.3 Economic Activity Estimates, 1977

	African (000)	(%)	European (000)	(%)	Total (000)	(%)
Residual sector	240	50	–	–	240	46
Commercial agriculture	50	10	6.5	18	56.5	11
Fishing and fish processing	7	2	0.5	1	7.5	2
Mining	19	4	3.5	10	22.5	4
Primary production	316	66	10.5	29	326.5	63
Manufacturing	10.5	2	3	8	13	3
Construction	13	3	1.5	4	15	3
Industry	23.5	5	4.5	12	28	6
Transport	11.5	2	1	3	12.5	2
Trade and finance	20	4	5	13	25	5
General government	17.5	4	16	43	33.5	6
Domestic	75	16	–	–	75	15
Services	124	26	22.0	59	146	28
Open unemployment	17.5	3	–	–	17.5	3
Total	481.0	100	37.0	100	518.0	100

Source: Derived from *Manpower Estimates and Implications for Namibia*, UNIN, 1977. For further details, see Annex Table 6.

against infectious diseases is available (indeed compulsory) for African cattle, in order to protect the European herds. Tinning facilities for African cattle (and a few recently inserted European ranches) have been developed in the north, in order to facilitate barring movement of African cattle into or across European ranching areas, which might spread disease, and to prevent their competing with European ranch offtake in respect to the quota for live cattle exports to the Republic of South Africa.[13] Indeed African sales of crops and cattle have sometimes not simply been neglected but actively discouraged or barred.

The backbone of African agriculture is cattle for both milk and meat. The main crops are millet, sorghum, maize and vegetables, but yields are apparently among the lowest in the world for the staple grains, except in the narrow Okavango Valley. Root, forest and bush fruit, and fish and game are significant in some areas (e.g. Caprivi) and to some communities (e.g. the San).[14]

Fishing, which has been badly hit by the results of recurrent overfishing, contributes about 2% of GDP (plus another 1% in processing) and a slightly lower share of employment (plus almost 2% in processing during the peak season). The fishing is largely carried out by seiners and trawlers owned by European small businessmen with 'Coloured' and African crews. The tinning and oil or meal extraction, located in Walvis Bay and to a much lesser extent Lüderitz, is dominated by four South African firms.[15] The contract price set by the firms and the quotas set by the South African occupation authorities dominate the industry. Virtually the entire catch is exported to or through South Africa. In respect to fish-meal (used primarily for fertilizer) the South African price is below the world price – a situation comparable to that for beef with the difference that no real global access and marketing problems exist for fish-meal. So export-oriented is the sector that it is impossible to buy Namibian fresh fish in Windhoek.

Mining[16]

In 1977 a third of Namibia's GDP came from mining, which provided about one-twenty-fifth of total employment. By 1979, with higher uranium oxide prices and output and higher diamond prices, virtually half of GDP was secured from mining but with about the same employment.

This sector is a clear example of John Stuart Mill's dictum applied to Britain that colonies were merely places in which it was convenient for her to carry out part of her business. Ownership, senior personnel, inputs of machinery and construction materials, markets and destination of product are 95–100% foreign; only wages and tax revenues (about 50% of Namibian revenues) remain in the territory. It is this sector which accounts for the bulk of the 33% divergence between domestic (produced in the territory) and national (retained in the territory) product.

Uranium ($275 million gross at 4 500 tonnes) and diamonds ($500 gross million at 1.9–2.0 carats) were the dominant mineral subsectors by 1979. Diamond production on a large scale dates to the 1940s, that of uranium oxide to 1976. Copper, lead and zinc ($150 gross million on perhaps 200 000 tonnes) are, like diamonds, older industries. They have been adversely affected by post-1974 prices, but are in a position to recover (to 250 000 tonnes and $300 million on present capacity) if the anticipated middle 1980s price boom occurs.

Until the 1970s Namibian mineral production was dominated by two companies with two more substantial second-rank firms. The leader was Anglo American (diamonds via Consolidated Diamond Mines) and American Metal Climax/Newmont (base-metal mining and smelting via Tsumeb). The former is South African and the latter United States-based and controlled. Second-line companies were the South West Africa Co. (SWACO) – vanadium, lead, zinc, tin – with Anglo/South African ownership, and the Iron and Steel Co. (ISCOR) – tin, manganese, base metals – with South African state ownership.

Three newcomers have appeared since 1966 (ironically the date of the revocation of the mandate and the beginning of the illegal occupation). Two are in copper and associated metals: Falconbridge of Canada (Oamites) and Johannesburg Consolidated-Johnies of the Anglo American Group (Otjihase) but the disastrous fall in copper prices between 1975 and 1977 forced the closure, on a care and maintenance basis, of the second group's mine at the turn of 1977–78. The largest newcomer is RTZ (formerly Rio Tinto Zinc, a British-based transnational corporation with global interests in base metals and uranium), the largest shareholder and, with the South African state Industrial Development Corporation (IDC), the controlling interest in the $300 million Rössing uranium mine and concentration plant. The oxide is airfreighted to Paris and, apparently via a swop or 'washing' arrangement with Niger or Gabon, analagous to those used in sanctions busting oil to Rhodesia, used to meet RTZ's basic contract with British Nuclear Fuels.[17]

TABLE 3.4. Namibian Mineral Resources

Major minerals (% of world reserve)		**Secondary minerals**	**Alleged deposits**
		Germanium	
Diamonds	(5)[1]	Semi-precious stones	Natural gas
Uranium	(5)[2]	Berylium	Oil
Zinc	(1)	Bismuth	Coal
Cadmium	(1)	Lithium	Fluorspar
Silver	(2)	Manganese	Iron
Arsenic	(5)	Molybdenum	Platinum
Copper	(1)	Phosphates and Salt	
Lead	(1)	Tin	
		Vanadium	
		Wolfram	
		Tantalite	
		Lime and Marble	
		Gold	

[1] 10–15% for gem diamonds

[2] 10% or more including discoveries through 1979

Sources: Adapted from W.C.J. van Rensburg and D.A. Pretorius, *South Africa's Strategic Minerals*, Johannesburg, 1977, and Odendaal Report, Pretoria, 1964.

Namibia's proven reserves (see Table 3.4) are significant in global terms for gem diamonds, uranium, arsenic and germanium.[18] They are significant in absolute terms for copper, lead and zinc. Manganese, vanadium and salts/phosphates may be absolutely significant. Coal, iron ore and oil are uncertain in global and absolute terms. While the colonial mining policy has been one of maximizing output (and South African foreign revenue and tax receipts) and not territorial product or coherent development, there is no reason to fear early exhaustion of resources. Proven deposits are good for fifteen to twenty-five years at present output and 'secondary' ones, identified but not fully proven economically, for perhaps another fifteen. While tentative findings, let alone unsurveyed areas, are not calculable, the results of 1960s' and 1970s' prospecting and geological surveys are promising.

Secondary sectors[19]

The secondary sectors, manufacturing, construction, electricity and water, generate about one-seventh of GDP and provide about one-sixteenth of employment. However, they are almost as dependent on exports as the primary sector because the bulk of manufacturing value added is fish and meat processing for export, the major users of electricity and water are the export sectors and supporting services, and the major markets for construction are the export firms and the state.

Fish tinning and fish-oil or meal extraction dominate the manufacturing sector. Meat processing is second in importance, despite the fact that 80% of the beef is shipped as live cattle (to the benefit of the South African packing industry) and only 20% packed or tinned territorially. Together they account for half of the manufacturing sector.

Other export processing is minimal. Karakul pelt preparation and wool scouring are done in the Republic. Similarly, quota and price measures prevented the continued growth of the once-promising butter and cheese industry. The same pattern exists in respect of mineral processing. Processing necessary before export (copper smelting, uranium-oxide separation and concentrating, lead refining) are partly done territorially, but other activities (copper and zinc refining, diamond sorting and cutting) are wholly carried out in the Republic. As a result the raw materials of Namibia are not available as a base for manufacturing in the territory.

Other manufacturing consists of some food processing (flour milling, soft drink and beer bottling); repair (fishing vessel, automobile, railway, although heavy maintenance is done at Upington and Capetown, not in Namibia); machinery; light engineering (tins, spare parts, simple fabrication and casting); and miscellaneous (printing, semi-artisanal furniture and boat building). The common characteristics are relatively high natural protection through transport costs, relative absence of economics of large-scale production and, in some cases, major advantages of speed and convenience to users of a nearby establishment.

Namibia is a small country in terms of population and, given the very unequal pattern of income distribution of its dual economy, it is an even smaller market for most products. However, this does not fully explain the minute role of manufacturing. Colonial policy has also been critical:

1 as a part of the South African Customs Union territory, South West Africa has had no tariff protection against the Republic;
2 the import and wholesale sectors are South African-owned and 'naturally' look to home-country suppliers;
3 tax and credit policy has been designed to favour mining and ranching, not manufacturing;
4 quotas and administered prices have hampered or barred pre-export processing in respect to meat and dairying;
5 railway rate policy basically favours manufactured imports and live cattle exports;
6 South African bodies, e.g. railways, do not treat Namibia as a separate territory and centralize planning, procurement, heavy repairs and manufacturing in the Republic.

Construction is dominated by the state and the mining companies on the market side, and by branches of Republic of South Africa groups on the production side. It too is highly fragmented, with most planning and design work, some personnel, and almost all plant and inputs secured from the Republic. Only quarrying is local; cement production, while long mooted, has never been instituted and present plans appear contingent on a political settlement, especially as the current phase of the liberation struggle is bad for long-term confidence and therefore for construction contracts. About 5% of GDP is generated in, and 3% of employment provided by, construction.

Power and water (1.3% of GDP) are basically inputs into primary production and the consumption of the European communities, and both are relatively scarce and expensive. Two thermal stations at Windhoek and Walvis Bay supply a national electricity grid with additional production by mines. The major hydroelectric scheme, Ruacana Falls, is theoretically operational, but the combination of lack of access to the storage and pumping units in Angola and liberation forces' attacks on transmission lines make its present contribution nominal. Adequate water development is similarly held up; Windhoek now uses a very complex recycling plant to supply at least a third of its water from purified waste water. 8 000 boreholes (7 500 European and 500 African) supply ranch water for human and animal consumption and for spot irrigation.

Services

The tertiary (services) sector provides 28% of employment and 35% of GDP (13% of employment and 34% of GDP excluding domestic service). The high ratio of GDP to employment, especially excluding domestic services, is not due to high productivity based on natural resources, as in mining, but to the fact that 60% of the very highly paid European employees are in this sector.

The aggregate sectoral figures do not show imbalances as dramatically as do those for the primary and secondary sectors. General government at 6% is low, but not radically so, while the other figures, except the domestic service estimate, are not particularly atypical of middle-income countries. The aggregates, however, conceal the nature of the services and their users. Transport, trade and storage are basically inputs into exports and import distribution – a fact following from the nature of production patterns. For the same reason, they are basically European services, given the restricting of Africans to hewers of rock and drivers of cattle (to paraphrase Hendrik Verwoerd's use of the biblical 'hewers of wood and drawers of water').

Public services, like infrastructure, are oriented to the European economy and to Europeans. Those available to Africans, some primary education and a very limited amount of technical and secondary education, some health services (especially in towns and at work places), a limited number of urban houses, and a larger number of prison-like single worker contract labour compounds, are basically inputs into the European sector labour force, perceived in the same way as cattle vaccination or mineral surveys. Other expenditure 'for' Africans, appointed 'chiefs' and 'Homeland' 'governments' and their 'homeguards',[20] administrators and police, sham development authorities (at best creating a coterie of dependent shopkeepers and officials),[21] are more accurately characterized as expenditures 'on' Africans, i.e. on holding them down. It is not accidental that all-weather tarred and gravelled roads were not built in the north and north east until the 1970s. They were not built to allow African development but to combat the armed phase of the liberation struggle.

The outward-looking economy

Namibia cannot be described as an open economy. With respect to all but one country it has high tariffs and tight exchange controls. The exception, of course, is South Africa. The tariff maintains Namibia as a captive market and the exchange controls ensure that surplus flows to the Republic and no further without South Africa's consent.

However, it is an externally-oriented economy and has been since the initial European conquest. Admittedly, both as a source of raw materials and as a captive market German South West Africa was not very successful; nor until the 1950s were South African efforts to create a settler economy with a mining backup any more successful. The perception has been consistent: the colonial territory of Namibia can save foreign exchange by providing goods which would otherwise be imported from abroad (e.g. fish and fish-meal), earn foreign exchange from its natural resource-based exports to the outside world (metals, diamonds, fish, beef, Karakul), provide a captive market for metropolitan exports of consumer goods (e.g. maize) and production inputs (e.g. mining machinery, construction materials), and provide a flow of surplus to the metropolitan economy from settlers, residents, firms and/or taxes. Beyond that it is of no interest and if it competes with metropolitan production it must be deterred (e.g. dairying) or subjected to controls (e.g. cattle).

The results are striking. Two-thirds of GDP are exported – 90% of physical goods. Of that, nearly 100% consists of uncut diamonds, uranium oxide, raw metal, ores and concentrates, unprocessed Karakul pelts, live cattle, unscoured wool, tinned fish, fish-meal and oil, frozen lobster, chilled or tinned meat, all unprocessed or very simply processed natural resource-based products. Equally, except for meat, beer and soft drinks, most milk, half of grain and a minor portion of other foods, Namibian consumption, production inputs, construction material, machinery and equipment demand is met by imports. A more extreme case of producing what is not consumed and consuming what is not produced is hard to imagine in a territory with substantial size, resource diversity and territorial demand.

TABLE 3.5 Namibian Exports in 1966 and 1977 (R000 000)

	1966	(%)	1977	(%)
Agricultural products	32.6	16	130	18
Karakul pelts	15.9	8	65	9
Meat products	16.7	8	65	9
Fishery products	48.9	23	65	9
Fish-meal	22.4	11	33	5
Tinned fish	14.0	6	20	3
Other	12.5	6	12	2
Mineral products	127.8	61	505	70
Diamond	85.0	41	280	37
Uranium	–	–	100	12
Copper	19.2	9	55	11
Lead	12.3	6	40	6
Other	11.3	5	30	4
Total	209.3	100	700	100
Exports as % of GDP	67%		62%	

Source: Derived from Annex Table 18.

The bulk of exports and imports are to or through South Africa. Uranium oxide and most of the base metals are the principal exceptions. In the case of exports, only cattle, a substantial share of tinned fish and fish-meal, and some base metals are kept in South Africa. The rest is either re-exported directly or processed, e.g. Karakul, some ores (concentrates), raw metal, some diamonds. The effect is to transfer income to South African Railways, South African processors, South African merchandizing operations and, in the case of fish products, South African consumers.[22]

Imports are 90% from South Africa and 60–75% of South African origin.[23] Namibia is probably South Africa's second largest market for manufactured goods (following Zimbabwe). The impact on Namibia probably is more in higher costs than lower production, e.g. South African cars at 125–150% of the landed cost before duty of Japanese, but the lack of protection and incentives has limited domestic manufacturing while the presence of South African maize subsidies has played a part in creating the grain deficit. Again, the near monopolization of import/export, wholesaling and transport (including the economically dubious Capetown–Namibia rail link[24]) transfers income from Namibia to the Republic, in contrast to a system based on direct imports from the lowest cost supplier by the cheapest transport route.

Equally striking are remittances, which are estimated at over R400 million (37% of GDP) in 1977.[25] About three-quarters are to South Africa and, since they are basically derived from Namibian foreign-exchange earnings on exports, represent a net foreign-exchange gain to South Africa of the order of R300 million. When added to South African exports to Namibia this gives a minimum annual foreign-exchange value of the colony to the metropole of R600 million. The success, in its own terms, of the colonial development and exploitation strategy is only too evident. Even allowing for the foreign-exchange cost of the war, Namibia still yielded a foreign-exchange surplus to the Republic of at least R300 million in 1977.

Predictably in an economy built to export, investment is equally external in generation. Of directly productive investment, 90% is foreign – slightly under half of this is South African and the balance non-South African transnational corporations and bank loans.[26] The incentives given to foreign investors are generous including, *inter alia*, exceptionally low tax rates, profitable depreciation rights, free exportation of revenues as well as raw materials without quantitative or qualitative restrictions, and above all a cheap and ample labour force. South Africa has encouraged foreign investment in mining[27] for three reasons:

1 to spread the risk, especially on high-cost operations such as uranium and petroleum exploration;
2 to strengthen the South African external balance position since the Republic herself has a net capital inflow;
3 to build up a group of firms (e.g. RTZ, Falconbridge) and states (e.g. those such as the United Kingdom with atomic fuel supplies dependent on Rössing) with vested interests in a continued colonial economy under South African management.

Government investment has followed a zig-zag course with a high inflow of funds from the Republic (probably the counterpart of its heavy external borrowing), following twenty years during which Namibian territorial surplus investments in South African securities more or less balanced South African state corporation railways and communications investment. However, with a fall in state investment and a rise in revenue derived from Namibia,[28] by 1977 the net inflow on government account was near zero and by 1979 the net surplus on government account probably exceeded the investment inflow of railways and communications.[29]

The colonial economy produced rapid growth between 1945 and 1965, more moderate growth over the period 1965–70, and has been near stagnation since (Table 3.6). The slowing down after 1965 relates partly to the peaking of ranching output and recurrent crises resulting from over-fishing and subsequent catch reductions. It also relates to a plateau in mineral production prior to the opening of Rössing, Oamites and Otjihase. The post-1970 stagnation[30] – negative growth if

TABLE 3.6. The Growth of GDP

Period	Nominal Growth	Real Growth
1946–1956	20.0%	14.3%
1960–1965	14.2%	9.2%
1965–1969	7.0%	4.5%
1970–1975	14.2%	2.5%

Source: W. H. Thomas, *Economic Development in Namibia*, Dortmund, 1977.

diamonds and uranium oxide are excluded – is secondarily related to depression in South Africa and economic disorder globally as well as to the most severe fishing crisis to date. However, primarily it is a crisis of confidence: the future of the colonial economy is in doubt so that additional or even sustained investment is not attractive and, for the smaller proprietors or enterprises, expatriation of capital as well as profits is increasingly practised.

This means that the productive forces base of the economy is in some danger of being damaged for the medium term. Doubts as to the future hardly help to impose control on fish catches or herd sizes. They may encourage grab-and-run mining although there is little evidence of that. Consolidated Diamond Mines' output build-up in Namibia parallels De Beers' output management, including rather larger new programmes or expansion in Botswana and the Western Cape. The lag in prospecting and exploration and near cessation of development expenditure in mining does mean that Namibia may not be well placed to cash in on the probable base-metal and uranium boom in the mid-1980s, but with fifteen to twenty-five years' proven reserves it can presumably be made up before present output levels are endangered.

In any event, the real challenge to the colonial economy does not relate to its ability to generate growth nor in relatively sustained growth. It lies in its externalization of markets, sources of supply, capital and capitalists, state and business; it lies in the exclusion of the majority of people from the income generated by the growing segment of the dual economy, while exploiting their labour to make possible the exploitation of natural resources to the benefit of external econommic factors.

Distribution: the anatomy of inequality

Any division of production and distribution is artificial. The nature of ownership, of decisions as to products and markets, of state intervention, of social and production relations determine both the structure of output and the distribution of the proceeds. The colonial economy does not separately happen to be based on private foreign-owned production for export and at the same time to have a radically unequal distribution of income including a large drain of surplus abroad. The two are as integrally related as the sides of a coin. A dual economy, even one less deliberately constructed than Namibia's, does not separately happen to have low productivity and low incomes in the excluded sector: the allocations of investment and services reinforce the production and the income disparities alike and create classes, bureaucracies and power structures with a vested interest in reproducing them.

Namibia's GDP in 1977 was approximately R1 135 million or $1 000 *per capita*, about the world average and higher than any genuinely independent sub-Saharan African state. Namibia is territorially a 'middle-income' economy, but, as in the case of production, distribution is dual.

The African and 'Coloured' communities number over 90% of the population, over 90% of the economically active population, and over 85% of the 'modern' sector employed and self-employed. Yet (see Table 3.7) they receive about one-eighth of GDP. Their total average household income (treating migrants and 'Homeland' dependents as single families) is about R150 million, giving personal figures of the order of $750 per year or $150 *per capita*. About 75% of that income is from wages, 15% from 'subsistence' (which nominally 'employs' more African and 'Coloured' people than the wage sector), and perhaps 10% from petty trade, craft and other non-agricultural self-employment.[31]

The European expatriate and settler community, including small and middle proprietors, receives about 28% or R315 million (see Table 3.7), that is, about R3 000 *per capita* or nearly R10 000 ($12 000) per household. Of this, about two-thirds is wage and salary income, averaging perhaps R7 000 per employee as against R400 for African and 'Coloured' employees. One-third is from small and middle businesses, primarily ranches, stores and service establishments, with an average supply of perhaps R10 000.[32]

TABLE 3.7 Distribution of GDP in 1977

	(R000 000)		(%)
Africans/'Coloureds'			
Subsistence economy	25		2.2
Wages and salaries	105		9.3
Small-scale production and trade	15		1.3
Total income	145		12.8
Per capita		R125 ($150)	
Europeans			
Wages and salaries	210		18.5
Self-employed income	105		9.2
Total income	315		27.7
Per capita		R1 975 ($3 470)	
Taxes on proprietors	175		15.4
Large company surpluses	500		44.1
Total GDP	1 135		100
GDP *per capita*		R850	($990)

Source: Derived from Annex Table 15 B – D; compare with Annex Table 17.

The apparent ratio of 23:1 ($3 500: $150) between European and African/'Coloured' *per capita* incomes is considerably higher than in

South Africa. It contrasts with perhaps 8 to 1 in an independent African state with a large resident European community like Zambia or Botswana.[33] The difference in income is mirrored by that in availability of public services (notably health and education) and in life expectancy, 65 and 72 years for European men and women, 37 and 33 for African. By comparison, the Tanzanian life expectancy estimate is 43 to 45.

South African official publications, firms and individual South Africans regularly assert that the average income of Africans in South Africa and Namibia is higher than in most independent African states. Even ignoring the question of whether this would go very far toward justifying the radical inequality, this claim is false.

Tanzania's 1977 GDP *per capita* was of the order of $160, roughly comparable to the Namibian African income.[34] Of this, about $135 *per capita* represented personal incomes of African Tanzanians. The cost of living in Tanzania appeared (admittedly on scanty evidence) to be at least one-quarter lower than in Namibia. Thus, on a comparable basis, the figure is of the order of $180. As noted above, Tanzanian life expectancy figures are better, which tends to confirm, at least in respect to food, the estimate of higher personal consumption power by Tanzanians than by Namibian Africans.

State expenditure, at least nominally, on behalf of Africans and 'Coloureds' in Namibia during 1976/77 was $65–75 *per capita* (see Table 3.10) but, of that, at least half represented European salaries and a high proportion covered administration over, not for, the communities. The comparable Tanzanian figure is approximately $65 which, adjusted for lower salaries in Tanzania, may be comparable. However, the provision of certain services is of a very different order of magnitude in Tanzania compared with Namibia: for example, the provision of pure water (40–45% of the population compared with perhaps 25% in Namibia), preventive medicine and basic curative medicine (an average of six clinic visits a year for rural and eight for all Tanzanians), primary education (85% initial-year enrolment as a step toward universal primary education), adult literacy and education (75% adult literacy compared with perhaps 25–30% in Namibia), secondary and tertiary education (a tertiary enrolment of 10 000 of which 3 000 is university in Tanzania, whereas in Namibia the tertiary enrolment for Africans is, at most, 100, of which none is university).

Even excluding issues of equality, participation in decision taking, power over officials and the state, Tanzanians have higher levels of combined personal consumption power and access to public services. But Tanzania is one of the world's thirty poorest economies. In 1977 it had a *per capita* level of productive forces barely over 15% of Namibia's. That it is able to provide higher personal consumption and public services to its citizens than those of Africans in Namibia is a fairly devastating comment on claims that the colonial economy is in the interests of the colonized Africans as well as the colonizing Europeans.

Personal incomes account for only about 40% of Namibian GDP, and wages, salaries, subsistence income for only 30%, whereas more normal figures would be of 70–80% and 60–70%. About 60% of GDP is accounted for by gross operating surpluses of large (foreign) enterprises. Of this, one-quarter (15% of GDP) is taken by the state and three-quarters (44% of GDP) represents depreciation (perhaps one-fifth) and post-tax profits (perhaps four-fifths or 35% of GDP). These calculations (see Table 3.7) are subject to error, but they do indicate basic proportions and orders of magnitude – stigmata of the pure colonial economy at its most profitable, externally oriented, unequalizing and rapacious. The form may be less naked than the initial land theft, the coercion slightly less brutal than the barbed whips and systematic genocide of the wars of reconquest at the turn of the century, but what is practised in the last colony is still the political economy of theft.

The pattern of GDP end use appears to be about 22½% (R250 million) current account surplus (net export of purchasing power), 33% (R365 million) personal consumption, 9% (R120 million) public consumption, 17½% (R200 million) gross state and parastatal investment, and about 17½% (R200 million) gross private investment. The investment rate is surprisingly high. Its private component is dominated by replacement investment, mineral exploration (at least a third of the total), and mine or associated development (the last stages of Rössing and its township, and the first stages of the Langer Heinrich mine).

As noted earlier, because of the disarticulation of the economy, the concentration of personal income in the hands of a few Europeans, and the high propensity to import in relation to investment, additional production for export has a very low impact on generalized demand for local goods for domestic consumption. Further, it does not generate significant employment growth for Africans or Europeans because not only mining and fishing but also ranching and services are highly land- and capital-intensive. Growth in Namibia produces generalized demand and employment in South Africa (and to a lesser extent other suppliers of imports or recipients of remittances) much more than in Namibia itself.

This contradiction actually cuts across the ethnic line; the interests of the large companies and of South Africa are not fully congruent with those of the non-ranching settler community. The ranchers occupy an intermediate position: South Africa is their main market, but price and quantity are controlled and development by their sector of external markets has been discouraged. Thus in recent months settlers have expressed territorial economic nationalism against the South African state and the main mining companies (Anglo in particular).[35]

Contrary to wishful thinking by liberals,[36] the contradiction within the European community does not constitute a basis for unified black-white territorial nationalism against South Africa and transnational corporations. The contradiction between the settlers (especially the ranchers) and the African workers and peasants is much sharper. The basic settler interest is in reallocating the gains from exploitation, not restructuring the productive system nor ending the political economy of theft.

The symbols and end products of the colonial, externally oriented nature of the economy are demonstrated by the gap between

TABLE 3.8 Divergence of GDP and GNP: 1946–77 (R000 000)

Year	GDP	GNP	GNP % of GDP
1946	22.2	20.4	92
1950	61.0	46.4	76
1956	141.6	85.1	60
1962	146.7	104.1	71
1969	368.9	278.0	75
1977	1 135.0	710.0	63

Sources: Odendaal Report, Pretoria, 1964; *Financial Mail*, 'Desert Deadlock', 2 March 1973.

GDP (produced in territory) and GNP (retained in territory) (see Table 3.8) and the level of remittances (see Table 3.9).

In 1946 the colonial economy was not, in its own terms, a success. There were relatively low surpluses to be extracted. Indeed, in the 1930s remittances were negative and, including subsidies, GNP probably exceeded GDP. From 1946 to 1977 the gap between GDP and GNP increased from 8% of GDP to 37%, and, although there were fluctuations (a peak divergence of 40% was recorded in 1956) this trend has continued.

The growth in the gap is no accident. One of the 'purposes' of the colonial economy, as opposed to the nationally controlled export economy, is to maximize the surpluses available to the metropolitan state, its firms and its nationals. The increase in the gap from less than R2 million in 1946 to R55 million in 1956 to R90 million in 1969 and to more than R400 million in 1977 is not evidence of the failure of South Africa's colonial political economy for Namibia but of its massive success.

Surplus generated in a colony is useful only if it can be remitted or reinvested to generate further surpluses. Again, the Namibian case is a success story. Individuals, firms and, on recurrent account, the South African state have been able to remit because of the export surplus and capital inflow.

In 1977 (see Table 3.9) about 20% of remittances were by individuals, 70% by large enterprises, 10% by the state. Given the proportion of European employees in transnational corporations and the dominant role of company-based revenues in state receipts, this suggests that about 85% of the remittances were derived from the transnational corporation/manager sub-sector of the colonial economy

TABLE 3.9. Remittances from Namibia in 1977 (R000 000)

Gross Domestic Product		1 135
Remittances:		
European wages/salaries	50	
Small enterprise surplus	35	
Large enterprise	300	
State net revenue	40	425
Gross National Product		710

Source: Derived from Annex Table 15 D.

TABLE 3.10. South African Recurrent Budget for Namibia: 1976/77

	R000 000		%
Revenue			
Income tax	26.5		14
Company tax	83.7		45
Value Added Tax	7.4		4
Duty	36.0		19
Repayment of loans, interest	7.0		4
Other income	26.2		14
	186.8		100
Expenditure			
White:	74.0		53
General administration		12.2	
Education		15.0	
Health		14.2	
Other social expenditure		8.3	
Economic services		24.3	
African:	53.6		38
Bantu administration		49.5	
Bantu education		3.5	
'Coloured':	13.0		9
Administration		12.0	
Education		1.0	
Total[1]	140.0		100
Security Police[1]	4.5		
Military expenditure[2]	250.0		

[1] Excludes Security Police which is in SWA Budgets.
[2] In RSA, not SWA, Budgets. Estimated expenditure in/on/against Namibia.
Source: Data derived from Annex Tables 32, 33; W. H. Thomas, *Economic Development in Namibia*, Dortmund, 1977. Compare with Annex Table 32 for years 1978/79 and 1985/86.

and 15% from the settler/resident proprietor sub-sector.

Data on Namibian state revenues and expenditure are difficult to compile both because they are partly on South African and partly on territorial account, and because the forms in which they have been published make it difficult to distinguish between capital and recurrent expenditure or to ascertain the object or beneficiary of expenditure. However, it is possible to derive an overall impression. In 1976–77 (see Table 3.10) the recurrent revenue (dominated by diamond-related revenues) exceeded recurrent expenditure by about R50 million or 50% of capital expenditure. This excludes expenditure on security police and the military of the order of R250 million (expenditure not for Namibians or Namibia but necessary to preserve the last colony).

Of recurrent expenditure of R140 million, about 53% was for Europeans (9% of the population), 9% was for 'Coloureds' (9% of the population) and 38% for Africans (82% of the population). Within these categories there are marked variations: 20% of expenditure for Europeans was on education compared with 8% of expenditure for 'Coloureds' and 7% of expenditure for Africans. The dominant category of 'administrative' expenditure for Africans and 'Coloureds' includes some for health and education but is dominated by payments to officials whose duty is repression or control and not service or development.

Expenditure *per capita* is about R50 for Africans, R125 for 'Coloureds', R675 for Europeans. In other words public spending is proportional to private income and reinforces rather than redresses inequality. The African/European gap of 13 to 1 and Black/European of 12 to 1 is striking, especially as at least half the expenditure 'on' the African/'Coloured' peoples is on repression. This would suggest that a more accurate *per capita* ratio of service provided is 25 to 1.

A new era?[37]

South Africa has repeatedly claimed that changes are occurring. First Odendaal, then the 'new' labour provisions after the 1971 strike, then Turnhalle, most recently the 1978 'elections' and 1979 'National Assembly' were claimed to mark the dawn of a new era. Now Odendaal, the post-strike variations on contract, and Turnhalle stand discredited and one is left with the events of 1978 and early 1979. Four things were promised:

1 removal of apartheid as to residence, choice of work, access to services and shops;
2 equal pay for equal work;
3 training and advancement opportunities;
4 free elections and National Assembly members.

On the face of it apartheid has been ended: Justice Steyn did not implement most petty apartheid laws; the 'National Assembly' has not only banned residential segregation but also made refusal to sell to Africans an offence. However, the Democratic Turnhalle Alliance (DTA) has decided not to desegregate schools and discrimination in employment is not an offence. While a few rich Africans can buy houses or shops in European areas, Windhoek City Council is cutting services to Katutura, pleading financial stringency. While the pass laws may have gone, new vagrancy legislation still restricts residence and employment changes and police raids go on.[38]

It is true that Europeans rioted against the housing legislation and were merely watched by a handful of police as they jostled Assembly members, but disturbing colonists is one thing and changing the structure of the colonial economy quite another. Moreover, Professor Gerrit Viljoen, President of the Broederbond, has succeeded Steyn as Administrator, apparently with a brief to defuse the ultra right-wing European reaction. He departed in 1980 with this facet of his mission at least partially achieved.

Equal pay for equal work and minimum wages of R50 plus food and lodging or R100 cash has not been adhered to.[39] Even the government does not pay the correct rates,[40] and only a few of the largest mining companies (Consolidated Diamond Mines, Tsumeb, Rössing, Falconbridge) appear to pay average African wages as high as the 'proposed' minimum.[41] That minimum is below the poverty line for an urban family.[42]

Opportunities for advancement have fared little better. There are still very few opportunities for education beyond primary school and virtually none at tertiary level. The one technical high school, opened in 1979, was paid for by Anglo American, not the state. Some large companies seek to have a least a token number of African artisans, junior firemen, clerks or bookkeepers (sometimes regrading the job so that a good deal less is paid than the R7 500 plus fringe benefits which a European artisan costs). However, such employment opportunities are few and there are fewer still chances to qualify for them.

There was an election in the sense that Africans could vote, but even the 'moderate' Namibia National Front denounced it, as did Church leaders.[43]

The new era is seen as a new charade for almost all Africans.[44] The settlers offer nominal wage increases and a few concessions designed to buy a collaborator elite, hoping to finance these by higher taxes on the major companies. The companies in general offer some advancement opportunities, somewhat higher wages, and slightly better conditions, hoping to gain a more skilled, more stable and more loyal labour force at the expense of squeezed-out settlers and expatriate Europeans.

Ironically, there is an exception which shows how much further a true neo-colonial policy would go. Anglo American:

1 pays, at least in its main unit, Consolidated Diamond Mines, the minimum wage to all employees and more to most;
2 has an in-service training programme and has financed the only technical high school;
3 promotes Africans and is seeking to provide a growing number with family or private room housing and has desegregated the company school;
4 *de facto* recognizes a workers' liaison committee which resembles a union branch;
5 refused to coerce employees into registering to vote in the 1978 election (only 6% did so);[45]
6 provides substantial data and comments on studies on its operations by outside bodies which are hardly self-evidently friendly to it.[46]

This example is virtually unique. Rössing only built a model 'works township' after RTZ's Chairman was heavily criticized in the United Kingdom and taken on tour by an Anglican bishop of what was then probably the worst mine housing in Namibia. Its main support for education is for adult literacy on a small scale and only now is it seriously evaluating environmental hazards.[47]

Of course, Anglo American is not engaged in philanthropy. It believes that a skilled, stable, African middle-level technical and managerial cadre will lower costs. It knows from experience elsewhere in Africa that colonialism is doomed and that if it acts prudently it can do profitable business with successor states. If these views were evident in the company sector as a whole then a neo-colonial settlement might be conceivable. It is possible that, if South Africa had had that vision in 1966, Namibia might well be independent, relatively conservative, internally inegalitarian, and externally a building block in a South African economic 'Pax Pretoriana'.[48] However, 1979 is not 1966 and Anglo American policy is not that of the other companies, let alone the settlers or the occupation authorities.

In summary, the verdict on the new era might be a generalization of a comment made about the 'new contract system':

> In the long run, it will thus depend upon the acceptance or rejection of a system which is based on migrant labour, differential wage rates on grounds of colour, and unilateral collective bargaining facilities.[49]

A valediction forbidding mourning

The colonial economy in Namibia prospered for the quarter century 1945–70 and has continued to produce exports and surplus at high levels during the period 1970–79. That Namibia did not develop as an economic unit, that Namibians were largely excluded, that inequality grew: these were the conditions for, and marks of success of, the colonial economy.

Whatever transpires in the 1980s, the colonial economy has run its course. If armed conflict continues for a decade, then the death of the colonial economy may be accompanied by the destruction of the levels of productive forces which are its one potentially positive heritage. If – a rather unlikely event – a settler-based white nationalism seizes and holds power with South African protection, then a transition to a more integrated, less external surplus maximizing political economy will unfold along the lines of the Rhodesian economy's evolution between 1965 and 1979. If a conservative African comprador elite succeeds to power – again unlikely – there will be similar moves to change the division of surplus going to foreigners and foreign firms as against that going to some Namibians, and to broaden the range of domestic production, following the Gabon pattern. If the liberation movement triumphs in a semi-agreed transfer before the base of productive forces is seriously damaged, the colonial economy will leave a surplus flow potential adequate to begin the task of restructuring.

In no case will the transition be short or easy. The contradictions which have rendered the reproduction, and will render the maintenance, of the Namibian colonial economy impossible will live after it to constrain, constrict and plague its successor.

Notes

1 See W. G. Clarence-Smith and R. Moorsom, 'Underdevelopment and Class Formation in Ovamboland 1845–1915', *Journal of African History*, 16, 3, 1975.

2 See Ronald Segal and Ruth First, *South West Africa: Travesty of Trust*, Deutsch, London, 1967, Chapters by Bley, Lovis, Bradford, Ngavirue.

3 For details see Innes, Chapter 4 below.

4 See Annex Tables which demonstrate statistically a number of these characteristics, especially Tables 7, 10, 11, 14, 15, 18, 20, 25, 27.

5 See Clarence-Smith and Moorsom, 'Underdevelopment and Class Formation in Ovamboland' and Rauha Voipio, Chapter 6, below, for an analytical and a more personal articulation of this point.

6 See Annex Table 15. GDP estimates normally value crops at farm gate prices. It might make better sense for household consumed food to value it at urban retail prices or cost of local purchase.

7 Cf. Gillian Cronje and Suzanne Cronje, *The Workers of Namibia*, International Defence and Aid Fund, London, 1979; ILO, *Labour and Discrimination in Namibia*, Geneva, 1977; Moorsom, 'Underdevelopment, contract labour and workers' consciousness in Namibia', *Journal of Southern African Studies*, October 1977; Voipio, Chapter 6 below.

8 Basic data on mining from Commonwealth Secretariat, *The Mineral Industry of Namibia*, London, 1978.

9 Cf. e.g. speech by I. J. Duncan of Western Mining (associated with BP), cited in *Financial Times*, 16 August 1979.

10 See *Africa Contemporary Record*, 'Namibia', 1977–78 and 1978–79, Africana, London, 1978, 1979; J. Stewart, 'Lessons from the pilchard debacle', *Financial Times*, 26 August 1978; 'Building up a ruined industry', *The Star* (Johannesburg), 23 September 1978.

11 Discussed and detailed in Christie, 'Who Benefits by the Kunene Hydro-electric schemes', *Social Dynamics*, 2 January 1976, and Nixon, 'Land Use and Development in Namibia – A Report Prepared for UNIN', 1978.

12 Department of Foreign Affairs, Republic of South Africa, *SWA Survey*, Pretoria, 1974. Mbamba, 'Possibilities for the Future Development of Livestock Ranching in an Independent Namibia', MA Thesis, University of Sussex, 1977.

13 The South African Customs Union is a 'one-way' common market. Namibia does not have free access for beef or dairy products; South Africa has the right to buy fish-meal at a price set below export parity and to dump maize in Namibia.

14 Even for Namibians, the San are particularly oppressed. Many Europeans do not regard them as human. Most are employed on seasonal terms on ranches and are dumped back into the desert to 'hunt and gather' for much of the year.

15 See Innes, Chapter 4 below, and Roger Murray *et al.*, *The Role of Foreign Firms in Namibia*, Africa Publications Trust, London, 1974, for details of fishing sector ownership.

16 See Commonwealth Secretariat, *The Mineral Industry of Namibia*, for more detailed data.

17 The British Nuclear Fuels (BNF) contract provided the base from which finance for Rössing could be raised. It was post-1966 and places RTZ and the British government in the position of knowing receivers of stolen goods. The swop is apparently to allow 'true' BNF statements that it has received no uranium oxide from Rössing. For later data on contract refining of Rössing concentrates in France, the Netherlands and the USSR, see *Sunday Times*, 'Revealed RTZ Secret Uranium Deals', 2 December 1979, 'Hijacking threat to illicit uranium trade', 9 December 1979.

18 According to a former United States government advisor, Anthony Harrigan, Tsumeb is of high strategic significance for the American military

industry being the largest producer of germanium after mines in Zaire. (A. Harrigan, Journey Report on South West Africa, 1963). See also Odendaal Report, Pretoria, 1964, p.25.

19 Odendaal Report, *SWA Survey*, 1974, gives the same description, but views it as natural. See also Murray *et al.*, *The Role of Foreign Firms in Namibia.*

20 Even Andreas Shipanga, the SWAPO defector, has termed the homeguard 'the real terrorists', citing specific cases. See *Observer*, 16 June 1979.

21 See, for example, the report on Rehoboth in the *Observer*, 2 June 1979. This is precisely what Rehoboth does not need at a cost of half the annual South West Africa estimates for all 'Coloured' education.

22 In the case of beef, who subsidises whom is not clear. The railroad loses money on an irrational cargo (live cattle instead of chilled beef) to the benefit of South African packing plants. While the Republic of South Africa market is less uncertain than the world, access is limited and Republic-controlled. Further, until recently exports of meat outside the Republic were discouraged; they are now hampered by lack of Namibian packing plant capacity.

23 The 60–75% range depends on treatment of goods, notably South African refined petroleum products, with a very high non-Republic content.

24 Direct shipment by sea, especially, but not exclusively, for non-RSA goods, would normally be cheaper. Live beasts are the least efficient form of meat shipment; chilled carcasses would allow more load per car and reefers – unlike cattle cars – can carry a return cargo, not be hauled back empty.

25 See Table 3.9 above; Annex Table 15.

26 See Innes, Chapter 4 below; Murray *et al., The Role of Foreign Firms in Namibia*; Wolfgang Thomas, *Economic Development in Namibia*, Grünewald, Munich, 1978, Chapter 1.

27 Outside mining there has been relatively little non-South African foreign investment. Barclays and Standard dominate banking, Shell and BP are the the largest petroleum distributors, Metal Box has the tin plant, but the Namibian operations in each case are branches of South African subsidiaries which are dominant in the Republic, not of the UK head offices. In ranching, fishing and commerce non-South African foreign investment is negligible. The general pattern is therefore colonial, not neo-colonial or generalized dependent economy.

28 The South West African Territorial and Republic of South Africa Consolidated Fund South West Africa account estimates are hard to consolidate. Further, the published expenditure categories are non-standard and non-revealing.

29 See Annex Table 28.

30 See *Africa Contemporary Record*, 1976–77, 1977–79, 1978–79 for more detailed coverage of stagnation.

31 For detailed listing of most available data see Cronje and Cronje, *The Workers of Namibia*, Chapter 4, and sources cited there; Thomas, *Economic Development in Namibia.*

32 Estimated from advertisements (*Observer, Rand Daily Mail*) indicating government salary scales, data cited in Nixon, 'Land Use and Development in Namibia', and A. M. Mbamba, 'Possibilities for the Future

Development of Livestock Ranching in an Independent Namibia', MA Thesis, University of Sussex, 1977.

33 If the foreign community were very small and comprised only highly skilled managers and technicians on technical assistance or TNC payrolls a wide difference would not be so damning.

34 On Tanzania, see e.g. R. H. Green 'Income distribution and the eradication of poverty in Tanzania' in I. L. Horowitz, *Equity, Income and Policy*, Praeger, New York, 1977; *Toward Socialism and Self Reliance Tanzania's striving for transition projected*, Scandinavian Institute of African Studies, Research Report 38, Uppsala, 1977. 'Tanzanian political economy goals, strategies and results, 1967–74' in B. U. Mwansasu and C. Pratt, *Towards Socialism in Tanzania,* University of Toronto/Tanzania Publishing House, Toronto/Dar es Salaam, 1979.

35 Settler anger at the large companies for exporting surplus and at the Democratic Turnhalle Alliance for its accommodationism is manifest in stories and letters to the editor in virtually every June–August 1979 issue of the *Observer.*

36 This is the line of H. Smith and G. Lister of the *Observer*, in columns and leaders: territorial nationalism across racial and class lines and against outsiders (including South Africa, Anglo, Marx).

37 The main sources for this section are Cronje and Cronje, *The Workers of Namibia*, ILO *Labour and Discrimination in Namibia*, and the *Windhoek Advertiser* and the *Windhoek Observer*, 1978–79 issues.

38 *Observer*, various issues June–August 1979, especially 23 and 30 June, 7 July 1979. See also ILO, *Labour and Discrimination in Namibia*, pp. 80–81.

39 See Cronje and Cronje, *The Workers of Namibia*, Chapter 4.

40 *Ibid.*, especially pp. 46–51.

41 Study by Pastor Gerson Max of United Evangelical Lutheran Church. Partially summarized in Cronje and Cronje, *The Workers of Namibia*, p. 47.

42 *Advertiser*, 21 July 1978, citing University of Port Elizabeth survey.

43 See Justin Ellis, *Elections in Namibia?* British Council of Churches/Catholic Institute for International Relations, London, 1979.

44. Even H. Smith of the *Observer* in his leaders rails against it as hypocritical, citing education (compulsory and integrated) and wages (higher and fair).

45 *Advertiser*, 2 January 1979, and communication from researcher who interviewed Consolidated Diamond Mines management at Oranjemund.

46 E.g. in regard to the Commonwealth mining study and some consultants for UN specialized agency studies.

47 Communication by members of international agency approached on environmental/worker safety issues.

48 The term is used by *New African,* July 1979, in describing Prime Minister Botha's attempts to build an economic dominance/dependence system from Zaire and Zambia to the Cape to defend South Africa.

49 Marcelle Kooy, 'The Contract Labour System and the Ovambo Crisis of 1971 in South West Africa', *African Studies Review*, 1973.

4 South African capital and Namibia

DUNCAN INNES

Imperialist domination in southern Africa, 1650–1900

The earliest period of capitalist development in Europe, the era of mercantile capitalism, was characterized by the expansion of international trading networks. During this period, South Africa was first colonized by the Dutch. They had established important trade links with the East, and occupied the Cape in 1652 to create a supply point for their ships. At that time South Africa was inhabited by a number of different indigenous peoples who had lived there for thousands of years.[1] Dutch settlers, sent to produce food and wine for the passing ships and to establish a garrison at the Cape, decimated many of the southernmost inhabitants and drove the remnants northwards.

During the eighteenth century, European capitalism underwent a transformation: mercantile capitalism gradually succumbed to industrial capitalism. With this transition, Holland was eclipsed by other developing industrial nations. Around 1800 Britain, which was emerging as the foremost capitalist nation, seized the Cape from the Dutch. Large numbers of Dutch settlers in the Cape rejected British rule and moved into the interior of South Africa. (This was the period of the Great Trek.) There, following a number of vicious battles, they gradually forced the indigenous inhabitants off the land and formed two states, the Transvaal and Orange Free State Republics, which were beyond British jurisdiction. The British, who at this time wanted the Cape only because of its strategic importance as guardian of the route to the East, were not particularly concerned with the two inland republics.

Thus the period from the mid-seventeenth to the mid-nineteenth centuries in South Africa was dominated by imperial requirements of a strategic kind. The capitalist centres in Europe had little interest in any of the use-values in South Africa. Consequently, the colony had no substantial international purchasing power and the local economy was chronically underdeveloped. In 1861 there were only 3.2 km of railway line in South Africa, no telegraph system, and total foreign investment stood at about £15m.[2]

In 1867 the Cape's importance to British capitalism altered dramatically with the discovery of large quantities of economically recoverable diamonds. Here was a use-value which had considerable international purchasing power because of the high level of demand for diamonds among fashionable circles in Europe, the United States and Russia. In 1886 an even more important use-value, from the point of view of international capital, was discovered in the Transvaal Republic – gold.

British capital's response was virtually instantaneous. Men and machinery were dispatched immediately to South Africa to develop diamond and gold mines, British capital poured into the area[3] and infrastructure expanded.[4] Within a short time conditions of monopoly capitalism were established in the mining industry and control was vested in the hands of a relatively small number of monopoly capitalists in Britain.

The prime aim of the monopolies was to keep costs as low as possible and to earn maximum profits. This required the creation and control of a large labour force which could be employed at low wages. It also meant that local groups had to be prevented from 'creaming off' too much mining revenue to stimulate their own expansion. The fact that the gold mines were in the Transvaal Republic caused much concern to the British because, in particular, the local state in the Transvaal was inadequate to organize and control the necessary black labour supply for the mines. The monopolists initially attempted to seize control of the state themselves and when this failed the British state intervened on their behalf and overthrew the independent Boer republics in the Boer War of 1899–1902. In this way, British imperialism extended its control over the whole of South Africa, as well as Bechuanaland, Basutoland, Swaziland and, further north, the Rhodesias.

Namibia: background to colonization

During the last century, the area known as South West Africa remained, however, beyond British control. The vast land mass of Namibia had supported a number of different tribes for centuries prior to the arrival of the first colonists. These people lived off the land and, particularly in the centre and north, produced a small surplus which enabled a trading network to develop. When, following the colonization of the Cape by the British, European traders and missionaries penetrated the territory from the Cape, they encountered not only a market for their goods, but also existing trade routes. Consumer goods and arms were rapidly absorbed by the African chiefs and tribal leaders in return for commodities, including cattle, copper, iron, ivory and ostrich feathers, for which there was a market in Europe. Thus capitalist market relations started to extend to Namibia on a limited scale.

However, even the limited extension of capitalist relations to the region was to have disastrous consequences for the local economies. First, the surplus value was realized in Europe; reinvestment of resources in Namibia did not occur. Second, changes in the composition of exports from the area eroded the local social structures. As the original exports dried up, sections of the African leadership, mainly some Ovambo monarchies, requiring European arms and consumer goods to protect the dominant position they had established for themselves, sought to replace them with cattle and then people (as slaves). The expansion of trade in these commodities served to undermine the local economies which were drained of means of production and subsistence (cattle) and labour power (people). Thus the underdevelopment of the local economies was a direct consequence of the extension of capitalist market relations to the area. A massive rinderpest epidemic, carrying off up to 90% of the north's cattle, completed the task of destruction. By 1900 these economies were no longer able to support their population.[5]

The gradual evolution of capitalism in Namibia, led by traders and missionaries, created pressures for the extension of capitalist state control over the area. In 1876, the British colonial government at the Cape sent a Commissioner

> to get a hold on the country between the Orange River and the Portuguese's settlements on the west coast in such a way as might lead to annexation, if the inhabitants desired it and our own interest made such a course desirable.[6]

However, British imperialism's own interests at that time made such a course impracticable. First, Britain was bogged down in inter-imperialist rivalry over Egypt and Turkey and was unwilling to undertake a major new annexation of a territory which, to all intents and purposes, seemed an arid wasteland. Second, circumstances related to the diamond fields (and later the gold mines) in South Africa fully occupied the local British colonial government. Third, the series of local wars culminating in the so-called Zulu War proved expensive and required British support for the colonial state. Fourth, very substantial opposition to imperial expansion, especially with respect to apparently unprofitable colonial wars, existed in the United Kingdom.

The failure of the British state to take the initiative in the 1880s gave German commercial interests in Namibia the opportunity to act on behalf of German capitalism. (Unlike the other advanced capitalist powers, Germany had no colonies of its own at the time.) British imperialism, which needed German support in its struggle for control over Egypt, was unwilling to resist the advance of German imperialism in Namibia. In 1890 the British concluded a treaty with Germany recognizing German annexation of the whole of Namibia, or German South West Africa. In this way, capitalist state control came to be exercised over South West Africa in order to defend and advance the process of capitalist exploitation and accumulation.

British imperialism gains control of Namibia, 1900–1919

Precisely because South West Africa did not produce any commodities for which there was large-scale demand in the capitalist centres, the initial years of German colonial rule did not produce major inflows of capital. A little capital was channelled into land and mineral speculation but this had only a minimal impact on local production. In 1906 and 1908, with the discovery first of internationally marketable copper and then of diamonds, large capitalist interests in Germany suddenly began to invest in the local economy.

The discovery of these commodities in South West Africa had an impact on economic development in many respects not dissimilar from that which had occurred in South Africa following the discovery of diamonds and gold, e.g. the influx of foreign capital and machinery, the development of basic infrastructure, and the expansion of the local market for agricultural goods. There were, however, important differences between the two experiences. First, initial discoveries suggested that there was not a particularly large supply of copper and diamonds in South West Africa, whereas gold and diamonds were known to be in large supply in South Africa. Second, diamonds in South West Africa were found mainly near the surface, hence only tools, some simple machines and basic equipment were necessary in the extraction process, whereas in South Africa diamonds and gold were to be found fairly deep underground thus requiring relatively more sophisticated machinery to extract them. For these reasons, German capital expenditure in South West Africa was much lower than British expenditure had been in South Africa. As a result, mining was carried out on a smaller scale in South West Africa and infrastructure was less developed. Furthermore, because mining was on a smaller scale, less black labour was required in South West Africa than in South Africa. This led to the development of different techniques of labour coercion by German capital. In particular, after an initial phase of military conquest[7] at the turn of the century which nearly wiped out the labour force, the German colonial regime sought instead to secure the collaboration of the African tribal leadership (a section of which was already addicted to capitalist commodity consumption) in providing the necessary labour force.[7] These chiefs selected migrants from among the tribe and sent them out to labour for capital. On their return, the migrants had to bring the chief a gift.[8] The basis for this collaboration had been laid by the undermining of the local African economies; instead of selling his tribesmen as slaves, the chief now sold them as wage labourers. Finally, there were far fewer settlers in South West Africa than in South Africa and, consequently, German capitalist interests appropriated and repatriated to Europe a higher share of the revenue from mineral production.

However, despite the smaller scale of economic activity in South West Africa (when compared with South Africa), the advances which did occur were, in terms of the country's own economic development, important. Between 1900 and 1910 the value of imports (mainly machinery, tools and equipment) rose from 7 000 to 44 000 marks, while the value of exports rose from 8 000 to 79 000 marks (almost all copper and diamonds) over the same period.[9]

Between 1908 and 1915 over 55 000 carats a year of diamonds were exported while the dividends of one of the German mining companies rose by 3 800%.[10] The development of the mining industry also provided the basis for the expansion of capitalist farming in the country and, in particular, for the cattle and sheep industries. By 1913 there were 1 331 European-owned farms in South West Africa. The means to this expansion was, of course, the theft of land from the indigenous inhabitants. Whereas the original land area of Namibia comprised some 82 million hectares, by as early as 1903 Africans had been confined to approximately 31 million hectares, while Europeans controlled

42 million hectares. The bulk of this European-owned land (29 million hectares) was controlled by international concession companies.[11]

These developments, in particular the theft of land, the development of mining and collaboration with the chiefs, set in motion forces which were to bring about the mass destruction of the peasantry and the development of a Namibian proletariat. By 1920 there were already 5 800 Africans employed on mines in South West Africa – 4 600 on the diamond mines, 800 on the copper mines, 300 on a tin mine and 50 on vanadium and salt mines.[12]

The outbreak of the First World War in 1914, South Africa's invasion of South West Africa in 1915, and the terms of the Treaty of Versailles in 1919 put an end to German colonial rule and transferred South West Africa to British domination. The inter-imperialist rivalry which had developed between the most powerful capitalist states – Britain, France, the United States and Germany – was the cause of the outbreak of war, and provided reason for Britain in snatching Germany's colony. But there was a more specific reason why German imperialist interests in South West Africa threatened British interests in South Africa: competition by German diamond merchants had brought the diamond price crashing down. Consequently, the British state had a specific reason, as did the South African state (which earned much of its revenue from diamond taxes), for ending Germany's hold in South West Africa. Unwilling to commit troops which were needed in Europe, the British government requested the government in South Africa to invade the colony on its behalf.

In the negotiations after the war, the British state's plans for her new colony to be annexed to her dominion, South Africa, were nearly thwarted by the United States. The American state, seeking to weaken the power of British capital, opposed the annexation of South West Africa to South Africa. Eventually a compromise was reached whereby South Africa was designated the mandatory power in South West Africa, responsible for the territory to the League of Nations. Although South West Africa still fell under British domination, exercised through South Africa, that domination was not absolute and the colony was, in principle, open to capitalist enterprises from other countries.

The South African state acted swiftly, in its own and British capital's interests, to transfer control of the country's diamond resources to a British-oriented company to consolidate the world market. Immediately after the Treaty of Versailles had been concluded, the Anglo American Corporation, a partly British-owned company registered in South Africa (and one of the monopoly mining groups in that country) was allocated control over the most important diamond mines in South West Africa. Anglo subsequently formed Consolidated Diamond Mines of South West Africa (CDM). The copper mine at Tsumeb, which did not threaten British interests, was allowed to remain under the control of its original German owner, the Otavi Minen und Eisenbahn Gesellschaft. From 1915 European settlers, farmers, traders and entrepreneurs from South Africa flooded in to establish themselves in the country, while many Germans were repatriated. By 1921 there were only 8 000 German settlers left, while South African settlers numbered 11 000.[13]

South African capitalism expands: Namibia stagnates, 1920–1945

A numerically strong settler population and the large-scale nature of mining operations in South Africa necessitated the development of a considerable infrastructural base. This included the building of roads, railways and housing, the provision of electricity and water supplies, and the development of certain industries providing inputs to the mining industry, e.g. engineering repair works, boot and shoe manufacturers.[14] To fulfil these requirements international mining capital had to channel a portion of the international purchasing power accruing from the mines through the South African state into local development.

By the end of the First World War the local settler classes had emerged as a powerful economic and political force in South Africa and over the next decade an even larger proportion of the international purchasing power was channelled into local economic development. The period after the depression saw a further intensification of this process of development and gradually, an industrial sector, based mainly on the iron and steel industry, began to emerge as an important part of the economy. By the time the Second World War broke out the industrial sector accounted for some 20% of South Africa's gross domestic product (GDP). The war temporarily severed international trade relations among the capitalist centres. With European industries unable to supply either their own or peripheral markets, South African industry expanded, filling the gap in the internal market and exporting to the ravaged European centres. By the end of the war, South Africa's industrial base had expanded from £141 million in 1939 to £304 million in 1945.[15] The country was developing into one of the more powerful peripheral economies.[16]

The rise of the mining, industrial and agricultural bourgeoisie in South Africa was to have important consequences for the future form of capitalist relations in Namibia. South African capital saw the importance of South West Africa's resources. Consequently, the settler bourgeoisie gave full support to attempts to bring the country within the British South African sphere of influence. Legislation enacted by the South African government during the 1920s aimed at securing that end.

The *de facto* racial segregation introduced by German colonial rule was rationalized and legalized. Africans were confined to limited geographical areas, the 'reserves', which effectively reduced existing landholdings sharply and denied access to new land. All land outside the 'reserves' was to become the domain of European mining or settler capitalism; the 'reserves' were to become labour reservoirs. The flow of labour to areas of capitalist production was controlled by the South West African Native Labour Association (SWANLA). Established in 1926 as a joint state–employers recruiting mechanism, SWANLA denied Africans the bargaining power and choice of employer which a free labour market would have allowed. In particular, it enforced contract migrant labour (with families remaining in 'reserves') for over half of all Namibian wage employees.

In 1925 the South West Africa Constitution Act passed a measure of political power to European settlers, who could vote for a local Legislative Assembly. Control over African affairs, police and defence remained the direct responsibility of the South African state and Africans were denied political rights. In 1928, the new Native Administration Proclamation gave the South African state the power to appoint and dismiss African chiefs and headmen as tribal leaders in the 'reserves' and therefore to control virtually all aspects of African life. In this way the collaborationist role of the chiefs was institutionalized and chiefs who had previously resisted this role could be dismissed.

The local settler bourgeoisie and the officially sanctioned African chiefs formed the basis of a local bourgeoisie which was to assist international capital in the control and exploitation of the declining African peasantry and the growing Namibian proletariat.[17]

Every effort was made by the South African state to facilitate the growth of settlement. Cash advances of up to £750 per settler were made for the purchase of stock, implements and seeds. Farm leases were made available on a rent-free basis for the first year, 2% of the purchase price for the second and third years and 3½% in the fourth and fifth years; after five years the farm could be purchased over a twenty-year period.[18] In 1927/8, £120 500 was set aside for European education, compared with £100 000 in 1928/9 for African education. By 1928 the European population had reached 28 000 while the African population stood at over 200 000.

Despite this considerable assistance to European settlers, agricultural activity showed litttle sign of expanding during the first decade of South African occupation. Mining activity did not fare much better.

The share of mining and agriculture in the GDP fell. After having gained control of De Beers Consolidated Mines, the largest diamond producer in South Africa, Anglo American controlled the

TABLE 4.1 The Distribution of GDP by Sectors of Economy 1920–1977 (%)

	Agriculture Fishing	Mining	Industry	Services	Total	R000 000) GDP
1920	13	59	3	25	100	13
1925	12	49	6	33	100	11
1930	5	44	8	43	100	10
1935	46	13	7	34	100	8
1940	48	4	6	42	100	10
1945	46	13	6	35	100	20
1950	34	33	6	27	100	61
1955	26	39	6	29	100	129
1960	15	34	13	38	100	142
1965	20	47	8	25	100	214
1970	16	31	14	39	100	379
1975	16	27	17	40	100	674
1977	18	33	14	35	100	1 135

Sources: D.C. Krogh, *The National Income and Expenditure of South West Africa;* W.H. Thomas, *Towards Acceptable Development,* Dortmund, 1977; United Nations, *Toward Manpower Development for Namibia*, 1978.

diamond industry throughout the capitalist world. The company's control over South West Africa's gem diamond fields, the richest in the world, was vital not only for the company but also for diamond interests in South Africa and Britain and for capitalist expansion in South Africa. Had these fields fallen into the hands of competitors, Anglo's hold over the industry would have been substantially weakened if not destroyed. The world-wide recession at the end of the 1920s caused a fall in demand for diamonds. In order to maintain prices, Anglo American reduced output sharply. The cuts included bringing production in South West Africa to a complete stop.

From the very beginning, Anglo American's monopoly control over Namibia's diamond resources resulted in these being developed in the context of the overall interests of a transnational company and not in the interests of the territory nor even of CDM considered separately. The company had gained control over the South West African diamond fields primarily to keep them as reserves and to prevent any competition and not necessarily to increase production. Hence, despite the recovery of the world market for diamonds in the 1930s, mineral production in Namibia did not expand but remained well below its 1920 level.

As the depression was affecting capitalist centres, South West Africa was experiencing its worst drought of the century. Stock farming was particularly hard hit. By 1930 the value of agricultural production had fallen to 5% of the GDP and, by the time the drought and depression had broken in 1933, cattle farmers had lost an average of 50% of their stock, sheep farmers had lost between 70 and 80%. After the drought and the depression the economy recovered and secure markets were found in South Africa. As a result of this recovery and the low level of mineral exploitation, agriculture contributed almost 50% to the GDP during the ten-year period 1935–45.[19]

This form of development resulted in Namibia's growing dependence on the South African economy. It produced a few internationally marketable minerals and agricultural products for the South African economy; it imported industrial goods from South Africa. Trade, transport and the bulk of other services were controlled by South African companies. The South African state benefited directly from its control over the country through taxation in excess of recurrent expenditures. New settlers had to repay the financial support they had received Thus the financial burden of settlement policy was shifted on to the underdeveloped economy. The burden was heavy: by 1934 South West Africa had accumulated loans from South Africa valued at over R4.7 million (87% of the GDP).[20]

Consequently, between the world wars the Namibian economy was characterized by stagnation and limited diversification and the country was in a state of chronic underdevelopment. Industrial growth was marginal and the contribution of the industrial sector to GDP was never more than 8%. It was not until 1938 that the Namibian GDP exceeded that of 1920, the year when South Africa was granted the mandate to administer and 'develop' Namibia. South African capital was too weak to exploit Namibia's resources to the full but it was unwilling to lose what promised to be a potentially valuable area. From a historical perspective, it is clear that the period of stagnation in Namibia was a phase when the South African bourgeoisie sought to find its own feet before launching a full-scale assault to appropriate Namibia's resources for itself.

The effects of this underdevelopment were felt most severely by the African population. Denied access to new land, the Africans' economic base continued to decline. At the end of the 1930s the African population (253 000) was eight times the size of the European population (31 000) but Europeans had more than double the amount of land (38 million hectares) allocated to Africans (17 million hectares).[21] Only a tiny fraction of the wealth created by African labour went to satisfy their needs. During the ten-year period 1928–1938 the South African state spent R1.3 million on the settlement of 2 100 European farmers in Angola, whereas only R1.1 million was spent on all services for the 262 000 members of the African population.[22] The continuing impact of the theft of agricultural and grazing land and the imposition of taxes accelerated the proletarianization of the African population. There was a growing stream of African migrant labour from the 'reserves' into the centres of capitalist production on the farms and mines and in services.[23]

South African capitalist domination in Namibia, 1946–1976

By 1945 the South African bourgeoisie was prepared to play a major role in the exploitation of Namibia. The establishment of the United Nations Organization threatened to undermine its intentions. The United Nations' scheme to place under trusteeship all those territories previously held under League of Nations' mandates was unpalatable to the South African state. First, it involved a far greater degree of supervison than had been exercised by the League. Second (and more important), the trusteeship system carried with it the clear intention that there should be a 'progressive development' of the trust territories 'towards self-government or independence'.[24]

Development towards independence in Namibia would have meant that the South African bourgeoise, which was still relatively weak, would have had to accept a far greater degree of independence from local classes in Namibia, as well as having to compete on more equal terms with other, more powerful, international capitalist interests. Under these conditions, it was unlikely that South African capital would have been able to retain its powerful position in Namibia. Its interests lay in gaining a political stranglehold over the country.

Consequently, the South African Premier, General Smuts, went before the United Nations in 1945 and 1946 to argue for the incorporation of South West Africa as a part of South Africa. To strengthen his case a 'referendum' was carried out among the chiefs and headmen in South West Africa. Given the collaborationist role of many of these appointed state functionaries (who were guaranteed revenue from fines imposed on their 'subjects', land distribution and labour migration), it is not surprising that they supported South

Africa. When the United Nations rejected Smuts' proposal, South Africa refused to accept the trusteeship system and announced that it would continue to administer the territory under the defunct League's mandate. General Smuts announced categorically to the South African Parliament that the relation of South West Africa to South Africa was 'more nearly approximated to that of a colonial possession than anything else'.[25]

In 1948 the National Party came to power in South Africa and introduced measures to intensify colonization. This can be directly related to events in South Africa at the time. The development of two major new gold fields, the Far West Rand and the Orange Free State (the latter field was the world's richest), gave a tremendous boost to the South African economy. Not only did the new government attempt to increase local distribution of international purchasing power; it also attempted to secure the production of maximum surplus value through intensified exploitation of black labour. Mass resistance by black workers was met with violent repression, their political organizations were banned (the South African Communist Party) or subjected to harassment and intimidation (the African National Congress). The 1950s were characterized by intensified class struggle as the South African bourgeoisie launched a sustained attack on the mass of workers and peasants in South Africa and Namibia. This attack was met by the armed resistance of the peasantry and the intensification of African National Congress resistance in South Africa. In Namibia mass resistance began to take on a more organized form as well: the immediate predecessor to the South West African People's Organization (SWAPO) was formed, and in 1959, sixty-five Namibians were shot (eleven died) by police in Windhoek, during resistance to the destruction of an established African urban area.

In the 1950s the bourgeoisie in South Africa was in a powerful position. Large-scale production of gold meant that South African capital had access to considerable new international purchasing power, much of which was secured by industrial capital and the state. Consequently, South African industry expanded rapidly. The manufacturing sector grew at an annual average rate of 10.6% between 1945/6 and 1963/4. By the period 1967–1971, the manufacturing sector accounted for 27% of the GDP compared with agriculture, forestry and fishing's 11% and mining and quarrying's 11%.[26]

Hence, in the two decades after the Second World War, not only were international mining interests in South Africa accumulating capital rapidly, but so too were other interests, such as manufacturing. In addition, the continuing international struggle being fought on the stages of the United Nations and the International Court of Justice added important political pressures for South African capitalism to establish a firm economic hold over Namibia. South African capital could not afford, nor did it need, to wait any longer.

The impact on Namibia

The result of South Africa's new economic involvement in Namibia was reflected in the high growth rate of the GDP over the three decades following the Second World War.[27] GDP grew six-fold in ten years (1945–1955), and during the subsequent twenty years it grew almost ten-fold (see Table 4.1). Growth has not been spread throughout the economy, but confined to particular sectors only: first, those involved in production of commodities with international purchasing power; second, those involved in production of commodities required by capital inside South Africa; and, third, those relating to strategically significant areas.

In the immediate post-war years, South African capital acted to exploit particular sectors through which to secure international purchasing power: mineral resources, fisheries and Karakul pelts. The importance of these, particularly minerals, to South Africa's own economic development has been underlined since the mid-1960s when South Africa's own major sources of international purchasing power, gold and diamonds, began to run down. Over the last decade, prominent capitalists in South Africa have continually stressed the need to find products which could be marketed overseas to replace gold and diamonds when South Africa's supplies of these are exhausted.[28] Otherwise the economy would be placed in jeopardy through, for instance, the inability to import necessary new technology for the expansion of industry. Consequently, South African capital involvement in Namibia was intensified.

Intensification was not just economic (as expressed in the higher GDP growth rate) but also political. Here, South African policy was determined largely by the growing strength of SWAPO and by the increased international opposition to its policies. The establishment of the Odendaal Commission was the first step in this process, and was followed in 1968 by the Development of Native Nations Act and, the following year, by the South West Africa Affairs Act. The latter provided for *de facto* incorporation of Namibia as a fifth province of South Africa: all major functions of government were transferred to Pretoria and all major state revenues were made payable directly to Pretoria. The former provided for the setting up of 'Homelands' with legislative assemblies constituted on a tribal basis, identical to the Bantustan system being introduced in South Africa.

The expansion of mining: diamonds and base metals

The most important developments after the war occurred in the mining industry. Its contribution to the GDP fluctuated around one-third over a period of exceptionally rapid economic growth.[29] Considerable absolute expansion occurred: from R2.5 million in 1945, total mining output rose to R48 million in 1960, and by 1977 had reached R375 million.[30] This expansion was based primarily on development of the diamond sector which consistently accounted for almost two-thirds of the total value of Namibian mining output. One company, the diamond producer CDM (part of the Anglo American Group), in conjunction with its subsidiaries, controls 99% of Namibia's diamond output. Following a decline in output of Anglo's other diamond mines and loss of much of the surplus share of other mines, as South Africa and other states (e.g. Tanzania, Botswana) increased royalty and tax levies and share participation requirements, CDM has revolutionized its diamond operations in Namibia. It has adopted a highly mechanized production process and in 1973 had a fleet of almost 300 earth-movers worth about R15 million and a labour force of over 5 000.[31] The highly capital-intensive techniques of production have generated much larger outputs and enormous profits for CDM: between 1943 and 1962 CDM's pre-tax profits amounted to R369 million. Of this, 28½% (R105 million) was paid out directly to the South African state in taxes and 37% (R138 million) went out of the country in the form of dividends.[32] Thus at least two-thirds of the profits (R243 million) were exported from Namibia. In one year, 1969, CDM earned gross profits of almost R70 million,[33] about 20% of total Namibian GDP. In 1974 CDM contributed 40% to the total profit of the De Beers group.[34]

These figures show clearly that CDM is a major source of surplus for De Beers, one of the three main components of the Anglo American Group. Namibia provides this monopoly corporation, which controls a large proportion of mineral production in Africa, with a revenue share critical to the Group's overall strategy. Anglo American acquired the diamond fields in 1919 for R7 million, perhaps 'the most profitable mining deal of the century'.[35] By the mid-1970s CDM was the world's largest producer of gem diamonds, producing around 80% of the combined total of gem diamonds from South Africa and Namibia.

Base-metal production was also revolutionized after the war. During the war, South Africa expropriated the German-owned Tsumeb mine. It was held by the Custodian of Enemy Property until 1946 when it was sold to the Tsumeb Corporation, a consortium comprising American Metal Climax (American), Selection Trust (British), Union Corporation (South Africa-based British), and Newmont Mining Co. (American). The consortium paid R2 million for the mine, an amount recovered in the first year of operation simply by working existing ore dumps.[36]

In 1962 a copper smelter was brought into operation followed, in 1963, by a lead smelter. The value of output rose substantially as blister copper and refined lead were added to concentrates. Between 1964 and 1973 the value of output rose from R33 million to R83 million. By the early 1970s the Tsumeb Corporation had expanded to three mines (Tsumeb, Matchless and Kombat) and produced 80% of Namibia's base-metal output.[37] It had become the sixth largest copper producer in the world, it controlled the largest lead mine in Africa, and it was the largest employer of labour in Namibia, employing over 5 000 Africans and 1 200 whites. The average black wage bill per annum in the 1960s was R1.46 million; the average white wage bill per annum was R14.6 million.[38] In 1969 and 1970 the company reported net profits of R13 million and R25 million respectively. By 1969 the corporation had paid out a total of R108.7 million to South Africa. A company director explained that the company's taxes were being used to finance both state development plans and the construction of the 'strategically important' road linking Capetown with Luanda in Angola.[39]

Between them, Tsumeb Corporation and CDM produced about 90% of the mining industry's output during the 1950s and 1960s. They were responsible for almost one-third of Namibian GDP and contributed about 50% of exports.[40]

In the 1970s several new companies sought opportunities to exploit Namibian natural resources. In 1972 thirty-four foreign mining and oil companies (sixteen South African, eleven from the United States, three British, two Canadian and one each from France and Greece) were granted prospecting rights. In the mid-1970s there were fifteen big operating mines and several dozen smaller ones in Namibia. They included three major new mines: Rössing (uranium) controlled by Rio Tinto Zinc, General Mining, and the Industrial Development Corporation (IDC), with a full capacity output value potentially equal to that of CDM; Otjihase (copper) controlled by Johannesburg Consolidated Investments; and Oamites (copper) controlled by Falconbridge and the IDC (see Annex Table 29 and Map 3.2).

In all, more than twenty foreign private-sector firms and a South African state company, the Industrial Development Corporation, control Namibia's largest mining companies. Four of the foreign companies (Anglo American Corporation, Charter Consolidated, De Beers and Johannesburg Consolidated Investment) are associated with the Anglo American Group. It also has shares in and joint mining operations with six other corporations (Selection Trust, Federale Volksbeleggings, American Metal Climax, Rio Tinto Zinc, Newmont Mining and Consolidated Gold Fields). Of the twenty largest mining operations in Namibia shown in Table 4.2, the Anglo American group directly controls seven and has minority share holdings in six others including Tsumeb Corporation and Rössing via Rio Tinto Zinc. The Oppenheimer Group also held a substantial share in SWANLA, the migrant labour recruiting organization. Until the commissioning of Rössing, Anglo alone virtually dominated the Namibian mineral sector.[41]

No single mining company is even partially owned by Namibians and no substantial shareholdings are held by settlers or expatriate Europeans. All mining surpluses accrue to foreign enterprises. Apart from replacement and expansion investments, these surpluses are removed from the country, either as profits by the companies or as taxes to the South African government. The goods produced (diamonds, copper, lead, uranium, tin, etc.) are largely exported to central capitalist economies and, to a much smaller extent, to South Africa.

Commercial and subsistence agriculture

While commercial agriculture expanded in the post-war period, it did so with fluctuations. During the war it contributed almost 50% to GDP, but thereafter this declined to less than 20%[42] (see Table 4.1). These fluctuations largely resulted from the industry's limited export-oriented structure. In fact, development of commercial agriculture meant development of one area only, the livestock industry.

Cattle and sheep account for 85% of the total value of Namibia's agricultural output.[43] They are produced mainly for export: 90–95% of cattle are exported, while sheep are bred for Karakul pelts and other sheep products and wool by-products, all of which are exported. The main market for cattle is South Africa: since 1961 South Africa has taken between two-thirds and three-quarters of all marketed

TABLE 4.2 Main Mines and their Ownership

Mine	Mineral*	Company	Ownership
Large Mines			
1 Oranjemund	D	Cons. Diamond Mines	De Beers Cons. Mines
2 Continental Self Orange River	D	Marine Diamond Co.	De Beers Cons. Mines
3 Tsumeb	Cu, L, Z, S	Tsumeb Co.	AMC, NMC, ST, UC, OCC, SWAC
4 Kombat	Cu, L, Z,	Tsumeb Co.	AMC, NMC, ST, UC, OCC, SWAC
5 Matchless	Cu	Tsumeb Co.	AMC, NMC, ST, UC, OCC, SWAC
6 Otjihase**	Cu, Z, S	Otjihase Mining Co.	JCI, Minerts (SA)
7 Rössing	U	Rössing Uranium	RTZ, GM, IDC
8 Langer Heinrich***	U		Federale Mynbow, GM
9 Berg Aukas	V, L, Z	SWACO	CGF, AA, Charter (UK)
10 Brandberg	T, W	Kilu Products	SWACO
11 Klein Aub	Cu	Klein Aub Copper Co.	GM, FVB
12 Oamites	Cu, S	Oamites Mining Co.	Falconbridge Nickel (Canada), IDC
13 Witvlei	Cu	—	Anglo Vaal (South Africa)
14 Rosh Pinah	Z, L	Imcor Zinc	ISCOR (SA), Moly Copper (USA)
15 UIS	T, W, Z	Uis Mining Co.	ISCOR (SA)
Medium-size Mines			
16 Asis Ost	Cu	Tsumeb Co.	Tsumeb Co., SWACO
17 Otjosondu	M	SA Minerals Co.	JCI
18 Onganja	Cu	Navarro Expl. Co.	Zapata Norness (USA)
19 Krantzberg	T, W	Nord Mining & Expl. Co.	Nord Resources Co. (USA)
20 Loreley	Cu	Loreley Copper Mines	Diam. MUC, Moly Copper (USA)

AA – Anglo American Corporation (SA)
AMC – American Metal Climax Inc. (USA)
CGF – Consolidated Gold Fields Ltd (UK)
DMUC – Diamond Mining & Utility Corporation (SA)
FVB – Federal Volksbeleggings Ltd (SA)
GM – General Mining and Finance Corporation (SA)
IDC – Industrial Development Corporation (SA)
JCI – Johannesburg Consolidated Investment Co. Ltd (SA)
NMC – Newmont Mining Corporation (USA)
OCC – O'Kiep Copper Co. (SA/foreign)
RTZ – Rio Tinto Zinc (UK)
ST – Selection Trust Co. (UK)
SWACO – South West Africa Company Ltd (UK/SA)
UC – Union Corporation (SA/UK)
* – (D) Diamonds, (U) Uranium, (Z) Zinc, (S) Silver, (Cu) Copper, (L) Lead, (M) Molybdenum, (T) Tin, (V) Vanadium, (W) Wolfram.
** – Shut down 1977: reopening dependent on world copper price.
*** – Under development.

Sources: W. G. Thomas, *Economic Development in Namibia*, Munich, 1978; FAO, *Namibia, Prospects for Future Development*, Rome, 1977.

TABLE 4.3 Distribution of the Gross Value of Agricultural Production in 1960, 1970 and 1977 (%)

	1960	1970	1977
Cattle and meat products	52	50	48
Karakul pelts	25	32	32
Wool and sheep products	9	7	6
Dairy products	7	6	5
Game	2	3	6
Cereals and vegetables	3	1	5
Others	2	1	2
Total	100	100	100
Total output: R million	34.5	65.4	157.5

Sources: Department of Agriculture, Government; W. H. Thomas, *Economic Development in Namibia*. Compare with Annex Table 22.

cattle.[44] The main markets for Karakul pelts are the fashion centres of Western capitalism via the auctioning centre in London; 60% of all pelts produced go to the Federal Republic of Germany, the remainder to France, Italy, Japan, Scandinavia and the United States.[45] Two-thirds of all cattle are owned by European settlers while over 90% of the Karakul sheep are to be found on approximately four thousand white-owned farms.

Agriculture is the only sector of the Namibian economy controlled by local settlers. But their independence is limited to the farms. Three South African companies, Suidafrikaanse Vleisprodusent, Vleis–Sentraal Kooperatief and Afrikaanse Sake–Ontwikkelings–Korporasie, have monopolized slaughtering, meat processing and marketing. These companies also control the sale of meat to European destinations. The export of Karakul pelts is controlled by two British firms, Hudson's Bay and Anning's Co. and Eastwood and Holt Ltd.

South African capital has made no attempt to develop a broad agricultural base which could support the population. Only those sectors which have markets abroad (Karakul) or which produce goods needed by South Africa (cattle) have been developed. The result is that agriculture is totally dependent on the vagaries of foreign markets. Combined with recurrent droughts, the market pattern explains fluctuations in sectoral growth. Basic food items, cereals, dairy products and vegetables, are only about 10% of total agricultural output. Namibia has been forced to import most of its agricultural goods, mainly from South Africa. Thus South African farming capital has secured an adjacent captive market for its goods.[46]

The revenue earned from agricultural output accrues to whites and, in a majority of cases, to South African whites. In 1965 cattle from Namibia supplied 17% of the South African market. Heavily dependent on South Africa as a market, the expansion of the cattle sector is controlled by South African livestock producers who lay down a strict quota for cattle imports from Namibia to protect their own interests. Furthermore, farmers in Namibia contend that beef prices in

South Africa are often as much as 15% lower than those overseas.[47]

No attempt has been made to develop any agricultural activity which might provide competition for South African goods. Prices and market access for Namibian products, and freight rates to and selling prices of South African products in Namibia, were controlled by the state to discourage crop and dairy production and encourage beef production in Namibia. This has resulted in the highly distorted and underdeveloped nature of Namibian agricultural development.

Finally, the agricultural industry in Namibia provides South Africa with another kind of advantage. Given the underdevelopment of Namibia's manufacturing industry:

> virtually all means of agricultural production have to be obtained from South Africa, including fencing materials, piping, creosote wood, building materials, concentrated animal feeds, fertilisers, seed, insecticides, fungicides, herbicides, stock remedies, farm tools, machines and implements, vehicles, tractors, fuel and lubricants and spare parts.[48]

In other words, Namibia's agricultural industry supplies South Africa with a growing captive market for manufactured goods. This market is protected by the inclusion of Namibia in the South African Customs Tariff, by South Africa's non-tariff barriers, and by South African domination of commercial infrastructure.

Crop production among the indigenous population is almost wholly for subsistence and only a minority of cattle offtake is sold. African agriculture is centred on cattle raising except in the north and north east where millet and corn are cultivated. In Rehoboth and Namaland cattle raising is partly commercialized.

Lack of water and seasonal instability of supply have always been problems for indigenous agricultural production, and land theft added to the difficulties. Because the Germans and South Africans had put down initial African resistance by killing over half the population, this was not fully evident until the 1940s, but as the population recovered and grew, pressure on land increased. Periodic droughts have also played havoc with agricultural stability and food shortages have become a regular cause of labour migration. Apart from being directly responsible for increasing the pressure on land, South Africa has systematically denied indigenous producers knowledge, tools, credit and access to markets, so as to prevent any expansion in this sector.

The fact that migrant workers' families had access to land made possible wage payments below family subsistence and gave rise to the single migrant (versus family-based permanent) labour system. Minimum contract rates hardly increased in real terms between 1920 and 1960, and by 1971 had risen by only a little over 50%.[49] The system of maintaining wages at an extraordinarily low level, in the interests of capital accumulation, means that migrant workers do not have the financial resources to develop the productive capacity of the 'reserves'. The overall impact of South African capitalist involvement on the subsistence sector has been to undermine its capacity to support the indigenous population.

The fishing industry

The fastest growing industry in Namibia during the period 1945–1975 was the fishing industry. Like mining and Karakul production, this industry is export-oriented and is almost completely controlled by South African companies.

The first fish factory was established in Namibia in 1948 by Ovenstone's Ltd, a South African company. At the end of that year, fish exports were valued at R0.8 million (3% of the country's total export income). From these small beginnings the industry expanded rapidly; during the 1960s fish consistently provided almost 25% of all exports [50] and became the second largest export industry in Namibia, surpassed only by mining. The basis of this expansion has been a rapid rate of mechanization. Whereas in 1950 the number of fishing vessels per factory was approximately twenty-three, by 1965 it had been reduced to eleven, although four times as much fish was being caught in the latter period.[51]

Investments in the industry continued to rise substantially from a total of R19 million in 1965 to R49 million in 1972 (R35 million in fish factories and equipment and R14 million in fishing vessels).[52] The value of fish caught rose equally sharply and investments made were recovered in a few years. Like agriculture, fishing is virtually a mono-commodity industry. Two types of fish, pilchards and anchovies, account for almost 90% of Namibia's fishing earnings, while rock lobsters, a luxury commodity, account for most of the rest. Fishing is therefore vulnerable to price fluctuations on international markets, although, as the period after 1975 was to show, uncontrolled fishing both inshore and by foreign fleets posed a more immediate threat through reduction of fish stocks and catches.

South African capital benefits substantially from control over this source of international purchasing power. The Namibian fishing industry is dominated by nine South African companies,[53] of which at least five are inter-linked through joint shareholdings, combined operations or other agreements. Two of the nine, Kaap–Kunene and SARASAS Corporation, are linked to Anglo Transvaal Consolidated and Federale Volksbeleggings respectively. These are involved in exploitation of Namibia's mineral resources and are linked to the Anglo Group through minority shareholdings and through joint mining operations in South Africa.

The underdeveloped manufacturing sector

Namibia's manufacturing sector is grossly underdeveloped. The most important branch of manufacturing is food processing (two-thirds of the total in 1971/2), with fish products the dominant sector (72%) and meat products less important (20%).[54] This sector was developed to process exports which could not otherwise be realized.

The South West Africa Survey for 1974 claims that there can be no scope for industrial expansion in Namibia because of 'the small size of the population, the great area of the Territory in relation to the population, and the vast distances between urban areas'.[55] These geophysical 'limitations' do not prevent South Africa's manufacturing sector from finding a worthwhile market for its goods in Namibia and South African policies undoubtedly have contributed to the underdevelopment of Namibia's manufacturing sector. The commodities which South Africa exports to Namibia (machinery, industrial and transport equipment, cement, building materials and consumer goods)[56] are largely products which South Africa, because of her weak competitive position relative to capitalist centres, and because of political constraints, is unable to sell on world markets. The closed markets of Namibia are doubly valuable to South Africa.

South African capitalism has sought, with systematic state support, to build a system based on investment in Namibia's major resources; sale of their products internationally or to South Africa; and expansion of South African manufacturing industry through sales to Namibia. It benefits by profits from production in Namibia, by purchases from and sales to Namibia, and by the net foreign-exchange earnings of Namibia. A central requirement of this system is that South African capital must exercise control over Namibia to ensure that more competitive products from other foreign states are kept out and that no incentives or protection are provided to industries within.

Those industries that exist in Namibia do so solely to serve the interests of South African capital:

> . . . the manufacturing sector largely confines itself to the processing of perishable products for consumption in the Territory and the Republic, to finishing and assembling materials obtained from South Africa, or to specialized repair and small-scale production work.[57]

The industry serves South African capital by exporting to South Africa those commodities not obtainable in sufficient quantities within South Africa, e.g. meat products; by assembling South African machinery and equipment; and by doing repair work on plant and equipment for South African-owned companies (or international concerns).

A first step in intensifying South Africa's political and economic involvement in Namibia was the establishment of the Commission of Enquiry into South West Africa Affairs under the chairmanship of F. H. Odendaal in 1962. One of the Commission's major recommendations was that 'a broad programme of capital expenditure' should be adopted in the country as this 'would result in a considerable increase in the gross domestic product to the benefit of all population groups'.[58]

One aim of political intervention was to stimulate the Namibian economy, but the Commission's claim that economic growth was to be 'to the benefit of all population groups' was pure propaganda, for, in the same breath, the Commission declared that 'Such a programme must largely be founded on the development which has taken place'.[59]

As indicated above, that development was in the interests of South African capital rather than those of all population groups. In fact, the Commission explicitly argued that:

> this development can best be achieved if the various population

> groups . . . are not unsettled unnecessarily by disrupting their existing strong traditional family and homeland ties.[60]

That is, economic development was to occur within the context of the political structures laid down by apartheid. 'Economic activities,' the Commission continued, 'must therefore be brought to the home areas as far as possible'.[61] In other words, an economic web was to be created, based particularly on the expansion of infrastructure, which would further enmesh the Namibian people in South Africa's political grip. The Commission was adamant that:

> The full financial responsibility for the development of the non-white population groups and their homelands, shall initially vest in the Government of the Republic of South Africa.[62]

Economic growth, which the state sought to promote, was intended as the means to reinforce the political domination of the Namibian people. Economic control was to be exercised absolutely:

> no authority in South West Africa shall grant special concessions direct to any commercial or industrial concern in its area except in full accordance with policy in the Republic of South Africa. . . .[63]

After the South African government accepted these recommendations, expansion of the Namibian economy was accelerated. The South African state pumped over R150 million into the economy between 1964 and 1969, almost R60 million going to a single project, the Kunene dam and hydro-electric power plant, R41 million to road building, and R5 million to transforming the African 'reserves' into Bantustans.

One sector of the economy, construction, immediately benefited: between 1961/2 and 1971 the gross value of construction industry output rose from R11.8 million to R51.4 million. However, this sector's contribution to the GDP rose only marginally from 3% to 6% between 1960 and 1970.[64] Although small- to medium-sized local construction companies benefited from this expansion, large-scale programmes were undertaken primarily by South African (in particular LTA, Murray and Roberts and Murray and Stewart) and secondarily by other foreign firms.

The highly cartelized nature of the South African economy meant that any major economic projects brought further involvement by dominant South African economic groups, notably Anglo. A major sub-contractor on the massive Kunene hydro-electric project is LTA Ltd, a subsidiary of Anglo American. The LTA–Edmund Lafrenz Group sells and services construction equipment in Namibia.[65] Anglo American also has an indirect holding in the engineering company, Stewards and Lloyds, of South West Africa. Gearing Ltd, a company undertaking ship and boat repairs and general engineering, is a subsidiary of Anglo Transvaal whose main Namibian operations are in mining and fishing. Freight Services (SWA) Ltd, a company with branches in three major Namibian centres, and a beneficiary of increased forwarding, clearing and transport resulting from the construction programme, is a subsidiary of Freight Services Ltd, part of the Anglo Group. Anglo American also has minority holdings in Barclays and Standard, the largest banks in Namibia. Most of the finance for these schemes was provided by South Africa since, according to the *SWA Survey*, 'it is evident that the Territory's revenue from all internal sources is progressively less able to finance the volume of governmental activities in the Territory'.[66]

South African state policy placed the Namibia government in a position of massive indebtedness. For example, in 1964/5 the South West Africa administration paid out 29% of its total revenue in repayment of loans (R15.8 million).[67] The debt has continued to increase: the officially stated deficit on the South West Africa administration's accounts rose from R11.9 million in 1969/70 to R43.3 million in 1973/74. This rising deficit has been met by South African loans: between 1971/72 and 1973/74 over R53 million was loaned from the Revenue Fund in South Africa. Thus Namibia is being sucked into increased financial dependence on South African capital through public-sector capital expenditure in excess of South West Africa administration and South West Africa account revenues from the Territory.[68]

Namibia is part of a common monetary area with South Africa, Lesotho and Swaziland, and uses the South African Rand as currency. Unlike Lesotho and Swaziland, Namibia does not have even a rudimentary monetary authority of its own nor receive a financial transfer for imputed interest on South African Reserve Bank assets financed by currency in circulation in the Territory. All Namibia's financial reserves 'are held and administered by the South African Reserve Bank which operates as the Central Bank of both the Republic and South West Africa'.[69]

South African (or mixed South African/international) finance capital dominates private-sector finance. According to the *SWA Survey*,

> the bulk of the Territory's banking services are provided by branches of South Africa's largest commercial banks . . . similarly, South Africa's large building societies operate through branches or agencies in South West Africa and make a substantial contribution towards the financing of housing in that area. A number of South African insurance companies operate in South West Africa. . . .[70]

Namibia has no legislation of its own to regulate and control the operations of these financial institutions which are free to transfer Namibian savings to South Africa and to international centres, subject to South African (not Namibian) exchange control. The contribution of the finance sector to GDP remained constant at 8% between 1960 and 1970.[71]

Namibia's wealth is derived from primary products sold in South African or international markets. Most exports are via South Africa, although there is a trend to ship minerals directly to Europe and North America. In 1966, 89% of total exports were channelled to South Africa, but only a small portion were consumed there. The route taken by overseas exports is of interest: diamonds and Karakul, for instance, which account for half of Namibia's exports, although destined for overseas markets, have been sent via South Africa. They thus become liable for customs duties, railway tariffs and (more critical for diamonds) intra-company transfer price margins. By these and related methods, South African enterprises and the South African state are able to appropriate a substantial part of Namibia's surplus.

Methods of taxation include mining income tax, diamond mining income tax, company tax, undistributed profits tax, diamond profits tax, diamond export duty, stamp duty, marketable securities tax, transfer duties, film duties, customs and excise, sales duties and prospecting and claim licences. Between 1969 and 1974 mines have been the major source of revenue, providing 38% and 34% respectively of the total. If customs and excise (at 14% and 13% respectively) are included, South Africa earns approximately 50% of all its revenue from various forms of taxation on mining. (In 1969 total state revenue from taxation was R98.6 million, in 1974 R128.1 million.)[72] In this way, the South African state has appropriated a part of the international purchasing power embodied in Namibian-produced commodities. Furthermore, since South Africa's expenditures in Namibia are not in foreign exchange, tax revenues from Namibia represent a conversion of domestic to international purchasing power.

The appropriation of international purchasing power occurs at two levels: first, to the section of the bourgeoisie directly involved in exploitation of natural resources and to the state and, second, to the section of the South African bourgeoisie which manufactures means of production (and, to a lesser extent, consumption) whose sale to enterprises and individuals in Namibia provides a second round of surplus acquisition and a second round of surplus transfer from Namibia to South Africa.

The process of importing the bulk of her requirements from South Africa is costly for Namibia since South African industries operate behind tariff barriers and import control measures. Many of South Africa's locally manufactured capital goods are more expensive than those which Namibia could buy elsewhere if she were free to do so. It is evident that South African capital needs continued South African domination of the local state. If commodities from other countries were allowed to compete, the relatively underdeveloped state of the production process in South Africa would in many cases render her commodities uncompetitive against those from the developed capitalist world or from the socialist industrial economies of Europe, and she would lose a substantial share of the Namibian market.

This set of economic relations is inextricably linked to political relations and both are backed by the South African state with its 50 000 odd police and troops occupying Namibia.

The present phase of the struggle

In analyzing Namibian opposition to foreign domination, the first point to make is that exploitation of Namibia's natural resources is carried out primarily by international monopoly groups, which, although based in South Africa, Europe and the United States, are inter-linked. The network is dominated by a few powerful institutions, particularly the Anglo American Group, which are able to put forward policies designed to serve their joint interests. The Namibian economy is thus characterized by an extremely centralized, monopolistic decision-making system.

Affiliated to the small but powerful group of monopoly capitalists are several subordinate capitalist groups. Most important are the small settler farmers and small and medium-sized business proprietors. The alliance between monopoly capitalism and the local bourgeoisie is not without problems as the settlers have had to subject their immediate interests to those of South African monopoly capital. The restrictions on industrial development in Namibia, on financial autonomy, and on the pattern of foreign trade all impede the process by which this group can transform itself into a local settler bourgeoisie. Too weak to dominate the indigenous classes on their own, these local settlers are forced to continue the alliance.

A third group also involved in this alliance consists of appointed chiefs and headmen and their attendant bureaucracies and para-military units. The basis for their alliance was their undertaking to supply the labour requirements of monopoly capital. Their incorporation into the structures of state control in Namibia seems to give them a power well beyond that which numbers suggest,[73] but it is a power which is almost totally derived from the state's power and not an independent one.

These three groups constitute the ruling class in Namibia and together form the basis for the alliance of capitalist oppression and exploitation in the country. The power base is monopoly capital and it is primarily in the interests of the reproduction of monopoly capitalism that the state functions, although particular policies favourable to the local arm of the alliance and expenditure items benefiting the collaborationists can also be identified.

Peasants constitute the bulk of the indigenous population and for most of them wage labour is necessary for survival.[74] The degree of proletarianization is shown by the fact that there are only two peasants in the subsistence sector for every one migrant labourer at any given time. (In 1971, it was estimated that about 80% of all African men in Namibia had been migrant workers at least once in their lives.) According to Moorsom, 'Wage labour was unavoidable periodically for most, continuously for some, for the first 25–30 years of adult (male) life, by which time sons could take over the cycles.'[75] A large proportion of the peasantry may be seen as a proletariat which is forced, through repressive state measures, to live and reproduce itself in rural areas.

In addition to peasant households with incomes largely supplied by migrant labour, the Namibian working class consists of permanent farm-labour households employed by white ranch owners and a relatively small, though growing, permanently settled urban proletariat.

A tiny section of the working class has managed to appropriate a small surplus and to transform itself into a commercial petty bourgeoisie. Since 1963 this transformation has been encouraged by the South African state. Initially, the recruiting agency, SWANLA, held a monopoly over all retail and wholesale trade in the northern areas of Ovamboland, Okavango and Kaokoveld, which enabled it to subsidize its recruiting operations in these areas. However, in 1963 the Odendaal Commission recommended that 'trade in the homelands should to an increasing extent be conducted by competent indigenous entrepreneurs'.[76] SWANLA lost its monopoly and a class of indigenous small traders was able to emerge.

Although the conditions for its emergence were created by the South African state, this does not necessarily imply that this class collaborates with the state, although the latter seeks to achieve this. The Odendaal Commission, for example, recommended that the state should grant 'financial and other assistance to competent indigenous entrepreneurs'.[77] As a result, the Bantu Investment Corporation (BIC) extended its operations to Namibia in 1964. However, it has made little progress and the petty bourgeoisie has reacted against it, with accusations of 'exploitation' and 'deception'.[78] This class appears to be divided, with a small minority increasingly dependent on the state and a large independent majority hostile to the state. To the ranks of the indigenous petty bourgeoisie must be added several thousand teachers, clergy, clerical workers and nurses. Most are increasingly hostile to the state and sympathetic to SWAPO.

The struggle between these classes characterizes political developments in Namibia: on the one hand are the settler farmers and small businessmen and the indigenous tribal bureaucracy allied to international monopoly capital; on the other hand there are the proletariat and declining peasantry, supported by the majority of the African petty bourgeoisie.

The Turnhalle Conference aimed at introducing constitutional reforms which, on the one hand, would attempt to reconcile some of the short-term differences between international capital and local capitalist interests and, on the other, would incorporate the indigenous petty bourgeoisie into the alliance of exploiting classes. It aimed at restructuring the alliance of ruling class domination in Namibia so that the proletariat and peasantry would be increasingly isolated and leaderless.

The problem facing the bourgeoisie was how to react to SWAPO, which had refused to become involved in the Turnhalle negotiations. Here a rift opened within the ranks of international capital: South African capital (except Anglo) sought to deny all political rights to SWAPO and to impose control by means of physical repression. Non-South African foreign capital (including, for this purpose, Anglo) sought to involve SWAPO at a political level in the hope that a neo-colonial solution could be found.

Since the Turnhalle Conference, the South African state has pushed ahead with its strategy of seeking a political and military solution based on the repression of the organizations of the masses: new political parties have emerged within the ranks of the capitalist class and its allies, the most prominent being the Democratic Turnhalle Alliance (DTA); South African-controlled elections have been held; and the war has escalated with South African troops embarking on deep raids into Angola. SWAPO, however, has remained defiant, refusing to concede to the South African state's demand that it lay down arms, and, consequently, the Western powers have refused to give formal support to the South African manoeuvres.

It is clear that so long as SWAPO is able to resist the South African state's efforts to defeat it both militarily and, even more important, politically, the rift within the ranks of capital will remain. Essentially, that rift represents capital's incapacity to come to terms with the threat posed by the alliance of oppressed and exploited classes in Namibia. While the Western powers seek accommodation with SWAPO in the hope that they will thereby be able to control the forward movement of the oppressed classes, this is not an approach which the South African state can adopt, knowing full well that should SWAPO come to power in Namibia then South Africa's profitable access to the country's resources will almost certainly be brought to an end. It is these different interests among the foreign exploiting states which lie at the heart of the rift between them.

However, the struggle for national liberation in Namibia is far from over. The South African state still has the economic, political and military power to hang on to its colony for some time. The forces of resistance will need to be considerably strengthened before that power can be decisively broken. And even when the era of South African colonialism is brought to an end, as it inevitably will be, this in itself will not necessarily mean an end to imperialist exploitation in Namibia. Yet it remains true that the mass of the Namibian people have, through a long period of struggle, reached the point today where they are closer than ever before to reclaiming their birthright.[79]

Notes

1 See Monica Wilson and Leonard Thompson, *The Oxford History of South Africa*, Oxford University Press, 1969.

2 Exports from South Africa averaged about £0.25 m per annum between 1821 and 1849; between 1846 and 1866 there was a small improvement with the commencement of wool production: the value of wool exports rose from £0.2 m in 1846 to £2.1 m in 1866; D. Hobart Houghton, *The South African Economy*, Oxford University Press, 1973.

3 *Ibid.;* by 1820 (i.e. after the discovery of diamonds) £33 m had been invested; by 1911 (i.e. after the discovery of gold) almost £400 m had been invested.

4 *Ibid.;* telegraph systems were introduced and roads and railways built in the interior. By 1910 there were 11 265 km of railway line in South Africa.

5 This section draws heavily on the important and perceptive analysis by R. Moorsom, '*Underdevelopment and Class Formation*: *the origin of migrant labour in Namibia*, 1850–1915', paper delivered to the Workshop on Southern Africa, Oxford University, 1974.

6 Quoted in J. H. Wellington, *South West Africa and its Human Issues*, Oxford University Press, 1967.

7 There were two cases of genocide, against the Herero and Nama tribes, but the process of conquest was briefer and on a smaller scale than in South Africa and the Ovambo country was not effectively occupied until the period of South African rule.

8 See R. Moorsom, *'Underdevelopment and Class Formation'* for details.

9 I. Goldblatt., *History of South West Africa from the beginning of the nineteenth century*, Juta's, Capetown, 1971, p. 198.

10 Wellington, *South West Africa and its Human Issues*, p. 113.

11 Leonard Lazar, *Namibia*, African Bureau, London, 1972, p.95.

12 *Ibid.*, p. 64.

13 Wellington, *South West Africa and its Human Issues.*

14 Between 1910/11 and 1917/18 the value of industrial production in South Africa rose from £22 m to £60 m; see C.W. Pearsall, 'Some Aspects of the Development of Secondary Industry in the Union of South Africa', *South African Journal of Economics*, 1937.

15 D. Hobart Houghton, *The South African Economy*, pp. 122–23.

16 It must be stressed that, despite this industrial expansion, South Africa remained a peripheral economy and did not automatically shed the twin yokes of underdevelopment and dependency.

17 The laws affecting the lives of Africans in South West Africa were modelled on those of South Africa.

18 Wellington, *South West Africa and its Human Issues.*

19 Sean Gervasi, 'The South West African Economy,' in R. Segal and R. First, *South West Africa: Travesty of Trust,* London, 1967.

20 Wellington, *South West Africa and its Human Issues*, p. 312.

21 *Ibid.*

22 *Ibid.*

23 R.L. Bradford, 'Blacks to the Wall in SWA', in Segal and First, *South West Africa.*

24 United Nations Charter, Article 77.

25 Wellington, *South West Africa and its Human Issues.*

26 *South African Statistics*, 1968, Bureau of Statistics, Pretoria, and South African Reserve Bank, *Annual Report*, 1973.

27 *Report of the Commission of Enquiry into South West African Affairs 1962–1963* (Odendaal Report), Pretoria; 1964, p. 319, and *South West Africa Survey 1974,* Department of Foreign Affairs, Pretoria, 1977, p. 33.

28 Quoted in *A Survey of Race Relations in SA*, South African Insitute of Race Relations, 1969.

29 W.H. Thomas, '*The Economy of SWA*: *an overall perspective*'. Thomas's figures are drawn from a Confidential Report prepared by the Bureau for Economic Research at the University of Stellenbosch and entitled, '*In Ondersrek na die Ekonomiese Struktuur van Suidwes Afrika, 1960–1970*'.

30 *SWA Survey*, 1974, pp. 39, 70.

31 *Financial Mail*, Supplement, 2 March 1973. Wage figures computed from the *Financial Mail* and figures given in E. de Sousa Ferreira, '*International Capital in Namibia: Tsumeb and the CDM*', paper delivered to the Namibian International Conference, Brussels, May 1972.

32 Odendaal Report, p. 331.

33 Ferreira, '*International Capital*', p. 9.

34 *Financial Mail*, Supplement, 2 March 1973, p. 57.

35 *Ibid.*

36 *Financial Mail*, 1967, p. 42.

37 Ferreira, '*International Capital*', p. 11.

38 *Ibid.*, pp. 10–11.

39 Quoted by Ferreira from an advertisement appearing in the *Wall Street Journal.*

40 Thomas, '*The Economy of SWA,*' p. 10.

41 Roger Murray, 'The Namibian Economy: An Assessment of the Role of Foreign Investment and the Policies of the South African Administration' in R. Murray *et al.*, *The Role of Foreign Firms in Namibia*, London, 1974.

42 *Financial Mail*, 1967, p. 40; Thomas, '*The Economy of SWA*', p. 13.

43 *SWA Survey,* 1967, p. 62.

44 *SWA Survey*, 1967 and 1974.

45 S. Gervasi, 'The South West African Economy'.

46 According to the *SWA Survey*, 1974, p. 34: 'An average of 300 000 bags (weighing 90 kg each) of maize and maize products are imported annually from South Africa at a subsidized cost of R1.2 m, as well as approximately 100 000 bags of wheat flour at a cost of R700 000 . . . Concentrated stock feeds and high protein roughages (mainly lucerne hay) at an estimated value of R2 m and other agricultural products such as fresh and processed vegetables and fruit, sugar, powdered milk, butter, etc. worth about R10 m are also imported from South Africa each year.' By 'subsidized' is meant 'below current world prices'. The crucial questions are whether South Africa would be able to sell this maize on world markets or whether Namibia is the only market she has, and what would be the true cost to the Namibian economy of home production.

47 *Financial Mail*, Supplement, 2 March 1973.

48 *SWA Survey*, 1974, p. 34.

49 R. Murray, 'The Namibian Economy', and Richard Moorsom, 'Underdevelopment, Contract Labour and Worker Consciousness in Namibia, 1915–72', *Journal of Southern African Studies*, October 1977, p. 67.

50 Thomas, '*The Economy of SWA*'.

51 *SWA Survey*, 1967.

52 *SWA Survey*, 1974, p. 37.

53 R. Murray, 'The Namibian Economy'

54 *SWA Survey*, 1974, p. 40.

55 *Ibid.*, p. 40.

56 *Ibid.*, p. 33.

57 *SWA Survey*, 1967, p. 71.

58 Odendaal Report, p. 333, para (v) f.

59 *Ibid.*, p. 333, para (v) f.

60 *Ibid.*, p. 333, para (v) d.

61 *Ibid.*, p. 333, para (v) c.

62 *Ibid.*, p. 107, para 416.

63 *Ibid.*, p. 459, para (d) g.

64 *SWA Survey*, 1974, p. 40; Thomas '*The Economy of SWA*', p. 13.

65 *Financial Mail*, Supplement, 2 March 1973.

66 *SWA Survey*, 1974, p. 43.

67 *SWA Survey*, 1967, p. 76.

68 See R. Murray, 'The Namibian Economy'.

69 *SWA Survey*, 1974, p. 42.

70 *Ibid.*, p. 42.

71 Thomas, '*The Economy of SWA*, p. 13.

72 *Financial Mail*, Supplement, 2 March 1973, p. 42; *SWA Survey*, 1974, p. 4.

73 It is difficult to indicate precise numerical strength but, according to Tötemeyer, in 1972 they numbered about 1 050, though not all were necessarily collaborationist.

74 R. Moorsom, 'Labour Consciousness and the 1971–72 Contract Workers' Strike in Namibia', *Development and Change*, Vol 10, 1979.

75 *Ibid.*

76 Odendaal Report, p. 487, para. 1514.

77 *Ibid.*, p. 487, para. 1515.

78 *Financial Mail*, Supplement, 2 March 1973.

79 For a more detailed analysis of the current phase of the struggle in Namibia, see D. Innes, 'Imperialism and the National Struggle in Namibia', *Review of African Political Economy*, No. 9, 1978.

5 The white man's burden: Africans under apartheid

MARJA-LIISA KILJUNEN

> The indigenous groups had to be protected against the private enterprise of the white man, whose capital, skills and business expertise the underdeveloped man could not match.
>
> – South West Africa, A Progress Report, 1970

Early history

The written history of Namibia is largely the history of the white man. Most books on Namibia begin with the Portuguese explorers Cão and Dias at the end of the fifteenth and the beginning of the sixteenth centuries and then go on to the late seventeenth century and initial European penetration from the Cape.

The history of the people of Namibia is, of course, broader and goes back much further than this European perspective would indicate. A brief indication of earlier Namibian history is needed here, not least to rebut claims that colonial rule brought peace, justice and prosperity to a land previously engaged in a Hobbesian war of all against all.

The first known inhabitants of Namibia were the San (usually designated 'bushmen') a hunting, gathering, wandering people with highly developed graphic skills. Later arrivals pushed them to the fringes of the Kalahari and the desert rock slopes of the Namib edge. Between the ninth and fourteenth centuries the surge of pastoral peoples southward in Africa brought the Herero (including the Himba), the Ovambo (including the Kavango), the peoples of the Caprivi, the Tswana, and perhaps the Damara, to Namibia from the north and north east.

The Nama came from the Cape in two waves. The earlier – Red Nation – migrants may have been retreating from pressure by peoples themselves displaced by the seventeenth- or eighteenth-century European penetration of the Cape. Possibly the Damara, a subject people who had lost their language and state system, came with the Nama. The Orlam clans' migration in the early nineteenth century was part of the *Mfecane*, the violent making and breaking of African states triggered by the emergence of the Zulu state and by the northward push of European settlers. The last pre-colonial African entrants were the Basters, a Nama/Boer 'Coloured' group, deliberately settled at Rehoboth by German missionaries and merchants as a buffer state and a pawn in German–Nama–Herero struggles.

The state systems of the pre-colonial peoples varied from group to group and time to time. The Ovambo and Kavango had moderately open, small-scale kingship states, similar to those common in the West African forest zone. These carried on smelting and trading. Their trade with Cape merchants moved from ostrich feathers to cattle and to people, their structures from semi-participatory to highly authoritarian, and their relations with neighbours from relatively amicable to hostile, with systematic raiding wars to collect cattle and people to sell for guns, powder and liquor.

The Herero had rather fragmented clan systems. Reports of chiefs' herds numbering as many as 25 000 suggest a high degree of inequality, a feature not atypical of early southern African pastoral societies. Grazing land, and intra-clan disputes over it, were at the centre of Herero politics. The Nama incursion led to a complex series of conflicts over land and herds, complex because each side frequently included some Nama and some Herero.

In the nineteenth century Namibia too experienced the late emergence of African state systems before the advent of colonialism. No state comparable to the Merina Kingdom of Antanarivo, the Fanti Confederacy of coastal Ghana, or the (rather different) *Mfecane* states such as the Zulu empire or Basotho kingdom emerged, but under the sovereignty of the Afrikander family, the Windhoek state was created. Basically Nama, it had significant Herero clan participation, with some Herero as members of council or as district 'governors'. A road to Walvis Bay was built to facilitate trade, and missionaries were encouraged, largely as education and technical assistance personnel. The concept of a written constitution was toyed with but none was adopted (unlike at Rehoboth and in one or two Orlam states).

Namibia was never Arcadian, pre-colonial inter-group and inter-state relations were not always amicable, and conquest was by no means unknown. But the eighteenth- and nineteenth-century picture is not one of continuous, aimless bloodstained brawls. The Windhoek Kingdom was, in many respects, comparable to a number of the short-lived Boer Republics, as was the Rehoboth state. The Nama–Herero wars were the result of European pressure which pushed the Nama into what was previously Herero country.

Pre-colonial European penetration involved sealers, whalers and guano collectors on the coast, and more importantly, traders and missionaries overland from the Cape and inland from Walvis Bay. Sometimes inadvertently and sometimes wilfully (as with arms sellers and cattle and slave buyers), they exacerbated intra-Namibian conflicts. Further, they began the integration of some Namibian groups into the world economy in a way which sapped their self-sufficiency, increased internal authoritarian tendencies and weakened egalitarian and re-distributive mechanisms. They set the stage for Lüderitz's German South West Africa Company to begin the conquest of Namibia.[1]

The German period

Initially the Germans used various methods to acquire land and cattle: the extension of credit, purchases of cattle, offers of 'protection' against other clans, raiding campaigns and fort building. The results were impressive in magnitude.

While most land was allocated to concession companies, these

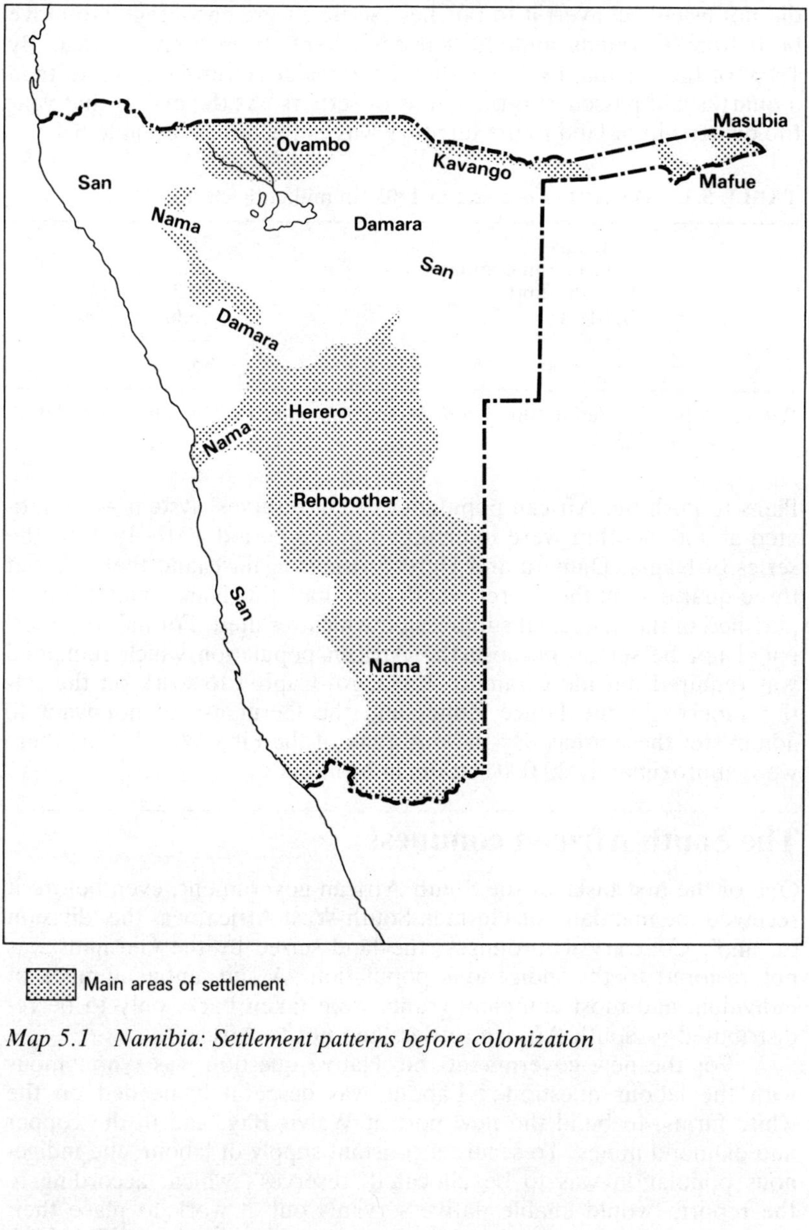

Map 5.1 Namibia: Settlement patterns before colonization

did not usually convert it to ranches. Settlers were encouraged to move both from Germany and, to a lesser extent, from South Africa. By 1903, of the original twelve million hectares of Hereroland, more than a quarter had passed into the hands of settlers. At the end of that year the ownership of land in the territory was estimated as in Table 5.1.

TABLE 5.1. Ownership of Land in 1903 (in million hectares)

Africans	31.4
Concession companies	29.2
Crown Land	19.3
Settlers	3.6
	83.5

Source: John H. Wellington, *South West Africa and Its Human Issues*, OUP, 1967, p. 123.

Plans to push the African populations to a 'reserves' system were initiated about 1900 but were interrupted in the period 1904–1910 by the series of Nama, Damara and Herero risings against land theft. About three-quarters of the Herero and over half the Nama and Damara perished in the genocidal suppression which resulted. Formal 'reserves' could not be set up because the African population which remained was required outside Ovambo–Kavango–Caprivi to work on the settler ranches in the Police Zone, and the Germans did not want to administer these areas. By the outbreak of the First World War, there were approximately 20 000 settlers in Namibia.

The South African conquest

One of the first tasks of the South African government, even before it received the mandate for German South West Africa, was the 'division of land'. Contrary to promises, the land seized by the Germans was not restored to the indigenous population. A substantial number of individual and most company grants were taken back, only to be redistributed to South African settlers and not to Africans.

For the new government the 'Native question was synonymous with the labour question'.[2] Labour was desperately needed on the white farms, to build the new port at Walvis Bay, and in the copper and diamond mines. To secure a constant supply of labour, the indigenous population was to be allocated 'reserves', which, according to the report, 'would enable native servants out at work to place their stock on the Reserves and collect there the old and infirm'.[3] This both limited the permanently resident African population in 'white' areas and reduced the level of wages to be paid to below a family subsistence level. Built into the system was the assumption that households could not survive on what they could earn or grow on the 'reserves'. The division of land in Namibia was based on the South African model of 1913. The Police Zone was treated as a white area. The areas suitable for ranching were allocated to settlers and the rest to the state. From the state land, 'reserves' were cut out (with the exception of Rehoboth and possibly one or two others on land notable for its submarginal or desert nature). The newly subjugated areas north of the Police Zone were treated as 'reserves', largely because they were either densely populated (Ovambo, Kavango), utterly unsuited to ranching (Kaokoveld), or totally isolated from the rest of the territory (Caprivi). In 1922 the Native Administration Proclamation Act formally established the 'reserves'. Where the Africans resisted movement from existing areas of residence to 'reserves', the administrators resorted to violence, burning dwellings, seizing cattle and destroying crops, or to threats of violence. The Herero, for example, who had lost all their land, were allocated eleven separate patches of land in the most arid parts of the Central Plateau and in the Kalahari Desert. At the same time, millions of hectares of sometime Herero pasture land, confiscated by the government from the German concession companies, were formally allotted to Afrikaner ranchers, many of them former members of the 1915 Expeditionary Force.

Led by their Chief, Hosea Kutako, the Herero protested against their banishment to barren reserves:

> We are a big nation and as such we shall not develop in a country like this where no human being ever lived before. It is a country only good for wild beasts.[4]

Taxes to be paid in cash (Grazing Tax, Dwelling Tax, Hut Tax, and even a Dog Tax in the case of some of the Nama) added to the pressure on Africans to seek paid work outside the 'reserves' For Police Zone residents, arrangements with individual employers were permitted. For the north, a recruitment and allocation company, the South West Africa Native Labour Association (SWANLA), was created as the sole legal channel for Ovambo and Kavango to secure labour contracts.

Racial discrimination, introduced by the Germans, was maintained by the South African administration, but on a more systematic and legally enforced basis; legal structures of discrimination operative in the Republic were applied to the mandated territory. Numerous laws to regulate the movement and residence of the indigenous population were implemented. They included the Vagrancy Proclamation 1920 (as amended), the Native Reserves Regulation 1924 (as amended), the Native Administration Proclamation 1922 (known as the Pass Law), the Extra-Territorial and Northern Natives Control Proclamation 1935 (as amended), and the Regulations for the Registrations Control and Protection of Natives in Proclaimed Areas 1955 (as amended).[5]

Despite these complex controls over the African population, sizeable urbanization took place. It is difficult to estimate accurately the number of inhabitants in these separate black and 'Coloured' townships that were created, partly because a substantial proportion remain there unlawfully. According to a recent estimate about 24% of the African population is urban (see Annex Table 3). In any case, only a fragment of the African population live in the 'reserves' within the Police Zone: the majority have settled in white ranches or urban areas.

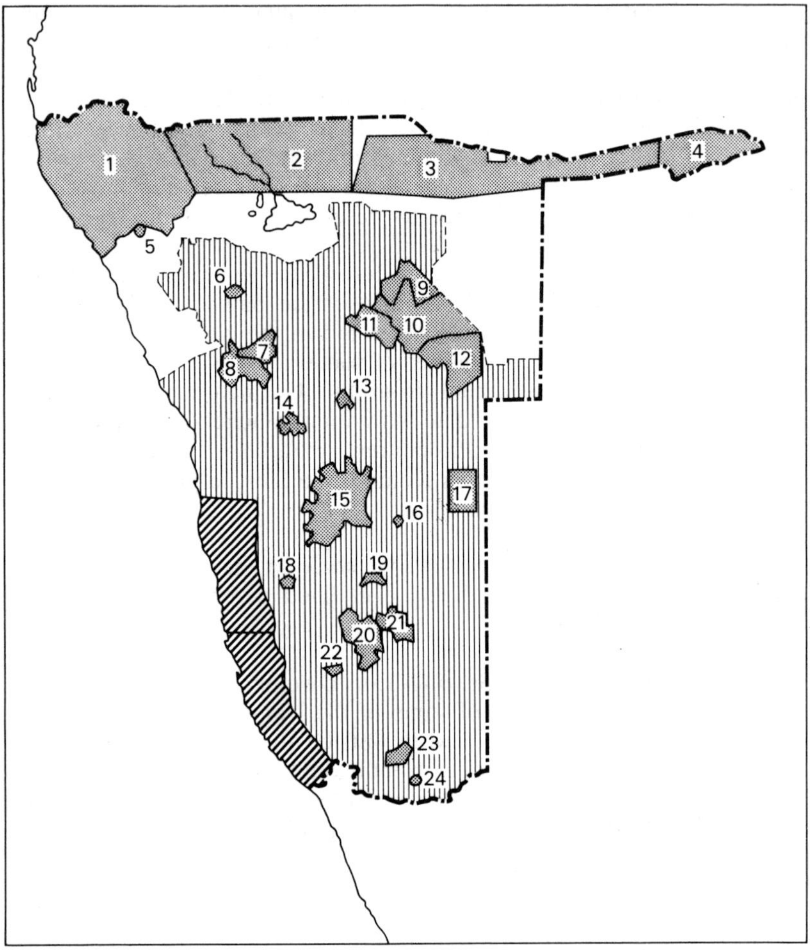

African 'Reserves'
Areas reserved for whites
Diamond areas
Boundary of Police Zone

1 Kaokoveld
2 Ovamboland
3 Okavango
4 East Capri
5 Sesfontein
6 Fransfontein
7 Otjohorongo
8 Okombahe
9 Otjituuo
10 Eastern
11 Waterberg East
12 Epukiro
13 Ovitoto
14 Otjimbingwe
15 Rehoboth
16 Hoachanas
17 Aminuis
18 Neuhof
19 Krantzplatz
20 Berseba
21 Tses
22 Soromas
23 Bondels
24 Warmbad

Map 5.2 African 'Reserves' in Namibia, c. 1920–1970

Katutura

One of the most tragic examples of apartheid in Namibia is the black suburb of Katutura outside Windhoek (see Map 5.3). In 1959 the black population was forced to move from their 'old location' which was close to the expanding city centre and, therefore, was designated as a 'black spot' in a 'white' area. The people had to leave their bulldozed dwellings for Katutura, even though houses, roads and public services were not completed. The new suburb was further from the city centre and involved rented municipal instead of owner-occupied houses. Living costs were substantially raised by the higher bus fares and rents. The move was resisted and the violent crushing of the resistance, Namibia's Sharpeville, was an important factor in the emergence of the modern liberation movement.

A tarred road from Windhoek leads to Katutura gate, situated next to a police station, and continues around the perimeter of the suburb (for the use of the South African police). The interior streets are all dusty tracks. The township is demarcated into sections for each ethnic group (see Map 5.3), each provided with separate schools. Attached to the main residential area is the migrant workers' compound with high fences, a patrolled security gate and perimeter floodlighting. Relatives and acquaintances have been smuggled in to live in Katutura. Katutura has been the target of repeated raids by the police to locate criminals, 'terrorists' or illegal residents. The last are frequently deported back to their respective 'Homelands'. The raids have often led to indiscriminate violence, beatings and mass arrests.

Africans living in towns do so under constant threat of being sent 'home' for almost any reason: arrears or disputes over rent, unemployment, disputes at work. While the townships often have extremely poor sanitation and sewage systems, the municipalities are concerned about dangers to hygiene because of poultry or other animals kept to supplement the food supply. In some cases people have been ordered to destroy their animals, again under threat of being 'endorsed out' of the township if they do not obey.

Divide and rule

South Africa, when forced to seek an internationally and internally acceptable strategy to show its intention to provide conditions which would facilitate the economic and social development of a majority of the population both within South Africa and Namibia, introduced the policy of 'separate development'. This was a further step in the progression from baaskap (domination) through apartheid (segregation). 'Homelands' were to be established for each ethnic group with the aim of self-government and finally 'independence' allegedly consistent with their own cultural and historical traditions.

The blueprint for the balkanization of Namibia was published in the Odendaal Report[6] in 1964. The Africans (including the Rehobothers and Nama) were divided into ten 'indigenous peoples' each of which was to be given a 'Homeland'. These were to cover 39.6% of the total area of the country. The urbanized 'Coloureds' were to be

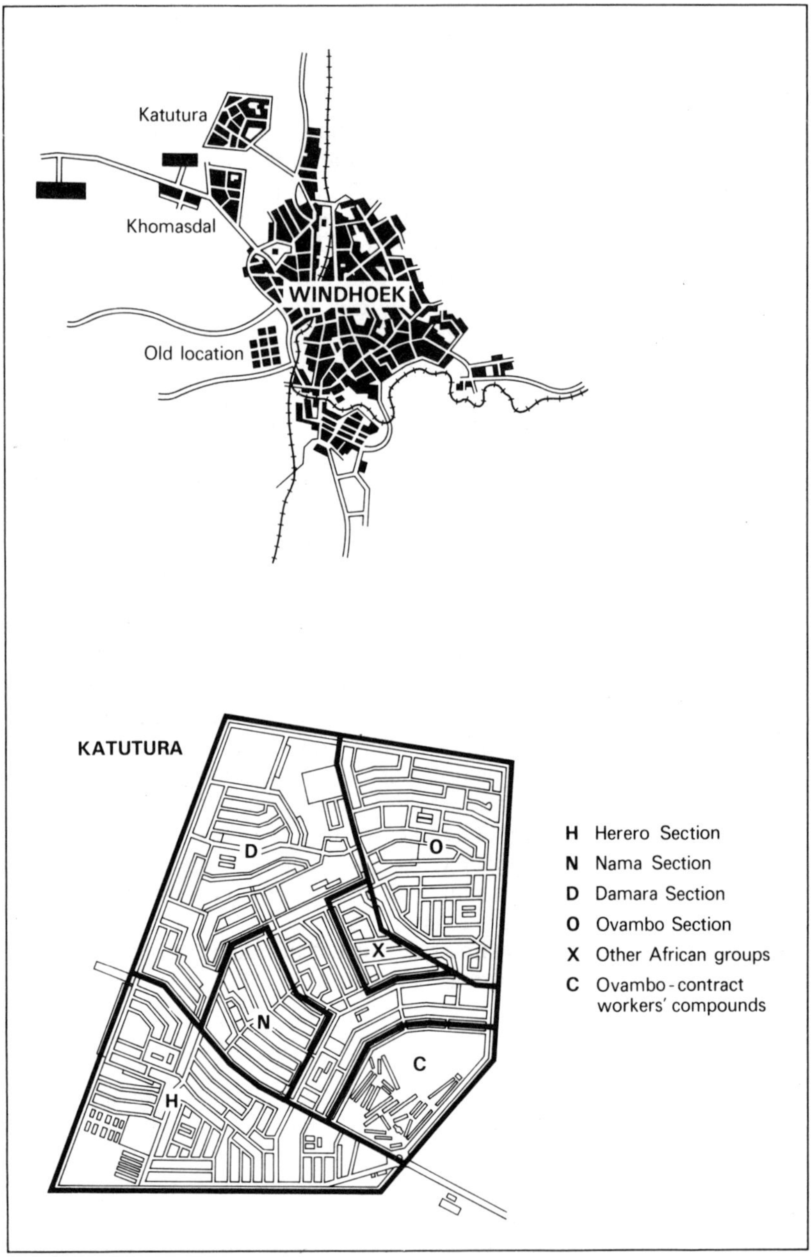

Map 5.3 Windhoek and Katutura

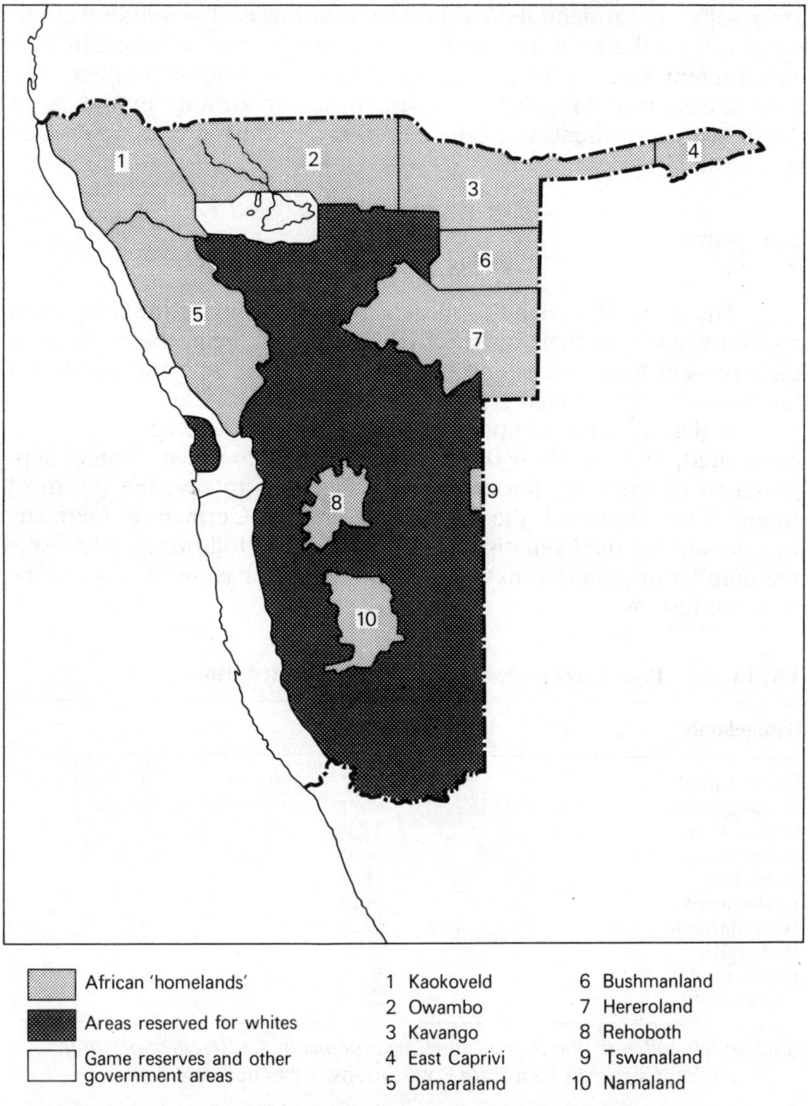

Map 5.4 African 'Homelands' according to the Odendaal plan

given separate residential areas in the major towns. The whites were to have 44% of the total area and the government was to retain 16% as 'government areas' (the coastal diamond fields, wildlife and National Park areas) (see Map 5.4). Expressed as proportions of the latest South African estimates of population, the country was to be divided as follows:

	% of Population	*% of Land*
Europeans	11.5	60.4
Africans	88.5	39.6

The term 'Homeland' is misleading since many of the designated areas are alien to their prospective inhabitants, being both far from their present home areas and equally inconsistent with the traditional territories of the African groups (see Maps 5.1 and 5.2).

If the residential implications of the Odendaal Report were implemented, at least 150 000 people would have to move to areas supposed to be their 'traditional homes'. Needless to say, the return of Boers to the Transvaal, the Cape or Holland, or Germans to Germany was not among the Commission's proposals. The following table shows the number of people who would be affected by having to move to the new Bantustans.

TABLE 5.2 Percentage of People Living in Designated 'Homelands'

'Homelands'	1970
Ovamboland	85.0
Kavangoland	96.0
Damaraland	12.0
Hereroland	54.0
Namaland	*6.6
East-Caprivi	99.0
Bushmanland	31.0
Rehoboth	*79.0
Kaokoland	97.0
Tswanaland	23.0

Source: *Homelands, the Role of the Corporations in the Republic of South Africa*, Chris van Rensburg Publications, Johannesburg, n.d.

* 1964; data from the Odendaal Report, Pretoria, 1964.

While the proposed reorganization of 'reserves' into 'Homelands' would have increased both total African land allocation and the fragmentation of groups among isolated pieces of land, it would not have made the African population any more able to live on the land allotted. It would, in fact, have reduced the quantity of even moderately usable land outside areas reserved for white ranchers. For example, the Hereros, who are traditional cattle farmers, are dispersed in eleven 'reserves'. Many would have had to move to an area in the northern part of the Kalahari Desert, which is probably of poorer quality than any of their present 'reserves'. Only about one-fifth of the land is suitable for grazing. The protein and phosphorus content of the grass is so low that cattle are prone to many diseases. The fact that neither Hereroland nor any other 'Homeland' would be economically viable or self-sustaining was quite openly stated in the Odendaal Report.

In fact, in respect of three 'Homelands' outside the Police Zone, Ovamboland, Kavangoland, eastern Caprivi, the present lack of viability relates in large measure to deliberate non-development or prevention of development, not just to land availability or quality. For example, Kavangoland probably has the highest crop-cultivation potential in the country but the present situation there is hardly impressive. The variety of crops grown with the help of simple tools and cattle manure is larger than in any other part of the country, but only a limited surplus of the staple crops, maize, millet, sorghum and vegetables (including beans, pumpkins, watermelons or groundnuts), is produced, and in some years the region is heavily dependent on imported maize. The cattle, which are critical to food supply (milk and meat) and cash income (sales to packing plant) are severely infested with parasites as a result of grazing in the grass-covered swamps.

This is despite African initiatives to increase productivity and to achieve a surplus rather than maintaining only a subsistence-oriented level of production. Small-scale irrigation, animal-drawn implements and new seeds have been introduced, but more despite than because of official policy or state services. Recent grudging support has not included efficient purchasing or input supply arrangements, nor has an overall water strategy been devised to deal with the problems imposed by the depth and steepness of the Okavango valley terrain.

Administration of 'Homelands'

After the passing of the Development of Self-Government for Native Nations of South West Africa Act, No. 54 of 1968, the following 'Homelands' and their respective authorities were set up: Ovambo Legislative Assembly, 1968 ('self-governing' status was granted in 1973); Kavango Legislative Assembly, 1970 ('self-governing' status was granted in 1973); Damaraland Advisory Council, 1971 (its powers were expanded in 1977); Caprivi Legislative Assembly, 1972; Rehoboth self-government in 1976 and the elected 'Kaptein' in 1977; Namaland, the Nama Council, 1976.

Whatever Odendaal may or may not have envisaged, there has been no change in the division of labour even after partial implementation of 'separate development'. The white economy still depends on black labour. The Africans still have no alternative but to sell their labour to the whites in order to secure a minimum level of livelihood. The 'Homeland' system has not in fact altered the 'reserve' pattern under which Africans had no economic, political or social rights within 'white' areas.

The 'Homelands' are responsible for guaranteeing a livelihood for the contract worker's family, as well as for education and health and for looking after the unemployed and the old. Traditional African tribal structures, institutions and characteristics, such as respect for old tribesmen, have been invoked in efforts to legitimize the inequality of the Africans. The South African government created an elite of minor administrators and tribal chiefs to work with the whites as an intermediary between white power and the Africans. This group has been granted limited privileges and a higher standard of living in the hope that it will develop a commitment to the continuation of the 'Homelands' as their destruction would mean loss of privileges.

More recent South African attempts, beginning with the Turnhalle Constitutional Conference in 1975, to find an internally and externally acceptable solution to the form of Namibia's independence, have not reversed the 'Homeland' principle. On the contrary, they have been based on it. All variants have provided for a weak confederal central government resting on a tier of 'Homelands' (including a 'white Homeland') or ethnic groupings, though the plan to divide the country physically into separate homelands was abandoned during the Turnhalle negotiations. As late as the fall of 1980, South Africa was pressing ahead with 'second-tier' (ethnic homeland) elections including one for the European 'Homeland'.

In the 'Homelands' the actual executive power is held by the South African government, the President and the Minister for Bantu Affairs, through whom all laws have to pass. Chiefs, who are nominated and paid by the government, have often had very little education or administrative experience. The most critical posts are still held by white administrators, who are placed as advisors and secretaries to the 'ministers'. The administrative bodies, legislative council and district and tribal councils, have been created by South African legislation with their powers limited to minor issues, and with their budgets almost totally dependent on government of South Africa allocations.

In 1973 a law was passed which gave the South African President the right to declare a 'Homeland', change their boundaries, decide on their official language, the Chiefs' duties and even their national anthem and flag, if any.

While all group members (wherever resident) over 18 have a right to vote in 'Homeland' administrative council elections, usually only part of the council is elected (in Ovamboland, for instance, 21) and the remainder is nominated by the Chiefs' Council (in Ovamboland, 35). Further, the procedures and pressures surrounding elections cast grave doubt on whether even elected members can be said to be representatives in any real sense.

The people have shown their resistance to the segregationist policies and to elections in which no real alternatives exist. In 1973 SWAPO successfully called on the population to boycott the elections in Ovamboland, so that only 2% cast a vote. Subsequently greater efforts to 'get out the vote' have been used to some effect: in 1975 50% of the electorate voted. But this was in a setting summed up by the Anglican Bishop as offering the Ovambo the choice 'vote or starve'.[7]

The economic development of the 'Homelands' is controlled by the South African government through the Bantu Affairs Council. The Council's main operating subsidiaries are the Bantu Investment Corporation (BIC) and the Bantu Mining Corporation. The BIC has granted loans to small enterprises, but has created very few new jobs in African areas: by 1975 it had created only about 1 500 new jobs in the whole of Ovamboland, in Kavango some 500, in East Caprivi a few hundred, and elsewhere a total of less than a hundred. This fell more than 50% short of the target to create 5 800 new jobs by 1975. The new job opportunities available in the 'Homelands' are mainly in construction, retail trading, health care and education; the number in industry is negligible. The economic development of the 'Homelands' has remained slow. To secure a sufficient work force for the mines and other parts of the southern sector and to limit increases in employment costs may be consistent with marginal job creation or petty bourgeois support; it is not consistent with creating flourishing 'Homeland' economies capable of sustaining their populations.

The consequences of the 'Homeland' policy were intended to be far reaching: the emergence of a common national feeling was to be slowed down and instead antagonism between different population groups was expected to be generated by 'Homeland' loyalties. The 'Homelands' were intended to be easy to control both militarily and politically. The development of political consciousness was to be retarded; social conflicts in the 'Homeland' could easily be seen only in their local context and interpreted as conflicts between tribes or population groups or between 'Homelands'.[8]

Attempts at 'liberalization'

The 'liberalization' in racial discrimination, widely publicized since the appointment in 1977 of an Administrator-General as chief representative (with dictatorial powers) of the South African government, has in fact been distinctly marginal. Some of the most glaring signs of apartheid were abolished during the preparations by South Africa for the Namibia 'Constitutional' elections of 1978. The Pass Laws were relaxed (obligation to carry passes was abolished), 'whites only' signs were covered up in parks, service areas and some restaurants were opened to all races, and the Mixed Marriages and Immorality Act was withdrawn.[9] But these measures barely changed the fact of continuing discrimination, or actual control of the African population, for to remain in employment special permission is needed and contracts must still be registered.

Similarly, the Abolition of Racial Discrimination, Act No. 3, 1979, is limited.[10] The act sets out to abolish racial restrictions on residence in urban areas, that is, buying houses in 'white' areas would become legal for 'non-whites', but it would benefit only a handful of Africans who could afford houses in European areas.

Other more important areas have been left untouched: the integration of education, statutory provision for the minimum wage recommended in the Turnhalle conclusions (but paid only by a few large companies and some government departments), and for 'equal pay for equal work' and 'equal opportunity for promotion'. Another Act passed at the same time is of interest; it reactivates residence control (under a new name) and makes failure to secure the new registration permit an offence.[11] The only obvious difference from the previous pass system, abolished in 1978, is that whites much also register, although which 'Homeland' they can be deported to if they fail to register is unclear.

• Municipal authorities, controlled by National Party members, planned to impede the integration of residential areas. Their meeting in Windhoek in August 1979 listed ways in which the Act could be implemented selectively: 'high standards of environment hygiene' should be preserved and 'strong measures against over-population should be taken, a premise must only be occupied by one family of father, mother and their own children.'[12]

South Africa's response to the settler backlash has been two-fold. Administrator-General Steyn was unceremoniously restored to the Free State Supreme Court and no less a figure than the President of the Afrikaner Broederbond, Gerritt Viljoen, was named as his successor. Administrator-General Viljoen at least appears to have promised that second-tier ('Homeland') elections will be held for the white 'Homeland',[13] and that removal of petty apartheid plus the installation of a 'white government with a black face' would not prejudice white domination. By his departure in mid-1980 he had reduced, though not eliminated, cleavages within the European tribes.

Migrant labour

The African 'reserves' and the white areas of the Police Zone are connected by the migrant labour system. Every year, tens of thousands of men leave their families in the 'reserves' for six to eighteen months because they have to go to work in the south, in mines, on farms, in factories, in hotels and restaurants. The number away at any one time appears to be of the order of 110 000. Thus up to two-thirds of the 150 000 'reserve' households are broken up at any one time and almost all over a three- to five-year period.

The basis of the migrant labour system lies in the insufficient means of livelihood in the 'Homelands' either to grow food or to earn money to purchase necessities, and in the numerous taxes to be paid in cash. Even given a good annual crop, the northern 'Homelands', Ovamboland, Kavango and eastern Caprivi, no longer produce enough food to meet the needs of their populations.

The largest, Ovamboland, is seriously overpopulated given present agricultural techniques and opportunities. The soil is of poor quality and the cattle suffer from endemic diseases. Vaccination to prevent diseases which might spread to white herds on the Central Plateau is provided; services to conquer non-epidemic parasites are not. Ironically a large European corporate ranch has been created as part of 'Bantu Development' and is receiving research and veterinary support – apparently rather successfully.

Ovamboland comprises only 7% of the total area of Namibia, but nearly half the country's population lives there. Only half of Ovamboland can be utilized agriculturally, which gives 9.6 hectares per person. In the main settled area the ratio is as low as 2 hectares per person. The figure in the rural white ranches is 1 625 hectares, that is, 170 times as much. Moreover, as the men must spend a large amount of their time away from home doing contract work, and are unable even then to afford implements and inputs, the return from the land is poor as it is tilled by women and children using primitive tools, at best oxen and unimproved ploughs.

The Odendaal Report points out the serious deforestation of central Ovamboland resulting from the fuel requirements of the concentrated population. Lack of official concern regarding the preservation of the ecological balance and the improvement of agricultural conditions has created a situation on which the Odendaal Report itself states that 'Soils in the Central area are already being intensively cultivated, so that it is doubtful whether any increase in grain yields can be expected in these parts'.[14]

Only some of the land at the disposal of the African population is usable, as figures for selected 'reserves' show (Table 5.3).

TABLE 5.3 Percentage of Usable Land in Selected 'Reserves'

Kaokoveld	30
Ovamboland	50
Kavango	10
Hereroland West	20

Source: FAO, *Namibia, Prospects for Future Development*, Rome, 1977, p. 27.

Overall, 150–175 000 African families, at least nominally active in 'Homeland' agriculture, have about 16.7 million hectares of usable land (say, 100 hectares per family, much of it able to support only one beast per fifteen to twenty hectares) and 6 500 European ranching families have 36.9 million hectares (almost 6 000 hectares per household) (see Annex Table 21).

In 1943, the South West Africa Labour Association (SWANLA) acquired, strengthened and reorganized the monopoly over recruitment and administration of migrant workers. SWANLA was shut down after the 1971–72 strike (nominally as demanded by the workers) and worker recruitment is now done through labour bureaux set up by 'Homeland' authorities. All unemployed men under 65 who are neither officially approved as being self-employed nor physically unfit must register as job seekers. Even though SWANLA was closed, and even though the formal classification of workers into categories A, B and C according to physical condition, age and work experience was discontinued, the contract labour system and the contents of the contract remained the same. Low wages, families compulsorily living apart, lack of choice of employer, restrictions on mobility, and poor worker accommodation remained its dominant characteristics. Changes were marginal: each worker now gets an individual contract; 'the master' and 'servant' were changed into 'employer' and 'employee'; the minimum length of contract became six months instead of the previous minimum of twelve months.[15] Before the strike, it was a crime for a black worker to break the contract: only the employer or the authorities in charge of African affairs were entitled to discontinue the contract. The contract worker remained, in effect, a prisoner of his 'master'; in isolated 'white' ranches the worker had no way to escape the whips, dogs, guns and barbed-wire fences of the farms.[16]

After the strike both parties gained equal rights to discontinue the contract. This somewhat increased the worker's legal rights assuming he could repay advances from his employer (including for his original travel to take up the job).

Not all workers are recruited through official recruiting channels, and illegal employment is probably fairly common. For instance, many earlier migrant workers on large farms are now more or less permanently living there, many with families (sometimes from and sometimes supplementary to their 'Homeland' households). Of the 110 000 migrant workers, some 80 000 are employed in industry, in the service sector or in mining, the remaining 30 000 are working in farms. Of the migrant workers an estimated 60 000 are contract workers from the northern 'Homelands' – though no exact figures are available.

The employer is obliged to provide food and accommodation for the worker for the duration of the contract. Accommodation can be a hut in the back yard or an animal shed on a farm. The food is often nutritionally very poor and usually badly prepared and served (e.g. with shovels from buckets). In urban areas housing is provided in prison-like compounds surrounded by high fences. Up to twenty men share the same dormitory hall and sleep in concrete bunk beds; no provision is made for workers on different shifts. Leisure-time activities are very limited: most workers have a choice between Bible readings and beerhalls. The workers are intended to be controlled twenty-four hours a day, thus including not only their working life but also living and leisure environments.

Health care is mostly not available, and any prolonged illness automatically means being sent back to the 'Homelands'. In 1975 only about 11.6% of the labour force was eligible for pension schemes. Contract workers are excluded almost by definition, their contracts are only temporary and not continuous, because of the compulsory time gap between contracts.

There are no signs that contract work will be abolished under the cosmetic 'liberalization' campaign: for instance, in spring 1978 the Matchless mine near Windhoek was planning 'family accommodation' for contract workers' wives to visit their husband for periods of a few weeks at a time.

Wages

There are no official published data available on wage and salary structures or cost-of-living data in Namibia. Figures normally quoted are based on fragmentary data obtained by interviews, some company reports, etc. The data available show that the African workers' wages in Namibia are even lower than in South Africa. The level of prices is lower than in Europe or Zambia but higher than in East Africa or South Africa. The minimum subsistence levels have not been officially calculated. In 1973 the so-called Non-European Affairs Department in Windhoek estimated that an average African family (five to six persons) living in Windhoek would need a minimum of R65 a month.[17] This was based on a technical estimate of minimum food, clothing, and shelter requirements and African patterns of meeting these needs, not on a European budget base. (Calculated on the basis of 'poverty datum line' (PDL) estimates made in South African urban centres and, therefore, not quite comparable with the Namibian situation.) Another estimate made in 1976 gave a much higher, and more realistic, figure of 'household subsistence level': R177 for 'Coloureds' and R151 for Africans.[18]

Inflation in Namibia has recently averaged 12% a year; wages, outside a few large employers, have lagged behind. Food prices alone increased by about 17% a year in the late 1970s. Many foreign companies pay the workers in their Namibian plants only half of what they pay in South Africa.

After the 1971–72 strike, wages were increased by mutual agreement between the employers. This agreement clearly augmented minimum wages, but at the same time limited competition over wages which would have led to new increases. In some sectors the post-strike increases were quite considerable. For instance, in Consolidated Diamond Mines, black wages increased by 200% in 1971–1972, the minimum wage to £30 and average wages to £46 a month. By 1979 average mining-sector wages for Africans (including payments in kind) may have reached R100–125 per month; those for Europeans, including fringe benefits, were almost certainly in excess of R1 000 (R750 plus fringe benefits for artisans).[19] Unskilled Africans do the dirtiest, hardest and most dangerous jobs, which, at the same time, are the lowest paid. Cash wages of R5–10 per month in domestic service and ranching are by no means a thing of the past.

The South African job reservation system is practised as rigidly in Namibia as in the Republic though it is not statutory: Africans are not eligible for certain kinds of jobs and in particular may not hold posts which would make them supervisors over Europeans. The formal legal position understates the pervasiveness of job reservation. White unions have succeeded in enforcing far broader and more rigid limits on black and 'Coloured' training and promotion than is statutorily required in the Republic. Further, the quality and quantity of African education debars them from most middle- to high-income positions. (For education and training pattern estimates see Annex Table 10.) In the mining industry Africans are deprived of access to the position of superintendent of a mine, shift-work foreman, engineer, or lift-shaft operator. Apartheid also includes a practice whereby, in certain sectors, only white people deal with white affairs (an African policeman cannot report or fine a white traffic offender).

Table 5.4 shows the type of employment in which whites and Africans are engaged. Most Africans do manual work; only about 1.5% of black and 8% of 'Coloured' employment can be regarded as 'white collar'. 97% of administrative, commercial and economic managerial positions are held by whites; of all unskilled workers, 98% are blacks. The less skilled the job, the higher is the proportion of blacks. The skilled workers are 60% white. Although the 'Coloured' labour force includes a higher proportion of 'white-collar', supervisory and skilled jobs than the black, it is also true that as many as a quarter of all 'Coloured' workers, including almost all 'Coloured' women employees, are house servants.

TABLE 5.4 Occupational Category Estimates (1977), (% of Total Labour Force in the Category)

Category	White	'Coloured'	African	Total (000)
Managerial/administrative	97	2	1	10
Professional/technical/ para-professional	60	15	25	17
Clerical/secretarial	42	25	33	6
Supervisory/foremen	32	16	52	12.5
Skilled – non-supervisory	60	20	20	5
Semi-skilled	5	15	80	50
Unskilled	2	9	89	90
Domestic	–	17	83	75
Small-scale non-agricultural self-employment	20	28	52	12.5
Small agricultural	–	4	96	240
Total (000) rounded	365	485	433	518

Source: Derived from Annex Table 7.

Farm workers are in the worst situation, both in terms of pay and of working conditions. They work six or seven days a week and usually ten to twelve hours a day; in Karakul farms the shepherds may work practically day and night during the lambing season. In 1976 an unskilled farm worker earned about R12.50 a month, according to a spokesman for the white farm producers' organization. The highest paid farm worker received R27. Wages are differentiated to the extent that contract workers and San are paid less than local workers, and women and children are paid less than men. According to F. B. Gebhardt, German-speaking farmers tend to pay slightly better wages than Afrikaans-speaking farmers.[20] In addition to their wages, farm workers receive payment in kind, such as maize meal, sugar, meat, tea or coffee, tobacco, soap and vegetables. On average about 50% of farm wages are believed to be in cash and 50% in kind. In some cases farm workers are allowed to keep a few fowl and goats and cattle but this is by no means very common. To be allowed to settle permanently in the ranches with their families some Ovambo migrant workers have sought reclassification to become local 'Damara' or 'Herero', whose 'reserves' are within the Police Zone.[21] A white assistant farm manager earned R500 a month in 1976. This is before standard fringe benefits which include a month's paid annual holiday, a gratuity of three months' pay every five years of employment, free accommodation, free life insurance and subsidized health services, reasonable transport and children's education allowances. These average at least 20–25% of basic pay.

Both in Namibia and in South Africa it is illegal for the Africans to go on strike: the minimum sentence for striking or instigating a strike is five months' imprisonment; the maximum is death. However, in defiance of these severe punishments, Africans repeatedly strike, demanding better pay, more humane working conditions, and – beginning with the 1971–72 general strike – the abolition of the contract worker system as such. The Namibian workers have no legal or institutionalized means of influencing their pay or working conditions: African trades unions like the most recent National Union of Namibian Workers cannot be registered, nor are they even informally recognised as representatives of the workers. Furthermore, the worker cannot, in principle, negotiate any terms of employment or pay directly with the employer; he can only refuse or accept the employment and pay as offered by the employment agency. In most cases the principle is the practice. However, some large firms (especially in mining) and some individual employers do bargain with informal workers' representative councils or individual employees.

The result is that Africans earn very little and contract workers are able to save less. A typical Ovambo worker returning to his 'Homeland' can hardly think of buying better equipment to improve the yield of his small plot or veterinary supplies to protect and improve his few beasts. Part of his wages has been spent during the contract on necessary personal expenses such as clothing, bus fares, free-time expenses, the ubiquitous fines for breaking racial or employment regulations, presents for the family, relatives and friends, the return fare home. Back in the 'Homeland' there are further expenses to be paid: a church membership fee, children's school fees, increasing amounts for food. More and more Africans have become trapped in the vicious circle of the contract labour system for most of their working lives, experiencing social conditions and other consequences of the system set out vividly in Chapter 6 by Rauha Voipio.[22]

Public health

There is little information on public health and health care in Namibia so it is impossible to give a systematic picture of the state of health of the population in numerical terms. But there is enough to show that there are not enough hospitals or clinics, particularly in rural areas, to provide a health service for all racial groups. The missionary hospitals provide most services in the African areas. They are subsidized by the government up to 100%. In 1969, there were 19 hospitals and clinics for whites, 21 for all communities, 117 for Africans. The ratio of one facility per 2 500 Europeans and one per 9 000 Africans is rather misleading as the standard of personnel and equipment is totally different. African health centres are frequently very modest clinics run by a couple of nurses in missionary stations. In sparsely populated areas the nearest health clinic may be as far as 40 kilometres away.

There is a great shortage of doctors, and of specialists in particular, as medical schools are in South Africa, and it is difficult for blacks to get study grants. Many do not want to accept government grants because they would be obliged to work in government hospitals for several years after they qualified. Ovamboland has no more than a couple of black doctors, and the government hospital in Oshakati has only a few white doctors: the number of black doctors trained in the Republic of South Africa does not exceed ten.

Hospitals are generally overcrowded: the official number of hospital beds in the Finnish Missionary Hospital in Onandjokwe is 246 but the actual number of patients at any one time is about 350. The missionary hospitals are also short of equipment: the Onandjokwe hospital, for instance, has no ambulance.

In northern areas the most common diseases are malaria, sleeping sickness, tuberculosis, various infections (such as meningitis), intestinal disorders, and, in children, diarrhoea. Because homes are broken up by the contract system, venereal diseases and, because of the increased consumption of alcohol and beer (often as a deliberate revenue-raising device), cirrhosis of the liver are also on the increase. In urban African districts, as well as in most 'Homelands' malnutrition is common, particularly in young children. Figures available for the Windhoek area show that the infant mortality rate was 163 per thousand among blacks, 145 for 'Coloureds' and 21 for whites in 1975.[23]

Education into inequality

One of the most visible aspects of apartheid, and a key factor in maintaining it, is the educational system, in particular so-called Bantu Education. Bantu Education is based on an official white educational theory that the purpose of black education is to bring up Africans to accept their oppressed social status and to be content with modest needs and access limited to the 'less demanding' duties in society. In 1953, the South African Minister of Bantu Education, introducing the Bantu Education Bill in parliament, made the following statement:

> Education must train and teach people in accordance with their opportunities in life, according to the sphere in which they live; Native education should be controlled in such a way that it should be in accord with the policy of the State.[24]

Education in Namibia is inegalitarian. Black, 'Coloured' and white education is differentiated by law, in terms of content and of operational framework. The curriculum, teachers' qualifications and salaries are different. The education of white Namibians is controlled by Namibian administrative authorities; the official responsible for African education is the South African Minister of Bantu Education; 'Coloured' education (Rehoboth, 'Coloured', Nama) falls under the Minister of Plural Relations.

In Namibia most schools for Africans were founded by missionary societies, which had full and sole responsibility for education of Africans until the mid-1960s. South African Bantu Education was officially introduced into Namibia in 1970, but in practice it had been followed since the early 1960s. The government has taken over most missionary schools. In 1960 there were 244 missionary schools but by 1973 there were only 36.[25]

In primary education, the main emphasis is on 'manual skills'; other subjects include natural science, biblical knowledge, history and geography. Mathematics is of secondary importance. In all Bantu Education, teaching for the first four years is in the vernacular. Although this is a positive point in developing cultural identity, in Namibia it is at the same time part of a policy of emphasizing racial and ethnical differences, and of making it more difficult for Namibians to communicate with each other.

TABLE 5.5 Education in Namibia, 1960 – 1973

	Number of schools	Number of teachers	Number of pupils	Pupil-teacher ratio
Africans				
1960	313	1 310	43 624	33.3
1966	415	2 071	78 295	37.8
1970	526	2 713	112 006	41.3
1973	592	3 453	138 890	40.2
Europeans				
1960	63	666	16 257	24.4
1966	77	979	19 893	20.3
1970	80	1 105	22 349	20.2
1973	85	1 233	23 195	18.8

Source: J. H. P. Serfontein, *Namibia*, Pretoria, 1976, p. 39. Republic of South Africa, Department of Foreign Affairs, *South West Africa Survey*, Pretoria, 1967 and 1974; W. H. Thomas, *Economic Development in Namibia*, Grünewald, Munich, 1978, p. 201.

The language question is serious, especially as the majority of children never go back to school after the first four years and thus never acquire fluency in any of the official languages of the country (Afrikaans, German, English). From the fifth year, all teaching is in Afrikaans, which meets with general opposition as it is felt to be the language of the oppressors.* English-medium schools for Africans – notably those of the Anglican church – have been suppressed. Because Afrikaans is spoken only in South Africa and Namibia, teaching it restricts communication with people of other countries, including other African countries. Namibian refugees have often faced great difficul-

TABLE 5.6 Educational Standard of African Teachers in Namibia, 1975

	'Coloured'[1]		Black	
University degree	16	2.1%	12	0.4%
Matriculation	233	30.8%	51	1.7%
Junior Certificate or equivalent[2]	359	47.5%	304	10.2%
Std. 6 (8 years' school)	–	–	1 606	54.0%
Technical or other vocational	27	3.6%	–	–
No qualification	121	16.0%	1 004	33.7%
	756	100.0%	2 977	100.0%

Source: W. H. Thomas, *Economic Development in Namibia*, p. 198.

[1] including Nama and Rehoboths.

[2] with additional teacher training.

* The Soweto protests were reflected in Namibia, too, where the student movement organized campaigns against not only the deployment of the Afrikaans language but Bantu Education as a whole. Exams were boycotted and hundreds of students fled the country to avoid police maltreatment and detentions.

ties with their studies and had to discontinue their education or had to take intensive language training. Despite this, and their poor general educational background, about 150 Namibian refugees have obtained university degrees, including several medical doctorates.

Table 5.6 gives the number of African (including 'Coloured') and European schools, the number of teachers and pupils, and the pupil–teacher ratio in these schools.

These figures demonstrate the wide racial differences in respect to the number of schools and to pupil–teacher ratios. For the Africans there are not enough schools; classes are big; distances from home to school are long; rarely are there organized school meals; there is a shortage of teachers. The level of education of most African teachers is inadequate; a third of black teachers have only a primary-school background without any vocational training. Black teachers are badly paid, getting perhaps half as much as white primary-school teachers.

TABLE 5.7 Expenditure on Education in the 1975/76 Budget

	White	'Coloured'	African
Total (Rand)	1 445 000	4 160 000	9 135 000
% of the total	52	15	33
per pupil (rand)	615	163	68

Source: based on W. H. Thomas, *Economic Development in Namibia*, p. 202.

In 1975/76 nine times as much money was spent per white as per African child. Education is compulsory for all 7–16-year-old white children, and for 7–14-year-old 'Coloured' children, but not for the blacks. In 1977, the percentage of 5–19-year-old African children attending school was recorded at 55%, the figure being as high as 72% for the 5–14 age group. However, these figures are based on the number of children registered for school. In practice it is not uncommon for children to be absent for long periods. The drop-out rate for Africans is high throughout the whole educational system, as shown in Table 5.8. Three-quarters of the children drop out during the first four years, and only 2% continue beyond eight years. In 1975, only 631 (0.4%) Afri-

TABLE 5.8 School Enrolment in Namibia in 1975

	African	'Coloured'[1]	White	Total
Lower primary	98 926	15 160	8 623	128 709
%	74.1	59.4	36.7	67.2
Higher primary	31 001	8 471	8 130	47 608
%	23.2	33.2	34.6	26.1
Secondary level	3 654	1 893	6 747	12 294
%	2.7	7.4	28.7	6.7
Total	133 581	25 524	23 500	182 605

Source: W. H. Thomas, *Economic Development in Namibia*, p. 200.

[1] Including Nama and Rehoboth.

can and 'Coloured' children attended the sixth form, as compared to 2 711 (11%) white children. It should be noted that a very large number of black Namibians have never been to school; illiteracy is common, 19% for 'Coloured' and 69% for black communities in 1977.

Africans have very little access to vocational training. There were 585 schools for the Africans in Namibia in 1975; including twelve junior secondary schools and eight secondary schools, seven teacher training colleges and five vocational schools. Most of the vocational training is for teachers and nurses. Northern Namibia has two agricultural colleges, but the student numbers are very low. The first genuine technical high school, oriented to mining, was opened in 1979 (and paid for by Consolidated Diamond Mines, not the state). There are no universities in Namibia, and those wanting to follow university courses have to go to South Africa. Only a handful of Namibian Africans have degrees from any of the 'tribal' universities in South Africa (see Annex Table 10). The following quotation from an interview with a former Namibian teacher illustrates pertinently the opportunities that Europeans and Africans have in education and in general in an apartheid society, and the conclusions the oppressed people have drawn from the circumstances they are forced to live in:

> Actually, my political development began when I started teaching at school in a rural district of Namibia north of Tsumeb. There I saw the needs of the African children and I began to understand the nature of our people's oppression. As a new teacher I felt that my students had to show immediate results and that I had to exercise strict discipline so that they could keep up. Some children were quite bright and very eager to learn, but most, I found, were weak and sleepy at school. After three weeks of teaching I decided to go around and find out where and how these children lived. I discovered to my horror that many had to walk over fifteen kilometres to school. Every morning at four o'clock they got up to work the land; then at eight they ran to school – literally ran, and without having eaten. When they got to school, of course, they simply collapsed.
>
> Later I went down south and saw the white children. All of them were living very near their school or staying at a boarding school. They were very healthy and wide awake, obviously lacking nothing in the way of food or transportation facilities. Seeing this big difference compared with conditions for African children in the rural area, I asked myself if it was really worth trying to teach African children under such circumstances, demanding that they keep up with the instruction. I decided then that before we could ever have a good educational system in Namibia we would have to liberate the country as a whole.[26]

Notes

1 For pre-colonial history W. G. Clarence – Smith and R. Moorsom, 'Underdevelopment and Class Formation in Ovamboland 1845–1915', *Journal of African History*, 16, March 1975, and Umar Al-Nagar, 'African

Initiative in Namibia in the Pre-Colonial Period', International Conference on Southern African History, Roma, Lesotho, August 1977; and Richard Moorsom, 'Colonization and Proletarianization: An Exploratory Investigation of the Formation of the Working Class in Namibia under German and South African rule to 1945', MA thesis, University of Sussex, 1973.

2 *Report of the Administrator 1920,* League of Nations Publications, Capetown, 1921, p. 13.

3 *Ibid.*, p. 13.

4 Quoted in Wellington, *South West Africa and its Human Issues*, OUP, 1967, p. 279.

5 See International Commission of Jurists, *Apartheid in South Africa and South West Africa*, Geneva, 1964.

6 *Report of the Commission of Enquiry into South West Africa Affairs 1962–1963*, Capteown, 1964 (the Odendaal Report).

7 There have been eyewitness reports of how people were threatened with loss of jobs, pensions, access to hospitals, identification documents, etc., unless they voted. Similar practices were reported during preparations for the 'constitutional' elections in 1978; see further K. Kiljunen and M-L. Kiljunen, *Report on a visit to Namibia*, 1978 (mimeo).

8 See Ruth First, 'The Bantustans: the implementation of the Odendaal Report', Paper presented at the International Namibia Conference, Brussels, May 1972.

9 Even these changes have not gone unnoticed in a country with such a deeply-rooted tradition of apartheid: white extremists showed violence to those of their own kind ('racial brothers') who in restaurants had the courage to dance with an African partner. Many licensed premises went back to their previous practice. Windhoek City Council shut its swimming pools in preference to integrating them.

10 For accounts of the legislation and reactions to it and the new residence permit and its initial enforcement see June–August 1979 issues of *Windhoek Observer.*

11 Even these minimal changes have outraged the settler community. A riot was staged against the Assembly members before the session at which the Act was passed. The National Party, which has the largest European following, walked out of the 'National Assembly.' A poll conducted through a newspaper opposed to segregated restaurants showed an overwhelming majority in favour of them (*Windhoek Observer*, 25 August 1979).

12 *Windhoek Observer*, 25 August 1979.

13 *Windhoek Observer*, 18 and 25 August 1979. The election was held and DTA lost to the right opposition – AKTUR.

14 Odendaal Report, p. 291.

15 For a renewed contract see John Kane-Berman, *Contract Work in South West Africa*, South African Institute of Race Relations, Johannesburg, 1972.

16 See V. Ndadi, *Breaking Contract*, LSM Information Centre, Richmond, Canada, 1974.

17 Heinrich-Georg Hubrich and Henning Melber, *Namibia – Geschichte und Gegenwart zur Frage der Dekolonisation einer Siedlerkolonie*, Informationstelle südliches Afrika e. v. Bonn, 1977, p. 140.

18 ILO, *Labour and Discrimination in Namibia*, Geneva, 1977, p. 61.

19 Advertisements in *Rand Daily Mail*, early 1979.

20 F. B. Gebhardt, 'The Socio-Economic Status of Farm Labourers in Namibia', *South African Labour Bulletin*, Vol 4, Nos 1 and 2, 1978, p. 158.

21 *Ibid.*, p. 150.

22 On labour, see further *South African Labour Bulletin,* Vol 4, Nos 1 and 2, 1978; Gillian and Suzanne Cronje, *The Workers of Namibia*, International Defence and Aid Fund, London, 1974; Jo Morris, 'The Black Workers in Namibia', in Roger Murray, Jo Morris, John Dugard, Neville Rubin, *The Role of Foreign Firms in Namibia*; Ray Simons, 'The Namibian Challenge', Paper presented at the International Namibia Conference, Brussels, May 1972; ILO, *Labour and Discrimination in Namibia*; Robert Gordon, *Mines, Masters and Migrants*, Ravan Press, Johannesburg, 1977; and the various publications by Richard Moorsom (see bibliography).

23 Wolfgang H. Thomas, *Economic Development in Namibia*, Grünewald, Munich, 1978, p. 23. See also G. Lachenmann, 'Perspectives for Decolonizing Health in Namibia', in *Perspectives of Independent Development of Southern Africa*, German Development Institute, Berlin, 1980, for a fuller account. This study suggests, if anything, that the reality is even worse and more integrally linked to the contract/reserve system than indicated above.

24 House of Assembly Debates, 1953, Vol. X, Column 3585, quoted in ILO, *Labour and Discrimination in Namibia*, pp. 42–43.

25 Marcia Kennedy McGill, 'Education Policy and Results' in Ronald Segal and Ruth First (eds.) *South West Africa, Travesty of Trust*, Deutsch, London, 1967, pp. 194–212.

26 Liberation Support Movement Information Centre, *Interviews in Depth, Namibia, SWAPO*, Richmond, Canada, 1973, pp. 3–4.

6 Contract work through Ovambo eyes*

RAUHA VOIPIO

The Contract system prior to the General Strike of 1971–1972

The Ovambo and the contract system

In December 1971, about 13 000 Ovambo contract workers went on strike in different parts of South West Africa against the so-called contract system.

Until the strike, common opinion among the whites of South West Africa was that the Ovambo fully accepted the contract system. They would point to the fact that for decades large groups of Ovambo had moved around in search of work. When the South West Africa Labour Association (SWANLA) started its work in Ovamboland in the 1930s the Ovambo left *en masse* for the Police Zone looking for work. At the end of the last century there were already Ovambo on the farms of German immigrants and in 1910 about 8 000 men were working outside Ovamboland. They walked the huge, barren Etosha Pan, taking at least six days to travel and facing hunger, thirst and wild animals. Every year some of them perished during that journey. Some settled down permanently at their new working places, but many came back and told exciting stories about their experiences in strange circumstances.

There were several explanations for their mobility. For example, traditionally Ovambo people had been to Otavi to fetch copper for their adornments, and young men in particular were accustomed to moving outside the borders of modern Ovamboland. They started to

* This chapter is based on a booklet written in Afrikaans during the strike of 1971–1972, addressed mainly to white employers and intended to be conciliatory. Its aim was to help them to see the conract-work system from the Ovambo point of view and to show the strikers not as criminals but as workers demanding their rights. My intention was not to make anyone angry but to touch hard hearts. The same things could have been said in a much sharper way, but in the circumstances it would not have helped.

The original booklet grew out of a lecture prepared for the Synod of the Evangelical Lutheran Church of South West Africa held at Otjimbingue in June 1970 on the theme 'The responsibility of the Church to look after the family life of the immigrant workers'. In order to obtain information on the effect of contract work on Ovambo marriages, the author sent out questionnaires to the workers and their wives and to some Christian workers in Ovamboland. Almost 1 000 were returned. They provided the basis for the lecture and subsequently for the booklet.

think that a youngster was an adult only after his first trip to the south. But if these had been the only reasons, there would not have been so many Ovambo looking for work in the south. The most important reason was the search for food. The travellers to the south tried to save their own lives and also to get provisions for the ones left at home.

Today when an Ovambo becomes a contract worker the reasons are the same. Although there are more opportunities for work in Ovamboland, population expansion has forced them to look for work outside their own territory. Many Ovambo resent the influx of large numbers of whites, 'Coloured' men, Herero and men from the South African Republic who have been given jobs that the Ovambo might otherwise have done. Even in years of good rainfall, cattle raising and agriculture do not provide sufficient income to live on and a salaried job is necessary to facilitate the purchase of food and clothes. An Ovambo man can get money only by making a contract, and going south. It would appear that this form of immigration work is generally voluntary, although there have been years when good crops have led to such a drastic reduction in the number of new workers that, following the instructions of SWANLA, tribal chiefs have sent messages to village chiefs that more men should sign up for contract work.

In actual fact it is misleading to talk of a willingness to do contract work when people have to choose between hunger and migrant work. As there is not enough work in Ovamboland, it must be sought elsewhere in South West Africa. Mobility has been made easier by the new way of thinking adopted by more and more Ovambo that Ovamboland is their home, the whole of South West Africa is their fatherland.

But this in turn has given rise to new questions relating to freedom of movement and freedom to find employment. Why do we have to go to SWANLA when we need work? Why isn't it possible for us to go ourselves and look for jobs where we want to? The Ovambo pastors complain that men try – even by doubtful means – to get the papers of a permanent resident in an urban area in order to be free from the strict laws of contract work. This is even more likely to happen when a young Ovambo with a contract falls in love with a girl and knows that he does not have any hope of taking her with him to Ovamboland.

It is not surprising that the Ovambo eagerly listen to claims that contract work is a new kind of slavery. Years ago a young Ovambo was seeking refuge in a home of a friend and complained: 'My master claims that he bought me and that he can do with me anything he wants. And he says he wants to throw me into the sea.' Naturally one can say that such a case is an exception. By talking in terms of buying workers the employers have acted without understanding. They are now reaping the harvest of their folly.

After the strike in 1971 it was said that Ovambo dissatisfaction with the contract system was a recent phenomenon. In fact, dissatisfaction had existed for a long time, but was only recently brought into the open. The Ovambo people have an amazing ability to bear difficulties and suffering. The contract-work system has been considered as one of the burdens under which man has to bow. The Ovambo Christians have, in the past, seen it as a cross that needed to be carried patiently. However, later on – partly as a consequence of information about conditions in other countries that many educated Ovambo got through the radio – the following questions have arisen: Do we have to stand the contract system for ever? Are there not any other ways to get work?

The questionnaires sent out in May 1970 did not originally ask for criticism of the system itself. In spite of this, some of those who answered added sharp criticism. One of them writes: 'The contract is the source of destruction of all that is human in man'.

The contract system and marriage

Contract work has shaped marriage and the family life of the Ovambo for over fifty years. Every year thousands of men have left Ovamboland and stayed away for twelve to eighteen months. It is surprising that Christian marriage has kept its place among the people at all. But one has to remember that the original moral standards of the people were strict and that the Ovambo themselves considered adultery and other forms of immorality as serious transgressions. In addition, the work of missionaries and the church had had a significant effect before the contract system was imposed in its present form.

Nonetheless, the contract system has created deeply-felt problems. In response to the questionnaire in 1970 a miner wrote:

> It is impossible for me to answer your questions, because God doesn't accept the break-down of christian marriage . . . We don't know why a man is separated from his wife for twelve months. It means a lot, a lot of homesickness, and later the man commits adultery because of the length of the contract time.

At the same time, an evangelist complained:

> I'm talking about a burden on my heart because I'm here on the spot in Hereroland. I don't have anyone here to discuss this matter with. Our young men and older men too, corrupt this parish of the Rhenish Church by begetting children, by rejecting them and returning to Ovamboland. The women here in Hereroland do not get married and live with one man, instead they have become objects of trade. The Ovambo who has committed fornication here is an unmarried man in Ovamboland, a Christian, as well as the woman with whom he has procreated a child. If he wants to marry her, the government refuses saying that he can well beget children but he has to stay unmarried. That is impurity. What can take away this difficulty? A change in the law of the government or the law of the Church?

The Ovambo people have a matrilineal system according to which the children belong to the mother's family. When a man marries he does not pay a bride price, but has to pay most of the wedding expenses and give obligatory gifts to the bride and her parents. He is normally unable to settle the debts incurred with savings from former contracts, and usually has to become a contract worker. While men tended to stay with their wives for at least twelve months after marriage during the 1950s, the time between the wedding and the husband's return to work has become shorter. Six months appears to be an average period by the early 1970s, although there are cases of a man only spending several weeks with his wife before returning to contract employment. Often the reason for a quick return is the hope of being employed again by the same employer. 'My master asked me to return within two months', is an answer you often get from a newly married man. In the answers the men sent me, the shortest time between the wedding and the return to work was three weeks. Nevertheless two of the wives state very clearly that their husbands only spent one week at home after the wedding.

Once the man has left home, problems of separation are sometimes aggravated by illiteracy. Not every Ovambo with a contract can write, or if he can his writing ability may be so poor that a real correspondence is impossible. Similarly, his wife may have to ask a sister, the wife of a neighbour or a friend to help to write letters. Yet the correspondence can be crucial: one pastor in a mining area has told of cases of men committing suicide after waiting in vain for letters from home. Letters do not always bring good news. One person writes: 'There are always complaints about the twelve months' separation in her letters.' Lack of money is often mentioned. It is true that many men try to send money home with those friends whose work contract finishes and who return to Ovamboland, but not everybody has that opportunity.

Frequently the young wife's health causes anxiety, expecially if she is pregnant. When a child is born, news of its birth often reaches the father only after many weeks, and then it takes several weeks before the wife gets a letter from her husband giving the child a name. Commonly, for the baptism of a child in Ovamboland, the father who is absent on contract work is replaced by a father's substitute who, together with the mother and the godparents, carries the child to the altar.

For the contract worker the threat of loneliness is very real. The picture of the home gets more and more faint. It is more a dream picture than reality. Twelve months is a long time. Continually people complain about the length of the contract period in their answers. There was nothing in the questionnaire that could have encouraged this kind of criticism. Many men hope that the church can help them in their social problems. Here are some examples from the answers: 'The contract time must be shortened, that's the answer'; 'It is necessary to have it changed so that a man doesn't need to be away for so many months or so that he can go there with his wife'; 'My wife is tired of waiting. Beloved is the Lord, let us be helped. The contract only for six months.'

Questionnaire responses referred to drunkenness and adultery as special problems for married men. The questionnaire asked whether the contract worker stayed faithful to his wife (emphasizing that there was no compulsion to answer this question). About half answered in the affirmative. However, answers to the questionnaire varied, depending on the different working places. Ten answers came from a small town. There was not any sign of infidelity in any of them, though three left the questions unanswered. In another work-place only two men out of seventeen had stayed faithful to their wives. But the negative answers also made it clear that adultery creates sorrow and unhappiness: 'I have the will but not the strength to do the good. I'm asking for intercession in this matter'; 'When a man gets involved with women in Hereroland, it happens because of sinful lust, the lengthy separation and especially drunkenness'; 'Yes, I've got a twelve month contract and very little good to say about it. The contract make people do wrong things. The soul breaks the commandment.'

Given the degree of dissatisfaction, it is surprising that many married workers lengthen their contracts and stay on for eighteen months. One possible reason is that they have not been able to save enough money. These six extra months can be very destructive in relation to the marriage.

The men themselves have made suggestions about how unity between man and wife might be strengthened. One possibility is the shortening of the contract time; another is that one partner might visit the other at weekends. Everybody understands that it is impossible for a wife to visit her husband in a compound. But in places where a worker has a room of his own, such a visit could be arranged. There are many masters who refuse to allow that because such arrangements are not included in the original contract. Here are some examples of the men's answers: 'Let the number of months be decreased and have it arranged so that I'll have an opportunity to visit my wife or that she could visit me'; 'It is necessary for the husband to go and help his wife every now and then.'

At the conclusion of the contract, the worker's homecoming may not be as happy as expected. Sometimes the home is in a poor condition and more dilapidated than expected; sometimes the husband has created an idealized picture of his wife and his home and, if it does not correspond to reality, there is disappointment. According to the answers: 'We find our houses in dilapidated condition, because the work contract had required an absence of many months'; 'Nothing had been done in the fields. The house was almost like a ruin, because the contract time was so long.' The help brought by the men is seldom sufficient. One of them writes: 'I find it difficult at home. My wife has been waiting twelve months for me to bring her what she needs; I didn't bring her anything.'

If the interval between the contracts is very short, one of the reasons for difficulties is that both the man and the wife think that they need a holiday. A long contract time often alienates the man and the wife from each other. 'We don't understand each other', complains a man. A psychologically difficult situation also arises when a wife has put her energy into getting everything into perfect condition before her husband's arrival and the husband, in low spirits, thinks that his wife has become too independent.

However, there are homes where man and wife work well together during his holiday, and, if the holiday is long enough, a new understanding and a new sense of unity develops. But the holiday time is often too short: half a year, three months, or sometimes only a couple of weeks. The reasons for a quick return to work vary: in most cases there is a desperate need for more money: 'The difficulty is that there isn't any money'; 'We got short of money, there was only hunger and lack of clothing.' In some cases the man wants to return to the old working place to avoid the insecurity of a new working place and an unknown employer. 'My master said that I can get work from him if I return within three months', is a common explanation.

After the first holiday time at home, new contract periods follow one another. Questionnaire responses indicated that some men had spent two-thirds to three-quarters of their married lives away from home; very few could afford to stay at home after two or three contract periods. Among the men there were those who had got married in 1962 and had just made their eighth contract in 1970. Even those who had been married for as long as twenty years still did contract work. The maximum number in the answers given was nineteen contracts.

The lengthy absences on contract work have consequences which have a direct influence on the man's marriage. If the man returns continually to the same working place, he sometimes develops a permanent relationship with a local woman, and comes to possess two wives and two families. It is his duty to look after the second wife and family as well. According to the Ovambo's way of thinking, such a permanent relationship is not at all less sinful than occasional relationships, rather the opposite: a man with two wives is *omushunimonima*, a man who has gone back to paganism, although there are probably few cases like this.

A further problem is the increase in venereal diseases. This is what a doctor said: 'When a young man gets married he often gives to his bride together with other presents also the venereal disease he's brought from the south.' There is a direct correlation between contract work and the spread of these diseases.

Ovambo people tend to have fairly large families and childless marriages are very unusual. In fact there are many contract workers who write that they have six or seven children. But such a big family brings again its own sorrows and worries. The salary that was just about enough to keep the wife and one child is hopelessly small for a family with several children. The father's absence creates predictable problems: 'Because of the contract my children don't know me any more', one complains. 'When I come home, my children run away from me'; 'I have become a stranger to my own children'; 'I left a small child at home. On my return he ran and asked his mother who this strange man was. This distresses me.'

Although some of the Ovambo wives bring up their children well, the lack of male influence has serious effects. The boys' upbringing suffers particularly from the father's absence. One miner writes: 'The upbringing of children is hard if the mother is alone.' Mothers experience particular difficulties when children reach their teens. Many Ovambo pastors in their answers to the questionnaire refer to this problem: 'The children leave school because their father isn't at home'; 'There aren't family devotions in the home any more'; 'Among the children there is disobedience, truancy, drunkenness, visits to work camps and to the Portuguese area of Angola'; 'Men turn to drink and don't want to stay at home any more'; 'There are often wives who come and say: "My home is in ruins. The girls have fallen into immorality".'

The problem of prostitution has also increased as workers have come in from South Africa to man large work plants and more and more Ovambo girls have become prostitutes; some women have also been attracted to alcohol.

The lonely wife

For the wives of contract workers, the system imposes particular strains. When a young man speaks about getting married he often puts it in terms of 'My mother needs help on the fields'; feelings are frequently not mentioned. The young bride is taken to the house of her parents-in-law and hard work, respect and submission are expected from her. When her husband leaves to undertake contract work she is left with people who are frequently strangers and who often think she is the most important worker in the house. When her husband returns for the first time, or maybe only after two contract periods, he acquires a field, builds a house of his own and takes his wife and children, and usually an older child from his own or his wife's family, to his new house. He usually leaves once the moving is over.

There was traditionally a strict division between men's and women's work in Ovamboland. For example, anything to do with cattle-raising was done by men. But in the contract worker's home the wife has to manage on her own. Most Ovambo pastors speak highly of the faithful hard-working wives, and point to the exceptionally heavy burdens they bear in the absence of the men. Some pastors complain that the burden of many wives is unbearably heavy:

> The wife is exhausted by the household work that she has to do on her own and that should be really done by two people. If the man is not at home, the wife toils almost until she kills herself with work. If the man were away for six months and the other six months he were at home, it would be more bearable.

The contract worker's wife feels privileged if her husband can stay at home after two or three contracts or if he can stay at home for two or three years between contract periods, but some husbands are still committed to contract work after almost thirty years of marriage.

For Ovambo women, their husbands' holiday times can also bring disappointments. A woman may not have any idea of her husband's real wages, and may expect more in the form of money or gifts than he brings home. Most of the wives answer that their husband brings them presents, 'even good ones', as a couple of them add. But very often they say: 'He doesn't bring anything.' The reason is usually drinking. It is also often difficult for the wives to see why the husband buys a radio, a tape recorder or anything like that when the wife does not even have the money for essential clothes. The fault can, of course, be just human weakness. But most of the time the contract worker's tiny salary is the only reason for the financial difficulties that darken the life of many couples during the husband's holiday.

As far as assistance with household work is concerned, there appears to be a wide range of experience. 'He gives himself to all the work at home'; 'He does it with real zeal and industry.' Those answers which stress the fact that 'we both have to work' are probably more realistic. 'There is no rest or holiday but we work together.' 'Very little', 'a bare minimum', 'seldom any at all', however, are also frequent comments about the man's contribution to the work at home. One wife writes: 'Yes, he helps to a certain extent, but he often says that he's come home for a rest.'

Wives' responses to a question in the 1970 questionnaire – 'Do you consider it a joy or a sorrow that your husband has to go?' – demonstrate some of the stresses imposed on Ovambo marriages by the contract system: 'I am happy when he goes abroad so that poverty can leave our home'; 'It is a grief because of the separation, but a joy because he gets money from his work'; 'In one sense it is a joy, because otherwise we suffer from shortage. In another sense it is sad. He leaves us like sheep without a shepherd'; 'I think it is a grief. He leaves us only because of need, otherwise he wouldn't go'; 'I feel miserable because the time is long'; 'It is good that he goes to earn money, but I'm not glad. I'm glad when he comes back.' All these answers reveal something of what goes on in the hearts of the women who have to stay alone at home year after year.

The effects of the contract work on young men

For young, single men who go to work in the south there are some benefits, in particular the financial help it enables them to offer their parents, and more general working experience. However, there are severe negative aspects as well. As the years go by, the bad example of the surroundings start to have an influence on them. Take, for instance, the bad example that hotel servants and servers have before their eyes year after year as they serve white customers. The environment where the contract workers mostly live is unnatural. Men are separated from normal society and for months at a time hardly see any women in the compounds where they live.

Homosexuality, which was previously unknown among the Ovambo people, appears to have been introduced in some mining areas in the compounds. All the former contract workers who gave their answers in Ovamboland gave a negative answer to the question on homosexuality. But the contract workers of today have a darker view of the matter. About three-quarters of the answers coming from a mining town reveal that there is homosexuality in the compounds.

A contract Ovambo and his employer

One of the basic characteristics of the Ovambo people is their friendliness, and some contract workers become quite attached to their masters. It is unusual for them to hate an employer and, even when faced with unreasonableness, they do not lose their sense of humour.

Employers have complained that 'their Ovambos' are lazy. Naturally there are lazy ones, but it must be remembered how much is demanded of them. The Ovambo leaves his own work pattern and has to adjust to the entirely new rhythm of work in a mine, a factory, a shop, or a hotel. The normal pattern in Ovamboland calls for hard work. When the fields have to be done people get up at four o'clock and work until late in the evening with only a short break at midday. The harvest period is especially busy. There are also times in between when the boys and the men have only the cattle to look after, and then they are able to rest more. Although work is not new to him, its pattern in a factory or mine can create difficulties for the Ovambo contract worker; the repetitiveness becomes monotonous, with the same work month after month.

The most difficult thing for an Ovambo is loneliness. In group work he is happy; if he is alone he is unhappy. On many farms this loneliness is aggravated by the living conditions, which are worse than in the homes of even the poorest of the Ovambo. According to an evangelist, young agricultural workers experienced particularly difficult conditions:

> Our little boys (15–18 years old) experience distress of both soul and body. There is horrible misery on the farms. When a young man goes to work on a farm he does not even have time to cut his hair. The young man sleeps under a zinc plate erected in a place that looks like an elephant path. When it rains, they get wet and very cold. They serve for far too many months with too little money. The misery is great on the farms. The whites torture people.

In the relationship between the employer and the Ovambo employee, much depends on the former's attitude, and, in particular, whether he views the worker as a human being or as a chattel. A humane attitude can make an enormous difference. Then the employer is no longer indifferent to his servant's living conditions. Then he is no longer made to sit on the platform of the lorry in the wind and rain while travelling, when there is enough room inside the lorry. The employer's attitude is tested particularly at times of family crises, for example if a worker's wife becomes ill and he needs time off to visit her. It is not always possible to grant time off, but at least the employer can discuss this and try to find a solution with him. He can do a lot through telegrams, phone calls, etc., and he can save many people from real misery by giving permission for a visit.

The contract Ovambo and his salary

Money causes a lot trouble in the marriages of migrant workers. The main reason for this is that the salary is so very small. Many men complained about the smallness of their salary in their answers, even though there were not any questions directly relating to the salary. Most contract workers are troubled by not being able to spend more on their families.

Some evangelists were asked to what extent the men send money to their wives or take it home when they return. Seven evangelists thought that at least half of the men used most of their money for their families. A couple of them added that three-quarters or more of the men spent only a small part of their money on anything else. Only one thought that many men spent their money on themselves at their working places.

There are many employers who consider the salary of their contract workers as only a kind of pocket money, defending a low salary level because workers get free food and lodging. But none of the contract workers works to keep himself only. Even the youngest shepherd boys go to 'get food for their parents and younger brothers and sisters', as one Ovambo pastor says. Many young Ovambo boys have to leave school because their parents tell them they are old enough to look after their parents and to earn money.

The duties of the men with families are even more onerous. Although their first duty is to look after their wives and children, the men's parents also expect something. On the questionnaire one contract worker wrote:

> I work for my home, my wife, my children, my father and my mother, for taxes, for the hospital and for the church collection. For my brothers and my sisters and for my neighbours, too. There is a lot of grief. We all work for whites. We don't get any money. As I've been working all these years without getting anything. Yes, I've got a little bit. I don't waste my money, not at all.

SWANLA has fixed the minimum salary to be paid to a contract Ovambo. Ovambo men are divided into three classes, A, B, and C. An A–man is physically strong and fit for heavy labour; a B–man is not quite as strong; and a C–man is either a young boy (under 16) or physically weak. As an illustration of salary levels: an unqualified young male house servant gets a minimum of R3.75 (about £2.50) a month for a 12-month contract; a cattle shepherd sleeping outside gets R5.25 (less than £4). The minimum salary of a qualified B–man is only R5, and if he comes back to the same employer it is R7.50. A beginner in the mines gets 30c (about 20p) per shift; by the end of the contract 40c. This works out at about R8.69 (about £6) minimum per month. It is true that many employers pay more than the minimum requirement. Thus the average salary of an unqualified miner worker was R17.58 in 1965, and the salary of a house servant in Windhoek was between 9 and 12 rands. The salary can be two or three times higher in hotels, some factories and some offices. The salary is, of course, higher where a worker has to provide his own food.

Having a definite minimum salary has the advantage, on the one hand, that every worker gets at least something and does not need to work for only beer or cigarettes. On the other hand, there are disadvantages. If the minimum salary is for instance R6 and if the master pays R7 he is happy with himself for he pays more than he has to. Another is that a worker is paid a slightly better salary from the beginning if he promises to stay for 18 months: R4.50 rather than R3.75 per month for an unqualified beginner. The rise does not look high. But although the sum is small, 75c (50p), it is a big percentage raise (20%).

Such a long work contract may suit single men who know what

life is like in the south and who have good employers, but it is too long for young men who work on farms and in other remote areas, and it is even more dangerous for married workers, as eighteen months' separation from their wives can be fatal for their marriages. However, under the pressure of poverty, a promised increase in pay frequently induces men with families to sign a longer contract.

The salary is effectively reduced by some masters who make the servant pay for anything he happens to break by accident. Perhaps something has to be taken from the salary if the servant continually destroys his master's property by carelessness. But it is unreasonable if the servant has to pay for every broken cup or for every old shirt torn in the washing. It is also sensible to leave the price label on items, like clothes, which the employer for one reason or another decides to 'give' to his servant in place of part of his salary. The servant can see the prices of these items when he goes shopping and he may question the price the employer quotes.

Many Ovambo men are bitter at the high penalties that they have to pay for failures of one kind or another. A fine that would be insignificant for a white man can represent a large sum for a contract Ovambo and can create misery for the whole family. An Ovambo man who misses one day's work has to pay a fine of R40 (£30), equivalent to four months' salary. At the beginning of the strike there were cases of punishment by flogging in addition to the imposition of a fine.

Many Ovambo men are bothered by having no say in the choice of the working place or employer. If a man wants to go back to a former employer, he has a good chance of doing so, but otherwise the officers of SWANLA decide the working place and the type of work.

Sometimes Ovambo workers compare their own salaries with the salaries of other parts of the population. They notice that black people living permanently in the white areas get more than Ovambo contract workers, even when it is taken into account that these contract workers do not have to pay for their food and lodging. Immigrant workers in Ovamboland (some from the Republic of South Africa) get higher pay than the Ovambo and it seems that their pay levels take more account of qualifications than is the case with Ovambo contract workers. It goes without saying that salaries quoted in newspaper advertisements for jobs offered to whites must give the Ovambo considerable food for thought.

During the strike all the newspapers praised the courage of the white schoolboys who were willing to do the work of the Ovambo who were on strike. The amount of money that they got was mentioned there and the boys were asked what they were going to do with the money. The boys, who had been working for ten to twelve days told about bicycles that they intended to buy with the money. An Ovambo man knows very well how much a bicycle costs and how long he would have needed to work before buying one. One week's salary for a white schoolboy is what an Ovambo man, who might be father of a big family, earns in a whole month or even two. No wonder that an Ovambo pastor wrote the following:

> The lack of work makes men go. On the other hand it must be said

that they are not given enough money. If the salary were sufficient they could help their families and fathers for a long time. Isn't it true that everywhere in the world a man is paid according to his knowledge and skill in his work?

Developments after January 1972*

The new labour agreement between the government of South Africa and the 'governments' of Ovambo and Kavango in January 1972 was concluded during a state of emergency. The economic situation in South West Africa was chaotic; Ovambo labourers had to be brought back to their places of work as soon as possible. Disappointment among the employees led to attempts at new strikes, but those were brought under control, at times by force. Employers' associations were formed to protect the interests of employers. In Ovamboland a state of emergency was declared, which made meetings of employees impossible. Labour bureaux were established and new labour regulations drawn up, first in April, and again in August. The main points were:

a Labourers would be issued with identity documents.
b Deserters would be held, and employers compensated for losses incurred.
c Better arrangements would be made for the repatriation of deserters.
d Employers would have the right to register complaints about workers whose performance was not satisfactory.

Thus the freedom of movement of employees was restricted, and the rights of employers guaranteed.

The trial of eleven Ovambo and a 'Coloured' man accused of playing a leading role in the strikes held the entire country in suspense for months. The outcome was a great moral victory for the strikers. Magistrate H. J. Kriel admitted that the strikers had a real reason for their conduct: 'When one takes the rising cost-of-living into consideration, it is difficult to imagine how someone could make do and remain satisfied with so little money.' Nevertheless, the Ovambo lost something through the strike: the goodwill of whites, and their reputation as easily-handled and the most reliable workers in the country. There is truth in the words of Dirk Mudge reported in the *Suidwes-Afrikaaner*, 29 February 1972: 'Opposition to Ovambo is developing, and there is an ever increasing number of people who say that they want nothing more to do with the Ovambos.'

Many employers regarded the strike as a personal insult and newspapers reported labour being brought in from neighbouring countries 'so that the Ovambos can realise that they are not the only people who are capable of work'.[1] As the difference between the wages of migrant labourers and local workers decreased, employers began to favour using permanent residents, creating considerable unemploy-

* The second part of the chapter describes working conditions after the strike. Sadly the new contract system does not differ essentially from the former one and the present situation is in many respects even worse than at the beginning of the 1970s.

ment among the Ovambo. Ovambo unemployment also increased as contractors from the Republic brought their own teams of workers with them, even for large development projects in the 'Homelands'.

The situation from the employers' point of view

Many employers regarded the strike as a punishable offence. To them the new labour agreement was a sign of weakness on the part of the government and stronger action was demanded against anyone who caused unrest. Whereas previously it had been possible for employers themselves to recruit their workers in Ovamboland and to transport them in trucks, a new order was issued to the effect that all transportation of workers had to be by South African Railways, bus or train. The cost of transport was a 'recoverable advance' which the employer could claim back, but the slowness of this method has caused considerable dissatisfaction.

A section (clause F3) in the new contract gave the employee the right to end his period of service after notice of a specified number of days, and after repayment of the recoverable advances. Many Ovambo understood this section to mean that they had the right to leave one employer and seek work elsewhere. 'Ovambos run loose in South West Africa like springbok', a somewhat merciless newspaper article announced. There was a period of several weeks when Ovambo men moved freely through the country until new labour regulations made this impossible.

Farms suffered most from the uncertainty. Few Ovambo wanted to work on farms (55% of all migrant labourers on farms come from Angola, and a large number of them are not Ovambo, but members of other African nations), but when other work was no longer available, some Ovambo signed contracts to go to farms, with the idea of leaving those jobs later and seeking other employment. When they 'bought themselves out', that is, repaid the recoverable advances, they wanted to end the agreement. Such action caused great inconvenience and large losses to farm owners.

The situation from the employees' point of view

During the Ovambo Executive Committee's visit to Capetown in May 1972, one member maintained that the Ovambo people were completely satisfied with the new labour agreement. This view was in strong contrast to the truth: dissatisfaction was stronger and more conscious than before the strike. One reason for this was that the Ovambo had the impression after the strike that big changes in their favour were on the way. They were disappointed on several counts. The following reasons for dissatisfaction were taken from letters written during the second half of 1972. (The words 'contract' and 'contract Ovambo' have returned and are generally used in South West Africa, despite their formal 'abolition'.)

Meagre wages

During the strike, even the National Party newspapers admitted that the Ovambo were being exploited by many employers, and that the time for cheap labour was past. Some employers reviewed the entire wage issue and accepted that the wage they paid was not merely pocket money. But ignorance remained as to the true needs of the Ovambo worker, for example, his obligation to take gifts to all his relatives on return from a contract. The following examples give a picture of changes in wages rates.

After the strike, the Tsumeb Corporation, one of the main employers of Ovambo labour, paid 65–70 cents (about 40p) per shift, that is, R17.60 to R19.60 (about £10) per month. If one takes account of inflation, however, there was no real increase.

For some mines wages were lower than at Tsumeb. For example, in one copper mine, a man operating a mining drill received 56c per eight-hour shift, that is, a monthly salary for 24 days of R13.44. (On days off many miners work in the gardens of whites, earning 50c for 3 hours' work.) Mine work is heavy and many men complained about the paltry compensation miners received when involved in accidents at work. For example: 'If a man has been crippled at work and has received a small sum as compensation, he is discarded by the company; he has no chance of being accepted back as an employee.'

Other manual labour continued to be badly paid; for example, a man who earned R6.50 per month in 1971, and R8.50 in 1972, writes: 'My work entails breaking up old foundations with a pick each day. Sometimes you hit a very hard stone which resists you. When you leave, your arms are very sore. Never here do you feel good. If we complain, terrible things happen. We only pray to God.'

The greatest disparities existed in wages paid to domestic servants. In Windhoek a survey was done covering 36 Ovambo. One-third of them had received no wage increase between 1971 and 1972. The average wage of the 36 was R17.62 in 1971 and R22.17 in 1972.[2] Someone who earns R12 per month writes: 'I do all the housework, gardening, washing, ironing and cooking. I get no free time, and nothing which makes me happy. There is a terrible lot of work, but very little pay. I also work on Saturdays and Sundays.'

Wages paid by hotels varied between R15 and R30. One hospital which paid R10 before, paid R12 after the strike. A large hostel for white children paid R15 in 1971; in 1972 the figure was raised to R23.

In Windhoek the average wage for 'kitchen-boys' was considerably higher than elsewhere. In Walvis Bay wages varied between R15 and R20, and in a small town in the interior, between R8 and R10.

Wages on farms were even lower, about R6 being normal. According to one farm labourer: 'The work is very hard, and there are many troubles. I started work in 1955, but I still receive now what I did then – R6' (about £4). It was reported from farms near the coast that new workers were being paid R7.50 to R8.50, while people who had worked many years for the same employer could earn up to R10 or R12 per month.

The best-paid jobs were some services for water provision – at one inland town wages ranged from 10c to 20c (about 10p) an hour – and lorry driving for mines which paid 20c to 22c per hour. One building contractor paid 20c per hour, and since employees were supposed to work eleven hours a day, the daily wages were R2.20 (workers had to buy their own food). Such wages were exceptional, however; of a sample of approximately 250 men only eleven earned more than R40 per month.

Only during the strike did the Ovambo become conscious of how low their wages were in comparison with those of other employees. An additional Ovambo complaint was that they did not always receive the money promised them. When I asked a group to write down on pieces of paper what they earned, someone asked completely innocently: 'Must we write the sum which was promised to us, or the money we actually get?' This complaint came from Tsumeb: 'It has been discussed that after six months we get paid up to R1.52, but until today no-one received it.' In another letter: 'We agreed on the wage. You get it once, maybe, and then it decreases.' When I asked how such unlawful action is possible, I was told that it was said that rising costs cause contractors, for example, to lose their profits, and this makes it difficult for them to pay the promised wage.

Furthermore, during the strike, Ovambo said that they would rather receive more money and pay their own travelling costs. The result was that they had to pay travelling costs, even in cases where wages were not increased. According to the agreement, train and bus fares are recoverable advances. The bus fare from Ondangwa to Grootfontein is R3.60 (for farm workers R1.20) and the train journey to Walvis Bay costs R6.41. This means that most farm labourers and some domestic servants receive not a cent of their first month's wages.

Before the strike, each contract Ovambo at Grootfontein was given a khaki shirt and shorts, and some factories (for example those in Walvis Bay) gave jam and tobacco or sweets to workers once a week. These privileges were stopped because of increased wages. Where there was no increase or only a nominal one, this loss was regarded as an injustice.

In some cases employers defended insufficient wages, saying that the municipality did not allow the worker to live with them but demanded R12 per month (R2 for accommodation, R10 for food). R10 is a large sum for food: in mission schools for adults where three hot meals and extra tea are served only R7.50 per person is spent monthly on food. There are indeed two hot meals, and a piece of bread which the men can take with them to their place of work, but many workers have to leave the compound so early that they miss breakfast. When such a man hears that his monthly wage – because of the higher pay – is decreased by R10 for food, he does not know with whom he should be angry: with his employer or with the municipality. In some cases no consideration was given to the qualifications of an applicant in job assignments or pay. Men who received good wages as truck drivers in 1971 had to work with picks and shovels in 1972 and earn only half as much. This, too, created dissatisfaction and frustration.

The length of the working day

New contracts specified starting and finishing times (Clauses E1 and 2) and a section covered overtime (Clause C2). Many Ovambo workers, however, were unable to calculate the length of their working day with the aid of these data. Contracts made no mention of work on Saturdays or Sundays. A hotel servant writes: 'We work from eight in the morning till twelve at night.' Another says:

> They tell us our wages are supplemented so that we get R27, but we weep. There is much work, and there is no Sunday and no public holiday or Saturday. We must work every day from six in the morning to seven-thirty in the evening. They say that we are working according to the contract, by means of which we came from Ovambo, but although we weep, we must work because there is nothing which can save us.

This aspect is apparently better in mines and factories where wages are calculated by the hour. Complaints also come from the mines, however: 'A man has worked for say twelve hours, of which four are overtime, but those hours are cut in half, ten hours are entered, and two are discarded.'

Additional rail costs and harassment during travel

The railways have a strange custom in South West Africa, whereby anyone travelling in a southerly direction need not pay anything for hand luggage. Going north it is different. When the train arrives at Tsumeb or Grootfontein, the centres from which contract workers are transported to Ovamboland, hand luggage is weighed and the Ovambo must pay for it. If he transfers to a railway bus, luggage is again weighed, and a second charge made. There have been many complaints about the double fee, and claims that the money paid is out of all proportion to the weight and value of the luggage. If the Ovambo send their goods in the trucks of fellow countrymen, police at Omuwelo (the border station of Ovamboland) demand money for all freight except the personal property of the truck owner. This makes even that form of cartage very expensive for Ovambo returning.

Border posts are places where the conduct of clerks and police is subject to little control. The following letter tells of this:

> The trouble we have at Omuwelo near Namutoni is something too terrible to speak of. In the South we find whites who are selling their property. We buy things from them, like chairs, tables and beds. That white man sells these things and goes to Cape Town or Johannesburg. Now I take my chairs to Ovambo. At Omuwelo I am asked for a paper. He who sold me the goods gave me no paper. The police hit me and the chairs are left at Omuwelo. I go to Ovambo; I am hit and my chairs are taken away from me. *Whose* property are these chairs? Why am I, who am found with chairs, but with no paper, taken to court and punished as a thief? The police at Omuwelo harass and rob the Ovambos of their good clothes. The police live off Ovambos' property which they earned with difficulty and by faithful work.

Problems at the labour bureaux

Clause F3 of the contract gave the Ovambo the right to terminate his period of service. The worker was then to report to his local labour bureau for a new job within seventy-two hours, with a 'reference' from his previous employer. However, a worker was unable to move from the area of one labour bureau to that of another. If he had worked at Okahandja (about 80 km from Windhoek) and wanted employment in Windhoek, he had first to return to Ovamboland (at his own expense) and from there try to obtain a post in Windhoek.

Before 1972 employers were more circumscribed by the contract; only in the most extreme cases would they send their Ovambo workers home during their period of service. After 1972 workers were easily suspended and any complaints or claims for overtime pay were regarded as rebelliousness. For example, one writes: 'If you ask the employer for more money, he says you are spoiled by politics'; another says: 'The Ovambos' case is no longer being investigated. He is not questioned so that facts can come to light. He is just chased back to Ovambo. He is mocked and not heeded. Just chased away from work.'

In seeking a new job, workers were totally dependent upon the inclination of the clerk at the labour bureau. A letter signed by a group of workers records:

> The Ovambo goes to the labour bureau and says: 'I am a driver and I want work as a driver'. He is told: 'You are going to build rooms and the pay is R5 per week'. If he says: 'I don't want building work, and I am not satisfied with R5 per week', he is chased back to Ovambo and there are no means of self-protection. Is this a good system in which to find work?

In some cases the Ovambo has himself found someone willing to employ him. But the following is written of the consequences thereof:

> If he goes to the bureau with the paper from his old employer, and that of the new employer, the clerk tears up both papers and the man's pass. If the man has money, he is sent back to Ovambo. If he does not have it, however, he is put in jail.

Personal contact between prospective employer and employee is completely forbidden.

Difficulties with housing and night-passes

While the label 'compounds' was changed to 'hostels' in South West Africa the lack of privacy in large dormitories remained. There were many complaints about the Windhoek compound in particular.

Ovambo workers who were able to live with their employers regarded themselves as fortunate, but even they had their problems; for example, in Windhoek they were not permitted to be in the street after 8 p.m., unless their employer gave them a special night-pass. Let an Ovambo speak for himself:

> I wish to speak of a matter about which I and many other people, especially members of our church, the Evangelical Lutheran Ovambo–Kavango Church, complain. These people would like to attend bible-study and youth meetings. But if you have no night-pass, you will sleep in jail. Night-passes cause nothing but trouble. Some whites don't always feel like giving you one. You are asked: 'Boy, where are you going?', or maybe the master has gone away. You want to go to a service, but are scared .... I don't know what that night-pass means because it is only demanded of certain people, especially Ovambos. One day I was arrested because I had no night-pass. After the police had put me in their van, they searched for others without passes. Every time they saw an Ovambo the policeman shouted: 'Come here. Where is your night-pass? If you don't have one, climb in'. They let Namas and Basters go, as well as whites.

Church attendance is made really difficult for many Ovambo. What hurts us missionaries is that the road to the beerhalls is made as easy as possible. The beerhall is situated so that the Ovambo has only to cross the road to reach it. His hard-earned money is thus returned to municipal coffers and men who previously drank beer very seldom have become hardened drinkers.

Complaints about the system itself

The above complaints are about details; the main complaint was that the system in reality remained the same after the strike. 'It is said that the contract system has been abolished, that it no longer exists. But there is still a very strong smell of that contract-system in the air.' The period of work continued to be almost always twelve months – on farms even eighteen months – except in factories doing seasonal work. According to the contract (Clause F6), an employee was permitted to take unpaid leave during his service period for the purpose of visiting his home, the duration to be agreed upon by him and his employer. The Ovambo text read '*Omulongi oku na okumona ompito....*', which should be translated as 'An employee *must* have a chance' to take home-leave. However, this chance was seldom given. 'If you ask for it, you are not answered, only chased away.'

For the workers the system is the same or worse. The supposed freedom of choice is an illusion. A worker writes: 'It is said that one has the right to work freely, that one works together with one's master. In reality it is like cat and dog. We are addressed sharply and are so scared that we no longer have the strength to work.'

One great change did occur. Those who work only five days a week — for example, those in the service of the municipalities — and live not far from Ovambo, go home at weekends. It is very expensive, and the actual time spent at home is only one to one and a half days, but much use is made of this chance. Such a journey is also dangerous; if something goes wrong and the man is late for work, he is suspended. Another improvement was that visits by women to their husbands were made easier, at least in large centres.

Unfortunately only a small number of Ovambo were able to

make use of these privileges. For most men the new system meant twelve months of separation from their wives and children. Family life continued to be disrupted, just as it was under the old system. This was further aggravated by Clause F4 which stated: 'An employee may after termination of the period of service enter into an agreed period of service with the same or another employer, subject to local registration.' This saved the employers recruiting costs, and apparently gave greater freedom to the employee. In practice, however, it meant that a married worker might stay in the south year after year without seeing his wife or children.

The new system also caused a split between the Ovambo 'government' and the migrant workers. Previously contract Ovambo only accused the white government: after 1972 harsh words were uttered against the Ovambo 'government' for having sanctioned such a system: 'The contract is a very bad thing, but it has been forced upon us by our headmen'; 'Our headmen in Ovambo trouble us in their collaboration with the whites, because they have good jobs and are paid enough. They no longer look after their people, their children, but have turned their backs on us, and give us a snake when we ask for fish.'

Before the strike, headman Filippus Kaluvi was appointed as a liaison official between the Ovambo 'government' and the contract workers. Although the Ovambo, as far as I know, originally had nothing against him personally, it became impossible for him to carry out his task. He was the personification of the hated system. It is reported from Windhoek that he refused, because of fear, to enter the Ovambo compound, or even address a meeting in a church.

In February 1972 the Walvis Bay municipality made it known that it held the Ovambo 'government' responsible for any damage caused by Ovambo workers in the compound.[3] On 18 August the Ovambo 'government' accepted a measure to compensate employers on a *pro rata* basis for Ovambo workers who deserted. As a result the Ovambo 'government' began to levy fines on deserters who return to Ovamboland. Where workers felt that the fine was unjust, the relationship between the government and the people weakened further.

Broader aspects

Almost everything said above about the Ovambo also applies to the Kavango. The Kavango 'government' accepted the new system and its attendant regulations. Many of the Kavango on the South West African side of the river took up the Ovambo cause. The Herero and Damara did not join the strikers as many Herero who are not herdsmen or have private enterprises at least have the advantage of being able to find work near their homes. Those who come from distant Herero areas and who work with the Ovambo receive the same treatment and have similar grounds for complaint. Although the Damara did not take part in the strike, they also had troubles, and expected that the new labour regulations would be applied to them as well. The stipulation that Damara women must register as workers aroused tremendous opposition. Damara women were told that, if women who could no longer work, old people for example, were sent away, working women would have more room and better homes. The solidarity of these women has led to conflict. Damara headmen also protested against the new labour regulations.

The migratory labour system has been practised for many years. The peaceful course of events is entirely due to the fact that the Ovambo had always been an agricultural nation where each man has his own land. The wife remained at home and tended the crops. Now, developments in the country are changing this completely. In the new circumstances people are beginning to ask why wives and children cannot accompany their menfolk to their places of work.

Among the Ovambo one still finds those who talk thankfully about how much better everything is now than it was forty years ago, when they had to walk to Tsumeb, and earned a few rand a month. The number of people who are dissatisfied, however, is growing fast. They are not only young radicals, but also middle-aged men for whom the growing distrust and hatred is a religious problem. 'The government has allowed us to enter hell. Yes, it is clear that if you have no peace of mind, then all you can expect is hell.' Among the youth, demands are growing at the same rate as suspicion and bitterness. The future of the labour situation is largely dependent on whether trust is still attainable, and this can only happen if the powers that be are able to satisfy the demands of the workers.

Notes

1 *Suidwes-Afrikaaner*, 24 March 1972.

2 The minimum wage for a kitchen servant was R6 per month in 1971 and R7.50 in 1972. The maximum was R36 in 1971 and R44 in 1972. (R10 of the latter sum was additional pay for ironing.)

3 *Die Suidwester*, 28 February 1972.

7 The church in mobilization for national liberation

JUSTIN ELLIS

The major Christian churches in Namibia have a combined membership of two-thirds of the total population. Today they play a prominent role in political development toward liberation. However, emergence of the churches as a significant part of the opposition to South African rule in Namibia – in an institutional sense – is a relatively recent occurrence spanning less than two decades. Much early nationalist sentiment was influenced by Christian teaching, and individual Christians, including priests, have been involved in political action for many years, but action through the churches and by their leaders is more recent. This chapter will focus on the nature of this transition and some of the tensions it has generated.

Complicity of the churches with colonialism

Missionary activity began relatively late in Namibia. Early in the nineteenth century the London and Wesleyan Missionary societies began extending their work over the Orange River, the northern border of the Cape. However, a Lutheran, Hugo Hahn, is generally looked upon as the father of missionary endeavour in Namibia. Supported by the Rhenish Missionary Society in Germany, Hahn established a mission to the Herero people at Otjikango (near present-day Okahandja in the central region of the country) in 1844. In spite of the unenthusiastic reception which his message received, he began establishing a network of stations, some of which became 'colonies' where converts, rejected by their own people, could find what the missionaries believed to be a civilized Christian livelihood. To support his work Hahn began trading with the local inhabitants. His greatest worry was apparently that his work could never prosper because of disruptive inter-tribal raids.

Having the territory made a protectorate of either Britain or Germany would, he felt, give the country the peace and stability needed for his mission to prosper. While the colonization of Namibia would have taken place whether or not the missionaries agreed to it, the historical fact is that they did agree, and in fact facilitated the process of colonization, acting as interpreters and using their influence as advisors to community leaders.

The deafening silence of the German churches in the face of the brutal policies and actions of the German colonial government was particularly regrettable. There were voices of disquiet and protest from the missionaries working in Namibia, but when private representations failed to change colonial policy it was accepted with servility to the Kaiser. Even the refusal to allow Africans to be baptized or to worship was passed over in silence. Grappling with this past guilt has been a significant task during the past decade for the independent Evangelical Lutheran Church of about 130 000 members which emerged from the work of the Rhenish Mission.

Significantly for Namibian church history, Hahn decided that work in the northern part of Namibia, largely inhabited by the Ovambo people, was too much for him, and invited the Finnish Missionary Society to join him there, which it did in 1870. The early Finnish missionaries were undoubtedly severely puritanical, but they had no colonial interest in Namibia. Their sincerity and devotion began to change attitudes, both among the Ovambo and among the Finns, and later also created a church–state tension, with the church increasingly on the side of the people and increasingly distrusted by the state.

From the beginning, the Finnish Mission gave high priority to the education of Namibians who soon attained responsibility within the church. Women were given status through the work of Finnish women in all fields, particularly medicine. Although the Finns saw themselves as religious and moral agents with a mandate over all aspects of life, they did not see their mission as political. Nevertheless, early South African commissioners were soon grumbling about their pervasive influence, which was blamed for the breakdown of the traditional authority of the tribal headmen (favoured by the South Africans because of the ease with which they could be manipulated), and of the (supposedly) economically efficient system of polygamy, thereby causing famine. The South Africans were particularly concerned about the spread of 'bush schools', a widespread education system designed to make converts and their children literate. Further, their teachings on justice and brotherhood, however intended, were often perceived by the Ovambo as necessarily leading to criticism of the secular political and economic order.

The Evangelical Lutheran Ovambo–Kavango Church (ELOK) which became structurally independent of the Finnish Mission in 1954, in 1980 had about a quarter of a million members, and a very competent and experienced indigenous leadership. Its oneness with its congregation has been significant in the evolution of its concern with secular affairs.

The Roman Catholic Church began work in Namibia at the beginning of the twentieth century. For the first twenty years its activities were limited and discouraged by the colonial government which saw Namibia as an area for Protestant Missions. It is interesting to note that when the Catholic Church was given permission to work in the densely populated northern areas, the government expected it to play a definite political role. The Administrator required in 1924 (by government directive which was applied to all missions) that missionaries were to support and promote government policy; encourage the Ovambo to work in the south; teach their members loyalty towards the administration; confirm the authority of the headmen and leaders in their territory; and emphasize practical education and only introduce new syllabuses into their schools after discussion with the Director of Education.

Over the years the Catholic Church has built up extensive services in medicine and education, doing more than the government in many areas. It is represented throughout the country and has perhaps done even more than other churches to provide an example in living communities and shared liturgical services of inter-racial harmony in contradiction to the apartheid ideology. Because of the high qualifications for ordination, the Catholic Church in Namibia is still dependent on expatriate priests for its 130 000 members. Their generous welfare activities often, and unfortunately, lead these priests into a paternalistic role which breeds alienation and dependence. The vulnerability of expatriates to deportation makes them reluctant to speak up against South African officials, though the Bishop of Windhoek and his senior priests have (albeit later than Lutheran and Anglican Church leaders) proved themselves exceptions to this rule in recent years.

The Anglican Church began missionary work relatively late, in 1924, under the same agreement as the Catholic Church had signed. By the 1960s it had begun to move towards open conflict with the state. Perhaps because of its connections with the Anglican Church in South Africa (at that time approaching a serious confrontation with the Nationalist Party government) the Anglican Church in Namibia was the first to emerge as a political force, in spite of its small membership of about 60 000.

It should be noted that the Lutheran, Catholic and Anglican Churches from the beginning agreed to work within certain areas only, avoiding inter-church rivalry which characterizes some countries. However, these major churches regularly find themselves at odds with the Dutch Reformed Church whose white Afrikaner members resent their attacks on government policy. The Dutch Reformed Church has little mission work in Namibia, but, as in South Africa, criticism of government policy, and of the collaboration of the Dutch Reformed Church in providing a rationalization for apartheid, is most strongly felt when it comes from a person such as Mission Secretary Rev. P. D. Strauss who has sought to inform Namibian whites of black attitudes.

There is another important white church, the German Evangelical Lutheran Church. After years of hesitation and debate it recently agreed to enter into a union with the two black Lutheran Churches.

The beginnings of change

In various ways the churches have been involved in the struggle for Namibian independence from the outset. Initially, however, this took place outside formal church structures and against leaders' wishes.

Two lonely figures who deserve mention are Michael Scott and Theophilus Hamutumpangela, both Anglican priests. Father Scott, through his petitions and lobbying at the United Nations from 1947 onwards (before there was any significant political party to represent black Namibian aspirations), helped to focus attention on Namibia. Father Hamutumpangela was arrested for writing letters to the United Nations (which were smuggled through Angola to Portugal) about the sufferings of the Ovambo under the migrant labour system, particularly their robbery by South African police 'border guards' at the gate between Ovamboland and the south of the country. Hamutumpangela was one of the founders of the Ovamboland Peoples Organization, soon transformed into SWAPO.

From an early stage the South African government was worried about the influence of the churches and consequent problems for its policies. The Odendaal Plan, published in December 1963, first brought this tension to the surface in a formal Church–State confrontation.

As Ovambo was to be the first and model 'Homeland' in terms of this plan, the South African Minister for Bantu Affairs, de Wet Nel, visited the area in February 1964. At a large public meeting for the Ongandjera people the Minister met with an unexpected public questioning from Bishop Leonard Auala, then in his fourth year as Bishop of the Evangelical Ovambo–Kavango Church.

'Were the Hereros', the Bishop asked, 'happy about being moved from their old homes to new?' The Bishop must have known that they were not. He had worked as a teacher at Okahandja, seat of Hosea Kutako, the defiant Herero chief who for decades had been the most prominent leader of Namibian non-acceptance of the legitimacy of South African rule. In 1959 the Herero had rioted rather than move to a new location (Katutura) outside Windhoek, planned and built by the South African government.

> If not, I fear that it will also hit us Ovambos, and there are thousands and thousands of us working in the old Damaraland and Hereroland. And this will also affect our Church which to this very day cooperates closely with Hereros in Church matters. Secondly, all three Lutheran Churches in South West Africa have formed a conference [the Bishop then listed the Churches and all the ethnic groups which belonged to each] of which I am the Chairman. We have a joint Seminary at Otjimbingwe. Now I fear that your new dispensation of 'Homelands' for the non-white people of South West Africa will promote apartheid between the non-whites of South West Africa. And such apartheid between the non-whites of South West Africa will also hinder Church cooperation. And what about our theological seminary?
>
> I am thankful that it is the aim of the Odendaal Commission to improve the standard of living of the non-whites of South West Africa and attempt to let the non-white people develop to self-government. Is it then your intention to give these people the opportunity to say something about this creation of division and the moving of people's homes? May the Ovambo nation, which is larger than any other group in South West Africa, be given the vote to say something about these new 'Homelands'?
>
> We non-white people fear that with these new 'Homelands' we will not be at home with one another in our South West Africa as a whole.[1]

Bishop Auala was trying to voice the opposition of his people, expose the South African government, and influence the course of events according to his Christian commitment. At the same time he was apparently having to struggle with the prevalent misconception of

Martin Luther's two–kingdom teaching: the Church should confine itself to spiritual and churchly matters; it should 'keep out of politics', unless the government had threatened the autonomy of the church in matters of belief.

The South African government refused to give up the Odendaal Plan. The black Lutheran Churches refused to be silent. In May the same year they sent the Minister a joint memorandum under the signatures of both church boards, describing the Odendaal Plan as 'a danger to the work of the Church', and opposing any division. They requested a formal meeting with the Minister. However, in spite of repeated reminders, this request went unheeded for four years. On 21 March 1968 the Private Secretary of the Minister wrote a long exposition of the Odendaal Plan, and gave an assurance that it was always the policy of the government 'to work hand in hand with the Churches . . . with the object of developing the Bantu politically and spiritually to independence'. The Minister decided not to grant an interview, considering that the letter ought to provide an answer to any questions the churches might have.

In the meantime SWAPO had launched its first military attack on a police post at Oshikango. Large numbers of Ovambo were detained and 'interrogated' by the South African police, resulting in a forceful (but private) letter from the Lutheran, Catholic and Anglican Churches to the Commander of Police at Ondangwa:

> We feel compelled to present you a combined letter of strong protest regarding certain practices which evidently are frequent during the interrogation of Ovambos taken into custody. Our hospitals have been called upon to give medical attention . . . to many of these cases . . . the treatment needed has involved broken bones, severe bruising, dog bites, internal damage, as well as reactions to electrical shocks through the head.
>
> We unanimously acknowledge the right and necessity of any police force to interrogate, particularly in matters which involve the security of the state. But as Christians we deeply deplore the use of torture and brutality as a means of obtaining information. We feel that we have thus been thrown back into the horrors of ancient pagan custom with these practices. We also feel that this kind of treatment is rapidly causing deep-seated bitterness, resentment, and suspicion of the Administration among our population as a whole. . . .
>
> We are not sure whether you are fully aware of these facts, and therefore we ask that immediate steps be taken by you so that this physical abuse may be stopped. Being convinced that terror can never be overcome by terror, or evil by more evil, we hope and pray you will receive our solemn protest and request in the spirit which we know you are honouring.[2]

A watershed

In June 1971 the churches decided to move toward public confrontation with the South African Prime Minister, Mr Vorster. This courageous move was precipitated by two events, the first the advisory opinion of the International Court of Justice that South Africa's presence in Namibia was illegal, and the second a broadcast on the network of the South African Broadcasting Corporation.

While the decision of the International Court of Justice was undoubtedly received with great joy by black Namibians, Mr Vorster announced that he would ignore it. A South African Broadcasting Corporation official interviewed Bishop Auala and broadcast that the Bishop had also rejected the decision, the exact opposite of what the Bishop had said. Although the interview had been taped and the Corporation apologized for the 'error', it refused to correct the broadcast.

The churches, feeling impelled to present the facts, on 30 June published the celebrated 'Open Letter' to Mr Vorster. In blunt terms, they pointed out how South Africa had infringed basic human rights and called upon South Africa to cooperate with the United Nations so that South West Africa could become an independent state in terms of the declaration of the International Court of Justice.

Simultaneously (and even more provocatively) the Lutheran Church boards wrote to their congregations a pastoral letter explaining the Open Letter. Here they were more explicit: 'The judgement of the World Court was the answer to the prayer of many of our people because this judgement involves the hope of freedom and recognition of human worth.' The churches, the letter asserted, could no longer remain silent as they would otherwise become liable for the life and future of their country. Finally they appealed to their congregations to keep building bridges between the different ethnic groups, to maintain the peace, and to pray for a change of heart in the authorities.

The Anglican and Catholic bishops supported the Lutherans. Mr Vorster found himself in an embarrassing situation. He summoned Lutheran leaders to meet him in Windhoek during August 1971. At the meeting the church leaders, with careful reference to the Bible, stressed their role as watchmen over society. They enumerated the grievances of black people: that they always had to call a white person 'master'; that the police were abusing their powers and torturing people; that the contract-labour system was breaking up families and creating many other social problems. Finally they warned that the future would be dark if changes were not made. Mr Vorster attacked the concept of human rights, swept aside the complaints of the churches, and demanded that they should keep out of politics. He then tried to 'introduce' the church leaders to the Ovambo 'Homeland' government. Rising with all his dignity, Bishop Auala said that if the chiefs wanted to speak to him, they knew where his home was.

Far from being browbeaten, the frustration generated by this meeting with Mr Vorster made the Lutheran leaders more outspoken in their criticism of South African policy. At a meeting with Commissioner-General de Wet on 27 November, they publicly described the contract-labour system as a form of 'slavery'. Angered, de Wet claimed that the system was voluntary, and that those who objected to it could leave their jobs.

It is widely believed that de Wet's response sparked off the general strike of Ovambo workers at the end of 1971. Having so recently been vociferous in their attack on this system, the churches came to play an important role in the strike, providing the international press with information, and paying for the defence of those charged in court with having organized the strike, the authorities suspected that the churches had a hand in organizing the strike, and later in 1972 expelled the Anglican Bishop, Colin Winter, apparently as a scapegoat. It is illuminating to quote Bishop Auala's answer to this accusation:

> We supported [the strike] but we did not start it. We thought that the only way the people could show their desire (because the government officials would not listen to spoken words) was to strike, to let the employers know the will of the workers. Our people . . . told one another that there must be no violence. If someone saw a car full of whites, they should not throw stones. Strikers must be quiet, or simply say, 'We do not like the old contract labour system. It is finished. We want a better system. Until then we will not eat the food of employers. We will sleep outside our quarters. We will have no violence. We will have morning and evening prayers. Thus we will show our feelings in this drastic matter.' When white police came along, the young people sang songs.[3]

The strike did not produce the desired changes, but it brought the economy to a halt for a month or more and certainly marked a turning point in the history of Namibia. Further it marked a watershed in the churches' views of their secular duty: from quietism they had moved to a critical prophetic role and to a pastoral and supportive role for those (largely their own members) who struggled for justice.

Attempted repression of the churches

To maintain its hold over Namibia the South African government intensified repression, but its actions against the churches tended to be counterproductive. The deportation of Bishop Winter, for instance, led to the unification of a troubled diocese behind him. His synod asked him to remain Bishop of his diocese and to work for the Namibian church around the world. The uncompromising attitude of the Anglican Church, which lost four leaders in succession through deportations (Bishop Mize, Bishop Winter, Suffragan Bishop Wood and Rev. Morrow), won it great admiration among black Namibians and served to bolster morale.

All the churches have been affected by deportations and refusals of visas and permits to enter black areas. Although this has weakened many church institutions, the results have not all been negative: African churchmen have been promoted to positions of responsibility before they might otherwise have been, and most churches have increased their lay training programmes.

The most significant physical act against the churches was the sabotage of the Evangelical Lutheran Ovambo–Kavango Church press at Oniipa, at 3 a.m. on 11 May 1973. An accurately placed charge blew up the two large presses and in the ensuing fire 2 000 Bibles and a stock of school and church books were destroyed. There is a general belief that the blast was engineered by the South African authorities, probably through the Bureau for State Security (BOSS), now renamed the Department of National Security (DONS), to silence the Church's newspaper *Omukwetu*. After the Open Letter this weekly vernacular newspaper had been publishing a page of political news and comment and the South Africans were obviously worried about its growing circulation and influence.

It is interesting to note how church authorities dealt with this crisis. Publication of *Omukwetu* was continued, though in duplicated form for many months. Congregations and schools were soon without books, demonstrating the need which the press had fulfilled. Three weeks after the explosion, 8 000 people gathered for a prayer service at the ruins of the press where a cross and pulpit were fashioned from the remains of the presses. A fund was started and just two years later a second service was held at Oniipa, with 10 000 people in attendance, to celebrate the reopening of the press.

In defence

Action against the churches was only a small, though integral, part of the reign of terror which South African government unleashed, especially in northern parts of Namibia, from 1972 onwards through Emergency Regulation R17 and through unlawful measures. However, people could still meet at church services, which were practically the only meetings allowed, although even these have been interfered with by the military.

The churches have also fulfilled a protective role through the courts, the most celebrated action being that brought by Bishops Wood and Auala to stop the (officially inspired) public flogging of SWAPO supporters by tribal headmen. This particular application dragged on for nineteen months, eventually ending in the vindication of the bishops in the South African Appeal Court in Bloemfontein. The churches have also funded the defence of several persons charged under South African security laws, not only for the sake of justice but to create public awareness of why Namibians enter the liberation struggle, to expose abuses such as torture, and to save people from vengeance.

The role the churches have played in combating the systematic use of torture by South African security forces should be noted in more detail. After failing to persuade Mr Vorster to appoint a judicial commission of inquiry into torture, the churches ended the dialogue with him. Then, in May 1977, they published a long pastoral letter.[4] This contained information on the extent and methods of torture in Namibia; a history of church attempts to get a judicial investigation and a warning that a 'chain reaction of brutality and inhumanity' could be set off by the practice of torture; and an analysis of South African security legislation, showing how this facilitated torture. A long section advised people on their limited rights and how they should behave if detained, and recommended that relatives and congregations try to visit the detained and to remember them in the prayers of the congregation, quoting the Epistle to the Hebrews: 'Remember those in prison as if you were there with them; and those who are being maltreated, for you like them are still in the world.'

This pastoral letter was soon banned by the South African authorities, but during the limited period of its circulation it attracted much attention inside Namibia, placed the reality before the world, and perhaps deterred some South African officials. On the subject of torture, one must note the heroic efforts of Heinz Hunke, a senior Catholic priest, to stimulate the public conscience by publishing irrefutable facts about torture, and his incessant pressure on the South African Administrator-General, Justice Steyn, to do something about this practice. His deportation by Justice Steyn in July 1978 served to prove the truth of what the churches have said about the use of torture in Namibia as an integral and planned, not incidental and accidental, part of the occupation forces' scheme of government.

On violence

The fall of the Portuguese regime in Angola was greeted with great joy by black people all over Namibia. It signified change, raised hopes that Namibia might be next, and opened an escape route out of Namibia, with many young people leaving for Angola. The fall of the colonial government in Angola also provoked an escalation of SWAPO's bush war against South Africa, as SWAPO guerrillas could infiltrate Namibia from Angola with comparative ease. This placed the churches in a difficult situation as their avowed policy was that differences should be settled through negotiation, and independence attained by peaceful means. They considered that support for strikers and victims of torture posed different issues than did armed revolution. As the war escalated, more suffering was inflicted on the Ovambo people. One of the first steps taken by South Africa was to move 50 000 people to create a no-man's-land and Free Fire Zone along the border with Angola.

It is instructive to examine how the churches dealt with this. Knowing that they were greatly concerned about the exodus of the young and able from the country, the Commissioner-General called upon church representatives to meet him for discussions on how it might be stopped. Church representatives arrived at the meeting with a long memorandum drawn up after consulting their congregations, listing sixteen grievances which had caused people to leave the country 'without permission'. Like strikers, those fleeing to escape terror or gain education were seen as within the churches' pastoral and supportive care and a ministry to exiles was begun.

Following the assassination of Filemon Elifas, Chief Minister of the Ovambo 'Homeland' government, in August 1975, Bishop Auala, the chief's godfather, was asked to preach the sermon at his graveside. Under great pressure to condemn SWAPO for this act, and in the presence of several top representatives of the South African government, Bishop Auala used as his text James 3:17–18:

> But the wisdom from above is pure first of all; and it is also peaceful, gentle and friendly; it is full of compassion and produces a har-

vest of good deeds; it is free from prejudice and hypocrisy. And goodness is the harvest that is produced from the seeds the peacemakers plant in peace.

While advising that people should seek wisdom from above, the main thrust of the Bishop's sermon was in the form of a question, clearly understood by all: 'Are we to continue along the road which brings deaths of this nature? Should we not rather stop and reason together, and then decide in which direction we should set out?' While not giving a *carte blanche* to SWAPO, the Bishop laid the blame for violence at the door of South Africa.

In a case in 1977, a Lutheran Evangelist, Nabot Iimene, was brought to court under the Terrorism Act, charged with having attempted to assist SWAPO guerrillas. On one of his rounds Mr Iimene had been confronted by a group of armed men who described themselves as 'the men of the bush', a standard term for SWAPO soldiers. They instructed Mr Iimene to write a letter to his church headquarters requesting clothing, food and a radio. Fearing a second meeting, Mr Iimene wrote the letter, which was intercepted by the Special Branch. During the trial, the Secretary of the Evangelical Lutheran Ovambo–Kavango Church, Pastor Petrus Shipena, was subpoenaed to give evidence. He said that he had received the letter but had not responded, and, to the judge's consternation, said that it was the church's policy that the head office would not give such aid, but that people in the field had to make their own decisions according to their own consciences and circumstances. Mr Iimene was sentenced to five years' imprisonment on Robben Island.

Another significant outbreak occurred in March 1978 when riots broke out in the Katutura township outside Windhoek between those (not all) Herero supporting the Democratic Turnhalle Alliance (DTA) and supporters of SWAPO, mostly (but by no means all) Ovambo. South African police gave the DTA Herero a free run but arrested any Ovambo found carrying an implement conceivably usable as a weapon. The Lutheran, Anglican and Catholic leaders issued a statement appealing for calm: 'After opposing division peacefully for so many years, and trying to achieve unity, do we now want to create hatred among ourselves by killing and doing serious injury to one another?'[4] The church leaders advised that those who had lost loved ones (at least twenty people were killed) should grant the forgiveness for which they prayed, 'For if each side is to seek vengeance we will bring upon ourselves an age of escalating destruction and misery'. The statement also insisted that the law should be consistently applied to all, and that people should not carry weapons on the streets. 'We also believe that all private bodyguards should be disbanded.' This appeal did not bring the confrontation to an end. At the end of the month Chief Kapuuo of the Herero was assassinated by unidentified assailants, and, at his funeral, members of his bodyguard shot into the Ovambo hostel killing five people. After the violence subsided, the churches again started working to heal the rift in their congregations.

In his most explicit statement to date, Bishop Auala said in Geneva on 21 September 1978 that if South Africa refused to cooperate with the United Nations in bringing independence to Namibia, South Africa could not blame SWAPO if the violence continued: South Africa itself would be responsible for stepping up the violence because it had rejected the plan for a peaceful solution.

Churches in resistance

Following their earlier call for United Nations involvement in the independence of Namibia, the churches in August 1975 rejected the Turnhalle Constitutional Conference, because certain political parties and political prisoners were not to be present. In a letter to Dr Henry Kissinger, American Secretary of State, at the time of his meeting with Mr Vorster in Switzerland in June 1976, the leaders of the Anglican, Catholic and Lutheran Churches said:

> The truth about these talks is that the vast majority of the black population has no interest or confidence in them. One reason for this is that black delegations which are said to represent various population groups there have no mandate from those whom they purport to represent . . . Another more important reason why these talks are suspect is the dominating influence of white officials . . . behind the facade of a promised new order. We can only conclude that the Turnhalle talks *in their present form* have a negligible chance of success. Certainly one cannot any longer sanely gamble with the future of a nation and subcontinent at such long odds.[5]

Similarly, the churches rejected the elections held in Namibia from 4 to 8 December 1978 and published a report on South African organized intimidation which lay behind an unexpectedly high turnout of voters.

More positively, the churches have given considerable support to a Western initiative to bring about a negotiated settlement between South Africa and SWAPO for elections under United Nations supervision and control. However, there have been growing misgivings about this plan as South Africa has succeeded in watering down its terms and the Western powers have apparently lacked the will to obtain South African compliance.

The churches and political involvement

Not surprisingly, individual Christians have continued to play an important role in the political life of Namibia. Towards the end of 1974 a group of young church people, many of them already holding responsible church positions, initiated the formation of a new united black front in Namibia, drawing their inspiration from the South African black consciousness philosophy. Although the overall strategy was largely unsuccessful, a small number of clergymen and church officials became executive members in SWAPO and the Namibia National Front.

Perhaps the most effective spokesman for this group is Zepahia Kammeeta, one of the pastors on the Executive Committee of

SWAPO. Following his release from three weeks' solitary confinement and interrogation under the Terrorism Act, he wrote a letter to friends and supporters telling of the great reassurance he had found reading the Bible in these circumstances. Although he could not reveal the content of his interrogation, he went on to a question which he must have been asked on many occasions:

> Can us preachers not leave this struggle to the politicians?
>
> The struggle in our land has to do not only with the liberation of Namibia, but it goes further and deeper than that. The presence of the South African government is not just a political question, but it is a threat to the Gospel of Jesus Christ! Thus I see it as the task of every Christian to see to the knocking down of this government.
>
> The South African Government and its supporters proclaim . . . especially by what they do . . . a message diametrically opposed to the Gospel. While God tells us that in Jesus Christ he has broken down the wall of separation between himself and us, and between us and our fellow men, the South African Government proclaims and builds the wall of separation which brings about alienation, mistrust and prejudice, fear, hatred and enmity.
>
> Therefore I see the struggle in Southern Africa and especially here in Namibia, not merely as a political struggle, in which only politicians may participate, but as a struggle in which all Christians are called to participate. And if this should happen, an armed struggle can be avoided, because the word of the cross is enough for us to be able to tackle this task . . . Or should God withdraw from the history of this world, hand it over to the Devils, and restrict himself to the temples and church buildings?[6]

However, there remains a good deal of opposition to the idea that the church should be partisan in its political involvement. At one extreme are some older ministers and missionaries who feel that the church should be 'neutral' in political questions.[7] On the other are younger theologians, who say that neutrality actually means silence and the condoning of iniquity. Dr J. L. de Vries of the Evangelical Lutheran Church has tried to develop an understanding half-way between the two, speaking of the role of the church as that of 'mediator between the fronts' working for reconciliation. Others have criticized this terminology, saying that while the hope of reconciliation must remain basic, one can only be accepted by South Africa as a mediator if one ceases a principled criticism of its policies.

Whatever the internal ideological struggle of the church over its role in society, the *de facto* situation is well enough established for South African propagandists to spend almost as much time attacking the churches as attacking SWAPO. Ironically, they acknowledge the power of the churches by desperately claiming that SWAPO, which has facilitated the organization of congregations with lay or ordained leaders in its refugee camps, is violently atheist and wants to burn all its churches.

The future

As long as South Africa refuses to withdraw from Namibia, pressure and attacks on Namibian churches and their leaders will increase in severity. Though the existing church structures may eventually crumble, Christianity, as an integral part of the daily struggles and hopes of the Namibian people, will continue.

When a popular government comes to power in Namibia there is likely to be a good deal of cooperation between it and the churches; certainly the latter could be enormously helpful in motivating people to participate in the government and development of their country during reconstruction.

Hopefully the churches in an independent Namibia will resist the temptation to accept places of power, and continue to promote the ethos of service to the poor and voiceless. Only by maintaining the values for which they now stand can they act as a credible influence with the right to speak out against any government which they feel is seriously in error or serving the interests of only a few.

Notes

1 'Questions about the Odendaal Report and the division of the country SWA among its inhabitants', document by Leonard Auala, Bishop of ELOC, Oniipa, 20 February 1964. Afrikaans original, translated into English by Justin Ellis.

2 Letter of 23 January 1967 to Captain van Heerden, South African Police, Ovamboland District Commander, signed by Bishop Leonard Auala of ELOC, Archdeacon L. Mallory of Anglican Mission, Odibo, and (illegible), priest-in-charge of Roman Catholic Mission, Okatana. Afrikaans original, translated into English by Justin Ellis. Partly quoted in H. Hunke and J. Ellis, *Torture – a Cancer in Our Society*, Windhoek and London, 1978, p. 13.

3 'Joint Statement on Torture in Namibia', May 1977, signed by Bishop L. Auala, ELOC, Dr J. L. de Vries, ELCSWA, Bishop R. Koppmann, Catholic Diocese of Windhoek, Rev. E. Morrow, Anglican Diocese of Damaraland. Also partly quoted in Hunke and Ellis, *Torture – a Cancer in Our Society*.

4 'Statement by Church Leaders in Namibia during time of Bloodshed in Katutura Township', 7 March 1978, signed by J. L. Vries, E. S. Morrow and R. Koppmann.

5 Letter to Dr H. Kissinger, dated 18 June 1976, signed by Dr J. L. de Vries, ELCSWA, Bishop L. Auala, ELOC, Bishop R. Koppmann, Catholic Church in South West Africa, Rev. E. Morrow on behalf of Bishop C. O'B. Winter, Anglican Diocese of Damaraland.

6 Quoted in Gerhard Totemeyer, *South West Africa/Namibia: Facts, attitudes, assessment, and prospects,* Fokus Suid Publishers, 1977, pp. 221–22.

7 In 1980–81 the churches' trajectory toward more overt opposition to the state and support for liberation continued. In addition the Catholic Church leadership passed to a Namibian bishop so that all three of the largest churches are now African-led. Parallel to the UN 1981 Geneva talks a Namibia Council of Churches' delegation including senior leaders from all major churches held an ecumenical meeting with national and world church leaders at the World Council of Churches headquarters half a mile away. (Editors' note.)

8 National resistance and the liberation struggle

KIMMO KILJUNEN

I have come to know that our people cannot expect progress as a gift from anyone, be it the United Nations or South Africa. Progress is something we shall have to struggle and work for. And I believe that the only way in which we shall be able and fit to secure that progress is to learn from our own experience and mistakes.

– Herman Toivo ja Toivo, 1967

Tribal resistance

National resistance in Namibia, currently manifest in the armed liberation struggle, dates from the nineteenth century. When the first colonists, the Germans, invaded Namibia at the end of last century, they were met with resistance by different groups. Initially the Germans sought to use sudden attacks to get control. However, these blitzkrieg tactics did not work well and it was realized that a more gradual colonization process would be necessary.

Effective occupation of the south and centre, the Police Zone, took the Germans about ten years. Even then they were continually engaged in armed conflicts, particularly with various Nama and Herero groups. Victory for the Europeans was due, above all, to modern weapons and military technique and to their ability to take full advantage of African inter-tribal frictions. The Germans succeeded not only in preventing any lasting cooperation or military co-ordination among the peoples but also often managed to incite one ethnic group or sub-group against another.

The Africans soon realized that only the colonial power benefited from their internal conflicts. In the early 1890s Hendrik Witbooi succeeded in uniting several Nama tribes, thus marking the beginning of a struggle for liberation from the white occupiers. The insurrection was suppressed in 1894 only after Germany sent military reinforcements. There were two insurrections by the Bondelswart, a small tribe in southern Namibia, at the end of the century. These too were cruelly suppressed.[1] The Bondelswart rose again in 1903, were joined by the Herero and later by the Nama, under the leadership of Hendrik Witbooi, and eventually the rebellion expanded into a nationwide war. Seven thousand African warriors, most without firearms, under the Herero chief, Samuel Maherero, forced the Germans to withdraw to their bases in Windhoek and on the coast to wait for reinforcements from Europe. After these arrived, General von Trotha gave his notorious 'Extermination Order':

Within the German boundaries, every Herero, whether found

> armed or unarmed, with or without cattle, will be shot – I shall not accept any more women and children. I shall drive them back to their people, otherwise I shall order shots to be fired at them.[2]

The war continued until 1907, ending with complete German victory. The Africans suffered great losses and bloodshed: the 80 000-strong Herero tribe was vastly diminished with only some 15 000 starving refugees remaining; half of the Nama and Damara had been killed.[3]

The Germans never extended their administration to the northern area of Ovamboland. They managed to isolate this area, with the highest population and the strongest tribal institutions, from the rest of the country and to use it as a labour reserve so that actual conquest and direct rule was not an early priority. German colonial rule ended during the First World War when South West Africa was invaded in 1915 by 43 000 South African troops.[4] The Africans hoped that with the ending of German rule their land, cattle and political rights would be restored; this had been partly promised by the South Africans. But while the British and South Africans were willing to reveal the brutal atrocities of the German colonial rule, they were not prepared to relinquish any of the privileges acquired by the whites. On the contrary, the new rulers were anxious to unite all the whites, including the Germans, to prevent any African resistance.

In 1915 a war had broken out between the Portuguese, expanding their colony in Angola, and the Kuanyama, the second largest Ovambo tribe. It resulted in the deaths of nearly 5 000 Africans. In 1917 the South Africans decided to intervene in this border dispute as if to protect the Kuanyama. This move ended the quasi-independent position of the Ovambo who now fell under direct South African administration. The South Africans confirmed the borderline drawn by the Portuguese, at least insofar as it affected Ovambo seasonal grazing and village intercourse. The border split the traditional tribal land of the Kuanyama leaving two-thirds of the tribe with the Portuguese and one-third in South West Africa. The Ovambo refused to recognize the arbitrary frontier. A punitive expedition led by South Africans was organized and over a hundred Ovambo were killed, including Chief Mandume, a powerful anticolonial tribal leader. From that time Ovamboland was fully colonized and split between the South African and Portuguese colonies.[5]

Compared to German colonial rule, the South African administration made no apparent changes, apart from expelling some German ranchers in favour of South Africans, and seizing and carrying out a similar reallocation of plunder in minerals. Nor were the Namibians any more content. In 1922 the Bondelswart again revolted, criticizing the system of compulsory labour for white farms and the atrocious conduct of colonial administrators. They were attacked by South African troops, assisted by aerial bombing and cavalry, and over a hundred Bondelswart men, women and children died, together with two government soldiers.[6]

In 1925 the Rehoboth people rose against land robbery, exorbitant taxation and the destruction of their community's autonomy. The uprising was cruelly suppressed and the remnants of self-rule, under their written constitution and treaties with the Germans, were wiped out. In 1932 an Ovambo tribe, the Kwambi, revolted against the high burden of taxes. The South African government replied with a punitive expedition devastating the tribe's capital, and exiling its chief.[7]

During the following years, African dissatisfaction with South African rule spread from one population group to another. The protests of a younger generation were added to the scattered revolts led by traditional tribal leaders. After the Second World War Africans looked hopefully to the United Nations which had inherited supervisory powers over the mandated territory from the defunct League of Nations. Beginning in 1946 with a petition from the Herero and Nama chiefs to the United Nations' Fourth Committee, the Namibians launched a diplomatic campaign which they were to sustain until the present. As many as 120 separate petitions were sent to the United Nations between 1946 and 1960. However, although a long sequence of petitions, discussions and resolutions has followed, they have yielded little in the way of concrete results.

Within Namibia, traditional tribal leaders such as Hosea Kutako and Samuel Witbooi continued to hold key positions in organizing resistance which took a tribal form during the early years. The outlet for dissatisfaction was often the chief's conclave with officials of the Bantu Affairs Department. However, it became more obvious that the Namibians should resolve their own problems instead of relying too much on outside initiatives or expecting changes to result from voluntary South African actions.

Organizing the national liberation movement

During the 1950s the resistance led by traditional chiefs and their councils gradually became secondary, and this decade saw the transition to national mobilization rather than tribal methods of protest. The contract workers began striking more widely, student societies and new types of political organizations were founded. It became evident that an organization was needed that was capable of mobilizing the whole people and of coordinating localized strikes, sporadic anti-colonial demonstrations, and individual or small group petitions to the United Nations into a united nationwide protest movement.

The wave of nationalism which swept over the African continent had its effect in Namibia. Ghana, led by Kwame Nkrumah, as the first independent country in Black Africa, was an inspiring example for the young nationalists. Equally, Namibians saw that colonies were becoming independent. In particular they knew that other ex-German colonies, Togo, Cameroon, Tanzania, were, by the late 1950s, on the eve of independence.[8]

In the early 1950s there were several strikes when African workers demanded pay rises. These were not the first manifestations of resistance by Namibian workers: as early as 1893 African workers at the Otavi copper mine struck for better working conditions and better pay; the first African political organizations and trade unions had been founded in Lüderitz in the 1920s (the most influential being the Universal Negro Improvement Association and the Industrial and Commercial Workers' Union) having branches also in Windhoek and Walvis Bay. But, on the whole, previous workers' protests had been limited to individual acts: absenteeism, desertions or sporadic cases of violence. After the Second World War larger-scale demonstrations by workers took place. In 1948 over 2 000 Ovambo contract workers went on strike at Tsumeb when a white foreman shot and killed a worker, and in 1949 a new and stronger union, the Food and Canning Workers' Union, was founded in Lüderitz, in the then centre of fish canning. It was basically a union for 'Coloured' workers and affiliated to similar bodies in the Republic. At the same time the contract workers from Ovamboland formed a union. Under the Suppression of Communism Act the police arrested and questioned the Union officials and banned all meetings.[9]

Activism increased in the early 1950s as did official retaliation. Trade unionism in Namibia was firmly suppressed after three large strikes of Ovambo contract workers occurred in 1952 and 1953 in Lüderitz and Walvis Bay. After these strikes African unions became illegal in Namibia,[10] but subsequent strikes have expressed the continuing discontent.[11]

In view of these occurrences, it became evident to some Namibians that a transfer of power would not occur without purposeful political actions. The few Namibian students who, in the early 1950s, had studied at schools and colleges in South Africa were strongly impressed by the civil rights movement and campaigns there. In 1952 they founded the South West African Student Body, which in 1955 became the first political party in Namibia, the South West African Progressive Association (SWAPA).[12] At the same time a group of Namibian migrant workers in Capetown, led by Herman Toivo ja Toivo, set up a political organization aimed at protesting against the contract-labour system.

Although students and migrant workers emphasized national objectives in order to overcome tribal divisions, the new organizations were initially tribally based. Nonetheless, all the national groups and parties to emerge later in Namibia have their origins in these student and migrant worker organizations.

The most significant of the new parties was the Ovamboland People's Congress (OPC) founded by Herman Toivo ja Toivo in Capetown in 1957. Toivo was arrested and sent back to Namibia to serve a long period under local arrest in Ovamboland and was thus unable to carry on his political activities. Subsequently OPC was reorganized within Namibia by Sam Nujoma and Jacob Kuhangua and changed its name to the Ovamboland People's Organization (OPO), with branches in Namibia and South Africa.

Initially OPO represented opposition to the contract-labour system. Since the majority of contract workers came from Ovamboland it soon became the interest group of Ovambo workers. Because a majority of Ovambo men must alternate between contract labour in the Police Zone and pseudo-traditional peasant farming in Ovamboland, an Ovambo workers' group began to reflect national demands of Namibian workers. Subsequently, as membership grew, it became less regional and less ethnic in character. In 1960 the organization changed its name to the South West Africa People's Organization (SWAPO), and developed into a national liberation movement. It broadened its programme to include demands for an end to South African colonial administration, the abolition of racial discrimination, rights to freedom of speech and free organization for all Namibians, and majority rule in Namibia. Sam Nujoma was elected president but soon after the movement was established he was forced into exile.[13]

During its early years SWAPO concentrated on building up a nationwide network of branches. The movement drew its support particularly from the northern parts of the country, migrant workers, urban Africans and youth and gradually formed a broad popular front. Military training was started in 1962. Four years later it announced that armed struggle would be launched to liberate Namibia from South African rule and in 1970 declared that it would place primary emphasis on armed struggle. To coordinate and lead this struggle the People's Liberation Army of Namibia (PLAN) was formed.

Two contradictions within the contract system have assisted mobilization. Massive prison-like compounds for single men who need permits to leave them at night give place and time for organization. Rotation back to the 'reserves' at the end of a contract takes the political messages back to the countryside. However, the organization of a national movement has met many obstacles, partly due to the physical conditions in a vast and sparsely populated country, and partly to attempts by the regime to suppress all signs of popular resistance. The division of Namibia into isolated 'reserve' areas and 'Homelands' has made it exceptionally difficult to keep any regular contact between different parts of the country. Persecution and harassment have made open, large-scale political activity almost impossible.

Furthermore, the transition from traditional tribally-based to newer political organizations created some friction. For instance, many chiefs were unwilling to surrender their influence or positions. The fact that many of the leaders were in exile has created additional difficulties, making communication slow and uncertain and sometimes producing different priorities at home and abroad. The necessity to operate on two fronts – both internationally, especially in the United Nations, and within Namibia – has not only been a source of strength but also a considerable weakness.

Other national movements

In 1959 Herero students set up the South West African National Union (SWANU) which aimed at creating a united national movement. Several OPO leaders, including Sam Nujoma, were initially elected to its leadership but the organization failed in its main objective. The SWANU President, a radical student leader, Jariretundu Kozonguizi, and the exiled Sam Nujoma met in Monrovia in 1960, and signed a letter calling for a merger of their organizations in Namibia, but the division remained.[14]

Another attempt at uniting these two organizations was made in 1963. The two executives decided to merge into the South West Africa National Liberation Front (SWANLIF) but again, unity was not achieved.[15] In 1963 SWANU refused to organize the military units recommended by the Organization for African Unity (OAU), thus losing its future OAU support. It was further weakened by a leadership crisis in 1966. Meanwhile SWAPO became increasingly influential both politically and militarily.

In their initial programmes SWAPO and SWANU did not differ a great deal. Personal and tribal conflicts seem to have been the major reasons for division, although it has been claimed that SWANU's pro – Chinese stance in Soviet–Chinese disputes of the 1960s revealed an ideological difference between the two as SWAPO did not take sides in the conflict.[16] In any case, by the 1970s SWANU had become essentially a student organization in exile, with an internal faction of rather more conservative leanings, almost totally Herero membership, and uneasily supporting 'third way' groupings between the South African-backed parties and SWAPO.

Initially the Herero Chiefs' Council (which had initiated petitioning to the United Nations) gave its support to SWANU, but gradually the tribal leaders began to fear the radical young men in SWANU. In 1964 a new organization was founded, the National Democratic Organization (NUDO), backed by such prominent personalities as Hosea Kutako, Samuel H. Witbooi and Clemens Kapuuo. There have been attempts to present NUDO as a nationwide organization but, in practice, it represents the Herero Chiefs' Council,[17] particularly since the main members of the (Nama) Witbooi family declared support for SWAPO in the mid-1970s.

Mburumba Kerina, who had been expelled from SWAPO in the early 1960s and had acted as a petitioner in the United Nations, announced in New York in 1966 that yet another unity movement, the South West Africa National United Front (SWANUF), had been established. It was said to be a merger of SWAPO and SWANU, but the leaders of both parties denied this. SWANUF seems to be merely a group appearing in United Nations lobbies and in some foreign universities, although a 'domestic branch' was established by representatives of Herero and Nama groups in Windhoek in 1974.[18]

In 1962 an independent liberation movement, the Caprivi African National Union (CANU), was formed in Caprivi. Because of the strategic importance of the Caprivi Strip, the South African government launched particularly strong repressive measures, banning the movement and arresting part of its leadership. As a separatist movement CANU had no chance of success and in 1965 joined SWAPO.[19] In 1980 a handful of ex-CANU members sought to recreate it and were in consequence expelled from SWAPO.

The last attempt to form a united front of political and tribal organizations actively opposing the South African administration was made in 1972. A joint National Convention was set up in connection with the visit to Namibia of Kurt Waldheim, Secretary-General of the United Nations. The National Convention brought together six political parties: SWAPO, NUDO, SWANU, the Voice of the People, NAPDO and the Rehoboth Volkspartei,* and it had the support of the Herero, Damara and Nama Chiefs' Councils and the African churches.[20]

However, the work of the National Convention soon became difficult, partly because of political differences, partly because of personal and tribal frictions. Furthermore, it did not recognize SWAPO as the leading national liberation movement. Subsequently in 1975 SWAPO and some other radical groups withdrew. These groups, SWAPO, SWANU, NAPDO, Rehoboth Volkspartei and the SWAPO Youth League, set up a more progressive Namibia National Convention (NNC) but this loose coalition disbanded in 1977. Within Namibia SWAPO has been prepared to support any umbrella convention which might promote national unity. However, internationally the movement has made it clear that it wanted to be recognized as the sole representative of the Namibian people, because it alone constitutes an effective opposition to South Africa.

There are currently some thirty parties or political groups in Namibia, including the white and Bantustan parties.[21] This proliferation is primarily due to the South African policy of separate development, which groups people on the basis of ethnic origins and has produced many political parties, all fairly insignificant, each representing only one ethnic group.

Several smaller local and tribal organizations have joined SWAPO, such as Rehoboth Volkspartei and NAPDO in autumn 1976. At the same time four other important groups in south Namibia, including the Nama Chiefs' Council, joined SWAPO. Together these

---

* NAPDO (Namibia African Peoples' Democratic Organization) is mainly supported by the Damara, whereas the Voice of the People has predominantly Damara and Nama support, and is closely linked to SWANUF. The Rehoboth Volkspartei, as its name implies, is active amongst the Rehobother. The parties are relatively small, even though they seem to have certain influence and significance among the people they represent.

Other parties in Namibia are, *inter alia*, the Labour Party (formerly the Federal Coloured People's Party of SWA) which claims to represent the 'Coloured' population. Rehoboth Baster Verening and Rehoboth Bevrydings Party have been in opposition to the larger Rehoboth Volkspartei. These three parties support the South African policy of separate development and self-determination for the Bantu homelands, and are justifiably afraid that the groups they represent will lose their existing privileges in a unitary state.

Whenever new self-governing homelands for Africans were founded, it was necessary to establish their own party machinery, partly based on previous tribal institutions. As an example, there are two Ovambo parties: Ovambo Independent Party (OIP) led by Pastor Ndjoba, which follows the government line, and the Democratic Co-operative Development Party (DEMCOP) led by Johannes Nangutuuala, which is in opposition. Similar types of parties are the Nama Organizations for South West Africa (NOSWA), Damara United Front (DUF), and National Independence Party (NIP) representing 'Coloureds'. These parties have been nothing more than instruments of South African rule, notwithstanding their shrill rhetoric during 'Homeland' elections.

Until the 1970s whites were almost unanimously behind the South West Africa Nationalist Party. Until quite recently there has been no progressive opposition (liberal or leftist oriented) to the apartheid policy of the government. The National Union Party failed in Namibia as it did in the Republic and the United Party became dormant before re-emerging as the Federal Party in the late 1970s.

groups represented 80% of the Nama people. In 1977 a group representing a substantial fraction of the Herero people also affiliated. This meant that the political influence of SWAPO covered the whole country, whereas earlier its sphere of influence was predominantly in the central and northern areas of Namibia.

Anti-SWAPO alliances

In 1977 the fact that South Africa had to recognize, however nominally, Namibia's right to independence as at least a federated unit (not a series of Bantustans), and to allow Africans to participate in general elections, however rigged, gave impetus to new political parties. Their objective has been to find an acceptable and effective counter force against SWAPO, and to protect a white-led, free-enterprise economy. Attempts have been made to replace the regionally scattered parties with new groups of a national character.

In that spirit, the tribally-based groups which took part in the Turnhalle constitutional talks formed a party called the Democratic Turnhalle Alliance (DTA) in 1977. In addition to the whites, led by Dirk Mudge and his all-white Republican Party, the alliance comprises representatives of the African elite from different parts of the country, mostly tribal chiefs, leaders of Bantustan parties and the 'Homelands' administrative elite. It is also supported (perhaps by a majority of) the Rehoboth and 'Coloured' communities who fear that their relatively privileged position vis-à-vis blacks will be changed with majority rule. The DTA enjoys official South African backing.

Its programme is based on the Turnhalle draft constitution and is in line with the prevailing system, except that it demands formal independence for Namibia and some reforms to improve the social status of the African elite (both traditional and modern). It aims to retain the tribally-based administration and a government consisting of representatives from the various ethnic groups, with each group (whether white or 'bushman') having the right to veto any decisions.

The DTA proposes higher wages, an end to job reservation and to residential discrimination, more posts for Africans within the upper salary brackets and business circles, as well as the removal of race bars on the purchase of land. The DTA's programme would protect the social *status quo* while introducing some reforms in apartheid legislation and offering Africans access to junior administrative posts. It would pave the way for the emergence of a loyal African middle class.

Among whites, the DTA has the backing of some ranchers and small businessmen, senior civil servants, 'Homeland' administrators and much of the professional and big-business managerial community. The English- and German-speaking white population supports the DTA as offering a chance to undermine Afrikaner hegemony. After a leadership struggle in the South West Africa National Party, Dirk Mudge founded the Republican Party, which joined to DTA.

The National Party fiercely opposes the DTA package as too radical and formed an electoral alliance called Aktur (Aksiefront vir die Behoud van die Turnhalle–Beginsels) with some 'Coloured' representatives. It is, in turn, criticized by the extreme right-wing Herstigte

Nasionale Party (HNP), a branch of the South African HNP. Between them, the Aktur and HNP hold the allegiance of a majority (mostly Afrikaners) of the white settlers and expatriates. They represent most white wage earners and ranchers, and some small businessmen. They also control the South West Africa administration, including the police and municipal services. For them, any changes in apartheid legislation or any black government more independent than a Bantustan one, would be real threats. Politically these parties, having lost the support of the South African regime, have no future.

Some small parties which had been left out of the Turnhalle talks, including SWANU, SWANUF and the Voice of the People, formed the Namibian National Front (NNF). A late affiliate was the small white-liberal party, the Federal Party, which is similar to the Republic's Progressive Federal Party, with a membership mainly of English-speaking senior managers and professionals. It is perhaps significant that it is apparently backed by the Anglo American corporation and the *Rand Daily Mail* as the means to achieve an orderly, multi-racial, liberal, capitalist 'solution'. NNF flirted with Andreas Shipanga's so-called SWAPO Democrats – somewhat misnamed as the Party's policy is mainly based on virulent hatred for SWAPO (see p. 167).

NNF wants to perform the role of a middle alternative between the right (DTA) and the left (SWAPO). To date it has primarily concentrated on accusations against SWAPO and on its own internal problems. In mid-1979 it appeared to be in a state of chaos, with the Federal Party at least temporarily disaffiliated.[22] It is seeking support, above all, amongst SWAPO's potential supporters. Because it is not immediately identifiable with the old regime and its programme aims at abolishing all forms of apartheid, it escapes being seen as an instrument of the South African regime. Its demands for political independence and for a non-racialist society are not supported by a programme of social transformation, and thus the party has escaped persecution by the government. The NNF has been in a state of flux for 18 months with the Federal Party apparently out and SWAPO(D) – which may itself have split – not quite in. It appears rather analogous to the Holy Roman Empire – neither Namibian, National nor a Front.

The NNF did boycott, and indeed denounce, the 1978 'election' and has declined to be co-opted to the resultant National Assembly. It does – or at least SWANU and SWAPO(D) do – call for United Nations-prepared and monitored elections.[23] The alliance supports rapid expansion of training and promotion of Africans, the phasing out of migrant labour, abandonment of racial discrimination in wages and salaries, help for African businessmen, as well as gradual land redistribution. But the NNF has remained a coalition of *de facto* racial and tribal parties; it has consistently rejected any resort to effective resistance; it has no clear political economic programme for transforming the role of the large companies; as far as agrarian reform is concerned, its aim is to pave the way for black agro-business. It would safeguard the long-term interests of big multi-national (mining) companies at the expense (relatively speaking) of the white wage and salary earners, ranchers, South African business interests and small white entrepreneurs.[24]

The role of the church

The church has played an important part in the evolution of resistance in Namibia, a country where a huge proportion of the population consists of practising Christians. African churches have taken an increasingly strong stand against apartheid, and have demanded the right of self-determination for the Namibian people. The multi-racial Anglican Church has most explicitly condemned government policies, and consequently been harassed by the authorities. Those working for the church have been persecuted and their activities limited.*

The attitudes of the Lutheran Ovambo–Kavango Church and the churches of the Rhenish Missionary Society changed gradually from apolitical to actively political. Formerly mission churches with totally African congregations, these churches have since the 1950s had a black clerical leadership. This process of politicization became overt in 1971 when the two bishops Leonard Auala and Paulus Gowaseb sent an open letter to Prime Minister Vorster and a pastoral letter to their congregations, strongly condemning the apartheid policy and urging members to further mutual understanding and cooperation between different races (see page 137).

Active participation in social affairs by the largest African churches has not only reflected the aspirations of their members, but has also directly led to their congregations supporting the national struggle for liberation in Namibia.[25]

The liberation struggle

While Namibian resistance has taken several forms and been institutionalized in many ways, and while there are many groups working against the apartheid system and for political independence and majority rule, in practice there is only one major national political organization, SWAPO. This has been recognized by several international bodies, in particular the Organization for African Unity and the United Nations. The latter recognized SWAPO in 1973 as the national liberation movement and authentic representative of the Namibian people. In 1976 this recognition was made exclusive and SWAPO was given full observer status at the General Assembly, with participation rights in all United Nations agencies.

Four stages can be distinguished in SWAPO's struggle for national liberation. First, in the late 1950s the national movement was established. Second, in the early 1960s popular political mobilization began.

* The other multi-racial church, the Roman Catholic Church, has been passive and maintained a good relationship with the government until quite recently. Its position has now shifted somewhat with the result that proposed publications have been banned and at least one member deported. The Dutch Reformed Church is a central ideological mainstay of white rule and provides the spiritual and moral justification for apartheid.

Third, in the late 1960s non-violent resistance and mass demonstrations were complemented by the establishment of a guerrilla network and by the beginnings of armed operations. Fourth, in the 1970s the armed liberation struggle assumed primary importance.

In the early stages it was most important to create a political organization to coordinate the previously spontaneous and scattered anti-colonial activities. Mobilization of the people could not happen spontaneously, but:

> a political organization was needed by which the politically conscious elements of society could come into a direct and constant contact with the broad masses of the people, to give articulate expression to the problems, aspirations and hopes of the masses.[26]

Initially the movement consisted only of some activists, students or migrant workers, whose influence was dependent on the extent to which they could reflect the needs and aspirations of the masses. To succeed it could not become an isolated elite, nor could it simply declare itself to be a vanguard fighting for the interests of the people. At first SWAPO concentrated on immediate problems such as arbitrary residential relocations and contract workers' problems as a way of involving people in political activities and of increasing their awareness and courage to organize.

Unlike some other colonial powers in Africa, but like the Portuguese and Rhodesian rebels' governments, South Africa was not willing to consent to any of the demands of the national movements. Consequently, African nationalists were left with no alternative but to organize for a liberation struggle. It took SWAPO a relatively short time in the early 1960s to establish a network of national branches, with the objective of organizing workers in towns and mines, and peasants, farm labourers, school children and women.

SWAPO's quasi-legal existence in Namibia has given it some advantages and South Africa, afraid of the international consequences, has not dared to declare SWAPO illegal. On the other hand, the South African government no doubt calculated that an organization with nominal freedom would be more 'moderate' than an underground movement and has tried to create a split between those freedom fighters who work within the country and those in exile. The government has been able to control SWAPO's activities, to restrict its freedom of action as far as publications and public meetings are concerned, and to keep the internal leaders under surveillance. Many prominent SWAPO leaders have been held in detention in Windhoek and Walvis Bay or deported to the prison of Robben Island in South Africa. In 1979 there were 400 SWAPO members imprisoned on Robben Island and several thousands detained in prisons and concentration camps in Namibia.

As a result of this repression, SWAPO has been forced underground to conduct its most strategic activities and to change its organization. The former open branches have been replaced by smaller cells whose activities are coordinated either directly at the local level or by regional leadership. The country has been divided into seven regions with regional leaders responsible to the national leadership. The supreme organ, the National Congress, elects as the policy-making body the National Executive and the Central Committee. In mid-1979 most members of the National Executive and the Central Committee were working in exile, mainly in SWAPO's headquarters in Lusaka, and virtually the entire SWAPO territorial and regional leadership based in Namibia had been detained. SWAPO closed its offices after the national headquarters in Windhoek had been raided allegedly by right-wing extremists, the 'White Resistance Movement'. One of the first issues on the agenda for the new so-called National Assembly in 1979 was formally to outlaw SWAPO.[27]

Non-violent action

Initially the national movement used non-violent methods, strikes, demonstrations, petitions and boycotts, to oppose the colonial regime. The regime, however, was not prepared to tolerate even minimal manifestations of opposition, and suppressed them. Methods of suppression were violent: in 1959 police and army opened fire on unarmed civilians during a peaceful demonstration in Windhoek, killing eleven and wounding over fifty people.[28] (See page 93.)

In 1963 it became almost impossible to hold public meetings and South Africa extended its 'security legislation' to Namibia. All publications became subject to censorship, the secret police and the security police widened their areas of activity and detention without trial was practised. SWAPO members were dismissed from jobs and schools, and expelled from urban areas. The absence of the most elementary political freedoms and rights, combined with police and military repression, made it increasingly apparent that the struggle for liberation could not be carried out solely by constitutional, non-violent means. As SWAPO's President Sam Nujoma stated:

> We have tried to solve our problems by peaceful means. In order to resolve this problem without bloodshed, we have repeatedly demanded that the South African Government should hand over the power to the Namibian people. We have tried peaceful manifestations in order to try to convince the regime of the unanimous nature of the African people's will to accede to independence and nationhood. South Africa either turned a deaf ear to all our attempts or met them with violent methods . . . it was after all our efforts to reach a peaceful solution had resulted in a stalemate, that my organization decided to embark upon armed resistance as the only remaining means open to us. The decision to initiate armed resistance is by no means an easy one, and I for one was at pains to agree to such a decision, but when my people have said 'enough', it is enough.[29]

When the International Court of Justice made its decision in 1966, stating that it could not hear challenges to the validity of the mandate because Ethiopia and Liberia had not the legal standing to raise them, SWAPO concluded that it could not expect any help from international law either. In August 1966 SWAPO launched the first attacks on the administrative centre of Oshikango in Ovamboland and on a South African military camp in Ongurumbashe in the extreme north-western part of Namibia. The South Africans retaliated with mass arrests of SWAPO members. In 1967 the South African Parliament enacted a new security law, the Terrorism Act, made retroactive to 1962, which authorized the death penalty and turned ordinary acts into major crimes if they had been committed with the intention of undermining 'law and order'.[30] According to the Act 'terrorism' is defined to include 'prejudicing any industry or undertaking or production or distribution of commodities or foods', encouraging 'social or economic change by force or violence' or 'causing financial loss to any person or the state'.

Several important political trials have been conducted in Namibia under the Terrorism Act. The first took place in 1967 and 37 men (Herman Toivo ja Toivo being one of them) were accused of 'terrorism' and given long prison sentences on Robben Island. In later trials some of the accused were sentenced to death and executed. In political trials it is common for the security police to be responsible for interrogation. Thus the cases are virtually decided before the accused are brought to court. There is increasing evidence of the use of torture to force the accused to give information or confess to the police.[31]

Guerrilla warfare

Arrests and repression by the government have not stopped the armed liberation struggle. Guerrilla operations spread in the northern parts of the country and rapidly advanced as far south as Tsumeb and Grootfontein. PLAN has had four operational zones in Namibia where guerrillas are well established and active on a day-to-day basis: the north-western (Kaokoveld), the northern (Ovamboland, Okavango), the central (Grootfontein District), and the north-eastern zone (the Caprivi Strip) (see Map 8.1). All these operational zones are in the north, where the majority of the Africans live, where geographical conditions are most favourable for guerrilla warfare, and where external support is available.

There are still vast areas where military operations have not begun, although between 1974 and 1980 PLAN extended its military activities towards the central and southern parts of Namibia, even attacking military installations near Windhoek. In 1979 attacks well south of Tsumeb–Grootfontein led to South Africa extending its 'operational zone' virtually to the Windhoek urban boundary. But, on the whole, the underground units of PLAN in the central and southern regions do mostly organizational work and training.[32]

PLAN tactics have been mainly to harass by sabotage, mine laying, ambushes and surprise attacks. Earlier, targets were mainly military convoys and patrols, bridges, strategic infrastructure and police stations; later some attacks were directed at larger military installations, such as military camps and bases and air bases. Mines on military roads have been particularly effective and have damaged the network of military roads built in the Caprivi and Okavango districts to such an extent that the South African army has been forced to rely more frequently on air and water transport. A military escort system has also been introduced for civilian travellers on the main roads from Tsumeb to Ruacana and to Kaokoveld. In addition more white settlers have sold their farms and moved away from SWAPO's operational zones.

In autumn 1977 Major General Black, Director General of the South African Defence Forces' military operations in Namibia, disclosed in Johannesburg that his troops 'were involved in about a hundred clashes with terrorists a month'. He estimated that the PLAN had 2 000 armed men in Angola, 1 400 in Zambia and 300 in Ovamboland,[33] an estimate that was probably too low.

Geographical conditions in Namibia are not very favourable to guerrilla warfare. There are only a few large forests, swamps or mountainous areas, most of the country being open grassland. This makes guerrilla units very vulnerable to air raids. Long distances and sparse population hinder communications. This means that the PLAN units must be small and extremely mobile, operating from constantly changing bases. The objective, naturally, is to extend the operational zones to cover the whole of Namibia:

> We do not, for the time being, claim to have liberated areas, but we do have large areas which are under our control. These areas contain hundreds of thousands of peasants. In these areas our fighters are running some semi-administrative functions such as medical and social services and as yet at a small scale they teach the people to read and write. It is true also, that up to now, the enemy does send its superior number of forces into these areas. But since it cannot maintain forces there permanently it naturally will leave a much weaker number behind which soon becomes an easy target of the guerrillas.[34]

It is doubtful whether SWAPO will be able, and indeed whether it will aim to create liberated areas – as the liberation movements in the former Portuguese colonies did – because the physical conditions are so dissimilar. However, SWAPO has more or less permanent control over an ever-increasing area. For example, there are some areas in Ovamboland which have been called semi-liberated by the local people, because SWAPO guerrillas have free access to them and the South African army and local administration have been unable to keep constant control over them (see Map 8.1).[35]

It has been important for SWAPO to establish military training centres and camps on a more or less permanent basis inside Namibia, especially as the guerrilla fighters trained or operating from abroad have found it difficult to get access to the country and to establish contact with local people. SWAPO guerrillas have been trained in Egypt (where the first group went in 1962), in Tanzania, Zambia, Algeria and in some European socialist countries. Most recently, independent Angola, in addition to Zambia, has become the central external base for SWAPO camps and military training. SWAPO's first military camp in Namibia was set up in 1964.

Those who have been trained abroad enter the country and aim to set up rural bases for training and organizing the local people. Often the best fighters are peasants who live and work at home but from time to time join the guerrillas. They know the terrain, the local people, the traditions of the area, and are not easily controlled and identified. Contacts with the local population are crucial as local support and protection are vital in guerrilla warfare. Most supplies, food, clothing and medicines come from the villagers. Thus the basic SWAPO units in the villages bear a large responsibility in ensuring that the guerrillas obtain material support.

Counter-measures by the South African regime

The expansion of the liberation struggle led the South African government to strengthen military counter-measures. Training of police and military personnel in tropical and counter-insurgent warfare began in Walvis Bay. In 1979 martial law was extended to cover all northern and central areas, including the capital, Windhoek, that is, practically half of the country, affecting 80% of Namibia's population.[36] At the same time a dusk to dawn curfew was imposed in the north where 50% of the population lives. The Caprivi Strip, of particular strategic importance, has been completely closed off and constantly patrolled by South African reconnaissance planes, helicopters and fast river launches.

The change of regime in Lisbon and the consequent independence of Angola intensified South Africa's concern about security along

TABLE 8.1 South African Forces in Northern Namibia in 1977

Permanent Units	
5 Infantry Battalions	3 500
3 South African Police 'coin' Battalions	2 100
1 Ovambo-Kavango Battalion	700
3 FNLA/UNITA, 1 ex-Rhodesian mercenary Battalions	2 100
Combat Support Units (light artillery, signals, engineer and medical units)	8 400
Reaction Force	
1 Armoured Battalion	500
2 Mechanised Battalions	1 000
1 Light Infantry Battalion	700
1 Parachute Battalion	700
Combat Support Units	2 900
*Logistic Support**	
Signal engineer, medical, quartermaster, technical and intelligence units	22 600
Air Force	
Helicopter and light strike, transport and liaison aircraft and supporting units	8 000
Total	53 200 men**

Source: *Namibia Today*, Vol. 1, No. 2, 1977, p.7.
* This does not include local police.
** 1980 estimates total about 70 000.

TABLE 8.2 Some of the South African Military Bases in Namibia in 1979

Northern Operational Area	
Northern Operational Zone Command, South African Air and Strike Force Headquarters	Grootfontein
Ovamboland	
Armoured Brigade and Infantry Brigade Headquarters, Parachute Battalion	Ondangwa
South African Police Battalion Headquarters	Oshakati
Mechanised and Infantry Battalions, Parachute Units and UNITA groups	Ruacana Falls
Mechanised Battalion	Oshikango
South African Police and Infantry Battalions	Eenhana
Infantry Battalions and Parachute Units	Nkongo
Infantry Battalions	Ombalantu, Onuno, Oshigambo and Oshivelo
'Homeland' Battalion	Oluno
Infantry Companies	Etale, Ogongo, Ohanguena, Okahau, Okankolo, Okatopeonjanja, Omungwelume, Otapi and Tsandi
UNITA groups	Elundu, Okalongo and Omundongilo
Kaokoveld	
Infantry Company	Ohopoho
'Homeland' Battalion	Opuro
Kavango	
Infantry Brigade Headquarters, Parachute Units, 'Homeland' Battalion and UNITA groups	Rundu
South African Police Battalion and UNITA groups	Kuringkuru
Infantry Companies	Katuitul and Bwambata
UNITA groups	Omauni
Caprivi Strip	
South African Air and Strike Force command base and Infantry Battalion	Katima Mulilo
Infantry Battalions	Andara and Singalamwea
'Homeland' Battalions	Mpacha and Omega
Police Zone	
South West Africa Command, South African Police Battalion, Mechanised and Infantry Brigades, air base, UNITA groups	Windhoek
Mechanised and Infantry Battalions, naval and air bases, Counter-Insurgency Training Centre	Walvis Bay
Infantry Battalion	Otjiwarongo
Infantry Battalion and air base	Gobabis
Infantry Battalion and air base	Keetmanshoop
Bushmanland Battalion	Tsumeb
Baster Battalion	Rehoboth

Sources: *Namibia Today*, Vol. 7, No. 2, 1977; *Current Events in Namibia*, No. 3–7, 1974–76; Kimmo and Marja-Liisa Kiljunen, *Report on Visit to Namibia*, Brighton, 1978 (mimeo); *Windhoek Observer*, 9 February 1980.

Namibia's 1 200-kilometre-long border with Angola. In June 1974, just after the Portuguese coup, the then South African Minister of Defence, Piet Botha, announced that police units in the Caprivi Strip would be replaced by permanent army units. It was also announced that African troops, previously used in a non-combatant role, would henceforth be armed and used to guard military installations and to take part in military activities.[37]

Mobile reaction forces were created to facilitate rapid intervention, and the army improved its general mobility, fire power, communications and reconnaissance capacity. In addition to helicopters and Land Rovers, the troops in northern Namibia used heavier weapons such as combat aircraft, tanks and armoured cars. The old bases in Walvis Bay, Grootfontein, Windhoek, Rundu, Ondangwa and Katima Mulilo were modernized and extended, and about twenty new military bases established throughout the northern parts of the country (see Table 8.2 and Map 8.1.)[38]

Grootfontein became the command base of the northern military zone and the most important air bases were situated in Ondangwa, Runtu, and Katima Mulilo. Furthermore, smaller bases and military camps were scattered along the border between Namibia and Angola. Microwave transmitters (installed by the British company Marconi and the German companies Siemens and AEG-Telefunken) connected these bases and camps with the commando base in Grootfontein and with Walvis Bay, Lüderitz and Windhoek, the latter the headquarters for South African military operations in the country. This massive armament runs completely counter to the provisions of the mandate, supposedly respected by the South African government, whereby South Africa has no right to set up military installations nor to have regular troops in Namibian territory.

South African military operations in Namibia have also destroyed the peace and security of neighbouring countries. The South African air force has used the Katima Mulilo base for frequent operations into Zimbabwe and Zambia, and Angola has been attacked from northern Namibian bases.[39] These attacks aimed both at destroying SWAPO camps and at destabilizing the respective governments.

In 1979 it is estimated that South Africa had some 60 000 men in Namibia of whom over 50 000 were in northern parts of the country (see Table 8.1). It is also estimated that there were a further 15 000 FNLA and UNITA elements, including those being trained and organized as strike forces to destabilize the Angolan state and those who were essentially resident mercenaries fighting against SWAPO. With Namibia as their base and South African supplies and air cover, UNITA troops have continually penetrated Angolan territory. There was even a rather fanciful plan to unite the Ovambo people in southern Angola and in Namibia and to form an independent UNITA-controlled buffer state[40] between Namibia and Angola or to seize the Calueque area, partly for the same reason, partly to allow operation of the Kunene power–irrigation scheme. Some civilians fleeing the fighting have been transported to Namibia to form additional troops for UNITA. In 1979 there were over 25 000 Angolan refugees in

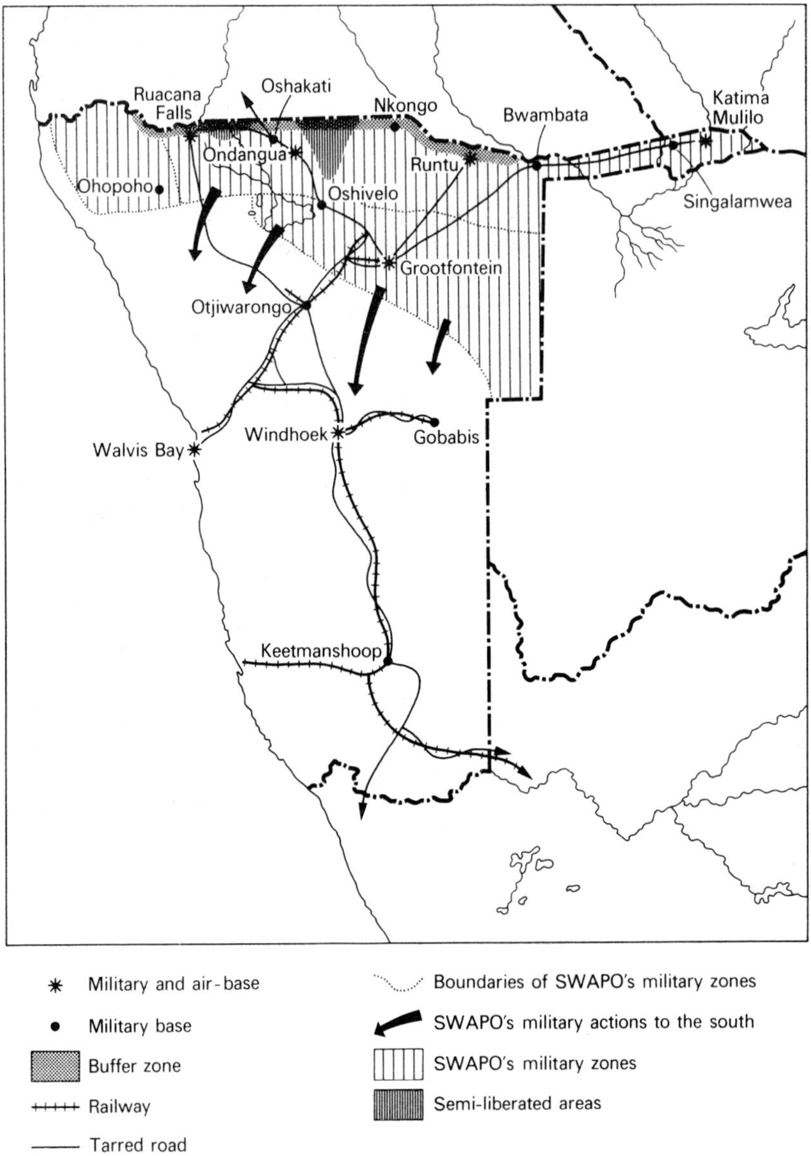

Map 8.1 The military situation in Namibia

Namibia, including 15 000 military.[41] It has been speculated that South Africa is trying to evacuate the countryside on the Angolan side of the border in order to facilitate the control of guerrilla movements. Tactics have included disguising UNITA men as SWAPO soldiers who attacked villages on both sides of the border, burning houses and stealing cattle. These are obvious attempts to turn the people against SWAPO and at the same time to transfer population from strategic areas to South African army-controlled 'security villages' in Namibia. Raids were stepped up, especially against Angola, in 1980. A major invasion designed to crush SWAPO's base forces and install a UNITA puppet regime in south-east Angola in mid-1980 was a failure on both counts. As a result Major-General Geldenhuys (who, ironically, advised against it and has indicated both that troops cannot bring security to white ranchers and that the future for Namibia is 'one man, one vote' with minority safeguards), was removed as head of the south-west command and re-posted in the Republic.

The South African government has also started to recruit Namibians for military service on tribal lines. In 1976 the first 'Homeland' armies were founded in Ovamboland and Kavango and in 1977 the recruitment of Africans for military service began in the southern part of the country, particularly among 'bushmen' and Rehobothers. The South African plan is for eleven tribal armies along the division of the 'Homelands', under SADF command.[42] The government has also transferred black troops from parts of South Africa such as Transkei. They have suffered heavy casualties, because they are always used in the more perilous situations such as at the front of convoys and in the front line during attack.

In September 1979 General Geldenhuys, then still commanding SWA Command, announced that 'in accordance with political developments in SWA a start had been made to create a SWA Defence Force which would be handed over to the government of the territory after independence'. The statement continued projecting the future:

> After independence it would be the exclusive prerogative of the government in power, whatever political force that might be, to conclude pacts, including defence pacts, with whatever country it wanted. If the Republic of South Africa is approached and the two parties find agreement, the possibility is not excluded that seconded (South African) defence units may find themselves in SWA.[43]

In addition to South African army and police structures there are several private white military organizations, such as local commandos and the Citizen Forces, and since mid-1970 private 'security firms' using mercenaries have rapidly expanded under the auspices of the South African security forces. Two all white Ku-Klux-Klan style groups have been organized, Blankswa formed by young Afrikaners and Wit Weerstandsbeweging by Germans. Those groups have drawn up a death list including several SWAPO leaders, churchmen and progressive intellectuals.[44] Some black members and supporters of DTA have also been issued with fire-arms by the security police. According to a local newspaper, 'there is no denial today that the private arsenals of the private armies far exceed the fire power in the hands of the police'.[45]

In 1975 South African forces started a comprehensive clearing of a 'no-go free-fire zone' along the Namibian border with Angola. A strip of land 600 kilometres long and between one and two kilometres wide was cleared of all inhabitants – some 20 000 people were resettled – and of all trees and bushes. Buildings such as schools, churches and hospitals were taken over for military purposes and security measures dictated that any unauthorized person moving in the buffer zone could be shot. A very poisonous plant, Mexican sisal, was planted in the area. This plant can give a deep cut which turns septic, and infection spreads through the body of a victim causing death.

Northern Namibia has also been subject to enforced resettlement schemes. In Caprivi and Okavango, according to different estimates, some 20 000–50 000 civilian Africans have been moved from traditional living areas into strategic hamlets guarded by the army. In many villages people opposed the order to move but were forced to do so. Nonetheless, houses and crops were burnt, hundreds of villagers arrested, and in several cases people were reported to have been killed, with reports suggesting total deaths to have been in dozens. At least 4 000 refugees moved from the Caprivi Strip to Zambia or Botswana.

Anti-guerrilla warfare has become increasingly cruel. Villages and forest areas where the presence of guerrillas is suspected have become targets of air raids and sporadic bombing; chemical warfare has poisoned rivers, ponds and cultivated land.[46] The paramilitary security forces have begun systematically to terrorize civilians and a network of detention centres and electric torture chambers has been established. Quite frequently ordinary people have been arrested by the security police and tortured or flogged, sometimes in public, especially in northern areas.[47] Penalties for imprisoned SWAPO soldiers, as well as villages thought to have given them help, are even more severe.

There is also evidence of massacres by South African troops. In 1968 sixty-three people were killed during forced removals of the population of a village called Linyant in the Singalamwe district of the Caprivi Strip. Over a hundred Africans were murdered during the State of Emergency proclaimed in Ovamboland in early 1972. A mass grave in Ohanuanga stands as a memorial to the returning men from the contract-workers' strike who became victims of the shooting. In September 1973 South African forces attacked a village in the Caprivi Strip killing a hundred and five people. In April 1977 the bodies of thirty women were brought to Oshakati; they had been shot when gathering food outside the village of Ikalongo. In the autumn of 1978 a church coach hit a mine near Nkongo causing the death of sixteen people.[48] The mine had probably been laid by South African troops trying to influence the negotiations of the Western Foreign Ministers visiting Windhoek and Pretoria by giving the impression of PLAN 'terrorism'.[49]

In 1978, on Ascension Day, the South African army and air force attacked Namibian refugee camps in Angola.[50] During that one day nine hundred people were killed in a transit camp in Kassinga, some 250 kilometres inside Angola, and nearly two hundred people are thought to have died in camps nearer to the Namibian border. Hundreds more were kidnapped and held in a concentration camp near Mariental in southern Namibia. It appears that the South Africans were taking 'preventive' measures, having calculated that it is better to kill a Namibian while he was still an unarmed refugee rather than wait for him to become an armed guerrilla. The attack would, it was wrongly supposed, also bring to a halt the increasing flow of refugees to Angola.

The escalation of resistance

If the aim of South African troops has been to stop popular support of the liberation movement by brutal reprisals, they have failed badly, for the opposite has happened. Peasant support has grown giving impetus to SWAPO's work of education and mobilization. The number of volunteers wanting to join PLAN has increased. In fact many young men leave their home villages and join in order to avoid punishment or recruitment into the 'Homeland' armies. School classes – often complete with teacher – contact PLAN and move *en bloc* to Angola.[51]

Popular resistance has also taken forms other than armed struggle, including demonstrations and strikes. The most important of these was the nationwide wave of strikes in 1971–72 against the contract-labour system, a show of collective strength, no longer simply individual protests or desertions. This was not the first mass action against the contract system; since the Second World War it is estimated that there have been nearly fifty strikes or go-slows by contract workers.[52] However, the nature of the strikes has changed from actions directed at individuals or against specific acts to broader, more general issues such as wages or working conditions. More recently they became protests against the contract system and colonial administration as such.[53]

In December 1971 Ovambo contract workers went on strike in Windhoek. From there the strike spread rapidly to other industrial and mining centres and by mid-January had affected twenty-three industrial centres, including eleven mines. A total of 20 000 men were on strike. To coordinate strike actions, workers' committees were formed throughout Namibia, the overall militancy and self-confidence of the people greatly increased, and more volunteers than ever before joined PLAN.[54]

The government arrested thirteen men and accused them of having led the strike and gave workers the choice of returning to work or being sent back home. The strikers refused to return to work and when returning home spread unrest in 'Reserve' areas. There were widespread demonstrations in favour of continuing the strike. Government efforts to recruit workers elsewhere failed and consequently a State of Emergency was declared in northern Namibia. Security police and army troops were sent in and there was a complete embargo on news. Over a hundred people were reported shot by the police, and several hundred men and women were arrested and tortured. To regain control of the situation, the government was forced to make some alterations in the conditions of contract work. These were mainly formal changes in terminology or slight pay increases (see p. 123). The restrictions on mobility, enforced separation from families, inadequate wages, and miserable accommodation in compounds all remained.[55]

Though the actual strike movement ended in summer 1972, the labour situation did not return to 'normal'. During the 1970s there was persistent industrial unrest and go-slows and strikes. The underground National Union of Namibian Workers (NUNW), established in the mid-1970s, gained ground and its influence grew particularly in urban areas and mining centres. In 1976 500 workers went on strike and halted work in the strategically crucial and strictly controlled Rossing uranium mine. Military police finally managed to bring the workers back to 'order'. In 1978–79 following the 'election' a series of strikes erupted. These were overtly quasi-economic and quasi-political.[56] However, the South Africans viewed them as political and as related to action by NUNW beginning with a secret organizing campaign in 1978 and including suggestions to workers on ways of demonstrating opposition to the 'elections'.

Popular resistance has also taken other forms. Severe rioting took place in spring 1973, involving some 5 000 African workers in Katutura.[57] This was a protest against the convening of a multi-racial advisory council set up by the South African government. In autumn of the same year a protest was organized in Windhoek against a visit by Prime Minister Vorster to the South West Africa Nationalist Party Congress. Tanks sealed off the area concerned, one protester was killed and at least 300 were arrested.[58]

Opposition to the policy of separate development and the Bantustans has been extremely bitter. In 1973 SWAPO called on the people of Ovamboland to boycott the elections for the Legislative Council. This resulted in massive abstention with only 2% of the electorate going to the polls.[59] In 1975 the assassination of the 'Prime Minister' of Ovamboland, Filemon Elifas, sparked off a series of arrests of SWAPO leaders and members. After the Soweto riots in South Africa in summer 1976 black school children organized and protested against Bantu education. Led by the SWAPO Youth League and the Namibia Black Students Organization (NABSO), the school children and students organized mass rallies and demonstrations and boycotted classes and examinations throughout the country.[60] Teachers in many places have also gone on strike, which has periodically disrupted work in schools.

Confronted with this growing resistance, the South African authorities have resorted to greater repression. Since 1973 mass arrests, raids and detentions have become commonplace and people have been accused of terrorism and detained indefinitely for police interrogation. SWAPO supporters have been expelled from schools and employment. The police have not hesitated to use violence: for example, in April 1975, when black workers in Katutura refused to show their pass-books at the compound gates, the police surrounded the area and fired into an unarmed crowd, killing five workers and wounding at least thirteen others.[61]

Katutura has been a centre of unrest. In spring 1978 conflicts between different political and population groups[62] broke out and at least twenty-six people were killed. These conflicts were partly provoked by the government, and partly reflected political confrontation between DTA and SWAPO supporters. Clemens Kapuuo, the Herero Chief and 'presidential candidate' chosen by South Africa, was murdered – by whom is unclear. In March 1978 some 2 000 workers in the Katutura compound participated in a strike, protesting against the increasing violence and repression.

In the summer of 1979, following the formation of the so-called National Assembly there were widespread arrests in different parts of the country. According to different sources, between 2 400 and 5 000 people were detained in Katutura and held in an open-air detention centre near Windhoek under the provision of Martial Law legislation. There were also reports from other areas that several new detention centres had been established.[63]

In the face of repression by police and army, Namibians have continued to leave the country. It is estimated that in 1979 there were perhaps 50 000 Namibian refugees in Zambia, Botswana and Angola (where the majority are). A high proportion are educated people, such as teachers, nurses and graduates.

The scale of the refugee problem has posed problems for SWAPO. In the mid-1970s young refugees criticized the party leadership, the standards of military training, and the poor conditions in refugee camps. They also demanded that the party congress should convene and that they should be given more influential positions within it. The consequent tension almost split SWAPO. In summer of 1976 the SWAPO leadership, wanting to show that they held full control, imprisoned Andreas Shipanga and ten other opposition leaders in Zambia and arrested several hundred party activists. The latter were soon set free and the leaders released in summer 1978. Shipanga then formed a new party, the SWAPO Democrats, which joined the NNF. Although South African infiltration has been blamed for this split, it was partly related to real material and organizational difficulties for SWAPO which had produced doubts in the minds of at least some refugees.

At the end of the 1970s, although South Africa has been forced to appear to consent to the basic demand for Namibian independence, the process of polarization continues and it appears that reprisals increase in brutality just as the strength of the South African regime in Namibia decreases in reality.

Notes

1 See examples in Helmut Bley, *South West Africa under German Rule 1894–1914*, Heinemann, 1971; J. Goldblatt, *History of South West Africa*, Juta Co., Capetown, 1971, pp. 111–28; Endre Sik, *The History of Black Africa*, Akadémiai Kiadó, Budapest, 1972, Vol. I, pp. 386–87.

2 Quoted in Randolph Vigne, *A Dwelling Place of Our Own*, International Defence and Aid Fund, London, 1973, p. 17.

3 Bley, *South West Africa under German Rule*, pp. 149–52.

4 Ironically, the most militantly nationalist Afrikaners opposed the invasion. They saw the South African government as violating the biblical text

against pulling down the boundaries of a neighbour and thereby bringing a curse on the Afrikaner nation. See J. H. P. Serfontein, *Namibia*? Fokus Suid Publishers, Pretoria, 1976, p. 20.

5 Ruth First, *South West Africa*, Penguin African Library, London, 1963, pp. 98–100; Sik, *The History of Black Africa*, p. 176.

6 Vigne, *A Dwelling Place of Our Own*, p. 17.

7 Sik, *The History of Black Africa*, pp. 176–77.

8 Peter Katjavivi, 'They fight to free a nation', *Anti-Apartheid News*, September 1970, p. 5.

9 Roger Gordon, 'A note on the History of Labour Action in Namibia', *South African Labour Bulletin*, April 1975; see also Keith Gottschalk, 'South Africa Labour Policy in Namibia 1915–1975', *South African Labour Bulletin*, January–February 1978.

10 In July 1978 the South West Africa Administrator-General announced that, in line with the policy of diminishing discriminatory measures during Namibia's independence process, workers of all races would in future be allowed to join trade unions. Black workers are in theory free to join white-dominated trade unions within the country. The Administrator-General had earlier stated 'To strike is a crime'; *Windhoek Advertiser*, March and July 1978, and G. and S. Cronje, *The Workers of Namibia*, International Defence and Aid Fund, London, 1979, pp. 71–76.

11 First, *South West Africa*, pp. 196–97.

12 Richard Gibson, *African Liberation Movements*, Institute of Race Relations, London, 1972, p. 119.

13 See, for example, Mishaka Muyongo, 'The struggle for Namibia in various fields', in *Namibia – Struggle for Freedom*, pp. 44–45.

14 Gibson, *African Liberation Movements*, pp. 119–22.

15 *Ibid.*, p. 135.

16 See Muriel Horrell, *South West Africa*, South African Institute of Race Relations, Johannesburg, 1967, pp. 82–83, and SIPRI, *Southern Africa*, Uppsala, 1976, pp. 79–80.

17 Gerhard Tötemeyer, *South West Africa, Namibia*, Fokus Suid Publishers, Pretoria, 1977, pp. 88–93; SIPRI, *Southern Africa*, pp. 79–80.

18 Tötemeyer, *South West Africa, Namibia*, pp. 93–100 and Jørgen Lissner (ed.), *Namibia 1975*, Lutheran World Federation, Geneva, 1976, p. 131.

19 Bengt Ahlsen, *Namibia*, Nordiska Afrikainstitutet, Uppsala, 1970, p. 32.

20 'Report by the Secretary-General of United Nations', *Objective: Justice*, No. 11, 1972.

21 See Tötemeyer, *South West Africa, Namibia.*

22 See *Windhoek Observer*, various issues, July–August 1979.

23 The NNF hopes to win 30–45% of the seats in a free election and form a progressive conservative coalition by attracting some DTA left dissidents as individuals and the SWAPO 'moderates' as a coalition member. The problem in this analysis is that NNF's projection–5% Aktur, 20–25% DTA, 30–35% NNF, 35–45% SWAPO votes – appears unlikely in a free election after an extended campaign. 5% for Aktur, 15% for DTA, 15%

for NNF, 65% for SWAPO seems more likely.

24 See, for example, African Bureau Fact Sheet No. 60, *Namibia's Political Economy* , July–August 1979.

25 IDOC project, *The Future of the Missionary Enterprise*, Rome, 1978, pp. 81–89.

26 SWAPO, Political Programme, Lusaka, 1976.

27 See *Windhoek Observer*, June 1979, and *Windhoek Advertiser*, June 1979. However, this was not in fact done – SWAPO remains *de jure* legal and *de facto* suppressed in Namibia.

28 See, for example, United Nations, *A Trust Betrayed: Namibia*, New York, 1974, pp. 18–19.

29 Sam Nujoma, 'The serious political situation in Namibia', in *Namibia – Struggles for Freedom*, pp. 23–24.

30 United Nations, 'Report by the Secretary-General of the United Nations', p. 30.

31 See H. Hunke and J. Ellis, *Torture – a Cancer in Our Society*, Catholic Institute for International Relations/British Council of Churches, London, 1978.

32 *LSM News*, SWAPO, No. 11–12; *Current Events in Namibia*, No. 2, 1974.

33 *Windhoek Advertiser,* 26 October 1977.

34 Sam Nujoma, quoted by Gibson, *African Liberation Movements*, p. 139.

35 According to Finnish missionaries, there are semi-liberated areas in the west from Omindamba to Okalongo, and in the east from Oshikango to Nkongo, reaching as far as Onankali in the south; Kimmo Kiljunen and Marja-Liisa Kiljunen, *Report on visit to Namibia, 1978* (mimeo).

36 Martial law (AG 27 of 1979) was extended on 10 May 1979 to six major white magisterial districts in the Police Zone: Windhoek, Tsumeb, Outjo, Okahandja, Otjiwarongo and Grootfontein. The new regulations gave the army and security police power to search premises and to interrogate and arrest any person without warrant and to prohibit any public meeting. The security forces were also empowered to hold detainees for 30 days, instead of 96 hours as before.

37 United Nations, *Decolonization*, No. 3, 1974.

38 Thus several small towns and villages were transformed into garrisons with access only by special permission of the army. See K. and M-L. Kiljunen, *Report on visit to Namibia*.

39 In July 1979 a United Nations Security Council document was published on the 'Human Casualties and material and other damage resulting from repeated acts of aggression by the regime of South Africa against the People's Republic of Angola'. It documents a chronological list of 193 attacks since 1976.

40 It is peculiarly fanciful because UNITA – even when a genuine liberation movement against Portugal – never had significant membership, organization or support among the Angolan Ovambo. Its base was among the Ovimbundu people of the plateau country.

41 *Windhoek Observer*, 11 August 1979.

42 In the 'Homelands' the 'homeguards' have earned a reputation as 'the real terrorists' even among supporters of such anti-SWAPO groups as the so-called SWAPO(D). See *Windhoek Observer*, 16 June 1979, *Focus*, No. 8, 1977 and 25, 1979.

43 *Windhoek Advertiser*, 7 September 1979.

44 *Windhoek Observer*, 28 April 1979.

45 *Focus*, July–August 1979; *Namibia Today*, Vol. 3, No. 4, 1979.

46 *Current Events in Namibia*, No. 3, 1974.

47 See Hunke and Ellis, *Torture – a Cancer in Our Society*.

48 See Ahlsen, *Namibia; Current Events in Namibia*, No. 3, 1974; *Namibia Today*, No. 3, 1978; *Windhoek Observer*, October 1978.

49 PLAN is careful to inform friendly persons and groups of where it has planted mines. It is most unlikely that a church group would not have heard rumours and avoided the route.

50 K. and M-L. Kiljunen, *Report on visit tc Namibia*.

51 *Windhoek Observer*, various issues, 1979.

52 Gordon, 'A note on the history of Labour Action in Namibia', pp. 12–14. See also G. and S. Cronje, *The Workers of Namibia*, Chapter VII.

53 Gordon, 'A note', pp. 17–18.

54 See G. and S. Cronje, *The Workers of Namibia*, Chapter VII.

55 *Ibid.*, Chapter VI.

56 In December–January 1978–79 Rössing uranium mine experienced the most serious dispute in its history when about 2 000 African workers stopped work. At the same time at the Uis tin mine, owned by the South African Iron and Steel Corporation, about 500 contract workers went on a three-day strike. 200 black workers were discharged at the Krantzberg Tungsten mine at Omaruru, owned by Noord Mining, and sent back to Ovamboland. At the Tsumeb mine there was also unrest and the South African Police were called in to raid the compounds. *Guardian*, 5 January 1979.

57 See, e.g. UNESCO, *Racism and apartheid in Southern Africa*, Paris, 1970, pp. 148–49, and United Nations, *Decolonization*, pp. 9–10.

58 UNESCO, *Racism and apartheid*, p. 149.

59 United Nations, *Decolonization*, p. 10.

60 *Focus*, No. 8, 1977 and *Namibia News*, December 1976.

61 *Namibia News*, July–August 1975.

62 These conflicts were not 'tribal' in any simple sense. Herero SWAPO members who were fleeing from DTA Herero armed and protected by security police, fled to and were protected in the Ovambo location of Katutura.

63 *Financial Times*, 27 June 1979; *Windhoek Observer*, June 1979; *Focus* July–August 1979. New detention centres had been established in June–July 1979, *inter alia* at Hardap Dam (near Mariental), Windhoek, Tsumeb, Oshakati, Ogongo, Okakarara, Runtu, Gobabis, Lüderitz, Onunu, Buffalo, Oshipata, Arandis/Rongwyn, Keetmanshoop, Mpacha,

Otjozundu, Katima Mulilo, Walvis Bay. The differing figures given in estimates illustrate how difficult it is to get reliable information about unrest or about government activities in Namibia. Foreign correspondents and independent local journalists do not enjoy full freedom to report and even when there are frequent reports of raids and disturbances, it is difficult to assess their scale or accurately to analyze their causes.

9 The state of the liberation struggle

AN INTERVIEW WITH SWAPO PRESIDENT SAM NUJOMA*

1 *What is the present state of the struggle for national liberation in Namibia?*

The current political situation in Namibia can be described under two main aspects or fronts; the first and leading aspect is the armed liberation struggle by the People's Liberation Army of Namibia (PLAN), the military wing of SWAPO. Our way of liberation began over thirteen years ago on 26 August 1966, under very difficult conditions. At that time, Namibia was sandwiched geographically between Angola under Portuguese colonialism in the north and racist South Africa in the south. The South African Bureau of State Security (BOSS) and the Portuguese PIDE, on the one hand, and the South African armed racist troops and the fascist Portuguese troops, on the other, fully cooperated in patrolling the border areas and fighting against SWAPO and MPLA forces in our respective countries. South Africa acted as the chief supplier of armaments and manpower in assisting the Portuguese fascists to suppress the resistance of the Angolan people in the same manner as it did in Mozambique, seeking to suppress the struggle for national liberation.

The Salazar–Caetano–Verwoerd–Vorster military alliance was aiming at the complete suppression of the war of liberation by the African liberation movements in Namibia, Angola and Mozambique. In the southern African situation, world imperialism with its multinational corporations, and NATO in particular, played a leading role in supporting the reactionary regimes in Portugal and South Africa. The Kunene and Cabora Bassa Dam projects are examples. They involved bringing in half a million and over one million Portuguese respectively to southern Angola and Mozambique, and more fascist South African Boers to Namibia. The intention was to strengthen the military, political and economic positions of the minority white regimes in southern Africa.

Despite frantic efforts by imperialists and multi-national corporations which practically financed racist South Africa's war machinery, the people of Namibia were more and more encouraged and, in fact, became more enthusiastic, joining SWAPO and the People's Liberation Army of Namibia (PLAN). This indicated that the Namibian population viewed PLAN as their defender and liberator and that PLAN strategy, as drawn up by SWAPO, is the only effective way to evict the forces of oppression and to destroy the overall pattern of South African colonial and racist institutions in Namibia.

* The interview was conducted by the editors in August 1979.

In 1966 when we launched the armed struggle, our guerrilla units were small in number and poorly armed. We were faced with many problems, particularly:

a shortage of arms and ammunition, and
b logistical problems due to the geographical position of Namibia at that time surrounded by territories which were either under colonial domination or about to attain independence.

Today, PLAN has grown considerably, to the extent that we can talk of battalions in numbers, of effective combat fire-power capacity, and of experience gained during actual fighting. Our guerrilla forces are in a position to frustrate and defeat enemy troops which are now better armed with sophisticated instruments of war such as tanks, armoured cars, helicopters and jet fighters. We also have to face UNITA reactionary elements trained by South Africa for use against SWAPO and the People's Republic of Angola. In short, our guerrilla forces are effectively operating in the eastern, northern, and north-western regions and are expanding our zones of operations into the central regions.

In fact, parts of these regions are semi-liberated. SWAPO cadres are providing social, medical and educational services to the people in the villages in these semi-liberated operational zones. The enemy still occupies some major centres, but in most cases is confined to its military bases because its forces are highly demoralized and afraid to fight face to face with PLAN forces.

The second aspect of our struggle, which is supplementary to the armed struggle but no less important, is the political mass mobilization of the Namibian people. Since its formation, SWAPO succeeded in mobilizing politically the mass of the people in Namibia, notwithstanding enemy harassments, intimidation, torture to death, imprisonments without trial, public flogging, restrictions and detentions under the notorious and obnoxious repressive laws, such as the Terrorism Act and Suppression of Communism Act, and the State of Emergency reinforced by martial law which is still in existence in Namibia.

SWAPO's political mass mobilization extends throughout Namibian territory from the Kunene to the Orange and from west to east. Because of SWAPO's effectiveness in political mass mobilization, fascist Vorster used delaying tactics, manoeuvres and intrigues by appointing, in 1963, the Odendaal Commission. Its findings were that Namibia can only achieve independence through tribal or ethnic ministates following the reactionary policy of Bantustan or separate development.

Later on these manoeuvres continued, with the racist regime appointing, in 1973, a so-called Advisory Council directed by Vorster's well-selected personal representative, Billy Marais. After that Vorster embarked on the formulation of the so-called Constitutional talks in Turnhalle, Windhoek, in September 1975. These involved hand-picked and well-selected tribal chiefs, on the pay-roll of the South African government, who did not at all represent the political aspirations of the Namibian people.

These tribal talks produced the so-called declaration of intent, issued by the Turnhalle puppets on 12 September 1975, and other subsequent statements. These unambiguously stated that any solution to the Namibian problem should take into consideration 'tribal or ethnic interests', which, in short, means the balkanization or division of Namibia on a tribal or ethnic basis. This has been totally and contemptuously rejected by the Namibian people. Most of the groups which were misled into these tribal talks have defected and joined SWAPO as the only salvation and effective fighting force to lead Namibia to genuine political independence. These manoeuvres have continued with the 'elections' last December and the self-styled 'National Assembly'. But they no longer convince anybody; not even the settlers in Namibia believe in them.

2 *What is the strategic aim of your struggle? What are the possibilities of negotiating with the South African government now and later?*

The main aim of SWAPO's strategy is to liberate Namibia from racist South African colonial oppression and to achieve genuine democratic independence, with a clear purpose of putting an end to the exploitation of man by man and to foreign interference in Namibian affairs. SWAPO continues to cherish and support efforts towards peace. Thus, despite the arrogance of the South African occupation regime and its oppression and suppression of our people, the possibilities for a peaceful settlement to the Namibian problem still exist. SWAPO has laid down the pre-conditions for such a settlement as follows.

1 SWAPO has been and is still ready to talk directly with the South African government regarding the modalities for transferring power to the people of Namibia under the leadership of SWAPO.
2 SWAPO demands that the participants at the Namibia independence conference be SWAPO, South Africa and the United Nations.
3 SWAPO demands that the United Nations convenes and chairs the conference.
4 SWAPO insists that, before any talks, the South African government must release all political prisoners, detainees and restrictees. Some of the leaders now in detention or restriction or in prison are likely to be part of the SWAPO delegation to independence talks.
5 South Africa must make prior commitments to withdraw all its armed forces from Namibia and to end its repression of the Namibian population.
6 The talks must be on an entirely new basis, reflecting the unity of the whole people of an independent and sovereign Namibia as a unitary state.

The whole question of Namibia's liberation by peaceful means depends on how the racist regime of South Africa responds to the above conditions. In the absence of a positive response SWAPO will continue to intensify its armed struggle until South Africa's regime is shamefully defeated in the same manner as Caetano was in Angola, Mozambique and Guinea-Bissau.

3 *What was the nature of the December 1978 vote? Why did a large*

number of Namibians register and vote? What kind of changes will take place in the strategy and tactics of SWAPO if Namibia is granted quasi-independence?

From the outset, the elections were held because of South Africa's fear of defeat at the ballot box under UN-supervised and -controlled elections. Needless to say, the results were predetermined. Throughout the registration and electoral process, people were forced to take out Democratic Turnhalle Alliance membership cards and to denounce SWAPO. Those who refused to do so faced physical assault, loss of jobs, pensions, cattle, medical treatment, education, etc. Thus it was an election at gunpoint and therefore totally invalid.

In view of the critical political developments occurring in Namibia as a result of increased repression by the racist South African armed forces, police and security services which are aiming to suppress the political aspirations and popular demands of the Namibian people, SWAPO will only change its strategy and tactics by stepping up and intensifying both its military operations and its political mass mobilization with a view to eradicate, once and for all, the direct colonial machinations and to crush any puppet regime which Vorster may create in Namibia now or in the future.

4 *Could you say something about the tactical principles followed by PLAN? Do you aim at creating liberated areas in Namibia? How are the units of PLAN supplied inside Namibia?*

The tactical principles followed by PLAN are based mainly on typical and scientific methods of guerrilla warfare. Ours is a people's war. Our basic aim is to liberate Namibia as a whole, with the support of the mass of the Namibian people, the exploited peasants and workers who form the backbone of our struggle against foreign occupation and exploitation. PLAN guerrillas, being part and parcel of the entire oppressed African people of Namibia, depend primarily on the support of the mass of the people who have come to look upon them as their liberator and salvation.

5 *How are the people recruited into the armed struggle? What kind of concerns and problems does SWAPO meet among the people? How do you educate your cadres and militants?*

Normally, new PLAN recruits are drawn from the organisation's membership. They are initially politicized so that they understand why they need to fight and make sacrifices to accelerate the liberation and independence of Namibia. Their major concerns include how and when Namibia must be liberated from the repressive South African racist occupation, although, all human beings, the new recruits have more personal concerns such as the well-being of their families.

Our cadres are educated politically within the framework of the Party Constitution and Political Programme so that they understand what SWAPO stands for and what contribution is required of them in the struggle for national liberation. This is done through party publications, speeches by the leadership, radio broadcasts by teachers in party schools, study groups, and among the fighting cadres of PLAN by the Political Commissars.

6 *Could you say something about SWAPO's activities inside Namibia, about your communication, propaganda work, etc.? How has SWAPO mobilized the people of Namibia? Why has the South African government not banned SWAPO?*

In deploying its racist machinery, South Africa makes frantic efforts to suppress SWAPO's political activities inside the country. These include encouraging white employers to dismiss SWAPO leaders and members from jobs, with the sole purpose of forcing them to capitulate to enemy networks and colonial machinations like the Turnhalle tribal talks. Other methods include arrests, detentions, restrictions, imprisonment and penalties of death or life imprisonment, all aimed at crippling SWAPO activities and propaganda machinery. The reason the racist regime of South Africa has not officially banned SWAPO is that, since its inception in 1960, SWAPO's popularity among the Namibian people has spread like the burning fire on dry wild grass. Thus there was nothing the enemy could do. However, this summer it has detained many senior SWAPO leaders in Namibia, so that we have been forced to go underground.

7 *Could you characterize SWAPO and its social basis? Who supports SWAPO? Do the whites give their support to SWAPO? How strong is SWAPO support in different areas of the country and within various groups of the population? What are the basic differences between SWAPO and other political organizations (DTA, NNF, etc.) in the country?*

We ought to be frank on this question of white support for SWAPO. The position to date is that the majority of the white population forms a privileged exploitative class with the fascist Botha regime fanatically behind it. This reactionary class, founded on the baseless myth of white supremacy, continues to perpetuate its ruthless exploitation and permanent enslavement of the African majority. The latter is being used as a source of cheap labour for the benefit of the minority white settlers who exclusively enjoy the riches and resources of Namibia. Meanwhile the African people continue to suffer from hunger, disease and ignorance and, above all, are denied fundamental human rights.

There are a few whites, alas very few, who started a few years ago to identify with the political aspiration towards national independence of the African majority. Among these are missionaries and clergy of the Anglican, Finnish, Rhenish and, of late, the Catholic, Churches who have recently started to fight against racist segregation by admitting black children into their schools, despite intimidation and a threat by the racist Pretoria regime to withdraw the government subsidy.

Other whites, more especially the rich, are strongly behind the regime's repressive machinery. More particularly, there is a group of business men and concerns which has formed a so-called pro-South

West Africa Fund. This aims at supporting and publicizing inside and abroad the activities of the reactionary tribal chiefs and puppets of the Turnhalle tribal constitutional talks in Windhoek. In turn, these rich whites are supported by multi-national corporations which are involved in the ruthless exploitation of the Namibian economy.

The 'political' organizations, which existed only on paper, have completely disappeared from the Namibian political scene. They offer no effective opposition to the illegal South African administration, because of lack of support from the Namibian masses (because of their own lack of political direction) and because they were afraid to make any sacrifices.

Occasionally one hears a statement made by individuals but, as they lack directives and do not act, the enemy does not see them as a threat to the *status quo*. One is not surprised that the top leadership of these so-called organizations (for example, Fannel Kozonguizi of SWANU, Gertzen Kerina of SWANUF) deserted the struggle long ago. Today such people are collaborators with the Vorster regime and on the BOSS–CIA pay-roll and were induced to participate in Vorster's deceptive tribal talks in Windhoek. SWAPO is a liberation movement organized on a national basis. It draws its support from all sections of the oppressed people of Namibia.

8 *Can you tell us something about the difficulties encountered during the development of the struggle in relation to tribal, linguistic, religious and regional problems, as well as difficulties with the traditional chiefs?*

At the time of SWAPO's formation we encountered no difficulties in politically mobilizing the masses. However, at the beginning, some of the oppressed African people were afraid to join the party, especially the elderly who had experienced years of bitter humiliation and suppression under the Boers after racist South Africa was given a mandate over Namibia at the end of the First World War. The elders asked such questions as, 'Where will you obtain weapons to fight against the white man who is not only well armed but vicious and who would not hesitate to use the might of his fire power to bombard or wipe out the African population itself?' We replied simply that we need not necessarily fight with guns. We would rely on our organizational ability and intelligence, uniting all the black people and forces to form a formidable and dependable base which the enemy cannot and will never destroy. We emphasized the importance of unity among the oppressed majority of our people, that our victory over enemy forces depends above all on unity of purpose and of action.

We also told our people that if the enemy continued its vicious attacks on an unarmed civilian population – as was the case during the struggle of the Bondelswart in 1924 when the fascist South African air force was used to suppress ruthlessly the resistance of the Nama people, and in 1959 when armoured cars were deployed against the residents of the old Windhoek African township who had refused to move to racially segregated locations – SWAPO would be left with no alternative but to seek assistance in the form of weapons and training from sympathetic countries. We would have to do this to resist, to defend ourselves, and to liberate our people and country through the barrel of the gun.

As regards the role of traditional chiefs, some of these became easy prey to, and instruments of, the enemy's colonial manipulations, manoeuvres and intrigues. In some cases they simply did not understand; in others they were selfish for personal gain. The racist regime was clever enough to place some of the greedy on its pay-roll. Today, these traitors are the bulk of those treacherous Namibians who are singing and dancing to the tune of Boer music in the DTA and the so-called National Assembly.

9 *What is the role of women in the liberation struggle?*

The Namibian women are part and parcel of the oppressed Namibian population. As such, like all other people who are deprived of their rights, humiliated and degraded, they identify themselves with the aims and objectives of the struggle, both political and armed, waged by SWAPO. Consequently, it is SWAPO's duty to educate and to mobilize politically women, youth and all sections of the Namibian population, in order to strengthen its manpower so as to fight effectively for the total liberation of Namibia.

Today, Namibian women are playing a very significant role in the national liberation struggle. For example, in the People's Liberation Army of Namibia (PLAN), women are not only active combatants at the front, but have also risen to positions of responsibility in the army. Those inside the country whose husbands have either been arrested, detained, imprisoned for life or killed, have taken over the burden of looking after the family, relying solely on their meagre incomes and resources to bring up their children and look after the elderly and the maimed. Those in rural areas till the land in order to produce sufficient food and the surplus to be able to obtain other household requirements, to send their children to school and, in fact, to ensure their general survival.

In SWAPO, we have adopted the principle of equality of the sexes. Therefore, our women can perform any duty or task in the party and, on the basis of ability and initiative, they can be elevated to the highest position.

10 *What has been the role of the church?*

The church is a foreign institution first introduced into our country by German colonialists and later by other church institutions from foreign countries. Although some of these religious institutions tried to introduce modern and scientific methods of teaching, the general tendency was to use the church and religion as a means of mental and psychological indoctrination and, therefore, colonization of the African population. One good example is the Dutch Reformed Church which holds to the 'pre-destination of peoples and races', and takes the line that those who are opposed to the government and the order of the day are also opposed to the teachings of God.

However, many missionaries and church leaders have come to support liberation. The South Africans have oppressed them too – burned their press, destroyed their churches, detained, tortured and killed even catechists and priests. Many PLAN members are Christians; some are priests or pastors. Services are held in their base camps.

11 *Could you describe how the political and military leadership is carried out? What are the relations of SWAPO working inside Namibia and outside? Are there any difficulties in coordinating actions? What kinds of roles do SWAPO organizations working inside and outside the country have in directing the struggle?*

The political leadership of SWAPO is in overall control of both military and political activities. In this respect, all SWAPO cadres, functionaries, commanders and combatants alike, whether outside or inside the country, receive directives and guidance from the political party leadership. Each and every member of SWAPO is bound to fulfil his or her responsibility within the framework of the Constitution and Political Programme of the Organisation.

Due to the imposition of repressive laws such as the so-called Suppression of Communism Act, the Terrorism Act, etc., under which many SWAPO leaders and members such as Ja Toivo, Tuhadeleni, Kahumba, and thousands of others, have been detained, imprisoned or sentenced to death, our comrades and the entire SWAPO leadership inside the country are carrying out activities such as political mass mobilization under considerable difficulties, practically at gun point. However, thanks to their iron-willed determination and dedication to the national cause, they have continued to intensify resistance. SWAPO is one, under directives from one and the same leadership; we coordinate our political activities inside, as well as our political and diplomatic efforts outside, in order to isolate the racist enemy internationally.

12 *What are the most difficult problems to be solved in an independent Namibia?*

The immediate preoccupation of an African government in Namibia is to destroy to their very foundations all the colonial and racist institutions which were created to facilitate the oppression and exploitation of the African majority by the white settler minority. These include social inequalities founded on discriminatory laws which deny Africans equal pay for equal work, adequate medical facilities, educational opportunities and other fundamental human rights. We shall embark on a crash programme of economic reconstruction and development and of social progress. More especially, we shall stress agricultural production in order to produce enough to feed the nation. Education and health being rights of each and every citizen, the African government in Namibia will provide free education, health and social facilities in every region, district, town and village.

13 *What kind of society will you start to build in a free Namibia? What lessons have you drawn from the past decade of African independence in relation to your own efforts for the future Namibia? What will be the share of foreign investments in independent Namibia? How will you deal with land?*

The basic ideological principle of SWAPO is to build a classless non-exploitative society which allows no room, no loophole, for the exploitation of man by man. We have gained some experience from seeing other African countries overthrow colonialism and foreign domination and initiate the building of institutions aimed at benefiting their peoples. But one should note two important points. The first is that most of these African countries obtained independence through a devolutionary or evolutionary process and only a few through a revolutionary process such as we are going through now. The second is that basically one cannot transplant a system from one country to another without scientific consideration of, for example, the ecology and the resources of that country. Thus, after the seizure of power, the Namibian people will establish their own governmental institutions, with a National Assembly as the highest organ to draw up Namibia's development programmes.

As one of the fundamental tasks of the new African government would be to destroy all colonial institutions aimed at exploiting and plundering Namibia's mineral wealth, logically, foreign investment would be allowed only in governmental joint ventures based on the principle of mutual respect and of benefit to the Namibian people. It must be borne in mind that the Namibian people are shedding blood to liberate each and every inch of Namibian soil (including Walvis Bay); thus each and every inch of Namibian land must and will belong to the Namibian people.

14 *What about the political system? Will the structure of SWAPO as a multi-class front change? What will happen to those who have cooperated with the South African administration? What about the white population?*

SWAPO fights to liberate Namibia from racist South Africa's colonial oppression and to establish a popular democratic government which will serve and defend the interests of all Namibians, regardless of colour, race, religion or place of origin. Every Namibian, including the whites, will be respected and protected by the national laws provided such a person also respects those laws.

15 *How do you think that Namibia as a small country can exist as an independent economic unit in the integrated world economy? How will economic relations with the Republic of South Africa be formulated? What kind of economic cooperation, and with which countries, would you be prepared to pursue?*

With its large territorial area and massive mineral resources Namibia cannot, in a true sense, be described as a small country compared to, say, Holland, Luxembourg, or Finland, but in relation to population one could say that Namibia is a small country.

However, we feel sure that with this small population we can utilize the abundant resources for the benefit of the Namibian people without leaving any loophole for foreign exploitation (as is the case today). Namibia could rank as one of the richest nations in the world on a *per capita* basis. Namibia would trade with all friendly nations on a basis of mutual understanding and respect so that trade would be beneficial to all concerned.

The South African economy is founded on inequality insofar as the sharing of national wealth among its people is concerned. The whites enjoy exclusive rights to the wealth of the country, thus exploiting ruthlessly the African majority. Therefore our relationship will be reformulated after that country is liberated.

16 *Since outside aid is so important to the national liberation struggle, which countries are giving aid to your struggle? Who are your allies?*

SWAPO appreciates the support given to the people of Namibia by all progressive outside forces. Our main source of political and material support is member states of the Organization of African Unity (OAU) and the OAU Liberation Committee, in particular the Front Line States; the Socialist countries; the Nordic countries, particularly Sweden and Norway; the Asian countries; some democratic organizations in Western countries, e.g. the World Council of Churches and the Defence and Aid Fund. Our allies are all the anti-imperialist, anti-colonial and anti-fascist forces struggling for the liberation of man.

17 *Do you see the United Nations (UN) as playing an important role with regard to Namibia? What would SWAPO expect from the UN at this moment? How should the UN act when Namibia is granted 'independence' manipulated by the South African government? What do you think will be the attitude of Western countries towards 'independent' Namibia as a result of recent developments?*

The United Nations Organisation has been and still is playing an important role in support of peoples struggling to free themselves from colonial oppression. The work of various UN organs has been relevant: the United Nations Council for Namibia, the Decolonization Committee, the Special Committee on the Question of Apartheid. However, the problem remains of the use of the veto by the United States, France and Britain, particularly with regard to Namibia, in efforts to perpetuate their exploitation of Namibian mineral resources through the racist regime of South Africa.

In view of the continued arrogance of racist South Africa in defying the 1966 resolutions of the United Nations Security Council, the General Assembly and the Advisory Opinion of the International Court of Justice in 1971 which revoked the mandate and made South Africa's continued occupation illegal and an act of armed aggression, the Namibian people expect the world body to take practical action under Chapter VI of the UN charter. That is, we expect an economic and an arms embargo, interruption of communications to and from racist South Africa, and a total boycott of the on- and off-loading of South African vessels and aircraft throughout the world.

The Namibian people also expect the UN Security Council to invoke Chapter VI of the Charter, especially articles 39, 41 and 42, and to call upon all nations of the world to deny recognition to the puppet regime which South Africa has imposed on the Namibian people under the aegis of the Turnhalle/Constitutional Talks arrangements, the 1978 'elections' and the 'National Assembly', and to support the active armed liberation struggle waged by the Namibian people under SWAPO's banner.

At present, the attitude of Western imperialist countries, especially the permanent members of the UN Security Council, towards the liberation of Namibia is negative, due to their massive economic investments in Namibia. However, no matter how racist South Africa and its imperialist allies try to manoeuvre, SWAPO will continue to rely on the actions of the Namibian people as the most decisive factor in the liberation of Namibia. Because of their negative attitudes, the imperialist countries helped the South African regime to perpetuate its colonial rule over Namibia. They have even lacked the political will to carry through their own proposals for a negotiated settlement.

18 *How can the UN ensure a free election? How can it ensure protection from coercion by South African troops, security policy and administrators?*

The UN plan for free and fair national elections in Namibia under UN supervision and control forms a sound basis from which we, the people of Namibia, might achieve our objectives. It ensures the withdrawal of the bulk of South Africa's troops from Namibia, the confinement of the remaining 1 500 to base, and their monitoring by a UN peacekeeping force. The South African administration would be superseded by the UN Transitional Assistance Group (UNTAG), which would include a special police unit. This is supposed to create the climate necessary for free elections.

Of course there is no guarantee that such a plan is fool-proof, although the fact that South Africa has refused to go along with it suggests that it provides an effective framework within which the people of Namibia might exercise their right to self-determination.

10 The ideology of national liberation

KIMMO KILJUNEN

> We in SWAPO have come to the realization that the decisive factor in our liberation struggle, now and in the future is the *conscious* participation of the people. By conscious participation, we mean a deep-going process of debate, criticism and self-criticism, that we are in the struggle to put an end to the exploitation of man by man in our society; that we are in the struggle to put an end to all forms of ethnic or national oppression; that we are in the struggle to make the *toiling* masses of Namibia, the workers and peasants, have direct access to the means of production; and that we are in the struggle to open wide all the doors to all the educational and cultural institutions to all Namibia's people without regard to race, sex, colour or ethnic origins.[1]
>
> – Sam Nujoma, 1976

Nationalism, liberation, social aims

This statement by SWAPO's President, Sam Nujoma, defines the specific nature of the national liberation struggle in Namibia. He emphasizes the need for people's consciousness to grow. He puts forward goals of social equality and basic human rights, and stresses that to achieve them structural changes in society are needed. The objectives are not restricted to furthering the interests of any ethnically, regionally, sectorally or socially distinguishable group, but are nationwide. This differentiates his movement from separatist, tribalist or class-based forces and makes it a *national* movement.

National consciousness does not prevent SWAPO from recognizing the existence of social conflicts and contradictions; rather, Nujoma's statement emphasizes the need for their solution. He does not speak only of achieving national sovereignty and the granting of economic and political power to Namibians, even though SWAPO, as the national liberation movement of Namibia, necessarily aims, in the first stage, at national self-determination. The fact that President Nujoma stresses not national aims but social progress as the basic criterion for SWAPO's action characterizes SWAPO not only as a national movement but also as a *liberation* movement.

In terms of national struggle, SWAPO's action is part of the general decolonization process in the African continent. Thus, its ideological roots and strategy are closely linked to the tradition of African nationalism, which provided the ideological framework for the general decolonization of the continent in the late 1950s and the early 1960s. In an analysis of African nationalism, four dominant ideological components emerge: *anti-colonialism, Pan-Africanism* and neutralism, *national unity* and *egalitarianism*.

Due to the lateness of national struggle in southern Africa there are some new and even qualitatively different elements in the liberation theory and social analysis of the national liberation movements. Those can be drawn, at least partially, from the experiences of the newly independent African states during their first years of political independence. While African countries had achieved formal political independence, a situation of dependence remained in structural social, economic and cultural relations with the former colonial powers. Thus a new concept emerged: neo-colonialism. The President of Ghana, Kwame Nkrumah, a leading exponent of African nationalism, ironically defined neo-colonialism as 'the process of handing independence over to the African people with one hand, only to take it away with the other hand'.[2]

Patterns of neo-colonial dependency were used by the liberation movement to explain why it had not been possible to provide an alternative to the present unequal international division of labour and to the consequent underdeveloped social structures in Africa. In reaction against these negative external forces, a strategic concept of 'self-reliance' emerged. This was based on mobilization and utilization of the community's own resources and capabilities to replace reliance on outside resources and ideas, and on the severance of existing external links of dominance and dependency. The strategy aimed to fulfil basic human needs and to democratize social structures and institutions.[3]

A social policy which emphasizes these objectives has thus come to complement the framework of traditional African nationalism. Together, they imply three new ideological components: *anti-imperialism; mobilization* of both material and human resources; and *social justice.* Subsequently these concepts have served to define the nature of social development in the post-colonial societies.

Social conditions in post-colonial Africa have therefore profoundly affected the liberation theory and objectives of the southern African national movements. Political independence can no longer be the final goal; it is only a necessary step towards a deeper and more comprehensive social and human emancipation in order to liberate from both underdeveloped social structures and repressive human relations. Anti-colonial struggle is directed against both the political and the economic power structures of the precolonial and colonial systems and it is at this level of social analysis that one can begin to talk about national liberation.

From anti-colonialism to self-reliance

The theory inherent in the process of national liberation in southern Africa is manifested in the Political Programme of SWAPO adopted in August 1976 by the General Committee. The paragraphs defining the general political goals state:

> The tasks before SWAPO at present and in the immediate future are:
> 1 The liberation and winning of independence for the people of

Namibia, by all possible means, and the establishment of a democratic people's government.
2 The realization of genuine and total independence of Namibia in the spheres of politics, economy, defence, social and cultural affairs.

In order to achieve these goals, SWAPO has resolved:

1 To persistently mobilize and organize the broad masses of the Namibian people so that they can actively participate in the national liberation struggle.
2 To mould and heighten, in the thick of the national liberation struggle, the bond of national and political consciousness amongst the Namibian people.
3 To combat all manifestations and tendencies of tribalism, regionalism, ethnic orientation and racial discrimination.
4 To unite all Namibian people, particularly the working class, the peasantry and progressive intellectuals into a vanguard partly capable of safe-guarding national independence and of building a classless, non-exploitative society based on the ideals and principles of scientific socialism.[4]

SWAPO's political goals and strategy for action as articulated here are *nationwide*; the movement remains faithful to the populist tradition in African nationalism. The Political Programme emphasizes *anti-colonial struggle* to achieve national sovereignty. The objective is to create a *unitary state* in which interests of different population groups and regions would be equally represented. The national movement is a *common front* combining separate interests of different classes, social strata and social groups.

At the same time, SWAPO's general socio-economic goals include social *liberation*, in the form of a strategy of self-reliance:

a in addition to political changes, social restructuring is required to abolish all relations of external domination, i.e. *anti-imperialism*;
b to realize 'genuine and total independence', and to form 'a democratic people's government' it is vital to organize the mass of the population and to raise general consciousness, i.e. *mobilization*;
c in a widespread liberation struggle involving different sections of the population with the workers and peasants actively engaged, the objective of social reform becomes a 'classless, non-exploitative society', i.e. *social justice*.

It is clear that SWAPO's programme is socialist in character despite the fact that the word 'socialism' appears in the party programme only in the section quoted above. In fact, it is more akin to main bodies of socialist thought and practice than several other ideologies or party manifestations that are classified under the value-loaded label of 'African socialism'.[5]

However, it must be noted that 'African socialism', 'socialism in

Africa',[6] and the socialist-oriented policies of the liberation movements – including FRELIMO and MPLA – of southern Africa have one common feature. They neither aim for a 'pattern of socialism' imported from outside, nor mechanically accept dogmas developed in other circumstances. Rather, their social analysis and strategy for action are based on local social and economic realities. 'The main burden for the liberation of Namibia rests solely on the Namibians and on their ability to understand their own society.'[7] This principle, repeated many times by SWAPO, clearly describes the attitude of the liberation movement to external influences both at the level of ideology and of practical policies.

Pan-Africanism and neutralism

What happens during the national liberation process depends on the historical, geographical, economic and social circumstances and conditions in each country. But its general character, both the ideological framework and political strategy, is comparable to other struggles for national liberation irrespective of time and place. This produces a feeling of solidarity among various liberation movements. Accordingly, SWAPO's programme also strives:

> To foster and strengthen the anti-imperialist unity amongst the national liberation, world socialist, progressive and peace-loving forces in order to eliminate all forms of imperialism, colonialism and neo-colonialism.

The Pan-Africanism of the early 1960s similarly stressed solidarity and the need for unity. Its slogan was 'Africa for the Africans' and it emphasized the similarity of problems in the continent. These were based on the struggle against the 'joint enemy', colonialism and white supremacy. SWAPO leans on this tradition and aspires:

> To support and promote the ideals of unity of Africa as provided for in the Charter of the Organization of African Unity (OAU).
> To work in close co-operation with all progressive governments, organizations and popular forces for the total emancipation of the African continent.[8]

The idea of a United States of Africa, vigorously sponsored especially by Nkrumah, never came to fruition. Instead, the Organization of African Unity (OAU) was established. While, in respect to independent states, it has supported the rather *status quo*-oriented solidarity of live and let live, the OAU has remained radical in outlook toward the remaining colonial territories. A central OAU activity has been its support, through the African Liberation Committee, for African liberation movements. This political and, above all, material support has also been of vital importance to SWAPO.

A logical continuation of Pan-Africanism has been the striving for neutralism and non-alignment:

> Africa should be free of all foreign military bases, nuclear and atomic testing facilities, and foreign military missions or pacts.... The foreign policy of African countries should in any case be guided by the principles of a most rigorous positive neutralism.[9]

This was stated by African leaders in 1963 when seeking a basis for African unity and not wanting to weaken this by aligning with any of the super powers. To stress neutrality and unity was essential to demonstrate the reality of newly achieved political independence.

In the same tradition, SWAPO's foreign policy emphasizes non-alignment and avoids involvement in conflicts between the super powers:

> SWAPO government will adopt a posture of neutrality and non-alignment enjoying friendly relations with all nations. We are Pan-Africanists, so we'll play a very active part in the OAU and will promote the objectives of closer economic cooperation and continental political unity.[10]

This was stated by Sam Nujoma, who went on to refer to the conflict within the socialist camp:

> You might expect some difficulty since this ideological conflict involves big powers who offer us considerable material support. But we accept only genuine support with no strings attached. Countries that are supporting us must accept the fact that they are supporting a genuine struggle for national liberation. If they give us support expecting SWAPO to side with them in conflicts with other countries, then we will refuse their aid.[11]

Egalitarianism and national unity

Another central ideological component of African nationalism has been the demand for equality of rights, the desire for personal emancipation. Throughout the colonial period, Africans have experienced discrimination in political, economic, social and cultural life, on the insistent ideology of natural white supremacy. 'Nationalism in Africa was primarily a claim for equality of status and of rights, for personal dignity, self-respect and full participation in the things of the material and spiritual world.'[12] In Namibia, inequality is sharply highlighted by the fact that the South African white minority government pursues statutorily enforced racial discrimination. For many people in Namibia the liberation struggle means, before all else, a struggle against racism and the system of white privilege.

The significant position of the church in Namibia, with the Christian ethic of equality and brotherhood, has added another dimension to the ideology of the national liberation:

> We are Namibians and not South Africans. We do not now and will not in the future recognize South Africans' right to govern us; to make laws for us in which we have no say; to meet our country as if

it were your property and us as if you were our masters. . . . Only when we are granted our independence will the struggle stop. Only when our human dignity is restored to us, as equals of the whites, will there be peace between us.[13]

We find ourselves a conquered people and the master does not discuss with the slave. And so we shall free ourselves and discussion will again take place between equals.[14]

Both these imprisoned SWAPO leaders, Toivo ja Toivo and Tuhadeleni, stress that for them independence and national liberation must carry with them equality between the conqueror and the suppressed, between the whites and the blacks. They both reach the same conclusion that personal liberation presupposes national liberation.

'You cannot become personally free, before you become an independent nation.' Independence necessarily implies national unity.

By national liberation we mean that the fight against colonialism in Namibia is first and foremost aimed at freeing Namibia as a single nation. By freeing Namibia as a single nation, it is postulated that the struggle does not aim at the reassertion of the authorities and power of the pre-colonial tribal kingdoms. This postulate concedes to the fact that, super-imposed as it is, colonialism is today a part of the Namibian history; and that history is nothing other than a series of eras, epochs, stages and forms.[15]

South African colonial rule has drastically changed earlier social conditions and structures. It is impossible to return to pre-colonial social and production relations, and autonomous tribal communities. Nor is the South African policy of 'separate development', which tries to revive tribal segregation by forming 'Bantu Homelands' and tribally-based nations, a real alternative. Instead, one has to start by acknowledging the fact that:

all of Namibia's tribal communities have been brought under the colonial order and thus suffered common oppression. This common oppression has dialectically shaped among those people a sense of collective destiny as a nation.[16]

In 1975 SWAPO published a discussion paper setting out possible elements of a constitution for independent Namibia. Defining central principles of the new constitution, the document states:

SWAPO has, over many years, repeated its essential conception of Namibia as an independent, unitary state. The borders of our territory are those of 'South West Africa', including Walvis Bay. Our experience of persecution and racialism over many years has deepened our unqualified commitment to democratic rule, the eradication of racialism, the establishment of the rule of law and the entrenchment of human rights. Moreover, we reject absolutely any notion of bantustans masquerading as federalism.[17]

Taken as a whole, the draft gives SWAPO's most detailed and

concrete ideas to date on administration of a future Namibia. According to the paper, the political system would be based on the principle of parliamentary democracy. Namibia would be a republic with a president with strong executive powers as the head of state. It is suggested that a single-chamber 100-member legislative parliament would be adequate, without excluding the possibility of an advisory second chamber consisting of traditional tribal chiefs. An independent judiciary and an impartial public service would guarantee minority rights. The cabinet would have a minister responsible for human rights, and a Complaints Commissioner would see to complaints about public administration. English would be the official language and Namibia would apply for membership of the Commonwealth.[18]

These constitutional proposals reflect Western principles of political democracy, expressing SWAPO's efforts to optimize national and international support for its programme. However, the document is not very precise as to the role of the national liberation movement, the position of the political opposition, or the status of the lower-level representative organs, such as people's committees, in an independent Namibia.

Social basis of the liberation process

It is important to examine the social content of Namibian liberation. This raises the question of how to differentiate between the concept of *national* liberation and that of *social* liberation.[19] Consequently one should examine which social strata form the leading elements in the anti-colonial struggle.

Each liberation movement reflects the specific conditions of its own country. Thus neither the vanguardism of a Marxist–Leninist proletarian party nor the Western democratic multi-party system has been able to provide a model for national liberation. What is required is a new, special type of political organization: a multi-class, united, nationwide political formation. In these terms, a liberation movement is the expression and embodiment of national unity in the struggle for independence.

Although some barriers against cooperation between different 'tribes', regional and social groups have been broken down, the Namibian people cannot be conceived as monolithic, without internal conflicts. SWAPO's liberation theory does not imply belief in a conflict-free society, or in Africa's 'classlessness', notions which have been typical of earlier phases of African nationalism. On the contrary, it recognizes social stratification and the attendant conflicts of interests within the united front, and realizes that, although they might not be explicit in the early stages of national liberation, they will inevitably become evident during the period of reconstruction.

The composition of a national liberation front and the position of different groups in it reflect the country's social structure, the level of consciousness of different social groups, and their positions in the colonial administrative machinery. The need 'to unite all Namibian people, particularly the working class, the peasantry and progressive intellectuals' is emphasized in SWAPO's programme. This expresses the general orientation of the Namibian liberation front firstly, against foreign, colonial domination and secondly, against internal inequalities and social subordination. As is typical of a national movement, there is no deeper analysis of social relations and the significance of different social groups in society – at least not in external mobilization-oriented manifestos.

In practice, the process of national liberation in Namibia was launched by a group of young, educated activists who had moved to urban areas. Some were contract labourers but others were school teachers or clergy. The young intellectuals and midde class do not, however, represent a sufficiently broad economic or social base to effect the seizure of power. They have to identify with the masses in order to mobilize an effective and widespread national liberation struggle. Nevertheless the intellectuals have had a significant role as instructors, organizers and leaders, especially in the first phase of the liberation struggle.[20]

The success of the liberation movement in Namibia has been based essentially on its ability to turn the interests of workers and peasants[21] all over the country into its own interests and thus to mobilize popular support. Those movements and organizations in Namibia which have been led by the traditional elite (NUDO, Damara Tribal Executive, Nama Chiefs' Council, etc.), or have limited themselves to fostering the interests of some specific social or ethnic group (Rehoboth Baster Verening, Rehoboth Volkspartei, The Voice of the People Party, Demcop, NAPDO), or have remained merely organizations of a narrow group of students and of political refugees abroad (SWANUF, and, beyond the special case of Herero land rights, SWANU) have thus not been able to become leading forces in the liberation process. SWAPO's success, on the other hand, can be explained by the following:

a its operations were originally mainly carried out inside Namibia and it has retained a broad network of branches and activists within the territory;
b it has been capable of uniting people of different ethnic or regional origins, and religious affiliations or beliefs into a cohesive, national organization;
c from its early beginnings, it found support not only among the intellectuals and the middle class but also, and most importantly, among urban (contract) workers and rural peasants and hence became a liberation movement.

The mobilization of the population has, in addition to national objectives, accentuated social aims, since the objectives of the liberation movement have been founded on the needs and aspirations of the lower social strata. Thus SWAPO was able to create a social basis for a successful liberation struggle supported by the majority of the population.

Social objectives of national liberation

What, then, is meant by identification with the interests of the majority of the people and what are the main policy issues in the independent Namibia? During the course of the liberation struggle the social objectives of the liberation movement have been refined continually. SWAPO's first political programme, dating from 1960, emphasized the right to self-determination and to political equality. The transformation process was seen primarily as political liberation, and consequently equal human rights and political freedoms were emphasized: 'Universal adult suffrage', 'full equality of the rights and responsibilities', 'freedom of speech, press, assembly, and religion', etc.

It would be wrong to assume that SWAPO no longer subscribes to these goals, but over time the emphasis has shifted from political liberation to social emancipation. The major objectives are social justice, nationwide economic progress, and people's participation in social decision-making. The 1976 Political Programme states the aspirations of an independent Namibia as follows:

1 Wage the struggle towards the abolition of all forms of exploitation of man by man and the destructive spirit of individualism and aggrandisement of wealth and power by individuals, groups or classes.
2 Ensure that all the major means of production and exchange of the country are [in the] ownership of the people.
3 Strive for the creation of an integrated, a national economy in which there is a proper balance between agricultural and industrial developments along the lines:
   a the establishment of processing industry;
   b a comprehensive agrarian reform aimed at giving land to the tillers;
   c the establishment of peasants' or farmers' cooperatives or collectives;
   d the establishment of state-owned ranching and crop farms, aimed at making Namibia an agriculturally self-sufficient nation, and
   e the cultivation of a spirit of self-reliance among our people.

As to education, culture and health services, the SWAPO programme aims to increase social justice and 'the development of the skills, knowledge and cultural creativeness of the toiling masses'. The programme proposes an extensive campaign for 'work-oriented, functional literacy', free and universal education, and, in particular, urgent training of technical and professional personnel. The health programme emphasizes free medical services, effective preventive medicine and health education.

The realization of SWAPO's political programme would imply profound social and economic reconstruction in Namibia. One is impelled to ask whether SWAPO would stand a better chance of carrying out its programme than have had other African national movements.

Social mobilization

Many African countries achieved political independence relatively painlessly. They did not experience violent anti-colonial struggle. Broad national movements were often established but were not forced to refine their goals beyond the single word 'independence', nor was there any need to raise general social consciousness beyond creating the belief that political independence was possible. In many cases, the mere replacement of the European administration by African counterparts did not change the privileged position of the elite or the prevailing economic power structures which were products of the colonial period. New bureaucracies have been corrupted and both civil and military elites have often used harsh methods to suppress attempts to extend the liberation process.

In areas where the people were mobilized on a larger scale, over a longer time scale, and with a more articulated set of goals and perceptions in the anti-colonial struggle, the independence movement became transformed into a liberation movement. In order to maintain and to extend mobilization, the political leadership had to tie the programme closely to the interests and aspirations of the people, which inherently presupposed social changes together with political independence.

The South African colonial administration in Namibia has not been willing to make concessions. Therefore the national liberation process led by SWAPO has been based on the broadest possible political mobilization. This strategy implies that SWAPO trusts in the political and social consciousness of the people themselves, and their willingness for active participation. This fact has not, however, been taken for granted; its development has required continuous political work, and eventually progress towards national liberation depends on its success. Consequently the political programme of SWAPO stresses:

> All sections and organs of SWAPO are called upon to make supreme efforts towards the building up of a reliable core of leading cadres who are capable of being in close and constant touch with the people at all levels.[22]

For political mobilization to succeed, SWAPO's programme emphasizes that one must constantly try to 'deepen political understanding' among SWAPO supporters and the people alike, to remove any doubts and suspicions concerning the possibility of change, and to show the strength of political organization:

> SWAPO shall involve the whole population in active discussion which is the main pre-condition for the people's explicit and conscious commitment to the policy of the movement.[23]

This is not an attempt from above, from an isolated vanguard, to lead the liberation process, but rather to show people the need to solve their problems themselves. The crucial strength of the liberation movement is based on everyday political work undertaken in villages and towns. Even when external support might be available and the preparation for resistance built up outside the colonial territory, the liberation movement cannot be successful without working inside the country and without having the active participation of the people.

Armed struggle

SWAPO holds the conviction that armed resistance to the South African occupation in our country is the only viable and effective means left for us to achieve genuine liberation in Namibia.

In many parts of Africa, bitter experiences of colonial wars and 'pacification' operations have led to serious attempts to find peaceful solutions. These have manifested themselves as quasi-pacifist ideologies, following the 'non-violent resistance' of Gandhi, or as only latently force-oriented tactics of mass demonstrations and/or non-cooperation such as the 'positive action' of Nkrumah.[24] In these circumstances, conscious acceptance of armed struggle has represented a long and difficult step:

> The brutal repressive policy of the South Africans caught us by surprise. We had thought that we should carry on our struggle with the peaceful methods used elsewhere in Africa. But our demonstrations, boycotts and strikes were met with brute force and many leaders of SWAPO were tortured and killed. At the same time our peaceful efforts on the diplomatic front were frustrated by the inactivity of the UN.[25]

> SWAPO itself was a non-violent organization, but the South African government is not truly interested in whether opposition is violent or non-violent. It does not wish to hear any opposition to apartheid. Since 1963 SWAPO meetings have been banned. . . . We have found ourselves voteless in our own country and deprived of the right to meet and state our own political opinions. Is it surprising that in such times my countrymen have taken up arms? It was not an easy decision. Another man might have been able to say 'I will have nothing to do with that sort of thing'. I was not, and I could not remain a spectator in the struggle of my people for their freedom.[26]

This is how Sam Nujoma and Herman Toivo ja Toivo describe the circumstances in which armed struggle became inevitable. The violence used by SWAPO is a direct response to the violence of the South African regime. Hence armed struggle is now integrally included in the general political strategy of the movement:

> However, much as we are convinced that armed struggle must now be the main form of our liberation activity, we do not beautify war as a purpose or regard it as a form of sport. We see war for what it really is – an extension of politics by other means. It is the continuation of political relations in the form of violence. But as in all other political relations one must seek to understand the nature of the politics being pursued in examining any war. As social relations, political acts are either just or unjust and just political acts are naturally to be supported.[27]

As resistance has grown and strengthened and the position of the regime weakened, there have been two complementary tactics in South African policy. On the one hand, the violence of the regime has become more intense, widespread and overt. On the other hand, a pseudo-solution has been attempted in the hope of dividing the national front.

Guerrilla activities have led to mass arrests, brutal retaliation and victimization. The South Africans hoped that the population would oppose the freedom fighters who were said to cause unnecessary suffering to civilians by continuing the guerrilla struggle. However, the effect has been rather the opposite. The violence of the government has strengthened the very challenge it had been designed to defeat. Those who until now had been cautious or undecided, but who have been punished or threatened, have been prepared to give full support to the resistance movement. The point has been reached where anything the government might decide to do against the liberation movement would weaken its own position: to reduce the scale of repression would facilitate progress by the movement; not to do so would fortify that challenge by expanding popular support.

This has forced the regime to revise its tactics, and to attempt to find a false solution to the problem. The government of South Africa, in convening the Turnhalle talks, in organizing general elections and in organizing a 'National Assembly', has apparently been forced to concede the basic demands of the national movement, those of political independence and African majority rule. In this new situation, SWAPO, as the leading national force, must re-evaluate its goals and strategy. Mass support inside Namibia and world-wide political support until now have been based primarily on *national* demands, which are generally recognized. In this context the political programme of SWAPO has provided the framework for a strategy of national struggle. After Turnhalle and the beginning of a move toward what are made to appear as national institutions and national independence, SWAPO should specify even more clearly its *social* objectives. Two senses of independence must be distinguished to demonstrate the difference between a national movement and a national liberation movement.

Notes

1 Sam Nujoma, statement at Dakar International Conference, 5–8 January 1976.

2 Basil Davidson, *Which Way Africa*? Penguin African Library, 1971, p. 126.

3 See, e.g., Raimo Väyrynen, *Interdependence vs Self Reliance: Two Approaches to International Economic Relations*, Tampere Peace Research Institute, Research Reports No. 16, 1978.

4 SWAPO, *The Political Programme*, 1976.

5 'African socialism' has been specifically rejected as a description of themselves or as a valid concept by Angola, Mozambique, Algeria, Ethiopia, Somalia, Guinea, Guinea Bissau and Tanzania. This is partly in reaction to its use to describe a particularly inegalitarian capitalist dynamic

(Kenya) and a more sophisticated gloss on a system combining external capitalist dependence, a secondary state capitalist sector and major bureaucratic and neo-feudal elements (Senegal). It is therefore a highly confusing term since different authors use it to classify very different policies and bodies of thought.

6 Sékou Touré's term and one less unacceptable to most Africans who reject 'African socialism' as a concept.

7 Richard Hall, ed., *South-West Africa, Proposals for Action*, The Africa Bureau, London, 1970, p. 23.

8 SWAPO, *The Political Programme.*

9 Davidson, *Which Way Africa*? p. 68.

10 Sam Nujoma, interviewed by *LSM News*, No. 11–12, p. 15.

11 *Ibid.*, p. 16.

12 Davidson, *Which Way Africa*? p.58.

13 Herman Toivo ja Toivo, Statement in the Supreme Court in Pretoria on 26 January 1968.

14 Eliaser Tuhadeleni quoted by Hall, *South-West Africa*, p. 26.

15 'On the Content of the Liberation Struggle', SWAPO, *Current Events in Namibia*, No. 7, 1976, p. 9.

16 *Ibid.*, p. 9.

17 SWAPO, *Discussion Paper on the Constitution of Independent Namibia*, 1975, para. 42.

18 Compare also with United Nations Institute for Namibia, *Constitutional Options for Namibia*, Lusaka, 1979.

19 See Amilcar Cabral's analysis in Lars Rudebeck, *Guinea-Bissau*, Scandinavian Institute of African Studies, Uppsala, 1974, pp. 82–83.

20 Cf. Amilcar Cabral, *Revolution in Guinea, An African People's Struggle*, Imprimerie Joseph Adam, Brussels, 1974 and Samir Amin, *The Class Struggle in Africa*, Africa Research Group, Cambridge, n.d.

21 Because of the contract-labour system the most politically conscious bodies of workers are also both past and future peasants.

22 SWAPO, *The Political Programme.*

23 *Ibid.*

24 See *Review of African Political Economy*, No. 4, 1975, pp. 9–11.

25 Sam Nujoma, interviewed by *LSM News*, No. 11–12, p. 5.

26 Herman Toivo ja Toivo, Statement.

27 SWAPO, *The Political Programme.*

11 The political economy of liberation

REGINALD H. GREEN

We do not believe in a system which sells people.

– Katutura Strikers, 1971.

Economic reconstruction in a free, democratic and united Namibia will have, as its motive force the establishment of a classless society. The social justice and progress for all is the governing idea behind every SWAPO policy decision.
- abolition of all forms of exploitation
- major means of production and exchange of the country are [in the] ownership of the people
- an integration national economy
- land to the tiller
- agriculturally self-sufficient
- a spirit of self-reliance

– SWAPO, Political Programme, 1976

Namibia is a special, or perhaps more accurately an extreme, case of a very small (economically and demographically), very dependent, very peripheral political economic unit confronted by both severe constraints on, but also the necessity for, radical political, social and economic structural change.[1]

The scant population is spread over a vast area. The usable land is in constant danger of degradation into desert and only a small fraction of it is suitable for crop cultivation. Namibia is heavily dependent on imported food, including up to 50% of staple grains. The rich fishing waters are now suffering from massive over-fishing and the mineral wealth is potentially in danger of being exhausted through unplanned mining. It is relatively expensive to supply additional water and power which, in turn, restricts the setting up of large industrial plants as well as extending crop cultivation by irrigation.

In technology the key sectors depend on foreign expertise and know-how, while Europeans – many of whom have no permanent ties with Namibia even under the present regime – hold 90% of the posts requiring high qualifications, even though they are at most a tenth of the population.

The economy is not internally integrated. The infrastructure (railways, communications, banking, commerce) does not cover the whole country and is centred on supporting exports and imports. The economy relies on a few commodities and is 90% export-oriented as to goods produced. By definition it is very fragile and, for several products, subject to sharp fluctuations in world prices and quantities demanded, and to problems of market access. Socially, the heritage of land theft, the so-called contract-labour system, residence control and apartheid have created a series of cumulative and cross-contradicting stresses on the economy and especially on the excluded, exploited and oppressed 90% of Namibians who are not white. All these factors make it difficult to create conditions in Namibia propitious for launching diversified economic development oriented toward meeting the basic needs of the Namibian people.

The resource constraints interact with that of size. Even if Namibia cut and polished diamonds and turned its blister copper into cables and pipes, the basic market would still be abroad. Even if every Namibian had as much meat, dairy products and fish as any dietitian would approve, over three-quarters of present production would have no domestic use. On the reverse side, fertilizer, pesticide, wire, implement, pump, vehicle and machinery plants can be viable in Namibia only if they serve markets broader and larger than its own ranching and farming sectors.

The lack of expertise and technical personnel can be remedied only gradually by training Namibians, but the course of Namibia's liberation struggle suggests a traumatic break in personnel continuity, like that in Mozambique or Angola or Algeria, not a relatively orderly and systematic transition like that of Botswana or Zambia or Tanzania. In the short term, keeping what is critical running and adding what is immediately essential may be more than the limits of the possible. Building up additions desirable in terms of medium-term priorities may have to wait.

Finally there are constraints on political economic choice: the advocates of a Transkei-type model or a Kampuchean one almost certainly live in an unreal world or at least in a non-existent 'Namibia'. The real struggle is between a Kenya/Botswana-influenced model and a Tanzania/Mozambique-informed one. The former requires Namibian capitalists of some competence and a high degree of worker acceptance of continued foreign dominance of their lives – conditions an observer may well believe to be contrary to fact. The latter requires, first, a fairly large, technically competent, committed Namibian public service; second, a party capable of mobilizing mass support and mass consciousness of the need for relative austerity (especially for elites); and third, a society and economy able to endure significant transitional disruptions. Even a sympathiser must have doubts as to how fully that set of conditions can be met.

Toward a political economy of liberation: SWAPO guidelines

The following is a presentation of the political economic guidelines toward a strategy for Namibian independence as presented or discussed by SWAPO. SWAPO is the only mass Namibian political movement with a nationwide support in terms both of geography and of community. In its external cadres SWAPO has both a substantial party and proto-government apparatus on the civil side and a military force.

The only other national bodies of significance in Namibia are the churches. They have been increasingly active in a struggle against perceived racial injustice and their teaching of the Christian gospel has been a major force in raising consciousness of injustice and of the possibility of change and of bringing Namibians together in groups.[2] The denunciation 'SWAPO Headquarters', scrawled on the wall of the Anglican Cathedral in Windhoek, was not random or mindless, at least to the daubers. The black churches have indirectly condemned also those Namibians who chose to cooperate with the government. However, because of their nature, the Namibian churches have not presented any very systematic guidelines toward a just political economy.[3] But it seems reasonable to assume that they are in broad agreement with the guidelines presented by SWAPO.[4]

The other political parties in Namibia are either European parties or small parties which draw their support from particular communities (ethnic groups). The whites' views range from 'what we have stolen we hold' (Aktur) through 'we'll give back a bit if we can keep the rest and *de facto* political control' (Democratic Turnhalle Alliance) to 'Let us build capitalism together – you take the small firms and posts and we'll keep the big' (Federal Party).[5] The black groups' statements tend to be fragmentary, with most of the few exceptions rather evidently written by American or South African public relations experts or lawyers. Both groups have stressed the importance of land rights almost to the exclusion of other issues. The white settlers, corporate officials, chiefs, would-be landed gentry and would-be inheritors of ranches all see access to, and secure control over, land as central.

SWAPO's political economic goals and strategies can be studied in four documents:[6]

1 the 1975 *Discussion Paper on the Constitution of Independent Namibia* (what its title implies and not an official programme or policy statement);
2 *Political Programme of the South West Africa People's Organization* adopted by the Central Committee in August 1976;
3 The 1976 *SWAPO Programme of Action*, a more detailed document largely articulating the published *Programme*;
4 *Manpower Estimates and Development Implications for Namibia*, prepared and published in 1978 by the United Nations Institute for Namibia but quite overtly seeking to construct a manpower development in the framework of the SWAPO *Programme*.

1 With the exception of one or two paragraphs, the *Discussion Paper* does not address itself directly to political economic issues, although seven themes do emerge:

a the potential for Namibia to become 'one of the richer states of Africa' is limited and thwarted by the pattern of territorial exploitation practised by South Africa;
b the policies of apartheid must be reversed and 'comprehensive and effective anti-discrimination legislation' must be used to preserve equality of access and prevent renewed communalism;
c educating and training of Namibian manpower are central needs and

must be met largely in Namibian institutions;

d 'the economic, social and political inequality imposed by South Africa is as profound as it is dangerous' and requires redress in terms of structural reduction of inequality of opportunity and of access to jobs, to housing and to land;

e 'genuine independence', including economic independence and in particular the rapid reduction of South African influence, are critical to structural changes in production (less imbalance and greater food production) and in distribution (less inequality and an end to enforced racial inequality);

f expatriate expertise (implicitly at least non-South African) will be needed for an interim period to fill the gaps until adequate numbers of Namibians have received education and training;

g property rights, 'including pension rights' . . . 'vested legal rights and titles in property', require legal protection.

The seventh principle does not appear to follow from, but rather to conflict with, the first six. Indeed it is not credible that its apparent meaning of Namibia vesting occupation land titles and land-use rights in their current holders was intended, as this would entrench settler and expatriate ownership of natural resources. What is clear in the *Discussion Paper* is the absence of any clear perspective on the mode of production either in respect to organization or to production relations. The statements do not lack content, but they are incomplete as compared, for instance, to the Kenyan 1965 *African Socialism*[7] or to the Tanzanian 1967 *Arusha Declaration*[8] which are coherent and relatively articulated presentations of capitalist and socialist strategies within the national contexts to which they pertain.

2 and 3 The *Political Programme* of SWAPO and the *SWAPO Programme of Action* taken together present a much more comprehensive and, in broad outline at least, articulated set of political economic goals and guidelines. They can be grouped in six clusters:

a mode of production (ownership patterns);
b rural development;
c distribution (exploitation and equality);
d national economic integration/self-reliance;
e basic services;
f participation.

a The basic *mode of production* set as a goal is socialist. 'Bringing all the major means of production and exchange into the ownership of the people' and 'planning and development will be governed by the principles of scientific socialism' are specifically set out as goals. However, a transitional period with state, cooperative, joint venture and private ownership is equally clearly stated. The initial minimum public (directly productive) sector is envisaged as including land, mineral and fishing rights, banking and finance, public utilities, mass media. Private ownership of productive assets will be allowed only within a national planning framework and subject to consistency with the interests of the people in the short term and economic development in the medium term. Arrangements renegotiated with existing private enterprises (implicitly as joint ventures) are specifically stated. Indeed full nationalization is neither specified nor clearly implied except in respect of land, mineral and fishing rights and South African state and state corporation assets. Continued private ownership of non-productive assets (dwelling houses, savings accounts) 'justly acquired' is guaranteed. It is clear that these reforms will radically change ownership relations. The nationalization of land, natural resources, finance, public services and transport would give the state the formal and economic means to pursue a transformation toward socialism.

b 'Comprehensive agrarian reforms aimed at giving the land to the tillers' are seen as a precondition for *rural development*. All colonial land 'rights' are to be extinguished and possible continued use of all or part of the land involved by present holders made subject to negotiation. Peasant and farmer cooperatives and collectives are presented as one form of organization to be developed and state ranches and crop farms as another. Self-sufficiency in food is made an explicit goal. Better knowledge, more inputs and agricultural industries (both to produce inputs and to process outputs) are cited as means to improve the productivity and the incomes of the rural sector.

c 'The abolition of all forms of *exploitation* of man by man . . .' is linked to aspects of *equality* including elimination of differences between towns and rural areas and regional balance in the distribution of wealth. Two sets of measures specifically cited are price control and general surveillance to prevent 'parasitic means' of making profits on the one hand, and opportunities for full, productive employment on the other. Linked to the latter are provisions for non-discriminatory wage and salary scales and protection of workers' economic and organizational rights. This protection is also to be undertaken by trade unions which are to be free to defend workers' interests and to participate in economic management. The contract-labour system, child labour and 'humiliating servant systems' are to be abolished. The degree of equality in earnings envisaged is not very clear; 'payment according to one's contribution' linked to a clear opposition to substantial unearned or property income and to broad rural/urban income equality implies narrower limits than those in a majority of African countries, but how much narrower has not received direct public consideration.

d *National economic integration and self-reliance* are treated as integral parts of national development. Equality of access to work, removing rural/urban inequalities, provision of education and training are seen as having an economic content as well as being necessary to making the SWAPO motto 'One Namibia, One Nation' a reality. The attainment of basic self-sufficiency in food and the building up of natural resource-based and/or input-producing industries is set in the context of increasing national economic balance and self-reliance. Public-sector control of fiscal, monetary and financial policy and institutions is one of the main means toward integration and planning set out.

However, neither autarchy – complete self-sufficiency – nor a drastic reduction of absolute levels of production for export are seen as realistic options. The programme, implicitly at least, envisages guidelines in mining, fishing and ranching production for export set in terms of long-term Namibian requirements. The processing of fish and meat will, in the first place, take care of Namibia's own nutritional requirements and also contribute to foreign-exchange earnings. Processing of raw materials to add to the value of exports and increase employment is a stated goal, as is the building up of a broader manufacturing sector, but these reforms do not, as presented, imply any drastic retreat from the world economy.

This is not an unusual stance even in the context of radical transformation of social relations. Autarchy, or even minimization of external economic contacts, has always been more an academic than an operational enthusiasm. The Soviet New Economic Policy, China's 1945–75 doubling of the ratio of external trade to national output, the central role of exports in Korean People's Republic development strategy, and the rapid post-1975 build-up of external economic relations by Vietnam suggest that selectivity and control are more likely to be the hallmarks of a socialist state's international economic strategy than general withdrawal from external economic relations. In the particular case of Namibia, almost any serious development strategy would be likely to reduce the ratio of external trade to national output, because the domestic market-oriented sub-sectors of production have been so systematically neglected rather than because external trade would be reduced absolutely or even systematically discouraged.

The most radical, and in the short term perhaps the most difficult, guideline relates to selective delinking to 'sever all relations with the South African racist regime until there is a democratic government in that country based on the principles of Majority Rule'. However, the wording appears quite deliberately to leave open the possibility of selective interim use of some personnel who are South African and renegotiated relations with some private South African firms on a case-by-case basis.[9]

e *Basic service* provision is presented in terms of health and education. Urban services, including housing, somewhat surprisingly given the shift from contract to resident household non-agricultural labour force patterns which is a recurrent theme, do not receive specific attention. Health is presented in terms of preventive as well as curative, paramedical as well as highly specialized, decentralized rural as well as urban. Indeed it is heavily influenced by SWAPO's own rural medical work in northern and north-eastern Namibia and the perspective that work has provided on needs and possibilities. Education is related to self-reliance (functional and literacy) and nation building (primary and adult, creation of a national cadre of educators). The balance of emphasis is significantly different from the standard European and UNESCO export models of the 1950s and 1960s especially in its emphasis on adult education, universality, variety of approaches and linking functional and 'broader' aims.

f *Participation* is a recurrent theme: 'The economic reconstruction aims at the creation of a classless society.' Trade unions are seen as workers' organisations to serve worker interests and to participate in economic unit management. Cooperative and community action are also stressed. In the political participation sphere SWAPO clearly seeks to become the single party: 'To unite all Namibian people particularly the working class, the peasantry and progressive intellectuals into a vanguard Party capable of safeguarding . . . and building.' This formulation poses a conflict of aims in emphasizing both the idea of a mass party and that of a vanguard party. On the one hand, the former offers broader scope for participation, a wider base for mass mobilization, a lower risk of the party developing into a state capitalist or bureaucratic socialist elite. On the other hand, the latter offers a higher average level of consciousness on the part of members, a membership more ready for sacrifice, reduced need for compromise in efforts to maintain unity within the party, a lower risk of neo-capitalist elites working their way up to the party leadership. In practice, both approaches, though with different balances of emphasis, have been used simultaneously among African parties aiming at socialism. TANU in Tanzania has put more emphasis on the mass side rather than on the vanguard role whereas MPLA in Angola has become a vanguard party and Frelimo in Mozambique seems to lie between these two.

Decentralization is implicit rather than spelled out and the word itself is not used. This is because South Africa's 'divide and rule' policy and attempts to create pseudo-territorial, pseudo-decentralized ethnic mini-states have required SWAPO to place central stress on attaining the unity of people, nation and state. It is not because a highly centralized bureaucratic model lies behind the strategy.

Women's participation is not explicitly treated in either the *Political Programme* or the *Programme of Action* but has received substantial attention within SWAPO. Indeed its secondary, technical and higher education programmes demonstrate a greater stress on equal participation by women at all levels than that achieved by any independent African (perhaps by any) state, while its initial work on new legal codes has concentrated on family law and on strengthening women's rights.[10]

4. *Manpower Estimates and Development Implications for Namibia* is a different type of document. It does not seek to present its own political economic goals but to articulate within SWAPO's. It is overtly political in that the framework constructed to identify probable structural changes and future personnel requirements is drawn from the SWAPO *Programme*. Further it deliberately poses a series of questions, e.g. urban transformation, creating a working national language, women's participation, production relations, urban/rural balance, income distribution policy, production relations, which are hardly the substance of technical manpower planning but do arise from seeking to carry the *programme* forward to the policy formulation and resource allocation stage.

By its nature a technical exercise does not define a political economic strategy, a primarily sectoral one does not articulate ways and means for an entire strategy, and an initial perspective exercise based on inherently inadequate data can only in part lead directly into implementation. However, the study does demonstrate a number of points in respect to SWAPO's strategy for a political economy of liberation.

a The elements of the strategy are broadly inclusive and coherent and have enough specific content to serve as a working frame for transitional and medium-term perspective planning.
b The strategy is both closely enough aligned to necessity and flexibly enough formulated in terms of phasing of detail that it appears technically feasible to devise a Namibian planning process able to achieve substantial implementation of the strategy.
c The major issues which arise in the course of working out technical documents, e.g. role of women, urban expansion, rural development, are ones already discussed within SWAPO, not blank spaces demonstrating lack of coherence or fatal internal contradictions.

Viewing the strategy presented in the four documents as a whole, several key points emerge.

a Economic and political relations are seen in terms of struggle and the state as an instrument in that struggle, not with the state as a neutral coordination mechanism within a broad harmony of interests.
b Liberation is perceived as requiring radical initial economic structural changes to set in motion a process of change towards socialism, equality, participation and self-reliance.
c The initial radical economic changes are set for the independence period (not several years later) but the phasing of the subsequent transition and the exact extent of the initial changes remain to be worked out.
d The magnitude of the implications and interactions of certain guidelines, e.g. 'ending contract' and urban population, removing urban/rural inequality and rural development, terminating South African links and interim personnel/knowledge procurement, do not appear to have been fully perceived to date.
e The guidelines' radical nature, both as to objectives and as to the requisite scale of initial changes, is coupled with deliberate flexibility as to particular initial priorities, sequences and sizes.
f Limited data, technical staff and ability to allocate energy from the immediate political liberation struggle have, to date, slowed the translation of the guidelines and protoplan framework into a more detailed and directly operational form. However, higher priority is now being given to such a translation in several areas.
g The number of elements relating directly to Namibian history and reality rules out any supposition that the documents are 'copied' from some external model, but the overall impression is that the greatest influences in shaping SWAPO views on strategic approaches and elements have been the Tanzanian and, more recently, Mozambican experiences. As between the Tanzania/Mozambique and Kenya/Botswana models there can be little doubt that the

Political Programme and the *Programme of Action* are basically congruent with the first and radically inconsistent with the second.

The political economy of accommodation

It is possible to advance a very different political economic strategy for a politically independent Namibia, that of slow change with major continuity (including with South Africa and settlers) and a basically peripheral capitalist ideology.

This is not the political economy of the Odendaal Report nor of the Turnhalle conference itself. Odendaal was an early attempt to continue the policy of separate development by founding 'Homelands' or Bantustans. Turnhalle merely sought to buy off a group of non-European traditional, professional and small business leaders, while slightly reducing the most blatant injustices of the system to prevent even gradual reform toward a more normal peripheral capitalist structure like that of Kenya or the Ivory Coast.

The strategy of gradual reform is the stated political economy of the Turnhalle Democratic Alliance organized by Dirk Mudge, and supported by some 'Coloured' and African politicians.[11] A similar approach is to be found in W. Thomas' *Development Strategies for an Independent Namibia*,[12] which is a coherent, forceful statement of the case founded on a detailed knowledge of official data. Thomas sees a need for more far-reaching change over time to prevent explosive change in the short term and to preserve the interests of large foreign firms, European managers and professionals as well as a reduced settler rancher and small business community.

This is also the strategy implicitly endorsed by large foreign firms, including Anglo American, American Metal Climax (Tsumeb) and Rio Tinto Zinc (Rössing), because they see it as requiring only minor accommodation on their part with any shifts of income or power to Namibians coming largely at the expense of settlers and expatriate civil servants. Fragmentary statements suggest it is also the scenario preferred by the so-called Contact Group (United States, United Kingdom, Federal Republic of Germany, Canada, France), otherwise termed 'the Gang of Five'. However, the Five and Anglo appear to favour a somewhat less glacial rate of change than do the Turnhalle Democratic Alliance and the other companies. Indeed, they seem ready to jettison the settler ranchers to save the mines and access to their output.

In principle this approach accepts that Namibia's history for the past century has been filled with injustices even if, unlike the political economy of liberation, it would not characterize injustice and theft as central and integral to that history. However, it also contends that a common interest basis uniting non-European Namibians, settlers, South African and European firms can and should be found. Harmony, not struggle, is at the core of its political economic model for Namibia.

Perhaps oddly, the basic principle of harmony is qualified by far greater emphasis on divergent sub-ethnic group conflicts of interest and far more emphasis on occupational and income inequalities among

Africans leading to potential clashes over policy than in the political economy of liberation. This is, at least in Thomas, combined with an emphasis on equality of opportunity and of personal rights. However, the heavy emphasis on ethnicity, combined with entrenchment of property rights, seem well designed to maximize conflict and to minimize equality of opportunity.

The case for relatively slow change is partly based on particular perceptions of economic and environmental constraints. The constraints themselves are real enough and are recognized in the political economy of liberation; it is the perception of their nature and implications which varies. However, more basically, this strategy is built on the foundation of commitment to a capitalist political economic and socio-political evolution. The model is a cross between Kenya (with South Africa playing the role of the United Kingdom) and Botswana (with the same combination of mining companies and citizen ranching entrepreneurs, multi-party system dominated by men of substance, and a state apparatus led by technical personnel cadres largely supplied by Europe and the Republic).[13]

The environmental and agricultural productivity constraints are outlined, including the danger of desert encroachment and loss of output and markets. The proposed solution is slow to very slow phasing down of existing settler farmers in favour of selected Namibian capitalist farmers combined with some sub-division of larger ranches. A fairly standard model farmer/smallholder support programme is proposed for the north with the gradual creation of freehold tenure as one of its priorities.

Transport, trade and monetary/financial dependence on the Republic (including the bland assumption that Walvis Bay will remain 'South African' until Namibia can convince the Republic it is 'responsible' enough to receive it)[14] are treated primarily as given facts in the short term, secondarily as providing valuable potential continuity and stability, and only tertiarily as too concentrated and requiring gradual diversification.

Maintenance of production is treated as vital to stable change because broad redistribution of the 75% of output estimated as going to settlers, expatriates and foreign firms is perceived as impossible. To keep output up requires experienced personnel, primarily settlers and Republic expatriates, but over time including trained Namibians and foreign aid technicians. Further, it requires continued investor confidence, access to private capital, and a climate conducive to large Western aid and only gradually decreasing Republic subsidy transfers.[15] The output and personnel constraints are of course real, but as *Manpower Estimates and Development Implications for Namibia* demonstrates, they can be viewed very differently depending on the degree of initial redistribution seen as essential, the speed and scope of Namibianization possible, and the degree of interim expatriate procurement achievable.

The greatest apparent factual disagreement relates to the fiscal position. The conservative perception is of a very large (up to R450 million) actual present deficit and a best possible result for an independent Namibia of domestic balance on recurrent account and total external financing of public sector investment.[16] Excluding 'defence' spending, the alternative calculations show a large recurrent account surplus now and no long-term need for substantial external capital (as opposed to personnel and technical assistance financing). Part of the divergence relates to very different – but not very clearly spelled out – tax and income-level assumptions. The political economy of liberation clearly envisages higher taxes and less generous salary levels. These basic assumptions interlock with those as to foreign firms, investor confidence, Republic relations, and dependence on industrial capitalist economy goodwill.

The political system envisaged is multi-party or broad party coalition. It is seen as led by men of substance, standing and traditional authority, in a way reminiscent of the daydreams of most colonial attempts to construct a *parti d'administration*. Foreign companies and governments are seen as its bankers plus settlers and expatriates, as its initial sources of expertise and personnel. The development of broader opportunities and a moderately rising share of output for Namibians within a gradually altered system are presented as aims, first to appeal to the leadership and its basic 'middle-class' supporters, and second to co-opt the main body of workers and peasants away from young, educated African leaders who are seen as largely committed to SWAPO.

The view of history and of property is rather special. No attempt is made to deny that the colonial regime was oppressive and exploitative, but no attempt is made to analyze how and why, as a base from which to propose strategic changes. Indeed the implicit view is that studying the past will envenom the present and hinder the future. This is especially true in respect to property. The issues of land theft and exploitative contracts, let alone the post-1966 illegal agreements with South Africa, e.g. Rössing, Oamites, Otjihase, Langer Heinrich, are blandly swept aside and all property rights except these of South Africa in respect of past infrastructure and operating transfers are entrenched.[17]

This strategy is not one of no change, nor are many of its detailed proposals unsound in themselves nor radically divergent from some of the projects and policies a political economy of liberation would choose. However, the context and direction of change are basically divergent: toward an externally dependent, internally divided, highly inegalitarian, peripheral state and economy. The actual results of implementing such a strategy would be even worse. The Republic is not the United Kingdom; a new Transkei, not a new Botswana, would be the likely outcome if the system survived. In fact, given the strength of SWAPO and the lack of global credibility such a regime would have, the only likely result would be a continuation of open warfare until the regime collapsed, a scenario which would make the process of transition to independence even more painful for all concerned.

Strategic choices: production, control, allocation, integration

Four strategic choices confront any attempt to work through a political economy of liberation in Namibia:

1 a national capitalist reconstruction or a transition to socialism?
2 a centralized or decentralized decision-making and implementing system?
3 a growth and modernization of basic-human-needs set of goals?
4 maximum integration into the existing international economic order or an emphasis on self-reliance and natural economic integration.

1 The mode of production issue is really a choice between transition to state capitalism and transition to socialism. The capitalism of the second half of the twentieth century is dominated by large economic units, and large private enterprises in Africa are inevitably dominantly foreign. A liberation-oriented strategy can, therefore, only choose between state capitalism and socialism as goals and, presumably, both would use joint ventures in large-scale and local capitalist/ cooperative/communal ventures in small-scale activity for a transitional period of moderately extended duration.

The difference is not necessarily in per cent of public sector ownership of means of production, but in goals in respect of income distribution, production relations and class responsibility of decision takers. In practice, overt state capitalism in Africa today tends also to seek to build up permanent alliances with transnational corporations and particular entrepreneurial/managerial allies and satellites around them and, on the whole, to have smaller and less profitable public, directly productive sectors than transition to socialism.

The SWAPO position is overtly one of transition to socialism and, while somewhat vague in respect of income distribution, is clear in seeking a non-capitalist pattern of industrial relations and a responsibility of leaders and state to workers and peasants.

2 Centralization/decentralization poses special problems in Namibia but perhaps more so in rhetoric than reality. Because of the use of divide-and-rule strategies by South Africa, political sub-division is at present seen as divisive ethnicity. In a country as small in population as Namibia federalism is in any event somewhat fatuous.

Administrative decentralization, with local and village councils and productive-sector managements and workers' councils with substantial decision-making powers, are another matter. The great physical size of Namibia, the multiplicity of production units in the rural sector, the inadequacy of centrally available data, the limited numbers of highly trained personnel, and the goal of broad participation in decision making all logically point to decentralization.

The need for political centralization built on local party units and national assembly constituencies should provide a framework for national strategies, programmes and guidelines within which village, ranch, district and company decisions can be taken and coordinated. The real problem will lie in achieving a working balance, identifying which policies must be central (e.g. probably almost all taxation and wage/salary-scale decisions), developing means for decentralized units to interact directly with each other rather than via Windhoek (e.g. northern grain growers and cooperatives with a food wholesale system), and ensuring that participation is real for workers and peasants rather than simply a decentralized exercise of official power.

3 Maximizing growth of output and of modernization is not a particularly relevant strategy for Namibia. Specific outputs (e.g. grain, dairy products), productive employment, and basic services need to be enhanced immediately and can be consistent with rather moderate growth of the overall level of productive forces. Indeed, modernizing large-scale economic activity and seeking to maximize the present high productivity sectors' output growth would probably have a negative impact on specific production, employment and services goals.

For this reason, *Manpower Estimates and Development Implications for Namibia* formulated a *basic human needs* approach to organizing and meeting development goals:

a creation of adequate employment (including self-employment) opportunities for all able-bodied Namibians of working age. Adequate in this sense means productive enough and fairly enough remunerated to provide at least basic household personal consumption needs;

b ensuring the availability to all Namibians of basic personal consumption goods (e.g. food, clothing, household necessities, shelter);

c providing effective access for all Namibians to basic communal consumption goods (i.e. primary and adult education, preventive and basic curative health services, water, urban services);

d maintaining and enhancing levels of productive forces adequate to meet the employment goals and to provide the basic goods and services (either directly by Namibian production or indirectly by production of exports) to purchase basic goods for Namibian use. This requires not merely production of basic goods and services but of the intermediate and capital goods to sustain them and of exports to meet basic needs indirectly by financing imports;

e creation of adequate physical (e.g. water, transport, power, urban), social (e.g. education, health), institutional (e.g. productive governmental, social) and financial (e.g. income distribution, fiscal policy) infrastructures to facilitate achievement of the other goals; and

f development of effective participation of all Namibians in decision making and review, as well as implementation, in respect of political, governmental, workplace and community bodies and groups.

This approach would require economic growth, but growth centred on particular goods and services. It would also require a fairly organized set of maximum and minimum objectives if rapid advances toward meeting basic human needs were to be made. In the medium term, increased output of minerals, and perhaps of fish, would be needed to provide surplus for investment and public services and to meet import requirements for goods which cannot be produced locally. This should not pose insurmountable problems on the export marketing side unless the entire world economy were to collapse or an unforeseen technical breakthrough were to render uranium redundant.

4 It is not useful to discuss Namibia's external economic relations in terms of trade versus autarchy. Its population and range of resources is too small for minimizing exports and imports in general to be plausible. The more positive and selective approach of maximizing self-reliance and national economic integration is the actual alternative to further incorporation into the world economy as an agglomeration of mining, fishing and ranching units.

Both insurance and bargaining power considerations enchance the case for less dependence on imports, especially basic foodstuffs and skilled manpower. Similarly, raising middle-level employment opportunities and domestic output levels constitute arguments for pre-export processing and for local market industries (e.g. cement, furniture) based on Namibian resources irrelevant to the world economy.

A more basic argument may turn on participation, especially in productive employment. The export sectors are quite incapable of generating full productive employment. Furthermore, a strategy of total integration into the world economy cannot provide the means to narrow rural/urban income inequality. Even if massive transfer payments were a plausible solution to the income side of the challenge, they would hardly do much toward creating a classless or a participatory society, much less to building self-reliance at community and workplace levels.

Elements toward strategic planning for Namibia

The use of the term 'elements' is deliberate as the list discussed here is incomplete and the inter-relationships among them incompletely worked out.

The *broad goals* have already been covered in the sections on the political economy of liberation and on strategic choices. In respect to basic human needs, more detailed targets need to be identified for use in actually drafting, implementing, and, especially, evaluating a planning process. Similarly, broad priorities and trade-offs among sub-goals need further consideration, e.g. a large foreign mining company role is a cost; the balancing benefits are gains in employment, foreign exchange and nationally controlled surplus generation. Further questions relate to levels of employment, foreign exchange and surplus and to the costs involved in attaining them.

From these goals flow rather far-reaching implications as to the necessary *role of the state, income distribution* and *production pattern*. Large-scale economic activity must be state-controlled and to a large extent state-owned. Neither Namibian (in any case non-existent) nor settler nor transnational corporation capitalists (except to a degree in joint ventures) can be expected to support a basic-human-needs strategy in Namibia. The resultant need to have expertise in the financial, managerial and negotiating fields heightens the urgency of Namibian manpower development.

If basic human needs are to include radically reducing urban/rural inequality and full productive employment, as well as expanding basic services, then it will be both financially and politically necessary to institute an egalitarian pattern of personal-income distribution and fairly detailed control over the use of enterprise surpluses. Control of production is urgent because so little is presently oriented to meeting basic needs.

Participation is likely to have three main avenues: production unit, government, and party. At the village and community level these may in practice overlap but their focuses are different: production relations (not simply industrial relations), government operation supervision, political guidance and review. The first will pose rather widely divergent specific problems for cooperative/smallholding villages, worker-owned and -managed large ranches, and union-based works councils and/or board of directors members. The second and third are – judging by Tanzanian and Zambian experience – somewhat hard to keep from overlapping in counterproductive ways unless clear guidelines are spelled out. Within each cluster issues of levels and structures will arise, e.g. do village production councils relate to any broader body? How do works councils and the National Union of Namibian Workers interact? What is the role of National Assembly members in village or urban neighbourhood councils? How should party units other than national ones direct their supervision of, and policy guidance to, government and public enterprise units?

Manpower development will pose problems quite different from those of less rapid and drastic transitions to independence. Of the present total of 36 500 non-African personnel it is likely that 7 500 must be replaced by newly recruited expatriates and over 20 000 by retrained Namibians within eighteen months of independence. For high and medium qualification personnel, broad parameters can be defined but details require more articulation. At the mass level, universal adult education (including both teaching a usable national language and literacy as well as additional work skills) relates directly to participation, to increasing productivity (especially of the rural self-employed), and to creating cadres to produce specific goods (e.g. housing) and services (e.g. basic health care) given priority in the basic-human-needs strategy.

Participation of *women* as a priority faces two specific barriers and has two special advantages in Namibia. On the one hand, women's educational and employment experience is so limited that for most women basic adult education and middle-level jobs will represent advances which require major effort, inadequate as they are to full participation. On the other hand, the fairly high proportion of women in present middle and upper qualification training programmes and the absence of any broad, all-male Namibian senior cadres to limit their progress are advantages compared to the standard colonial pre-independence pattern.

Public services pose three quite different challenges: converting high-cost, limited-access facilities to broader use at lower unit cost;

creating basic health and education services for rural areas; coping with the growth of urbanization. The first is critical not simply to break the elite/mass division but because attempts to continue and replicate these services as now run will be prohibitively costly. The second is self-evident as to nature but requires practicable elaboration as to methods; the need for paramedical and adult education personnel is equalled by the limited number of qualified candidates and lack of back-up support. The third has only recently come to the forefront of attention, surprisingly given the role of 'ending contract' in the liberation struggle. Reuniting the separated families will presumably mean that about 300 000 people will move to towns. The minimum requirement will be nearly 100 000 new housing units and radically expanded community services.

Public enterprises in foreign trade and finance are vital to effective Namibian economic control and planning. In wholesale trade they are likely to be vital to delivering basic goods to families, communities and small production units. In manufacturing they will carry the main burden of enlarging the sector. For fishing and mining at least, state majority joint ventures are needed both for surplus collection and control reasons. This is in addition to the standard transport, communication, power and water utilities. In the cases of ranching, inshore fishing, local transport and commerce, small-scale manufacturing construction (especially of houses) and services, the absence of Namibian capitalists (desired or not) requires that attention be paid to encouraging and providing back-up services to village, cooperative, worker self-management or other decentralized public sector ventures. Experience in Algeria, Tanzania and Mozambique suggests this task to be more complex and harder than creating large, nationwide units in the fields for which those are suitable.

Planning is critical in conditions of rapid transformation, massive dislocation and great uncertainty. It must be flexible and contingency-solving, without losing sight of long-term goals and how short-term actions affect medium-term progress toward them. This suggests low initial priority for a detailed comprehensive plan as opposed to broad strategic planning, and rolling one- to three-year programmes for key sectors. Speed, not sophistication, and approximate correctness in direction, not precise certainty, are needed. In that respect, some aspects of Chinese planning between 1950 and 1967 and of Tanzanian planning between 1974 and 1977 seem more relevant than either Soviet or the more orthodox African experiences. Two special problems are coordination of decentralized production units (perhaps via finance and wholesaling as in China and, to a degree, Tanzania) and ensuring that worker and peasant initiatives and proposals are actually heard and acted on (perhaps easier where, as in Namibia, technocrats will have few arcane techniques and numbers with which to brush aside the would-be contributions of others).

Law, laws and the legal system require, again unlike the typical post-colonial transition, immediate reconstruction. Until a body of laws compatible with Namibian goals is created there will be no adequate framework for administration and management and, probably more important, no clearly legitimate public system of norms for conduct. The present system, by its naked injustice, casts not only individual laws but law itself in the role of oppressive exploiter and thereby illegitimizes all laws, even those which, considered in isolation, are socially useful or necessary.

The drafting of an interim code has begun, starting with family law guidelines radically improving the status of women. The most intractable problems are likely to be in devising systems giving real access to the legal system for serious issues, adequate defence for the accused, and a parallel set of more informal arbitration and reconciliation bodies. The formal Western systems, whatever their merits at home, cannot possibly be applied for the majority of disputes. Lack of lawyers, of finance, of equality of access, of ability to perceive that the procedures do approach justice, and of speed in reaching decisions would be fatal defects if that were attempted. Equally, the colonial perversion and manipulation of traditional law has largely poisoned those sources and institutions, far more than in West or East Africa.

Agriculture falls into two sectors: former European ranches and former 'Homeland' areas. For the first, continued provision of services and support to worker-managed ranches based on present employees plus families has a good deal to commend it politically and technically. However, politically it may pose divisive land questions relating to precolonial rights well known to present sons and grandsons who are not now working on ranches. Technically it may raise problems over stock levels and land use akin to the potentially disastrous post-1965 expansion of Botswana ranching and the very bad experience of many Algerian worker-managed farms immediately after independence. A state farm alternative would face problems of recruiting managers, of cost, and of giving Namibians the impression nothing much had changed since foreign managers would still live in 'the big house' and give orders.

The African ranching and farming sub-sectors pose even graver land problems; to avoid long-term disaster some members almost certainly must move to the ex-European ranches. A strong case exists against freehold tenure and for substantial community activity, but probably not for the abolition of smallholdings and family plots. The 'traditional' land allocation system has been so perverted under the Republic as to be no longer usable and some decentralized system of allocating rights of land use will be needed urgently. Knowledge at all levels and by both peasants and technicians, personnel, and infrastructure pose major obstacles to rapid growth of crop production but these must be overcome if self-sufficiency in basic food (versus only 50% in half the years recently) and an assault on the agricultural/urban income gap are to be achieved. Indeed this is probably the most difficult challenge facing an independent Namibia on the production front.

Fishing will be another reconstruction sector in two senses. First, overfishing has seriously depleted stocks so that Namibia must assert a 322-km zone and enforce low interim quotas to allow revival of stocks and determination of long-term sustainable levels. Second, the fishing fleet will probably sail away to the Republic. This would keep catches low to allow restocking, but would create a major sectoral employment problem especially in respect of canning and processing, Namibia's largest manufacturing industries. Interim foreign charter or contract fleets and a rapid acquisition of trawlers, and training, would appear to be the only plausible response.

Manufacturing can build on existing processing to meet local needs (e.g. dairying) and altered export patterns (e.g. beef). Construction materials (e.g. cement, wood products, furniture) and overhaul and repair facilities (e.g. vehicles and machinery) are initial priorities related to urgent, early needs. The meeting of a broader range of local needs (e.g. garments, sugar, wheat, flour, textiles) and development of pre-export processing (e.g. copper refining, Karakul pelt processing, hides tanning and conversion into leather products) are probably less urgent and require detailed study as to feasibility, scale, and location.

Mining, especially diamonds and uranium, but also copper/lead/zinc, must be kept running near present levels to generate the surplus and foreign exchange for political economic transformation. In the short term this requires a substantial degree of foreign management and technical (as opposed to ownership and strategic) control. How to achieve this is subject both to experimentation and to negotiation with the present owners of Tsumeb and Oranjemund operations (copper/lead/zinc, and diamonds respectively) over provision of knowledge, division of ownership, and overall surplus allocation. In a rather different position are the unlawful post-1966 ventures of Rössing and Langer Heinrich (uranium), Oamites and Otjihase (copper). Further prospecting and development, as well as deciding on optimal long-run output levels, can be tackled in the medium term. The establishment of a core of Namibian state expertise on technical, managerial and marketing aspects is much more urgent.

External trade poses short-term problems quite different from the standard debate on 'delinking'. First, in the absence of Namibian bodies, many of the non-mineral exports cannot be sold except to or through South Africa. Second, the same problem arises in respect to procuring key imports as supplies and import houses are dominantly South African. Third, getting value for exports and plausible prices for imports (the 'transfer pricing' problem) will pose acute difficulties given sharply changed sources and destinations and the absence of a Namibian-based foreign trade sector. Fourth, without public sector handling (or at the least regulation) of all major foreign transactions, the degree of economic control possible in an economy like Namibia's is negligible. Except for minerals and petroleum, public-sector import and export corporations appear essential to keep trade flowing. Beyond that, a unit able to collect commercial data is needed to locate low-cost sources of supply and to monitor prices paid and received, with special attention to diamonds and uranium oxide ('yellowcake').

Finance, in the sense of financial institutions and management, will be critical to external trade and internal economic control as well as to the normal operations of the domestic economy. The Tanzanian experience between 1966 and 1978 strongly suggests that, given commitment, willingness to take risks, a limited cadre of skilled citizens and priority attention to training, a diversified, efficient, locally oriented financial system is one of the less intractable institution-building exercises in a developing country.

Finance in the sense of surplus generation to pay for public services and productive investment is unlikely to be Namibia's most severe constraint. Radical loss of surplus will mean major failures in production and/or external trade which cannot be rectified by simple contraction of spending. Because Namibia's present economic structure is so grossly exploitative, moderate output losses, significant redistribution of ownership, increased living standards for Namibian workers, expanded government service spending, and increased (as well as redirected) productive investment are compatible targets, unless very heavy burdens of military expenditure are imposed by South African intransigence (as is the case in Angola today) or a small, high-income Namibian elite carves out a large chunk of the potential surplus. This is not to say Namibia will not need foreign aid, especially in respect to personnel and especially during the first few years of independence. However, its ability to achieve financial self-reliance is potentially much greater in the medium term than is that of, say, Tanzania.

Conclusion

It is easy after preparing or reading even a rough list of main heads for planning the political economy of liberation in Namibia to wonder whether the exercise is possible. These doubts can be deepened by the lack of detailed data and the need both for radical structural changes and for great speed. The authors of accommodationist strategies are either overwhelmed by, or pander to, these doubts in arguing for limited, slow change and what, to their critics, seems a shift from South African occupation to neo-colonial dominance jointly by South African and transnational corporations. However, five more hopeful points can be made.

1 The political economic principles and strategy of SWAPO are remarkably coherent and clear for a liberation movement before independence (as a comparison with those of Ghana's Convention People's Party in 1950, two years before it became the government albeit seven before independence, or Tanzania's TANU in 1959 demonstrates).
2 SWAPO's strategy is based on perceived needs and aspirations of Namibian workers and peasants and seeks to relate these necessities to the constraints imposed by nature, locally created physical structures, and world order. In no meaningful sense can the strategy be criticized as inflexible or utopian.
3 Pre-planning has begun and is more inclusive than has traditionally been true in colonial transitions. Politics is (properly) more in command; the need to identify the practically plausible as well as the economically desirable is more clearly seen; the technicians are less convinced that they alone are the repositories of knowledge and more ready to look to people for information and advice.
4 The total unacceptability of the present occupation system and the evident impossibility of a return to the pre-colonial past, limit daydreaming and build in both a greater tolerance of transitional costs and a greater commitment to basic change than has often been the

case in more fortunate states e.g. Ghana between 1957 and 1965.

5 The resource base, much of the basic physical infrastructure, and a substantial production/surplus generation capacity for building a Namibia able to move rapidly toward meeting basic human needs do exist.

Ultimately, both for observers and, much more basically, for Namibians, the judgement turns on will and commitment. Pessimism of the intellect based on the evident (and less evident) obstacles is likely to prevail unless it is tempered and controlled by optimism of the will based on a commitment to radical change. The record of the liberation struggle, especially over the past decade, has both demonstrated and contributed to the building of a broader, more conscious and deeper commitment than has characterized the people of most small countries at independence. That consciousness and that commitment have been bought at a great price in human suffering and lives. The political economic strategy of SWAPO is designed to ensure that that price really is the downpayment on 'One Namibia, One Nation' and not merely the key money for marginally transformed external domination and exploitation.

Notes

1 The main South African sources (including some semi-confidential ones) are summarized and presented in Wolfgang Thomas, *Economic Development in Namibia: Towards Acceptable Development Strategies for Independent Namibia*, Kaiser, Grünewald, Munich, 1978. A more broadly based attempt to collate and to estimate from scattered date is *Toward Manpower Development for Namibia*, United Nations Institute for Namibia, Lusaka, 1978. Additional recent basic sources include R. Moorsom, 'Underdevelopment, Contract Labour and Worker Consciousness in Namibia, 1915–72', *Journal of Southern African Studies*, 1976; R. Murray, J. Morris, J. Dugard, N. Rubin, *The Role of Foreign Firms in Namibia*, Africa Publications Trust, 1974; R. Christie 'Who Benefits by the Kunene Hydro-Electric Schemes', *Social Dynamics* 2(1) 1976.

2 Because Christianity came to Namibia as a European religion and because, as preached in Namibia, it has usually placed a high value on avoiding violence and been somewhat ambiguous about the degree of detailed involvement of the church with the secular struggle for justice there has been a somewhat parallel ambiguity of relationships between Namibian Christianity and Namibian nationalism. See also Moorsom, 'Underdevelopment, Contract Labour and Worker Consciousness', and Chapter 7 above.

3 The Bishop in Exile of Damaraland is an exception. However, even the Right Reverend Colin O'Brien Winter's exposition of a Christian duty to transcend capitalism is much more explicit as a prophetic condemnation than as prophetic guidelines toward the economic aspects of reconstruction. Further, Bishop Winter, and some other Anglican leaders, have followed a much more overtly activist interpretation of the political duty of a Christian as a believer in the gospel than have the leaders of the numerically dominant and African-led Lutheran churches.

4 See for example 'Developments in the Churches' in J. Lissner (ed.),

Namibia 1975 Hope, Fear and Ambiguity, Lutheran World Federation, Geneva, 1976.

5 Aktur is analogous to the *verkrampt* (inward-looking) wing of the Nationalist Party in South Africa, DTA to the *verligte* (outward-looking) wing and the Federal Party to the Progressive Federal Party.

6 'Discussion Paper' partly reprinted in Lissner, 'Developments in the Churches'; *The Political Programme* and *Programme of Action*, SWAPO, Lusaka, 1976; *Manpower Estimates and Development Implications for Namibia*, Lusaka, 1978.

7 Kenya *Sessional Paper No. 10, 1965*, Nairobi.

8 TANU, *Arusha Declaration*, Dar es Salaam, 1967.

9 The most important question is that of the Anglo American group and, more specifically, of the Oranjemund Diamond Mine. Anglo is probably the least oppressive of the major employers in Namibia and has a record of willingness to adjust its style and its division of surplus to reach agreement with independent African states. A marginally changed Anglo role at Oranjemund would leave a very high proportion of surplus generation, foreign exchange earnings and single transnational external economic contacts under the control of a single transnational corporation based in the Republic. Alternatively, a 'most favoured nation' conversion of the Oranjemund regime to the pattern of the Jwaneng mine in Botswana, with high tax, 50–50 joint venture arrangements, citizen training, the promotion of domestic purchase requirements, and local cutting would go a good deal further and would significantly reduce the external control as well as the surplus drain risks.

10 The Namibian women directly involved perceive these changes as necessary to redress both pre-colonial African and colonial European structural subjugation of, discrimination against, and exploitation of women.

11 Recent speeches of 'Turnhalle Democratic Alliance' leaders especially Dirk Mudge, the late Clemens Kapuuo, Cornelius Ndjoba and, until his loss of position in the 'Coloured' DTA affiliate, Kloppers, are certainly consistent with this strategy. However, partly for reasons of mobilizing particular groups, they do not spell it out either as a broad, coherent panorama or a series of detailed vignettes.

12 Thomas, *Economic Development in Namibia.*

13 This summary is too brief to be more than a caricature of Kenya and Botswana. In particular, Botswana can hardly be said to have 'chosen' this strategy. However, it is precisely such stylized perceptions of Kenyan and Botswanan experiences which inform the minds of most advocates and critics of applying the Kenya–Botswana model in Namibia.

14 Walvis Bay illustrates South Africa's tendency to become bemused by its own propaganda. SWAPO fairly clearly has no desire to give naval base facilities to any state. However, it cannot afford to have its external contacts channelled through an enclave controlled by a hostile power. If South Africa continues to occupy Walvis Bay, Namibia will need a new deepwater port. One can be built at Hentiesbaai (about 80 km north of Walvis Bay) or Cape Cross but at a cost of perhaps $100 million. An offer to build the port in return for fishing rights and port facilities – including naval ones – would be very hard for a Namibian government to refuse so long as South Africa occupied Walvis Bay. Thus the South African claim (initially intended for external consumption) that SWAPO in Walvis Bay

meant Russian warships there has led to the attempt to keep Walvis Bay South African which in turn greatly increases the likelihood that some state could secure naval rights on the Namibian coast by building the port as a substitute for Walvis Bay!

15 E.g. Thomas, *Economic Development in Namibia.* Thomas's data are internally inconsistent. His external accounts projections show a total required inflow of capital from abroad very much less than his supposed state external borrowing requirement and do not appear to be based on the assumption of substantial inflow or outflow of private investment.

16 Compare, Thomas, *Economic Development in Namibia* and 'Namibia', *Africa Contemporary Record 1977–1978*, Rex Collings, London, 1978.

17 See for examples, D. Innes, Chapter 4, this volume; R. Moorsom, 'Underdevelopment, Contract Labour and Worker Consciousness'; S. Gervasi, 'The South West African Economy' in Ronald Segal and Ruth First (eds.), *South West Africa: Travesty of Trust*, Deutsch, London, 1967, and contrast with W. Thomas, *Economic Development in Namibia.*

12 Transnational corporations in the future of Namibia

CONSTANTINE VAITSOS

The issue of SWAPO's relations with foreign firms is founded on two major strategic political objectives which will significantly affect relations with transnational enterprises as well as other issues that SWAPO and Namibia will face in the future. The first is the commitment of SWAPO to provide support to the oppressed people of the Republic of South Africa even after Namibian independence. The second is the attempt to transform Namibian society towards socialism.

The first objective implies a very definite commitment to and an awareness of continued conflict with the Republic of South Africa after Namibian independence. This will in turn affect the economic and social structures in Namibia. It will significantly affect relations with foreign enterprises, particularly in the mining sector where practically all foreign mining is subject to the intervention of the International Development Corporation (IDC), a branch of the South African government which controls, either through equity or other means, a significant part of the operation of the mines. In addition, it will influence the presence of expatriates running the mines or activities in the rest of the economy. It is estimated that after independence Namibia will need approximately 15 000 expatriates to manage the economy (compared with 36 000 under the occupation regime). The financial cost will be high: if one assumes an average annual salary of $20 000, expatriates will cost $300 million annually. The presence of highly paid foreign personnel will have other critical implications for Namibia's future policies of social restructuring and will pose difficult issues in relation to its commitment to support the oppressed in the Republic of South Africa and elsewhere.

The second objective, to establish a socialist state in Namibia, has two major implications. The first is the nationalization of the means of production by the Namibian government. While a government can nationalize physical assets and mining rights, it is important to note that it is difficult to nationalize decisions if decisions are subject to certain constraints, as it is possible for ownership and control in a firm to be quite distinct.

There are three important issues related to the nationalization of decisions. The first is that there will be continuing heavy dependence on foreign manpower. Even where the mines, or the companies running the mines or the mining rights, have been nationalized, there may be conflicts over decision-making by, say, managers or engineers.

The second issue concerns the marketing of commodities. The industries related to diamonds or uranium are vertically integrated in the international economy and Namibia would be unable to avoid a situation of dependence in a world marketing system where, for example, De Beers deals with more than 80% of all diamonds traded in the Western world.

The third issue concerns the possibility that minority holders in the equity of a firm might be able to obtain, or retain, control even when majority control is in the hands of the local government or local companies. There are cases where the by-laws of specific enterprises state that decisions regarding procurement of technology or investment above a certain ceiling must have, for example, 80% approval from equity holders. This means that 51% ownership or 75% ownership by the local government does not give actual control for positive changes. Control through veto rests with the minority. Thus there are important considerations regarding legal and technical commitments made by the government in the process of nationalization where ownership and control might not coincide.

In summary, it is not so much the form in which nationalization takes place (taking the assets or shares of an enterprise), but the involvement in the operations of the firm which counts. Nationalization has to be seen in a complex framework which encompasses manpower requirements at technical and managerial level; vertical integration in the international economy; and the form in which voting control is exercised in the company.

The second commitment implied by the orientation towards socialism in Namibia is to provide basic health, education and nutrition for the mass of the population. This in turn implies that the realisation of socialism will depend initially on the availability of surplus finance from mining. The need for a surplus from the mining sector could well pose difficult choices where nationalization was being considered as against continuing relations with foreign firms.

These two major political objectives – supporting the oppressed in the Republic of South Africa and moving towards socialism – also carry with them certain defence requirements for Namibia, externally vis-à-vis South Africa and possibly internally for security reasons, which might consume a very significant part of any available surplus.

There are certain characteristics of the economy of Namibia which should be noted as background to what follows.

1 About two-thirds of Namibia's gross domestic product (GDP) and 90% of the goods component is exported, with the bulk of exports from the mining sector. The average for developing countries is between 25% and 30% and for countries like the United States or India below 10%. This gives particular importance to the management of external trade, especially given that half the food consumed in Namibia is imported.
2 About 40% of GDP is what might be called gross corporate surpluses, that is profits of companies, tax payments, depreciation allowances and other reserves concentrated in four sectors: diamond mining, uranium mining, base-metals mining, fish and fish processing. The surplus of these four sectors accounts for 40% of the GDP of Namibia and the numbers of companies involved are small, seven of substance in mining and about the same number in fishing.
3 The value of GDP exceeds gross national product (GNP) by at least

30%. The produce of Namibia is being remitted abroad through company dividends, royalties and tax payments to the government of the Republic of South Africa, and the difference between GDP and GNP indicates the degree of exploitation in Namibia. In this context, technical issues might become very important for the survival of the country in recovering the surplus currently being remitted abroad. For example, there may be choices between granting accelerated depreciation to foreign companies and granting tax holidays (the former might involve postponement of the tax intake by the government while the latter might involve complete foregoing of it), and other technical questions regarding tax leasing, equity participation, and corporate income-tax management.

4 Namibia's economy has been structured to depend on the Republic of South Africa, in productive structure, in marketing, in external trade, in management relations, and in labour practices with *de facto* enforced labour.

5 Potentially, Namibia is a fiscally viable economy. It is estimated that, if uranium and diamond mining operate more or less at full capacity and if base-metal prices do not drop as in the period 1976–1979 but average out at more acceptable levels, the recurrent fiscal revenues that Namibia could obtain are of the order of $700–800 million or approximately $500 *per capita*, a higher level than is available to most developing countries.

Elements in an integrated policy for mining

The most complex policy issue after independence will be the disentangling of the economy of Namibia from that of the Republic of South Africa. A number of major policy issues will be involved.

1 One is the renegotiation of the contracts of existing mining operations with foreign firms with respect to equity, tax considerations, rate of exploitation of the ores, and so on. Namibia has certain strengths in this context. First, it has proven reserves in gem diamonds, uranium, copper, zinc, lead and other minerals, and some of these are strategic for the economies of the Western world. In addition, there are important precedents from which Namibia might benefit if it is able to apply a 'most favoured nation' approach to dealings with foreign firms. One may cite the important legal issues raised when Chile nationalized its copper mines. These included the interpretation of international law on the forms of renegotiation and contractual and other agreements made with foreign firms.

In the case of Namibia there is a very important consideration: in 1966 the United Nations revoked the mandate of the Republic of South Africa to control the economy and the territory of Namibia and in 1971 an advisory opinion by the International Court of Justice strengthened the 1966 position. Other United Nations declarations have reaffirmed that the presence of South Africa in Namibia is unlawful. This is important because all contracts signed by foreign firms after 1966 are null according to this opinion, as is all South African legislation passed after 1966 which is applicable to

Namibia, including tax legislation and mining legislation. The main Act regulating mining operations in South Africa dates from 1968, two years after the revocation of the mandate. The future Namibian government will possess important legal advantages in renegotiating conditions imposed by contracts which the International Court of Justice has held are not valid. This is different from what happened in Botswana or Kenya, for example, where previous contracts had a degree of legitimacy in that they were legally signed by an acknowledged sovereign power, even if a colonial one.

2 A related element of strategy is the take-over and efficient management of the mines, to ensure the collection of surplus. This will depend on the solution of certain technical problems in existing operations by foreign firms, e.g. by Rio Tinto Zinc Co. in the Rössing uranium mine, and on dealing with possible efforts to undermine the efficient functioning of the mines, e.g. non-continuation of investment in exploration or in maintenance of equipment, both of which could have very serious repercussions for the future and the productivity of mining operations.

There are, in addition, various accounting procedures which companies under threat of nationalization may employ which would have to be confronted after independence. For example, it is traditional before nationalization takes place, particularly if (as is true in Namibia) the accounts of the subsidiaries are part of the consolidated statement of parent firms in the Republic of South Africa, to transfer funds through internal company transactions. These are very difficult to detect afterwards even if it is known that they have taken place. Another gambit is to revalue the assets of the subsidiary through accounting procedures and to claim compensation on the inflated values. There are also operations to maximize accounts payable by the subsidiary so that there are many lenders, in addition to the equity of the parent company, whom action of nationalization might appear to or actually threaten.

3 There are important questions concerning the take-over and management of railways and ports, especially for the transport of base metals. (Diamonds and uranium are exported by air rather than by rail or sea.)

4 The management of external trade and the establishment of sectoral or national enterprises needed for procurement (e.g. of grain) and sales (e.g. for mining, fishing, livestock) will be critical.

5 It will be vital for Namibia to establish quickly national resource surveying agencies and to manage existing resource records (maps, geological, chemical and physical property evaluations) which may constitute a very important asset. It will be necessary to ensure that existing records remain in Namibia.

6 The forward integration of processing in Namibia could increase national value added. Kunene hydro-power may provide a basis for further processing and, in the case of base metals, for product manufacture.

7 The management of surplus generated through mining or processing for the benefit of the whole economy, rather than for the benefit of the particular state enterprise involved in running the mines in

Namibia, will raise complex issues. There are cases of state enterprises operating like states within a state, with major conflicts between the state corporation as a producer and the state as a regulator or planner. This has to be managed very carefully in the case of Namibia in view of the high concentration of resource generation from a few companies.

These are the main factors in an integrated strategy for mining. Complex options are involved. The objectives of the revolution for independence in Namibia must take account of these issues which are central to the management of Namibian resources for the benefit of the Namibian people.

At a much more disaggregated level certain characteristics can be defined as strategic in the mining sector. If human capabilities or bargaining power are limited, they should be concentrated on these crucial issues. The two key products are diamonds (The Consolidated Diamond Mine Co.) and uranium (Rössing and Langer Heinrich).

Diamond industry

There are two main areas for consideration. The first is the surplus generated through diamonds. The second is marketing. With respect to earnings, publicly available sources would indicate that the potential under a new set of contractual, ownership, and tax arrangements with De Beers would be approximately a quarter of a billion dollars annual net surplus accruing to Namibia.

Regarding taxation, the existing tax structure of the Republic of South Africa applying to occupied Namibia has two characteristics, both adverse to the interests of Namibia. First, it gives very generous allowances for depreciation, capital exemptions and other capitalizations undertaken by all mining companies (whether in Namibia or in South Africa). Given the high capital intensity of the mines in Namibia a completely different tax system is appropriate for that country. Second, the mineral taxation system is regressive, so that as the profitability of firms goes up the percentage share of government earnings declines. This is important for Namibian diamonds, since they are of very high quality and hence offer the possibility of high profitability.

The tax system in South Africa includes a proportional export tax and a mining leasing tax which have a very mild progressive rate structure and a proportional corporate income-tax component (two such taxes for diamonds). Because diamond mining costs tend to be less variable than diamond output or prices, high revenue leads to a lower share of taxation in surplus.* While the degree of regressivity may be lower than supposed for diamonds, which have an abnormally high combined set of company/dividend taxes compared to other minerals within the Republic of South Africa, what Namibia should seek is to have a progressive tax system with surplus share taken, rising as profitability increases. This has been applied in other countries. For example, the Botswana government negotiated with De Beers a system of earnings sharing whereby De Beers is, to a large extent, a diamond extracting and marketing agent with a fixed percentage return on its mining investment.

There is another important precedent in the case of the Bougainville mine (a Rio Tinto Zinc group enterprise) in Papua New Guinea which also embodied a minority state ownership participation, in this case 20%. As profits increased, the government obtained part of the surplus through dividends, and in addition to other tax considerations traditional in mining operations, when return on investment – as defined in the contract – exceeds 15%, the tax applicable on the additional profit is not at the 33% standard rate but at 70%. The higher profits resulting from price or unexpected cost/output ratio savings go largely to the government.

An important consideration is the combination of tax rates and equity participation; equity sharing can be used as a trade-off against fiscal management. Each has its own particular constraints but the combination allows the government certain options not available otherwise. For example, a fixed fee plus interest payment to the company may not be consistent with efficient operation of a mine, because if the firm is assured of a particular return and no more then it might run the mine in a manner unrelated to generating surplus. A progressive system of taxation is likely to apply differently to existing mines with proven reserves as contrasted with new mining contracts where reserves are unproven.

A related issue is transfer pricing in diamonds which are sold by the Consolidated Diamond Mines to the Central Selling Organization (CSO) of De Beers. Transfer pricing can take place through at least two different channels:

1 Price differentials. The sales of diamonds from the subsidiary to the trading company could be at prices which are different from the market price set by the cartel, which is a monopoly price. This does not take place – or rather the CSO margin is openly negotiated – since CSO prices are published and can be checked.
2 The quality assigned to diamonds. This is the crux of the matter for diamonds. There are two thousand complex quality categories for diamonds at CSO sales level, varying in price per carat from $1.70 to

---

*	*Year 1*	*Year 2*
Revenue	$ million	$ million
a 1.5 million carats at $100	150	
b 2.0 million carats at $150		300
Operating cost	40	50
Surplus	110	250
Export tax (15%)	22.5	45
Lease	3	7
Company and dividend taxes	40	94
Total tax	65.5	146
Tax as % of surplus	60%	58%

more than \$3 500. There are fifty people employed at De Beers to grade diamonds, some with fifteen years' experience, taking critical decisions on the quality of diamonds sold. (The main non-De Beers or joint venture enterprises – e.g. USSR, Tanzania, Botswana, Angola – all employ independent expert valuers.) Thus the valuer who determines the quality assigned to each diamond determines the earnings of the producing companies, and grading can totally alter sales and surplus and thus the declaration to and the tax cut of the government.

On the issue of marketing, the main question is whether Namibia will choose to participate in the sellers' cartel organized by De Beers. There are good arguments in favour of it doing so. The CSO is a very well-run and strong sellers' cartel and it controls 80–90% of the international market. It operates on the principle that supply should never exceed demand at going prices and has established what would appear to be a potentially buoyant price structure linked to inflation and confidence in gems, with prices moving up at least in line with inflation. However, Namibia would pay a price: probably 10–15% of the wholesale price as commission to De Beers.

Uranium industry

Issues relating to uranium are more complex because they involve not only specific companies, but also at least six governments of developed countries, all seriously involved or interested in Namibian uranium production and marketing.

There are several technical issues to be considered. For the particular type of uranium in Namibia (low grade but in large quantities) specific technology has been developed but it is in the hands of a few companies, mainly in the United States, the United Kingdom and the Federal Republic of Germany. There is therefore the question of how Namibia might obtain the technology. A second characteristic is that uranium mining is a capital-intensive activity. The completion of a second mine at Langer Heinrich, in addition to the Rössing mine, will require major capital investments. Further, there are important safety issues for people working in the mines and uranium-mine management requires particular expertise.

Further problems relate to involvement by foreign governments. For example, the government of Brazil, seeking uranium from a source not controlled by the United States, has an agreement whereby uranium ore is exported to South Africa in exchange for uranium for Brazil's atomic energy activities.

In addition, other governments are involved. Canada participates at a government level in a *de facto* company/government grouping which runs a uranium cartel. The ownership of Rio Tinto Zinc's interest in Namibia is not directly through Rio Tinto Zinc, but through a Canadian subsidiary.

The French government is also involved in three ways. The first is financial, with respect to the sale of uranium enrichment plant and equipment worth billions of dollars to the Republic of South Africa, and the 10% equity stake of a French energy company in the Rössing mine. The second is political, the issue of ensuring sources of uranium outside United States' control for the *force de frappe*. Third, uranium relations appear to have been tied to the sale of nuclear weapons and delivery systems like Mirage jets and Crotale guided missiles.

The United States is involved since sales policy of oxide affects the policy of non-proliferation of nuclear armaments and related atomic energy issues.

The Federal Republic of Germany is also involved in two ways. First, there is (or has been) substantial interaction and cooperation in atomic research between German enterprises and state entities in the Republic of South Africa. After the Second World War the Federal Republic of Germany was prohibited from undertaking research on military issues and hence research had to be arranged abroad. Second, Germany's nuclear power programme has sought to build up assured sources of uranium oxide by joint ventures and by research abroad.

The United Kingdom is heavily involved and, as a direct result, is mistrusted by SWAPO. Regardless of the party in power, the United Kingdom government has played a consistent and major supporting role in creating Namibian uranium policy. It was involved from 1968–70 on through a long-term contract with Rio Tinto Zinc which, on the one hand, underwrote the mine and, on the other, gave the United Kingdom a low-cost oxide source. When the Labour Party went into opposition there were accusations that information had been withheld from the government by Rio Tinto Zinc, and Labour in opposition indicated that they would revoke the uranium deal, but no such action was ever taken or, it seems, even seriously considered. The United Kingdom government is one of two (the other is that of South Africa) which do not accept the validity of the 1971 International Court of Justice opinion on Namibia, especially the section which makes post-1966 natural resource projects such as Rössing analagous to 'contracts' between a thief and a receiver. At a meeting between SWAPO and James Callaghan when he was Foreign Secretary, there was nearly total disagreement. In general the United Kingdom has argued that the existing contract with British Nuclear Fuels and the existing Rio Tinto Zinc role are in Namibia's interest – a perception not shared by SWAPO.

This gives some impression of the complexity of sale, security of supply, technology, defence and financial issues involving the United Kingdom, Canada, France, the Federal Republic of Germany and the United States. Japan and the Netherlands are also interested in sources of uranium. As has been indicated, the national interests of these states are not identical or harmonious; further, state and company concerns are not self-evidently the same in each state. SWAPO, a liberation movement which is seeking to establish a rational policy for the management of uranium reserves, for its negotiations with foreign enterprises and the safeguarding of surplus and foreign exchange, is faced with this complex of issues and conflicting interests and the interests of the industrialized countries concerned with Namibia are likely to impinge on Namibian decisions.

In conclusion, some indication of the potential financial scale of uranium operations will demonstrate how vital decisions related to uranium will be. At capacity operation, the Rössing mine will produce 5 000 tonnes of oxide (it is now producing about 4 000)* worth about $500 million (at world market prices); if the comparable unit at Langer Heinrich is completed, the potential gross earnings will be $1 000 million. Recurrent operating cost at capacity is probably 25–30% of potential revenue. Depreciation would, for Rössing, come to about 10% of revenue at capacity output. Thus the surplus would be of the order of, say $300 million for Rössing and $500–550 million for the two mines. Not only decisions on future ownership, management and sales policy of Rössing but also on when to complete the Langer Heinrich mine and to arrange for its management will require urgent attention and action soon after independence.

* 1978. Capacity production was reached in mid-1979 and has been sustained. (Editors' note.)

13 Agrarian change

ROBERT CHAMBERS AND REGINALD H. GREEN

> If the people are to develop, they must have power. They must be able to control their own activities within the framework of their village communities. . . . At present the best intentioned governments – my own included – too readily move from a conviction of the need for rural development into acting as if the people had no ideas of their own. This is quite wrong . . . people do know what their basic needs are . . . if they have sufficient freedom they can be relied upon to determine their own priorities of development.
>
> – Julius Nyerere

IMP QUOTE

Toward further inquiry

With genuine independence, agrarian change in Namibia is inevitable. It is likely to be far-reaching, not cosmetic. It will be determined by Namibians on the basis of their views as to what is desirable and what unacceptable, what is practical and what unrealistic. The roles of the expert and of the outsider will be limited. That is as it should be.

In the meantime, agrarian change in Namibia is not a topic which can be set aside for consideration later. The issues are not so simple and straightforward that pre-independence discussion by Namibians is needless. Hence the purpose here is, albeit modestly, to map out the contours of some of the issues and perspectives which bear on action and policy for agrarian change. This task is undertaken with reservations: data are scrappy; neither author has carried out field research on land, in the villages, amidst the herds or with the peasants of Namibia.[1] But policy cannot wait for full and perfect data, and it may be helpful to review what is available and also to examine alternatives in the light of experience elsewhere in Africa.

Some assumptions and constraints

A major problem in projecting issues and possible trajectories for agrarian change is the lack of a clearly ascertainable context for the political transition. The assumptions used hereafter are:

1 the incoming government is a liberation movement one, committed to the broad principles of SWAPO's 'Political Programme'[2] and 'Programme of Action';[3]
2 the transition takes place before 1985 following a semi-negotiated transfer of power involving an election and not a war *à l'outrance*;
3 the agricultural sector has not been devastated by the course of the war prior to independence nor has the departure of settlers involved

systematic destruction of fixed assets and herds on a broad front;
4 significant numbers of European ranchers complete with bank accounts, herds, vehicles, tractors and other movables are in South Africa, not Namibia, at or soon after independence and therefore abandoned ranches are likely to be significant in numbers and as a proportion of total ranching area;
5 similarly, while agricultural training, research, services, planning, marketing and control bodies have not been systematically destroyed or evacuated, large numbers of staff have departed, records and data files are not in good order, and the general handover process is less than complete, efficient, orderly or cordial.

These assumptions rule out certain options, such as leaving European ranchers in undisturbed possession. They also increase the urgency of the need for immediate action by the incoming government which should have carried out at least a preliminary review of options and a tentative identification of initial policy measures and means for acting on them.

The options will also be constrained by many other factors. These include economic and political relations with the outside world, especially South Africa and the Western countries with interests in mining; the attitudes of the white population of Namibia; the administrative capacity that can be mustered for agrarian change; the degree of popular demand and support for agrarian change; the degree of willingness of present ranch employees to continue in that sector; and the priority given to maintaining exports of livestock products.

To examine the various scenarios and the options they present would be a lengthy exercise; and actual events would be unlikely to fit exactly into any postulated scenario. It seems more useful, therefore, to focus on other aspects: to outline the baseline conditions; to compare these with conditions and experience of other African countries which have undertaken agrarian change; to list some possible objectives of agrarian change and to weigh these against alternative forms of production organization; and finally to note some special problems of transition.

The existing European and African sub-sectors

The main emphasis is on the present European ranches. This choice is made for three reasons. First, they account for the bulk of rural output and encompass the bulk of the usable land in central and southern Namibia. Second, because they are at present European-owned and -run, using complex technologies and integrated into the territorial exchange economy, the necessity for and the problems of transition are more immediate than in respect to African small-scale mixed farming or herding. Third, there are no African parallels of immediate post-independence reform of a European ranching sector of the size of Namibia's, absolutely or relative to the economy. The problems of creative thinking from first principles and of relating principles to physical and human realities will be more demanding than in the African sub-sectors of the countryside.

The African or 'residual' agrarian sub-sector will be covered in the discussion of baseline conditions and some brief comments on possible issues and approaches made in a separate section. In the future, it will interact with the present large-scale ranching sector and the challenges it poses in the long term are no less important or easily resolved. However, they are different and, unlike the large ranches, are not such as to generate a national crisis if not tackled immediately after independence.

The setting

Ecology

The ecology of Namibia is hard and unyielding.[4] This was true for pre-colonial societies, has been true for European settlers, and will remain true for participants in agrarian transformation.

Rainfall is low and uncertain. In the north and north east it is adequate for crops in good or normal years. The Oshana (temporary watercourse) and Okavango Valley areas are also watered by drainage systems rising outside Namibia. The combination of rainfall, some permanent surface water and a high water-table also permits cropping in the Tsumeb–Grootfontein areas. The balance of the central plateau – with local exceptions – is sub-marginal for cultivation with natural water availability. Its northern and central areas are suitable for extensive cattle raising – at ten to twenty-five hectares per animal – and its western and southern zones for sheep – again at ten to twenty hectares per animal.[5]

The coastal area constitutes the Namib Desert and between the desert and the plateau runs a range of hills and mountains which are largely bare rock. On the extreme east Namibia runs into the Kalahari Desert; over a wider area the Kalahari Sandveld limits the usefulness of the rainfall and the fertility of the soil.

Soils are mixed. The north east has moderate soil quality but also a large swamp area. The Okavango Valley, the Tsumeb–Grootfontein area and the Central Plateau north of Windhoek have relatively good soils. The Oshana country presents special problems related to its combination of sandy ridges and clay proto-pans at the bottom of watercourses. The balance of the Central Plateau is very mixed.

Stable pasture management is difficult; overstocking or failure to rotate herds can set off degradation which is difficult to reverse. This is especially true of the south and the desert margins and in drought years.[6]

Water is a central problem: boreholes and check dams (usually with sand-filled reservoirs to limit evaporation) are critical to ranching and to spot irrigation. Major dam and channel irrigation at Hardap near Mariental in the south has encountered severe problems of increasing salinity. The area north of Windhoek, the Okavango Valley and, if the drainage and pan formation problems can be overcome, the Oshana country appear to be more suitable for large-scale irrigation projects.

Water for large-scale irrigation would have to come from the Kunene (and for its own valley, Okavango). In the south the Orange

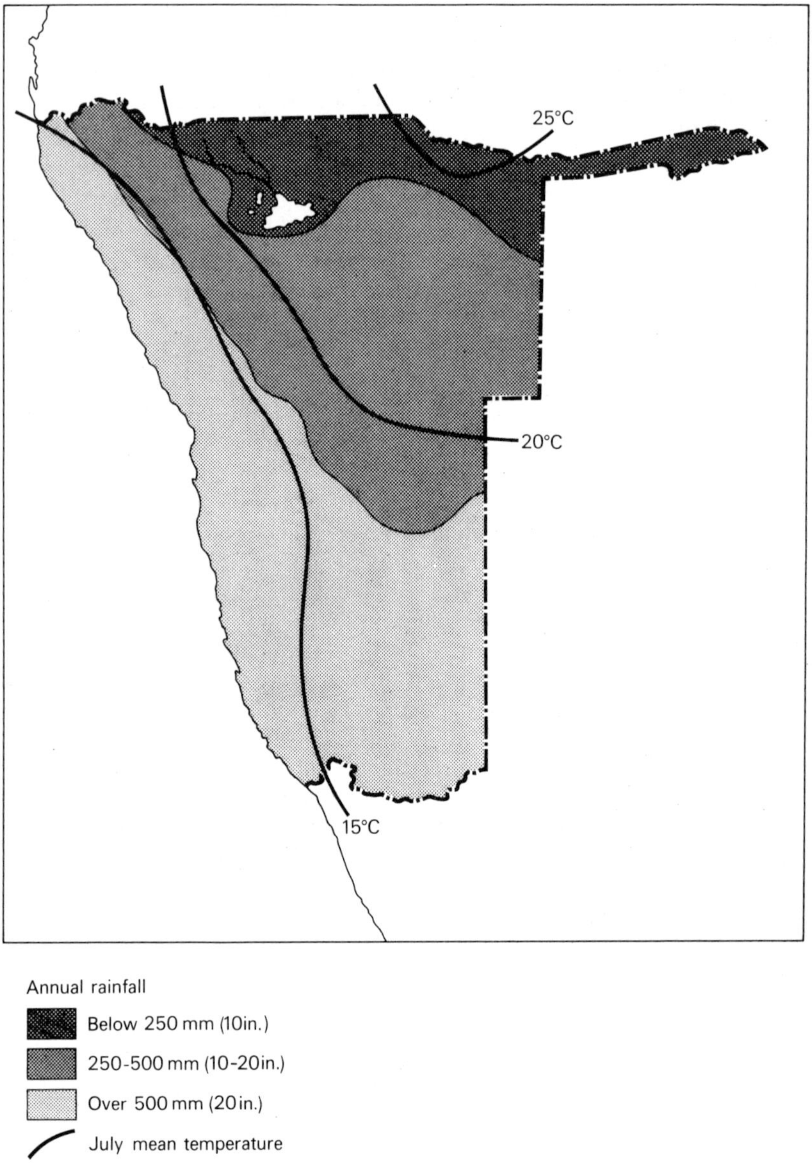

Map 13.1 Namibia: Precipitation and temperature

River is a possible source.[7] Across the Orange River at Upington irrigated agriculture is successful. No perennial rivers are located within Namibia. The largest seasonal ones, Swakop and Kuiseb, have underground flows which might be usable for spot irrigation at their mouths but the Kuiseb is probably already overtapped for mine and Walvis Bay urban demand.

Land use

Of a surface area of 82 400 000 hectares, about 53 000 000 is permanent pasture. Given present technology, water supply, and methods of exploitation, this is almost fully utilized. About 700 000 hectares (7 000 under irrigation) is now suitable for crops; of this, perhaps 650 000 is cultivated (see Annex Table 21).

The land-use pattern is in large measure, but by no means totally, the product of the ecology. The concentration of 37 700 000 hectares in about 6 500 European ranches and farms has created a set of production units oriented to maximizing marketed production and operating surplus, considerations which bias them toward commercial livestock. Further, state (South African) policy has been to encourage livestock (live cattle exports) and discourage both dairying (to protect South African dairying) and crops (to provide a market for maize from the Republic of South Africa).

In respect to African agriculture, the state influence is even more dominant. The African population has been confined to holding grounds for dumping families and spare workers. This has created a parody of pre-colonial herding and cultivation which is a residual, not a subsistence, sector. Further – with recent and limited exceptions – African production for household consumption has received no supporting services and that for marketing has not only received few services but been actively discouraged or even banned.

The sandveld area to the south and east of the Ovambo and Okavango Valley areas is a special case. It was utilized extensively on a seasonal basis in the pre-colonial period and smaller-scale seasonal, long-distance cattle migration is still practical. Provision of permanent water points (e.g. by pipelines from Kunene and Okavango) might render it suitable for year-round cattle raising as rainfall is adequate for pasturage.

The European ranches[8]

The European ranches number about 6 500 production units. About 5 500 are managed by resident proprietors, another 500 by Namibian (but not ranch) residents, several hundred by individual Republic of South African residents and a handful by corporate owners. Typical sizes range from 5 000 hectares in the cattle zone to 15 000 in the extreme south of the Karakul area. Their total area is 37.7 million hectares.

Employment is of the order of 6 500 Europeans and 50 000 Africans. The average permanent labour force is about ten on cattle ranches and five on Karakul ranches, in both cases augmented by seasonal labour. The pattern of production relations is social, not household, but extremely hierarchical, with a traditional colonial master/servant or baas/boy relationship usual.

In general, ranches have at least one artificial permanent water site, in total 6 000–7 500 boreholes and 5 000 small dams. These serve the fenced 'camp' (200 hectare paddocks) system used to rotate grazing. About one-third of the ranches have a tractor. Total capital investment per ranch is high, being in the order of R200 000 including land and R100 000 excluding land.[9]

Cattle herds are around 2 million, sheep 4 to 4.75 million. Assuming the lower figure for sheep, both herd sizes have been fairly constant–with drought-related fluctuations for cattle – for at least a decade and a half (see Annex Table 23). Goats, pigs, poultry and horses, asses and mules, are of minor significance.

Crops are also of limited significance (see Annex Table 26). There are a few exceptions, for example, two or three successful market gardening enterprises established by Portuguese from Angola; the Hardap irrigation-scheme units, and the irrigated company farm of Consolidated Diamond Mines; and a handful of mixed farmers near Tsumeb and Grootfontein producing wheat, vegetables and fruit, as well as cattle. Most cattle farms grow some maize for cattle and for a portion of the wages in kind given to African workers, but very little grain is marketed. In good years perhaps half the territory's requirements of maize and 95% of wheat are imported.

Commercial agricultural output in 1977–78 was probably of the order of R174 million (see Annex Table 22) of which R164 million is from the European sector. On the revenue side about half comes from cattle (400 000 animals) and a little under a third from Karakul sheep ('Persian Lamb') (nearly 3 000 000 pelts) and wool (see Annex Tables 25 and 26). Most of the balance is small stock, poultry, dairy products, hides and skins. Only about 5% would appear to be derived from commercial crops, including wages in kind.

On the cost side European wages in 1977–78 were probably of the order of R4 million (500 persons) and African R15 million (50 000), half in cash and half in kind. Expenditure on implements and recurrent operating inputs was of the order of R45 million and gross fixed investment was R15 million. Financial charges were of the order of R10 million and net operating surplus R76 million.[10] Value added was about R125 million.

There appears to be a fairly wide range in proprietors' surplus, with the top 20% securing perhaps R15 000 and the slightly below average R5 000.[11] The mean is likely to be of the order of R10 000. A 1969/70 estimate for five cattle districts showed an average surplus of R9 223. Net income per ranch probably peaked in 1973/74. Since then costs are said to have risen 96% and revenue 2% for cattle;[12] for Karakul the price has, however, risen by almost 100%.

The management skills required for a 5 000-hectare ranch with 500–600 cattle or a 15 000-hectare one with 1 500–2 000 sheep are considerable. While most physical work is done by Africans, often without close supervision, the general planning and decision taking, for example, on rotating 'camps', seeking veterinary assistance, timing of fattening and delivery to market, is in European hands. This may, however, not be the case on the up to 10% of ranches which have no resident European. In those cases the senior African, however designated and paid, may be serving as a manager with, at most, weekly inspection visits.[13]

Ranches exist within a dense supporting network. Planning is done by the government, which pays 50% of the capital costs. Veterinary services are of high quality as are research and advice on pasture management and water development. Marketing is rigorously regulated by the state in respect to the 80% of cattle shipped to the Republic of South Africa. Domestic marketing is managed by three abattoirs for the 20% slaughtered locally (8% local market, 12% tinning or direct chilled meat exports).[14] Karakul purchase and export through the Republic are in the hands of three firms. The availability of inputs including fuel, food, implements, fencing, borehole equipment depends on a smoothly working import, wholesale and local distribution and transport system. Transport of animals also depends on maintenance of roads, of rail services and of the road haulage fleet (largely run by South African firms).

The residual sector

The African (including 'Coloured') residual sector is much less homogeneous than the ranches. Rehoboth is to a degree a smudged copy of the European ranches, at least for its elite. Most of the Police Zone Reserves are heavily over-stocked and have little or no crop potential. The Oshana country poses special ecological problems but has substantial potential despite present low yields. The Okavango Valley has high potential for irrigated cropping but for a limited area, unless lift irrigation is proved to be viable. The Caprivi Strip is analogous to southern Zambia.

What these areas have in common is that they are the products of a process of wilful underdevelopment by the colonial power. This is aimed at low productivity and limited market production to help sustain the families of 'single' term contract workers. Viable African subsistence farming or ranching was not wanted because it would have drained the labour pool. The resulting social, production and economic patterns are therefore warped and residual. They are not simply 'natural' systems; much less are they traditional. Rather they are the result of conscious policy measures.

About 700–750 000 persons at any one time live in the residual areas, of whom 240 000 are, or attempt to be, economically active. At the same time over 100 000 migrant labourers from the sector's 150 000 households work in European agriculture, mining, construction or urban employment (see Annex Table 3).

The 'reserve' areas total 32 600 000 hectares (see Annex Table 21). Of this perhaps 16 100 000 hectares are usable for pasture and 600 000 for crops. Given the low carrying capacity of the pasture (an average even lower than the ten hectare per beast of the European ranches) and the very low yields (one bag of grain per hectare on some reports),[15] 100 hectares of grazing and four hectares of arable per household is hopelessly inadequate at current levels of investment and technology.

In the drier areas water is a very serious problem; there are 500-odd boreholes and a handful of check dams. So is technology: agricultural knowledge, improved seed, and adequate implements are all lacking. The absence of many adult men creates serious labour constraints for their households.

African cattle herds are probably between 800 and 900 000 and sheep between 300 and 350 000. The cattle numbers have fluctuated over the past twenty years with, if anything, a declining trend; sheep holdings seem to be increasing. Goats are relatively more important to African than to European herding: approximately 1 250 000 with a moderate upward trend (see Annex Table 23).

In the north and north east crops are relatively important, although, in most cases, less so than cattle. Total grain production may be of the order of 25–30 000 tonnes, with root crops 100 000 tonnes, vegetables 17 500 tonnes and beans and pulses 6 000 tonnes. These estimates (see Table 26) are highly speculative but show the food deficit nature of the sector. In several years grain imports have exceeded 100 000 tonnes.

Cash income from agriculture, largely cattle with some from sheep and goats, is of the order of R10 million. Food consumed by households is probably worth about R20 million in normal national accounting prices and R40 million at cost of purchasing imported grain. This gives a total sectoral income of either R30 or R50 million, that is R200 or R300 per household. Remittances from migrant workers total perhaps R15 to 20 million.

Specialized skills are not available to the residual sector either from its own members or the state. Vaccination of livestock is provided to prevent reservoirs of disease developing which might be transmitted to European cattle. (It would not be too cynical to suspect a similar motivation for human vaccination; very little else is provided in rural medical services or education.) There are several recent showpiece research and extension ventures (including, ironically, European corporate ranches in 'reserves') but there is no serious agricultural development goal. Plans for water use call for taking Kunene water several hundred kilometres across the most densely populated African area (Ovambo) to European ranches. Proper planning for water has not been included in a rural development plan for the north where half Namibia's population lives.[16]

Criteria for choices in agrarian policy

The criteria brought to bear on discussions of agrarian change, and the relative weights attributed to them, are influenced by the conscious or unconscious ideologies of observers. What follows is no exception, but it is felt that the explicit statement of these criteria provides a useful starting point for discussion, revision, and consideration of alternatives, even if others would wish to add or subtract criteria, or to give them different weightings.

Five criteria may be especially relevant to choices concerning agrarian reform: equity, employment, productivity, marketed output, and administrative feasibility.

Equity

SWAPO's strategic framework is integrally concerned with equity.[17] An economy based on historical land theft, on current labour theft, on gross inequality by race and on naked exploitation (in the colloquial as well as the technical sense) inevitably and properly leads to popular and political priority to equity.[18] Similarly a long and bitter liberation struggle both solidifies and radicalizes the determination to act and to act rapidly in furtherance of equity. The contrast between the 'big house' and the hovels, the R5 000–20 000 rancher net income[19] and the R75–300 cash and perhaps R200–500 cash-and-kind incomes of full year (perhaps half as much for seasonal) African workers underlines why equity is a priority.[20]

SWAPO views 'comprehensive agrarian reforms aimed at giving the land to the tillers' as the precondition for rural development. An end to all colonial land 'rights', that is, nationalization of land ownership, is envisaged as an early step. Tactics on land use are more flexible. Continued use of land by present holders (presumably subject to higher wages and worker organization) is at least tentatively envisaged. Peasants' and farmers' cooperatives and collectives and state ranching and crop farms are envisaged as institutional patterns to be developed.

At least by implication – 'the abolition of all forms of exploitation of man by man' – existing capitalist farms are seen as transitional and the creation of a new Namibian rancher capitalist class ruled out. Certainly the role of many chiefs and headmen in using their intermediary and collaborator roles to amass cattle and exploit other Africans, and the similarity of 'Coloured' (especially Rehoboth) ranches to the white pattern in terms of oppression of African labour, have created a deep mistrust of any large capitalist ranching approach whether white, brown or black.

Regional and urban/rural equity, meaning reduced inequality, are stressed. To implement this requires increases in ranch vis-à-vis urban and mining incomes; increases in present African ranching and farming incomes vis-à-vis both; and provision of basic services to rural Africans. It interlocks with the goal of food self-sufficiency which, *inter alia*, can be one route to increasing rural income through providing outlets for augmented or new crop and dairy production.

Employment and population support

It is a common belief that the 'Homelands' are overpopulated. Overpopulation is a relative concept, and concerns more than just population and resources. It depends on the level of technology, the distribution of resources, the structure of the population, and other factors. 'Homelands' with severely impoverished populations now might become prosperous with changes in technology, investment and infrastructure. This is particular true in respect to the north and north east. The extent to which the present white ranching areas should and can support additional population in the long term, is a question for further investigation.

In the short term, migration of families from the 'Homelands' to join workers on white ranches seems likely, so that the population physically present and supported in the present white farming areas would rise. The numbers of workers supported per ranch is not large. According to the Agricultural Census, there were in 1970–71 30 100 regular workers, 15 500 casual workers, and 4 100 domestic servants, plus some 500 white employees on white-owned and Rehoboth farms. In a survey of a sample of 330 farms it was found that

> Most of the farms below 5 000 ha in size have less than seven labourers, and more than one-third of the farms in the survey which are over 21 000 ha in size have more than sixteen labourers. The average number of labourers on farms under 10 000 ha, is given as six, on farms over 10 000 ha, nine to ten.[21]

Gebhardt also mentions that:

> More than half the farms with over sixteen labourers have not undergone decisive structural change during the last 45 years. They have not changed owners, remaining in the hands of the same family. On many of these farms there are a few extended families of labourers whose descendants have been employed on the same farm for generations.[22]

Recent estimates indicate a large ranch population of the order of 200 000 (of which 20 000 are European) and a total employment of the order of 56 500 (of which 6 500 are European).[23] They also suggest that 'ending contract' and reuniting households could raise the population by 50% to the order of 300 000.

Gebhardt's figures and the recent estimates taken together suggest stagnation in employees (excluding Europeans) over the past decade. If anything the trend has been downward. The substitution of capital for labour has proceeded at least as rapidly as expansion of operations.

On the Karakul ranches in the south (which have to a great extent been enclosed with jackal-proof fencing), there are often only three permanent labourers to a farm.[24] Similarly, 'camp' systems (fenced) have been substituted for free-range grazing to allow more effective rotational use of pasture.[25] The levels of capital investment in fencing and mechanization substituting for labour and the retention and support of past population increases, suggest lower rather than higher future potential for absorbing and supporting more people. Nonetheless, the provision of acceptable and adequate livelihoods for a larger number of families is an objective to be weighed in considering options of agrarian reform.

Two factors can be expected to increase the potentially economically active population on the large ranches. First, the reunification of families will raise the number of adult women by perhaps 30 000. Second, families (and herds) from the more desolate 'reserves' clearly will, to a greater or lesser degree, move to the adjacent ranches on a 'self-help' basis. A potentially economically active African population of 100 000 [26] (twice present employment) in the large-ranch sector is highly likely a year or two after independence.

Employment choices interact with production pattern choices. Almost any change in output mix would raise employment potential. This is true for dairying and dryland grain cultivation. It applies even more forcefully to spot irrigation on basically ranching units and to irrigated farms carved out of present ranches.

Productivity

Agrarian change often reduces productivity, at least in the short term. In the case of ranching, this can result from the running down of livestock numbers by ranchers before changes take place, sabotage, disruption of disease control, and lower levels of herd management. Choices of type, of scale and speed of agrarian change are likely to affect all these.

Productivity in Namibia is complicated by two other factors. First, it is not clear that existing levels of beef exports can be maintained. To do so would require that domestic abattoir and cold-store capacity be raised about three-fold, because significant live cattle exports other than to South Africa are unlikely to be feasible. South Africa would be unlikely to give an independent Namibia, which has carried out agrarian reform, quotas anything like the past levels. Even if capacity for killing, processing, and shipment can be achieved, gaining access to some markets e.g. European Economic Community, Japan, United States, European socialist states and identifying and building up market channels to others (e.g. Nigeria, Gabon, Kuwait, Saudi Arabia) is difficult, time consuming and costly in terms of specialized personnel.

Second, it is not clear what the appropriate output mix should or can be. The present context of prices, quotas, services and concentration on ranch-owner surpluses has created a bias in favour of beef and Karakul. But, because experience in Namibia (especially by Namibians) with most other products (dairying is an exception) is limited, how rapidly the mix can be changed, how far and at what cost in short-term losses of productivity, is very much an open question.

Marketed production and exports

In addition to affecting productivity, agrarian change is likely to affect the volume of production that is marketed, and the volume of marketed production that is exported. The former may be diminished by higher consumption on the ranch; the latter may be diminished by higher demand on the domestic market. Such higher demand can be predicted if the purchasing power of African workers rises, on the basis of the high income elasticity of demand for meat.

Lower marketed output and lower exports – unlike straightforward falls in output – are not necessarily bad things. They may even be goals. Namibian ranch workers reunited with their families should eat more meat, drink more milk, and grow more food, and more varied food, for themselves. Namibian urban and mine area demand for food will rise, again influenced by the reuniting of households on 'ending contract'. At least in respect to dairy products and, to a lesser but unclear extent, in respect to grains, fruits and vegetables, it is possible to substitute domestic market-oriented production for exportable beef. How urgent such action is considered to be depends more on considerations of focusing employment on present ranches and reducing food dependence than on pure output or surplus calculations.

However, a loss in total marketed output, especially of dairy products, poultry and eggs, grain, vegetables and fruits, will reduce domestic supply to urban and mining area markets at the same time that demand is increasing sharply. This will generate additional demand for imports and thus foreign exchange. More seriously, perhaps, it will impose added strains on the new foreign trade and distribution institutions.[27] Finally, because the only existing import channels run to South Africa, it will either require greater priority (and personnel) allocations to locating new import supply sources or hamper progress toward the goal of reducing dependence on the Republic.

Livestock exports in 1979 were roughly 13% of the total – R130 million. They were divided more or less equally between Karakul pelts (6.5%) and beef (6%).[28] If mining exports (85% of the total in 1979) hold up well, or grow with positive price trends and related quantity increases for copper, then lower exports from the livestock sector resulting from agrarian change may not be serious in themselves. On the other hand, if it were important nationally to maintain the level of livestock exports, then the scope, form and speed of agrarian change might have to be modified.

A total collapse of ranching exports would be a sign of disaster for a quite different reason. Present beef production is about 100 000 tonnes. Especially given fish, small stock and poultry availability, it is inconceivable that more than 25–30% (compared to 8% at present) could be consumed domestically. Karakul pelts are not of any domestic use and conversion to lamb and mutton for domestic consumption on any large scale would merely substitute for beef. The short-term prospects of radically altering the output mix toward domestic foods, that is dairying and crops, are limited. Therefore, a collapse of ranching sector exports would also mean a sharp fall of rural incomes, even allowing for increased rural household subsistence consumption of meat.

Administrative feasibility

Agrarian reform is usually administration-intensive, involving topographical surveys (sometimes), enumeration and valuation of assets and payment of compensation (usually), subdivision and settlement (usually), and farm planning (sometimes). Long and technical administration is often required, especially where there are strong legal safeguards and systems of appeals.

In Namibia, the base of information from surveys is probably much more detailed than with most agrarian reform programmes, certainly in Africa and Asia: for example, about 90% of the white farms have been planned by the Department of Agricultural Technical Services.[29] This should make initial operations comparatively quick and straightforward. On the other hand, Namibia is expected to be severely short of medium- and high-level manpower.[30] The manpower and administrative capacity that can be mustered will be one major factor constraining choice in approaches to agrarian change.

Further, it must be recognized that the present large-ranch sector does not, in fact, consist of self-sufficient units. An elaborate support and control mechanism exists in the state sector ranging from ranch planning through veterinary services to facilitation and regulation of marketing. The takeover and administration of this set of activities will place heavy demands on the new Namibian state. Similarly, the maintenance of present processing facilities and the safeguarding and/or substituting for present export markets and marketing channels will not take place automatically. While not narrowly part of ranch reform, these institutions, areas and problems necessarily interact with it.

Some comparative experiences

In making comparisons and drawing on the experience of other countries in Africa, information is most readily available on Kenya, Tanzania, Zambia and Botswana. However, in terms of historical experience and ideological commitment, the experience of Mozambique and Angola is likely to be more relevant to a SWAPO government. However, it is so recent that little data and still less reflective analysis is available. Socialist experience in Asia, for example, Mongolia and Vietnam, may also be of use, but is difficult to study and has taken place in radically different historical, ecological and cultural contexts.

There is, however, a similarity with Kenya, Tanzania, Zambia and Botswana in that they all became independent while some of their land was being farmed by white farmers and foreign-owned companies. Tanzania became independent in 1961, Kenya in 1963, Zambia in 1964, and Botswana in 1966. All have worked out and implemented new agrarian policies which have affected those farmers and companies.

The four countries had in common: a peaceful transition and transfer of power (though not without tensions, and, in the case of Kenya, qualified by the preceding Mau Mau rebellion); a policy of attempting to maintain the confidence of white farmers and foreign-owned companies (though least in Tanzania); a transfer of farming units with payment of compensation, either for a valuation of the farm as a going concern (Kenya, Zambia) or for assets excluding land (Tanzania), except in Botswana where there was no systematic programme of transfer; and maintenance of production under new forms of management, with settlement schemes (especially prominent in Kenya), at levels which, while sometimes lower than before, did not entail major adverse effects on the national economy.

All four at independence, though decreasingly thereafter, depended on the white farming and foreign-owned agricultural sector for a substantial proportion of their foreign exchange earnings through agricultural exports (Kenya, Tanzania, Botswana) and/or for a substantial proportion of domestically marketed food (Kenya, Zambia). Namibia is similarly placed in its reliance on white ranchers for the supply of most of its domestic and export-marketed livestock produce. It might appear, then, that the transfer of European ranches with compensation with orderly and phased settlement schemes maintaining production, presents a tested and reliable model which could be used in Namibia.

Botswana

The differences are, however, as significant as the similarities. Botswana is the closest to Namibia in its ranching economy: the similarities between the ranches of Ghanzi and those of Gobabis must be very strong in many respects. But white settlement in Botswana covers a small proportion of the country (the Ghanzi, Molapo and Tuli farms) and there has been a safety valve since independence in the open frontier for Botswana ranchers to expand into the Kalahari. There has been no pressure of population and stock to compare with Namibia's where half of the country and much of the ranching area has been occupied by white farmers and where no comparable frontier for settlement exists. Botswana was more neglected than exploited during the colonial period. It therefore lacks the political pressures for agrarian change which are so powerful in Namibia precisely because it never had a large, highly developed, European, capitalist ranching sector.

Zambia

In Zambia the European farming community, while dominant in tobacco, dairying and market-oriented maize production at independence, numbered less than 1 000 families and occupied less than 5% of usable land. Their presence did not in itself constrain either peasant access to land or state programmes to raise African output; indeed in one sense it made such change less risky by providing a stable basic commercialized food supply. Therefore, while the European farmer group has shrunk with departures and/or Zambian private and state acquisitions, this has never been seen by decision-takers as a matter of urgency: indeed seeking to delay it or to cause European farmers to remain as citizens has been as strong a tendency. Nor, given absence of acute land shortage, is there generalized peasant/European farmer conflict although particular local and personal tensions are not uncommon.

Tanzania

In Tanzania, too, the white farmers were insignificant compared with Namibia. Much of the land which they occupied was marginal, situated below higher potential areas at higher altitudes. They were neither so important to the economy, nor so numerous in the commercial and government sectors, that they were a major force to reckon with.

The dominant European farming unit was the plantation, in particular the sisal plantation, not the resident farmer. The sisal plantations were largely, although by no means all, nationalized between 1967 and 1972[31] and operated as state-owned corporate enterprises. Similar in size to Namibian ranches, they are quite different in size and organization of labour force and in degree of tolerance to mistakes. Their ventures into cattle and dairy farming have, with minor exceptions, had rather poor results.

Other European farms – coffee, mixed and dairy farms on Mount Kilimanjaro, a handful of small mixed farms and ranches in the northern plains and southern highlands, a few tobacco growers in the centre – were significant producers of coffee, wheat, pyrethrum and tobacco at independence. However, they did not take up so much land or labour as to be seen as an immediate hindrance to African rural development. In the early 1970s they were nationalized, usually into the hands of local communal bodies, for two reasons. Negatively, they had become fairly insignificant in total output (no longer holding a dominant position for any crop), and it was no longer critical to let them continue as an archaic enclave tolerated for its output. Positively egalitarian rural development was perceived as requiring an end to the anachronism of comparatively rich capitalist islands in the midst of a peasant and state farm system. Racial tension was not a major factor: Asian and African capitalist farms were also nationalized. Compensation was paid, largely out of a specially negotiated British grant, on the basis of assets valued at the net surplus they had been generating. Land was not included as an asset because ownership had been nationalized (without compensation) a decade earlier and revocable land-use rights substituted.

Kenya

The Kenya case might be considered the closest to Namibia. Land theft leading to land scarcity had been practised on a large scale, and reaction to it was at the roots of nationalism in Kenya where a prolonged and bitter armed struggle preceded independence. The European- and foreign-owned plantation sector was vital for foreign exchange earnings. In 1964 it accounted for over three-quarters of agricultural exports, partly because African production of export crops (tea, coffee, pyrethrum) had been discouraged or prevented, partly because settlers had received the lion's share of agricultural credits, inputs and advice. There was strong political pressure for land to be returned free to landless Africans. There were foreign interests, mainly the British government and the World Bank, anxious to maintain stability and prepared to pay for it. There was also an outlet for disaffected white settlers who could uproot and trek south to Rhodesia and South Africa. Equivalents to all these factors can be identified in Namibia.

But the differences are also deep. Independence was negotiated but not with the guerrillas or a 'land army'. The new Kenya elite wished to inherit the fruits of capitalist development and of the large farm sector,[32] whereas SWAPO is opposed to such a course. The dangers to the Kenya economy of disruption of agricultural production were greater than in Namibia. The Kenya settlers were also less 'Kenyan' than the Boer and especially German-speaking settlers' descendants in Namibia are 'Namibian'; they were also fewer in proportion to the country's population (in 1964 under 5 000 families – say 20 000 persons – in a population of 9 million compared with 6 500 – say 25 000 persons – in 1.25 million in Namibia today). They were more ready to leave and there were relatively fewer of them to resist leaving.

A final difference was that the demand for settlement schemes came from agriculturalists and focused on mixed farming areas, while the extensive European ranching areas were not subject to the same pressure, and most remained under white ownership for many years. But in Namibia it is precisely ranches that are the focus.

Mozambique and Angola

The transitions in Mozambique and Angola are very recent, have not yet attained stable or fully operational forms to replace the colonial ones, and are not well documented.[33] However, they afford examples of massive initial settler dominance in commercial agriculture, rapid withdrawal in the context of strife, and major efforts to prevent a collapse of the commercial side of the agrarian economy.

In Mozambique commercial production (other than cashew-nut and cotton) was dominated by plantations (sugar, for example) and Portuguese farms. The farmers largely decamped before or soon after independence, in many instances after stripping or sabotaging their holdings. The plantation experience has been more varied, but inability to adjust to a new environment, non-cooperation and low output has led to nationalization in most cases.

To date both funds and personnel have been concentrated on the ex-Portuguese farms which are large with fairly high levels of productivity. These have been operated as state farms albeit with more worker participation and collective management than is usual with that form of organization. Output initially declined sharply and recovery has proven hard to attain.

Peasant farming has been reorganized on the basis of village communities with fully communal (relatively rare), mixed (common) and individual peasant (also common) crop production, plus some communal services and economic activities. While seen as strategically central to agrarian change, peasant farming did not receive substantial skilled personnel or finance before 1978 because salvaging the ex-European sector had top tactical priority. Food output has been affected by very bad weather. Cotton and cashew output fell radically at independence – both were labour-regulation and tax-payment imposed crops – but has since recovered toward previous peaks.

The Angolan transition must be seen in the context of continued war. Insurgency, backed by South Africa, in the central and southern highlands, not merely limits agrarian activity in, and transport through, substantial areas of Angola; it also cuts off the previous source of labour for the northern coffee districts.

Almost without exception European planters and ranchers left Angola and most corporate plantations were abandoned. In the case of coffee, a mix of state farms and workers' cooperatives, plus an 'Operation Coffee' to recruit urban dwellers for seasonal harvesting teams, has been introduced. Production fell during the liberation struggle by perhaps 80%. Recovery has been slow, perhaps between 40 and 50% of previous peak output (that is, double the low point) by 1979. Workers' cooperatives, backed by highly experienced Cuban management teams, have fully restored sugar output after a moderate slump at independence. Plantation cotton production has apparently nearly vanished; the remaining third of peak output is basically peasant. Food production has been disrupted, as has its transport to cities, but because of the continued insurrection it is hard to identify how, if at all, this relates to agrarian transition.

The livestock industry has virtually ceased to exist. Up to 90% of 4.4 million cattle were eaten by combatants, killed during fighting, died of disease with the breakdown of veterinary services, were driven to South Africa, or were killed by departing settlers. Cattle slaughter was, for a time, banned and a minimum of five to ten years for reasonably full recovery is anticipated.

Mongolia and Vietnam

Mongolia appears to have the only extensive system of communal ranches.[34] However, data are scanty[35] both on its present operation and, more particularly, on the nature and problems of transition in the 1920s. Two differences exist: in pre-socialist Mongolia, large herds were owned by Mongolians using methods similar to smaller herders, not by foreigners with different technologies; and Mongolian herding is nomadic (or cyclical) to a much greater degree than herding in Namibia which, except in the north, is characterized by rotation of pasture but not seasonal migration over longer distances. However, Mongolian experience does demonstrate that relatively large, partially market-oriented communal ranching is, under some circumstances, possible.[36]

Vietnam's agrarian transition is widely known but has not been examined in detail in accessible sources.[37] It was, of course, in the context of an agrarian sector which was primarily directed to irrigated crops (albeit also in a rather harsh and demanding ecological setting) and one in which the initial techniques of landlords were not radically different from those of peasants. On the whole it may be of more comparative relevance to northern and north-eastern crop and mixed farming transition than to ranching.

However, several general elements have some applicability. First, agrarian transition was an integral part of an overall social transformation affecting town (and mine) as well as country. Second, mass mobilization and mass commitment leading to community self-discipline was vital. Third, despite the dependence on local initiatives and actions, a central framework was essential to achieving coherent results. Beyond the local level this framework, provided by the Vietnamese Communist Party and its state, was relatively centralized and hierarchical, especially in respect to determination of crops and levels of delivery for commercialized output. Fourth, belief by peasants that they could play new roles and not simply rebel against old ones was critical and was seen to require an extensive and intensive technological and ideological adult education campaign.[38] Fifth, the process of transformation was related to current peasant aspirations. In the Vietnamese case this meant a sequence of partial land reform, radical land reform, mutual aid teams, low-level cooperatives, high-level cooperatives, large-scale cooperatives extended over the period 1930–1976. Sixth, the challenges of the environment, including the social nature of rice production under irrigation and the challenge of sustaining the population, informed and supported efforts to achieve transition.

Future forms of ranching organization

Published sources on the experience with different forms of organization for ranching in anglophone East and Southern Africa are not particularly helpful. Forms of 'cooperative' ranching in Kenya undertaken after independence were in effect company ranches in which absentee 'shareholders' bought shares either in cash or through contributing livestock. The Group Ranches of Kenya[39] have had a chequered history and have not mastered the problem of controlling livestock numbers. It would be a retrograde step for Namibia to allow the 'tragedy of the commons' to occur in the white ranching area, but this could occur if several owners of stock took over a ranch and then competed with one another for grazing. The result would be ecological degradation, declining carrying capacity, and declining production.

Nor does Tanzania have a tested and replicable model to offer. The *ujamaa* philosophy and movement might, in principle, have lent itself to collective herds, but implementation had to start from a situation of family ownership of livestock. Ranching Associations were formed in Masailand but there was evidence that they were dominated by richer members.[40] In Upper Kitete village settlement, a prototype *ujamaa* village, there was a communal herd but it was provided by the Village Settlement Agency, not by the farmers who retained their own herds outside the village. Anthony Ellman reported in 1971 that 'there are as yet no *ujamaa* villages in which members have contributed any significant number of their own cattle to a communal herd' [41] In Dodoma, a major ranching region, a precondition of support for massive *ujamaa* village development was that, except for specialized village dairy herds, cattle would remain totally in the individual peasant sector.

The Tanzanian situation was, however, different from that in Namibia. In Tanzania, the objective was to build up communal herds out of individual herds. In Namibia, the starting point is different. Instead of small individual herds, there is on most white ranches one large herd in a single management unit. Problems of aggregation should therefore not arise, and the Tanzanian experience, while providing a warning that communal herds may be difficult to maintain when several families have interests in them, does not indicate that such herds are impossible to maintain.

Two particular interactions of villagization and cattle may be of relevance. First, creating villages when combined with a nightly round-up of cattle (e.g. for protection against vermin) has created severe spot environmental degradation and radically interfered with homestead vegetable and fruit production in a number of cases. Similarly, provision of permanent water points for ranching communities has led to increased herd size, and perhaps decreased herd migration, less than conducive to sustaining pasture quality,[42] and to especially severe problems in drought years. Second, while village herds for meat are almost unheard of, small dairy herds and improved bulls for breeding are not uncommon in communal villages. In both cases the value of a collective as opposed to an individual approach is clearer and in both the activity, when communal, is usually a new one not previously carried on by individual households.[43] The main body of Tanzanian experience is much more relevant to the residual sector than to the ranches. It is also a complex and controversial one which cannot be copied or used as a model without careful study.[44]

Botswana's experience has relevance for Namibia's 'Homelands' but less for the white-settled area. Botswana's Tribunal Grazing Land Policy (TGLP) was designed to secure and protect access on the part of owners of small numbers of livestock to communal land, while permitting owners of larger herds to undertake ranching on land designated as commercial. The policy has been implemented slowly and cautiously, with public consultation[45] and a considerable debate[46] about implementation and equity, reinforced by a survey of rural income distribution in Botswana[47] which found greater inequalities than had been previously supposed (indeed, on the face of it, among the widest in Africa).

For the white farming area in Namibia this experience would only be relevant if the forms of organization for Botswana's communal areas had been developed and tested, since these, with suitable adaptation, might have provided models for Namibian ranches. But these forms of organization are, in 1980, only in the process of experimental development although a highly organized programme for monitoring and evaluation of the TGLP should ensure that lessons of the experience will be available in due course.

There are three problems in ascertaining the direct relevance of the Botswana experience. Even with recent changes, the African rural sector will continue to be characterized by major inequality and in that context the richer and stronger are often able to co-opt programmes which appear technically neutral on equity grounds. Second, the Tswana capitalist ranching class, while it has engaged in very rapid expanded reproduction since the 1960s, is one which has evolved out of Tswana society and history. Because of the nature of colonial conquest and rule in Namibia, there is no convincing evidence – despite the existence of a few 'chiefly' herds of some size – that a Namibian social formation of comparable scale or productive efficiency exists or could easily be created. Third, the ecological viability of expansion into the 'Kalahari Frontier' in Botswana (or Namibia) will become less difficult to assess when a period of drought[48] has run its course.

Given Namibian conditions, four future forms of organization appear to present the main options for the white ranching area.

1 Family ranching as at present. This would maintain the *status quo*, either with the same European families or with a substitution of African families for white.
2 State ranching. This would entail a state employee as manager of one or more ranches, and payment of labour by the state. (As secondary – and neither dramatically successful nor totally unsatisfactory – sub-sectors, such ranches exist in both Zambia and Tanzania.)
3 Subdivision into smaller family units. This would entail a subdivision also of the herd, possibly the transfer of new families and herds from 'reserves' and perhaps additional fencing, and water supplies.

4 Production cooperatives or collectives. These would differ from state ranching in that members would increasingly become responsible for the management of and would share in the profits of the enterprise. (No examples are known in Africa, but the Mongolian *negdel* may repay study.)

A fifth option is a return to the semi-nomadic pattern practised 'before the Germans came'. This would not, strictly speaking, be subdivision as the present ranch-based field system would cease to exist. However, as this system is almost certainly inconsistent with ecological stability and sustantial production at or near present herd levels, and would entail conflict between present ranch workers and 'Homeland' residents, it has been ruled out of further consideration.

If these four types of organization are set against the five criteria – equity, employment and population support, productivity, marketed production and exports, and administrative feasibility – it is a matter of judgement how they should be ranked. Ranking is also sensitive to conditions which are difficult to predict. However, although only tentative judgements are possible, a matrix may clarify the costs and benefits of alternatives.

Forms and Criteria: Schematic Diagram
Degree to which criterion satisfied in the medium term

	Equity	Employment	Productivity	Marketed production and exports	Administrative feasibility
Family ranching on current lines	nil	medium	high or low[1]	high or low[1]	high or nil[1]
State ranching	medium	medium	medium to low[2]	high	medium
Subdivision to smaller family ranches	medium	high	medium to low[3]	low	medium to high
Production cooperative or collectives	high	high	initially low[4]	medium	low[4]

[1] This option could well generate such explosive social tensions as to be totally destructive of output. Livestock are easy to kill and grazing lands to encroach upon.

[2] Initial experience in Zambia and Tanzania was poor. This might not pertain in Namibia if managers with local experience were available and acceptable.

[3] Whether the present technology – including rotation and water – can readily be subdivided is less than clear. The long-term ecological stability of small units is open to doubt.

[4] Partly dependent on availability of skilled and experienced back-up and services personnel. Also dependent on whether a cadre of experienced ranch workers remains on ranches.

Some issues in transition

It is not practicable to survey here all the issues that can arise in agrarian transition; rather, a few issues will be noted which almost certainly will arise, together with some of the problems and opportunities they are likely to present.

Initial takeover

The fewer stock which stray or are killed and the less property that is run down or destroyed, the better start transition is likely to have. Similarly, the more ranches that are handed over by the outgoing proprietor with an overlap with the incoming manager or committee, the fewer initial mistakes are likely to be made.

As to fixed assets and stock, the answer may lie in compensation and, more particularly, early announcement of compensation. If it were announced that compensation at a willing buyer/willing seller price (less state capital subsidies) would be paid for improvements, implements, vehicles and livestock, this would create an incentive not to destroy wantonly and to take care of assets. If added to this were a reward for remaining (or a penalty for not) for at least three months after the arrival of a new manager or after the formation of a management committee, to advise the new operators, handover might also be facilitated.

The case for compensation here is based not on acceptance of the validity of colonial land titles but on the lower cost of paying for assets handed over in working order than that of taking over abandoned or smashed ranches with no stock. It does not apply to land. First, the European rancher cannot run off with or destroy the land, and second, the political cost of buying out 'land rights' based on a history of very primitive accumulation indeed would be too high.

These compensation/handover principles apply even if takeover is phased over, say, two years or even if it is only partial. Since ranches clearly will be acquired, it is better that they be handed over in good running order.

Ranch population and labour force

Ranch work is not popular and some observers believe the present ranch labour force will leave at independence. That would be a disaster for the sector and, as 50 000 jobs could not be generated elsewhere, also more broadly. The ranch workers know the bulk of modern ranch operations; whereas there is no guarantee that new settlers from 'reserves' would.

Inducing ranch workers to stay probably requires four conditions:

1 the right to bring their families and perhaps assistance in arranging transport and securing materials for constructing dwellings;
2 a clear guarantee – and initial action to make it credible – that medical care, primary education and adult education will be made available to ranch families as a matter of urgency;
3 a guarantee that work and production will be rewarded either with a living wage or with a share of the unit's operating surplus;

4 provision for workers to have an effective say in their working conditions and the general management of the ranch.

Reuniting of families is desirable and, if the ranch workers are to stay, inevitable. How many additional families, whether farmer-ranch employees 'off contract' at independence or 'reserve' herdsmen, can be accommodated is unclear. If at all possible, such moves should be discouraged until present ranch workers and persons with technical expertise can survey and consult on the situation.

Women in newly reunited households will probably wish to engage in work beyond 'household tasks'. If so, that is an added reason for early evaluation of cultivation possibilities, both rainfed and with spot irrigation, on a district (and ultimately ranch by ranch) basis.

San ('bushmen') may require special protection. Experience in Botswana suggests that there are dangers of their being both misunderstood and displaced in agrarian change. Their seasonal jobs should not disqualify them from better wages or communal ranch membership and the practical aspects of combining ranch work at one season with hunting at another should be discussed by all the workers with a view to finding equitable solutions.

Output mix

Fewer cattle may be desirable, if only because of interim marketing problems. There is a case for more dairying, and revival of the dairying industry is probably possible. However, more stress on fluid milk and less on butter would be appropriate and may raise collection problems although these should be solvable at district level in conjunction with ranch managers or representatives. Nationally, what is needed is a roughly appropriate price structure.

Where feasible, spot irrigation should be used to raise fruit, vegetable, pulse and bean output, both for ranch-resident use and also to make improving urban diets consistent with phasing out the import of 15–20 000 tonnes (including tinned equivalent) of South African fruit and vegetables. The labour force required for this is likely to be available in the reunited families and new entrants for whom cost considerations are quite different from those of outgoing ranchers. However, data on present successful growing need to be secured and made available to interested ranchers new to these crops. Further, marketing will need attention, in the form, for example, of encouraging institutions and firms to make contracts direct with ranches or of offering the ranch advice on fair 'farm-gate', or, if the ranch has a lorry, 'buyer's door', prices.

What can be done on grain is unclear. A price equivalent to world (not South African) import parity would be a start. Beyond that more data are required.

Irrigation – beyond spot irrigation, keeping research going, ensuring the continued operation of the Hardap test scheme – will take time, money and personnel. It is not clear that Kunene water should be brought to Okahandja, rather than used in the north. Little data exists on drawing on the Orange. The only urgent decision needed is to collect data including existing Portuguese and South African studies.

Adequate data collection and project design, securing finance and actually constructing works will necessarily extend well beyond the initial transitional period.

Ranch services

Ranches are dependent on services ranging from planning improvements through advice on pasture use to provision of vaccines. The need for these services will be greater during transition when there is less experience available of the complex decisions involved in ranch management.

Therefore research, planning, extension, veterinary services must be maintained. A foreman, as an acting state ranch manager or an elected communal ranch chairman, may be able to do 90% of his duties very well and to mobilize his fellow workers better than an outside manager. But it is probable that, if he cannot get advice and support regularly, the other 10% will cause failure of the ranch. This is not the Namibian's fault – it is that of the colonial history – but during agrarian transition it is Namibia's economy and ranch workers' livelihoods which will be at risk.

In addition, the ranching sector depends on other services. Ranches require transport: lorries and facilities to maintain them, rail services, cattle-holding grounds. They are dependent on abattoirs and packing plants. They will require new external markets for beef and a continued access to the world market for Karakul perhaps directly via European auctions. They need the import and delivery of fuel and fencing wire.

These requirements of the agrarian sector in transition must be made clear in discussions regarding transport and trade and must be put before those responsible for action in those sectors.

Staff

There are probably 8 500 European staff today, including managers and officials providing services to ranches. If all leave at once, the ranching sector as a series of modern high-productivity units cannot be preserved. If some leave, questions of how to replace them and by whom are of paramount importance. The optimal solution when technically viable is by present experienced Namibians on the ranches with maintained or enhanced supporting services.

A significant number of officials are believed to be willing to stay.[49] If they are personally acceptable, they should be encouraged to do so, e.g. by offering immediate two-year contracts on their present terms and conditions, with longer period renewal and its terms open.[50] There are also believed to be some proprietors who would stay as managers. Here, the view ranch workers have of them is critical. Subject to workers' agreement, they should be encouraged to stay, in their present homes and at a reasonably attractive initial two-year contract. If many gaps exist, each could perhaps supervise one to three adjacent ranches.

One method of filling the gaps is to recruit technical assistance personnel. For some posts with exacting professional requirements this is the only way. For others it would be helpful but not essential. But technical assistance personnel take time to locate, are expensive, are not available in thousands in ranching and ranch services, are not always competent, and will not know Namibia or Namibians, much less specific ranches and workers.

Thus there is a compelling case for maximizing short-term instruction on particular technical competences to allow promotion of African assistants, foremen, and experienced workers.[51] They do have direct operational and human experience, and they are, presumably, eager to advance to more responsible roles in the sector they know.

Attention should be paid early to the problems of supporting and managerial staff as they themselves perceive them.[52] The classic problems are lack of experience and continuity (that is, frenetic repostings), difficult and ill-supported assignments (for example, in a physically isolated district hard hit by sabotage and near total loss of ranch proprietors and senior staff), organizing services and routines for administrator not rancher convenience (an endemic danger even with newly promoted assistants and workers), inability to comprehend ranchers' and ranch workers' value systems and outlook (a great danger for new technical assistance personnel, perhaps unusually low for the upgraded Namibians).

Social Services

The need for action in respect to housing, education, and health was cited with relation to the ranch labour force. Much can be done by the ranch workers themselves, especially in respect to construction. However, personnel and training will be needed so that first aid and perhaps some elements of basic education and construction can be carried on by ranch workers and their family members.

Adult education in rural areas, both literacy and specific skills, is likely to be critical. One aspect must be 'gap filling' courses for the present unofficial foremen and artisans who will need to broaden their knowledge of when and why to use their applied experience. Identifying the gaps to be filled and the candidates for courses will presumably need to be an early duty of the new agricultural service.

Ask the workers

The need to achieve agrarian transition is national, but the Namibians most affected will be those who live on the ranches. They are also the Namibians with the best day to day knowledge of what needs to be done at ranch level and, perhaps, of what is needed from beyond the ranch.

Common prudence and not merely SWAPO's commitment to participation and a worker voice in decisions directly affecting them, argues for involving ranch workers in decisions on transition. If workers are not involved, the chances of their self-mobilization to make transition succeed are low.

For example, if one considers a technocratic solution seriously canvassed by an expert genuinely committed to liberation, several questions might arise from a ranch worker's point of view. The scheme calls for grouping ranches in units of 20–40 000 hectares, say 2 000 in all, each with an expert manager and a total staff of fifteen. This implies a 67% reduction in managers and 50% in total labour. One might well ask whether ranch workers would see this as a genuine transition and whether so few would wish to remain under the new terms and conditions that a reduction of labour by 50% would be practicable. It is also difficult to see how the manager/worker relation could be seen to be different, especially if many managers were ex-ranchers, present civil servants, or technical assistance arrivals. There may be simple answers but they cannot be known (as opposed to hoped or guessed at) until the ranch workers are consulted.

Timing

There are costs of going slow and of going fast. Barring a medium-term commitment to keeping most European ranchers in place on most of the land, the sector will not operate very well under the outgoing Europeans. The cost of that commitment in terms of political credibility would presumably be bankruptcy; its human cost to ranch workers and their families would be high.

The cost of not being prepared to act fast could be very high, however evaluated. There is no guarantee that a combination of hasty self-started exits and expulsions by ranch workers would not leave two-thirds to three-quarters of the ranches without managers in a few weeks, at or soon after independence.

In both these respects – the very high general political and worker socio-economic cost of allowing the *status quo* to continue and the danger of facing a sectoral collapse – the Namibian transition differs in degree from East African experiences with rural and agrarian change during transition and after independence. However, even in the East African states, the costs of action not fully thought out strategically, much less tactically, were high, as Jon Morris reflected in his evaluation of East African settlement programmes at the time:

> In fact, many of the problems of settlement seem to stem from the crash programme basis of national efforts in all three countries (Uganda, Tanzania, Kenya). Uganda was offered tractors by the hundreds when it had no programmes requiring them; Kenya was in political turmoil over the demands for more land at a time when thousands of landed European farmers were leaving; and Tanzania had released a frenzy of localised, self-help activity in agriculture when it created a new structure of regional and area administration. Agricultural technicians were faced with immediate political demands which left little time for planning or preparation. As a consequence, settlement programs ignored all of the lessons of the past. It is embarrassing now to read Arthur Lewis' (1954) comments on land settlement from twelve years ago, and to discover that most, if not all, of his guidelines were blithely ignored in contemporary programme planning.[53]

The micro-efficiency costs of rapid change are high. In the likely context of inadequate data, weak institutions, and probably not very focused consciousness by ranch workers as to what they wish to achieve (as opposed to what they wish to change), significant falls in output are likely. This is as true of a transition to Namibian capitalist ranches as to communal ranches, to smallholder ranches as to state corporation ranches.

However, the macro-efficiency judgement may be different. Until a strategy is adopted and a set of means toward its operation put in hand, micro-measures may reduce costs in the short run but raise them in the long. To take an extreme example, strengthening existing 'Coloured' and African 'headmen' capitalist ranches would be micro-efficient. But it would also make any subsequent structural transition for that sub-sector harder. Micro-efficiency is best used to capitalize on the gains made possible by macro- (systemic) change.

However, only a few systemic changes can be handled at once. If ranching has top priority, or if its transition cannot be put aside for a year or two, then it may be cheaper to act radically at once, bear the cost, and build on firmer foundations, rather than to devote time and energy to patching a structure known to be scheduled for replacement, or putting in place a stop-gap system (for example, state managers replacing ranchers and acting like the present ranchers with few other changes) that has little present credibility and no future viability. Even in a thoroughgoing transition, interim measures and least bad expedients will be necessary. The danger is that there will be only stop gaps and expedients and no coherent strategy or general policy framework.

From residual to peasant sector

In one sense it appears both easier and less urgent to commence a dialogue in respect to African agriculture. There are experiences of some comparability in other African countries. No great fall in household or national output would ensue if nothing much were done in the first year or two after independence.

However, that appearance is deceptive. Experience in Algeria, Mozambique, Angola and Tanzania is to a degree relevant. But not only can it not be copied, it is not uniformly successful enough in any of these states for Namibians to wish to copy it. Further, it is a double illusion to suppose that the residual sector can or will go on as before because both physical and political realities will cause change.

First, it can be expected that the families of most ranch and urban migrant workers will move to reunite households. This will reduce the population of the small agricultural sector by up to 300 000 and its economically active population by up to 100 000, perhaps within a year of independence. In itself that is a good thing. However, it will increase the urban demand for food and, unless something happens in the production and sale patterns of the remaining 50–75 000 peasant households, there will be no additional supply.

Second, if there are no signs of changes in basic services or chances to earn a decent living in small-scale agriculture, the sector will remain residual. In that case a second mass exodus to ranches and urban areas will be likely despite Namibia's urgent need for enhanced domestic market food production, and despite the improbability that the urban or ranching sectors could provide this second wave with meaningful job opportunities.

Third, the above case, while realistic, is rather narrowly economistic. The residual sector households are very poor. Many of them have participated directly in SWAPO's programme and believe that it includes them and their communities. The political, moral and mobilization capacity cost of delaying the start of transition from residual to peasant small-scale agriculture (no matter what the reasons for the delay) seems likely to be very high.

Small-scale agriculture in Namibia has suffered grievously from enforced isolation, both of the sector and among the households comprising it. The key to transition lies in breaking that isolation in a manner which integrates peasant agriculture in the Namibian economy on fair terms and integrates peasants in the Namibian polity as effectively, as well as nominally, equal citizens.

It is not possible here to draw up a blueprint. However, without any pretence of comprehensiveness, seven areas for discussion, explanation and dialogue can be listed.

1 Provision of basic community and social services by the state, e.g. adult and primary education, preventive and simple curative health care.
2 Provision of those productive services, e.g. vaccines, dips, known to be suitable, and identification or development of appropriate additions, e.g. improved seed, better hand- or ox-drawn implements.
3 Creation of a transport and a purchasing system backed by coherent purchase-price determination to allow and to encourage grain, dairy, vegetable and fruit production for the urban markets. While desirable in principle, direct village transport and sale is unlikely to be feasible in the first years of independence.
4 Concentrated attention to training villagers, preferably chosen by their village communities, in skills which can be used communally, e.g. community health, first aid, implement repair, carpentry and masonry, improved building and agricultural techniques, bookkeeping, dairy-herd care and management.
5 A serious rural water-development programme articulated to fit varied local possibilities, e.g. spring protection, shallow wells, tube wells, check dams and short pipelines as well as boreholes.
6 Selective development of communal self-help activity with social and economic benefits. Here the first priority should be given to areas in which communal effort will be demonstrably more effective than individual. Examples include small-scale irrigation works, soil protection, drainage and feeder road works, improved housing and community buildings, storage (including drought reserves) and marketing and small-scale workshops for repair and maintenance.
7 Considering encouragement of moves toward community-oriented settlement patterns to facilitate the provision of services and the marketing of output, providing such movement is voluntary and consistent with sound agricultural practice, e.g. Oshana-area dispersed settlement patterns are related to ecological realities which appear to militate strongly against large villages.

In preparing for transition, Namibia can find relevant experiences and training facilities in Tanzania, Angola, Mozambique and Botswana and systematic exploration of their potential would be a useful first step.

A parallel step should be to ask peasants how they perceive their own needs and aspirations; what action they wish to take to fulfill them; what sort of primary community and organizational structure they want; how they think state action can fill gaps in their own and their primary communities' capacities. Certainly not all the answers will be 'correct' or 'feasible', but nor are many of the answers of tradition-bound agronomists and desk-bound planners. Even if changed approaches by the peasants are needed, it is quite impossible to start a dialogue in support of change until the starting point is known. Unless participation includes strategy design and basic decision, effective mobilization and sustained commitment on the part of peasants will be the exception and not the rule. This process of dialogue cannot take place fully until independence, or at least during a United Nations-supervised transitional period. It can, however, begin now; there are thousands of past and future Namibian peasants in refugee camps in Angola and Zambia.

In beginning

It is normal to open a concluding section 'in conclusion'; in this case, if it truly is 'in conclusion' the present exploratory effort has been fruitless. What we have tried to do is to set out some of the existing knowledge on Namibia's agrarian sector and, thereby, to show some of its gaps; to sketch parallel or partially comparable transitions which suggest where detailed study of Namibians might be useful; to sketch the nature of the goals the agrarian sector is likely to be asked to serve in order to stimulate dialogue among Namibians on appropriate sub-goals, priorities and balances; to pose a series of organizational options and their limitations in order to provoke a realistic assessment of what is practicable and what is necessary by Namibians, particularly those who are, or will again be, involved in the agrarian sector as residents, community members or participants; and to outline some critical challenges of transition thus encouraging consideration of how they can be met and reflection on which ones have been left out.

The lesson of comparable experience appears to be that, whether fast or slow, early or late, radical or moderate, transition should be thought out and debated in advance as well as during its course. 'The unexamined life', Socrates asserted, 'is not worth living'; the unexamined agrarian transition is all too often barely worth having.

If this paper seems to convey a sense of urgency, it accurately reflects its authors' perceptions. President Nujoma in a recent interview stated:

> It must be borne in mind that the Namibian people are shedding blood to liberate each and every inch of the Namibian soil, thus each and every inch of the Namibian land must and will belong to the Namibian people.

Those words and the situation they express are not consistent with a long delay. But, if it is to belong truly to the Namibian people, the Namibian ranching sector must be radically transformed. There are choices of degree, of what to do, how, when, at what speed, and in what sequence. As events unfold and pressures develop, the practicable options may narrow. Thus the extent to which choices are real depends partly on anticipation, on the examination of options in advance, and on being prepared ahead of time. This chapter has been written in the hope that, in however small a way, it will contribute to that preparedness and to making those choices real.

Notes

1 Neither has a majority of other writers on the topic, but that is, at best, only a partial defence.

2 SWAPO, *The Political Programme of the South West Africa People's Organisation*, Lusaka, 1976.

3 SWAPO, *Programme of Action*, Lusaka, 1976.

4 See J. Wellington, *South West Africa and its Human Issues*, OUP, 1967; FAO, *Namibia, A Preliminary Note Towards a Country Development Brief*, Rome, 1975, pp. 1–4; FAO, *Namibia, Prospects for Future Development*, W/K9407, Rome, 1977, pp. 1–5. See also Chapter 2 above.

5 See C. Nixon, 'Land use and Development in Namibia – A Report Prepared for UNIN', 1978; also verbal communication from Nixon.

6 *Ibid.*, pp. 2–3.

7 A dispute will arise. South Africa claims the boundary runs along the north bank. This is the result of standard German colonial boundary denotation in Africa which stated the land under German suzerainty not the boundary. Ironically, on the Kunene, South Africa has always claimed a median line boundary.

8 Based largely on FAO, *Namibia, a Preliminary Note* and *Namibia, Prospects*; Nixon, 'Land Use and Development'; A. Mbamba, 'Possibilities for the Future Development of Livestock Ranching in an Independent Namibia', M. A. Thesis, University of Sussex, 1977; W. M. Thomas, *Economic Development in Namibia*, Munich, 1978; Republic of South Africa, *SWA Survey 1967*, *SWA Survey 1974*,

9 Derived from data in Nixon, 'Land use and Development' (especially p. 6a), and Mbamba, 'Possibilities for the Future Development of Livestock Ranching', especially pp. 55–56.

10 Calculated from various sources including Nixon, 'Land use and Development'; W. S. Barthold, *Namibia's Economic Potential and Existing Ties with the Republic of South Africa*, Berlin, 1977, pp. 21—25; Mbamba, 'Possibilities for the Future Development of Livestock Ranching', pp. 57–60; E. Berg, 'Namibia, Economic Growth, Structure and Prospects', paper for African American Scholars Council Namibia Study for USAID, 1977.

11 Cf. Nixon, 'Land use and Development', pp. 3–4.

12 A. P. Pretorius, Chairman SWA Meat Control Board, quoted in *Windhoek Observer*, August 1979, p. 4. In 1980 cattle prices improved.

13 Cf. F. B. Gebhardt, 'The Socio-economic Status of Farm Labourers in Namibia', *South African Labour Bulletin*, Vol. 4, 1 and 2, January–February 1978. Also discussions with Namibian ex-ranch workers.

14 Nixon, 'Land use and Development', p. 61, quoting Mr Heydenrick, Manager Meat Marketing Board. Reports in the *Windhoek Observer* of 1 and 8 September 1979 indicate that new abattoir capacity to slaughter all Namibian offtake in the territory is planned. A large cold store linked to exports outside the Republic is reportedly under discussion with French promoters.

15 South African Agricultural Reports cited by R. Moorsom in unpublished manuscript on Ovambo class consciousness.

16 Cf. Nixon, 'Land use and Development', pp. 5–6a; R. Christie, 'Who benefits by the Kunene hydro-electric schemes', Social Dynamics, 2, 1, 1976.

17 Cf. R. Green, Chapter 11 above for a fuller discussion.

18 Cf. R. Green and K. Kiljunen, Chapter 3 above for a fuller discussion.

19 Estimated from Mbamba, 'Possibilities for the Future Development of Livestock Farming', pp. 59–60; Nixon, 'Land Use and Development', pp. 3–4.

20 From a survey by Pastor Gerson Max, partially cited in G. and S. Cronje, *The Workers of Namibia*, London, 1979, p. 47, and from discussions with Namibians during 1978 research visits to Namibia.

21 Gebhardt, 'The Socio-Economic Status of Farm Labourers', p. 149.

22 *Ibid.*, pp. 149–50.

23 Cf. UNIN, *Manpower Estimates and Implications for Namibia*, Lusaka, 1978; pp. 7–14, 60; Thomas, *Economic Development in Namibia*, p. 310.

24 Gebhardt, 'The Socio-Economic Status of Farm Labourers', p. 149.

25 Nixon, 'Land Use and Development', p. 3.

26 Cf. UNIN, *Manpower Estimates and Implications*, pp. 51–62, 66–67.

27 Existing institutions are not oriented to these requirements and new private ones are most unlikely to be launched at independence. Thus there is little option at independence but to create significant state trading.

28 See Annex Tables 18, 24, 25.

29 Nixon, 'Land Use and Development', p.1.

30 UNIN, '*Manpower Estimates and Implications*', pp. 23–27.

31 For more detail see R. H. Green, 'A Guide to Acquisition and Initial Operation', in J. Faundez and S. Picciotto, *The Nationalisation of Multinationals in Peripheral Economies*, Macmillan, London, 1978.

32 Cf. Van Arkadie Report, and Colin Leys, *Underdevelopment in Kenya:: The Political Economy of Neo-Colonialism*, London, 1975, pp. 63–117.

33 SADCC, *Angola* and *Mozambique*, London, 1979.

34 There may be parallels on China's Gobi Desert margins but there is no available mention of any.

35 But cf. C. Humphrey, 'Pastoral Nomadism in Mongolia: the role of

Herdsmen's Co-operatives in a National Economy', *Development and Change*, 9, 1, January 1978.

36 The implication may well be to send a team to Ulan Bator and beyond to the nomadic communal ranches.

37 See A. Bhaduri, 'Decentralization and Self-Reliance in an Agrarian Economy: an analysis based upon agricultural co-operatives in North Vietnam', *IFDA Dossier 3*, Nyon, January 1979, and Len Phuong, 'Agricultural Co-operatives in Vietnam – Which Lessons to Draw', *IFDA Dossier 7*, Nyon, May 1979.

38 Verbal presentation by Vietnamese Adult Education Officials at June 1976 World Conference on Adult Education and Development held by the International Council on Adult Education.

39 Cf. Van Arkadie Report.

40 A. Ellman, 'Development of Ujamaa Farming', *Kronick Van Africa*, April 1971, p. 114.

41 *Ibid.*, p. 121.

42 Personal communications between 1972 and 1974 by USAID personnel associated with Masai Scheme.

43 See Mascarhems, 'After Villagization – What'; McHenry, *Tanzania's Ujamaa Villages: The Implementation of a rural development strategy,* California, 1978; also personal communications.

44 See J. Connell, 'The Evolution of Tanzania Rural Development', *IDS Communication* 110, Falmer, 1973; A. Ellman, 'Development of Ujamaa Farming', *Kronick Van Africa*, Assen, April 1971; O. Mess, *The Establishment of Cattle Ranching Associations Among the Masai in Tanzania*, Rural Development Committee Occasional Papers No. 7, Cornell University, N. Y., 1975; D. E. McHenry, *Tanzania's Ujamaa Villages: the implementation of a rural development strategy*, California, 1978; B. Mwansanu and C. Pratt, *Towards Socialism in Tanzania*, Toronto, Dar es Salaam, 1979.

45 Republic of Botswana, *National Policy for Rural Development*, Gaborone, 1973; *National Policy on Tribal Grazing Land*, Gaborone, 1975; and *Preliminary Report on Public Consultation on the National Policy on Tribal Grazing Land*, Gaborone, 1976.

46 M. Odell, *Village Area Development Programme*, Gaborone, 1978; 'Seminar Report on socio-economic monitoring of the Tribal Grazing Land Policy', Gaborone, 1977. R. D. Hitchcock, *Kalahari Cattle Posts: a regional study of hunter-gatherers, pastoralists and agriculturalists in the Western Sandveld Region, Central District, Botswana*, Gaborone, 1978; 'Meeting Communal Needs in Commercial Areas: Integrated Land Use Planning and the Communal Service Center Concept', Consultancy Report, Gaborone, 1978.

47 Republic of Botswana, *The Rural Income Distribution Survey in Botswana 1974/5*, Gaborone, 1976.

48 For analysis of drought in Botswana and of measures to deal with it, see S. Sandford, *Dealing with Drought and Livestock in Botswana*, Gaborone, 1972, and the proceedings of the symposium on drought in Botswana held by the Botswana Society (M. T. Hinchey [ed.], *Proceedings of the Symposium on Drought in Botswana*, Gaborone, 1979).

49 Personal communications from persons who have talked to them in 1977, 1978 and 1981.

50 A problem will arise if the Republic of South Africa seeks to call them back on penalty of loss of career contracts.

51 Cf. UNIN, *Manpower Estimates and Implications*, pp. 15–16.

52 Cf. Chambers, 'Administrators: A Neglected Factor in Pastoral Development', *Journal of Administration Overseas*, April 1979.

53 J. Morris, 'The Evaluation of Settlement Schemes Performance: a sociological appraisal', in R. Apthorpe (ed.), *Land Settlement and Rural Development in Eastern Africa*, Kampala, 1969.

Statistical Annex

REGINALD H. GREEN

Tables

A Population, Employment, Education

B National Accounts Estimates

C Sectoral Data: Agriculture, Fishing, Mining, Budget

TABLE 1
Census Based Population Estimates (1960–1980)

Year	Northern African[1]	Central/ Southern African[2]	'Coloured'[3]	European[4]	Total
1960 Census	238 047	110 695	58 771	73 464	526 004
1960 Primate[5]	320 000	122 500	60 000	73 500	575 000
1970 Census	427 732	165 773	78 096	90 583	762 184
1975 Projection[6]	497 500[7]	200 000[7]	92 500	100 000[8]	890 000
1977 Projection[6]	532 500[7]	212 500[7]	100 000	102 500[8]	947 500
1980 Projection[6]	582 500	235 000	110 000	107 500	1 035 000

[1] Persons of Ovambo, Kavango, eastern Caprivi origin.

[2] All other African persons.

[3] Nama, Rehoboth, 'Cape Coloured' persons, South African definition of 'Coloured'

[4] Afrikaans, German, English-speaking communities including contract and short stay.

[5] 1970 Census date adjusted backward to 1960 assuming population growth rate actually about 2.9%.

[6] Projections from 1970 census using approximately 3%, 3.5% and 1.75% growth rates African, 'Coloured' and European communities. (3.5% includes immigration, 1.75% includes change in number of expatriates *except* military forces.)

[7] Includes refugees outside Namibia.

[8] Excludes post-1970 military occupation forces expansion.

Note: All data highly approximate and incomplete. Base used is 1970 Census.

TABLE 2
Alternative Population Estimates[1]

Year	Northern African	Central Southern African	'Coloured'	European	Total
1970[2]	600 000	245 000	90 000	90 000	1 025 000
1977	735 000	300 000	115 000	102 500	1 252 500
1980[3]	802 500	327 500	127 500	(30 000)[4]	1 307 500
'1985–86'[3]	900 000	400 000	150 000	(50 000)[4]	1 500 000

[1] Based on numerous informal estimates ranging from 1 000 000 to 2 500 000 with most from Namibian sources in the 1 200 000 to 1 500 000 range for mid-1970s. Also related to employment and labour force estimates.

[2] 1977 estimate adjusted backwards at 3.0% per annum for African, 3.5% for 'Coloured', 1.75% for European communities.

[3] 1977–80 – '1985–86' pro-forma population growth estimates for African and 'Coloured' communities 3.0% and 3.5% per annum. Actual shifts resulting from immigration from Angola, Botswana, RSA are not subject to serious estimate.

[4] Assumes 7 500 long-term or citizen European households of an average size of 4 and 7 500 to 10 000 expatriate and volunteer households of an average size of about 3. Estimate includes expatriates from Asia, Africa, Latin America as well as Europe.

Note: All estimates highly approximate.

TABLE 3
Population Projections '1980–1981', '1958–1986'

A *Population*

Year	Small Agri.	Large Agri.	Urban Non-Agri.	Total
1977[1]				
African 'Coloured'	700 000	175 000	275 000	1 150 000
European	–	20 000	82 500	102 500
Total	700 000	195 000	352 500	1 252 500
'1980–81'[2]				
Namibian	407 500[4]	275 000[4]	575 000[4]	1 257 500
European/Expatriate	–	3 000	47 000	50 000
Total	407 500	278 000	622 000	1 307 500
'1985–86'[3]				
Namibian	375 000	350 000	725 000	1 450 000
European/Expatriate	–	3 000	47 000	50 000
Total	375 000	358 000	772 000	1 500 000

B *Namibian population shifts* (excluding Europeans)

Sector	1977	Ending 'Contract'[5]	Natural Growth[6]	Other Moves[7]	'1985–86'
Small Agriculture	700 000	– 400 000	+ 100 000	– 25 000	375 000
Large Agriculture	175 000	+ 100 000	+ 60 000	+ 15 000	350 000
Urban (Non-agriculture)	275 000	+ 300 000	+ 140 000	+ 10 000	725 000
Total	1 150 000	–	300 000	–	1 450 000

C *Population categories '1985–86'* (excluding Europeans)

	Pre-school	Full-time Students	Labour force[8]	Household[9]	Aged Disabled	Total
Male	200 000	150 000	325 000	–	40 000	715 000
Female	200 000	150 000	235 000	100 000	50 000	735 000
Total	400 000	300 000	550 000	100 000	90 000	1 450 000

[1] See Table 2.

[2] '1980–81' is a nominal year. What is intended is a 'target' for the end of the first year of independence. The population is 1977 estimate plus 3% a year growth.

[3] '1985–86' is again a nominal year – in this case the target for the end of the sixth year (transition year plus five) in independence. The population is 1977 estimate plus 3% a year growth.

[4] These projections assume most reuniting of households and some 'other moves' have taken place but neither shift is complete. They may overestimate shift in first year, given housing constraints.

[5] Population shifts resulting from reuniting of households divided by contract/other migrant labour regimes..

[6] 3% a year growth of population in sector adjusting for ending contract over 1980–85.

[7] Other moves from one sector to another. Projections are net – gross would be somewhat higher.

[8] Full-time equivalent numbers are used for part-time large agriculture and urban (see Table 5) employment.

[9] Persons not engaged in any activity generating income on standard definitions. (Individual producing substantial food or housing for self-consumption are included under 'Labour force' *not* 'Household'.)

TABLE 4
Labour Force Estimates (1977)

	Households[1]				Individual migrants[5]	Economically Active Persons			
Group	**Total**	**Small Agri.[2]**	**Large Agri.[3]**	**Urban[4]**		**Small[8]**	**Large**	**Urban**	**Total[9]**
Northern African	147 000	127 000[6]	6 000	15 000	75 000	195 000	20 000	96 000	311 000
Central/ Southern African	60 000	25 000[6]	15 000	20 000	22 500	35 000	23 500	63 500	122 000
'Coloured'	23 000	8 000	5 000	10 000	12 500	10 000	6 500	32 000	48 500
European	30 000	–	6 500[7]	23 500	–	–	6 500	30 000	36 500
Total	260 000	160 000[6]	31 500	68 500	110 000	240 000	56 500[10]	221 500	518 000

[1] Primary family units. Assumed average sizes 5 except for European estimated at about 3.5 because of 50% short-term expatriate element. Individual migrants are treated as having home households in Small Agricultural sector not as constituting single-person households elsewhere. However, they are included in urban and large agricultural (*not* 'small agricultural') total and economically active population estimates.

[2] All non-European ranching and farming as of 1977 falls in this class. Neither subsistence nor traditional is an accurate term because some produce is sold (and more bought) and the present system is by no means the traditional pre-colonial one.

[3] As of 1977 *de facto* the European ranching (and very secondarily farming) sector.

[4] All non-agricultural activities classed here.

[5] Workers who have base household units which remain in 'small agriculture'. Worker is single, short-term, outside home household. Contract labour is the dominant but not the only form, e.g. official fishery labour which is seasonal.

[6] Includes refugees outside Namibia.

[7] Relates to household's basic economic activity residence in a substantial number of cases is urban.

[8] Includes adults, children over 12 not in school of households in sector less migrants. Therefore includes *de facto* unemployed. (Adjusted from East African peasant sector data.)

[9] Implied labour force participation rates: 42.5% 'Coloured' and Northern African: 40% Central/Southern African sector.

[10] Domestic service in Large Agriculture sector is *de facto* omitted thereby understating total economically active population and Central/Southern African economically active relative to other groups.

Note: All estimates exceedingly approximate. No usable direct Small Agriculture data exist. Data for other sectors are incomplete and out of date. Previous estimates all appear to understate both Small and Large Agriculture and (urban) Domestic Service by large margins.

TABLE 5
Labour Force Projections to '1985–1986'

A *Total Labour Force[1]*

Year	**Small Agri.**	**Large Agri.**	**Urban (Non–Afri.)**	**Total**
1977[2]				
African/'Coloured'	240 000	50 000	191 500	481 500
European	–	6 500	30 000	36 500
Total	240 000	56 500	221 500	513 000
'1980–81'[3]				
Namibia	200 000	110 000	200 000	510 000[5]
European/Expatriate	–	2 000	13 000	15 000
Total	200 000	112 000	213 000	525 000
'1985–86'[4]				
Namibian	175 000	140 000	245 000	560 000[6]
European/Expatriate	–	2 000	13 000	15 000
Total	175 000	142 000	258 000	575 000

B *Namibian Labour Force Calculation*

'1985–86'	Small Agri.	Large Agri.	Urban (Non–Afri.)	Total
Potential Labour Force[7]				
Male	85 000	85 000	155 000	325 000
Female	90 000	90 000	155 000	335 000
Total	175 000	175 000	310 000	660 000
Actual Labour Force[8]				
Male	85 000	85 000	155 000	325 000
Female[9]				
Full time	90 000	30 000	45 000	165 000
Half time	–	1/2(50 000)	1/2(90 000)	1/2(140 000)
Total	175 000	140 000	245 000	560 000

[1] Includes 'open' urban unemployed. Categorized by sector of employment not residence, i.e. rural resident engaged full time in construction is classed as Non-Agricultural (Urban) and full-time farmer resident in a small town as Small or Large Agricultural.

[2] See Note 1, Table 3.

[3] See Note 2, Table 3.

[4] See Note 3, Table 3.

[5] Low growth 1977 to '1980–1981' is caused by sectoral shifts and increased full-time students.

[6] As calculated part B, this table.

[7] All persons over 12 minus full-time students and aged, disabled (estimated at Table 3–C).

[8] In Small Agriculture calculated as equal to potential labour force. (See Note 8, Table 1.) In other sectors adjusted for part time or non-participation of women in labour force (see Note 10, Table 3), following standard labour force/economically active definitions. No implication that household work is not work is intended.

[9] Very rough estimates. These are markedly above any recorded female participation ratios in non-agricultural labour force in Africa (though not necessarily above West African probable actual ratios) and above present Namibian urban (non-agricultural) levels.

TABLE 6
Economic Activity Estimates (1977)

Activity	Northern African	Central/ Southern African	'Coloured'	European	Total 1977	Thomas 1970[1]
Small Agriculture[2]	195 000	35 000	10 000	–	240 000	87 500
Large Agriculture[3]	20 000	23 500	6 500	6 500	56 500	36 500
Fishing and Fish Processing	3 000	2 000	2 000	500	7 500	7 500
Mining	15 000	3 000	1 000	3 500	22 500	18 000
Manufacturing, Electricity, Water[4]	5 500	2 250	2 500	2 750	13 000	12 000
Construction	8 000	2 750	2 500	1 750	15 000	12 000
Transport, Communication	7 500	2 500	1 500	1 000	12 500	11 500
Commerce & Finance[5]	10 500	6 500	3 000	5 000	25 000	19 500
Government	8 000	3 500	3 500	15 000	30 000	(25 000)
Domestic Service[6]	27 500	35 000	12 500	–	75 000	(8 000)
Other[7]	1 000	1 000	1 000	500	3 500	(3 000)
'Urban' Unemployment[8]	10 000	5 000	2 500	–	17 500	(17 500)
Total	311 000	122 000	48 500	36 500	518 000	259 000
Agriculture Total	215 000	58 000	16 500	6 500	296 500	124 000
Small Agriculture	(195 000)	(35 000)	(10 000)	(–)	(240 000)	(87 500)
Large Agriculture	(20 000)	(23 500)	(6 500)	(6 500)	(56 500)	(36 500)
Non-Agriculture Total	96 000	63 500	32 000	30 000	221 500	135 000
Mining/Fishing	(18 000)	(5 000)	(3 000)	(4 000)	(30 000)	(25 500)
Secondary Sectors[9]	(13 500)	(5 000)	(5 000)	(4 500)	(28 500)	(24 000)
Tertiary Sectors	(54 500)	(48 500)	(21 500)	(21 500)	(145 500)	(67 000)
Unemployed	(10 000)	(5 000)	(2 500)	(–)	(17 500)	(17 500)

[1] W. H. Thomas's 1970 estimates based on collection of scattered sectoral and enterprise is the best previously available source. For urban sectors – unless otherwise noted – these estimates are built up from Thomas's estimates adjusted for later bits of micro-data (e.g. 4 500 increase in mining employment related to Oamites, Otjihase and Rössing). Figures in ( ) are estimates in cases in which Thomas's sectoral division is not the same as that of this table. Subsequent 1977 estimates by Thomas are broadly consistent except for Small Agriculture and Domestic Service.

[2] See note[8] to Labour Force Estimates Table for method of estimation.

[3] Assumes 5 000 to 8 500 ranch units with average 6 to 10 of employees (other than European owners and managers) per unit. Excludes short term seasonal workers, i.e. 10 per ranch at 5 000 estimates and 6 at 8 500.

[4] Includes fish tinning and fish-meal production.

[5] Includes non-European traders. Estimates as high as 12 500 have been made for this sector e.g. 4 500 for Ovambo. However, it seems unlikely that those actually earning their basic household income from this sector can exceed 7 500–10 000. Overlaps exist with Small Agriculture, teachers, tribal officials.

[6] Assumes 25 000 urban-located European households typically with 2 to 3 full- or part time domestic employees each plus 'institutional' domestic employees e.g. cleaners. Previous estimates on order of 7 500 appear absurdly low. However, the present estimate may be too high. Rural domestic employment not estimated (see note 10 to Labour Force Estimates Table 4).

[7] Nominal estimates. Includes clergy.

[8] Nominal estimates. Suggest 6–7% open unemployment among economically active in sectors other than small agriculture from Central/Southern African and 'Coloured' communities and 8–9% Northern African. This may be 'true' given numbers forced back to 'reserve' and nominally engaged in small-scale agriculture. It is not, however, an estimate of numbers actively seeking urban sector jobs which is much higher – perhaps of the order of 60 000–75 000 including 42 500–57 500 who are nominally or actually economically active in small agriculture.

[9] Manufacturing, water, electricity, construction.

[10] Transport, communication, commerce, finance, government, domestic.

Note: All estimates are approximate. There are no usable comprehensive official data. All estimates (including those of Thomas used as base for urban sector) are built up from fragmentary micro-sectoral data plus rough estimation.

TABLE 7
Occupational Category Estimates (1977)

Category	European	'Coloured'	African	Total
Managerial/Administrative[1]	9 700	250	100	10 000
(Including: Large Agriculture	(5 000)	(–)	(–)	(5 000)
Other)	(4 700)	(250)	(100)	(5 000)
Professional/Technical/Para-professional[2]	10 300	2 500	4 250	17 000
(Including: Teachers	(2 500)	(800)	(2 800)	(6 100)
Nurses	(800)	(1 000)	(1 200)	(3 000)
Mining	(1 500)	(50)	(50)	(1 600)
Other Engineering	(1 500)	(100)	(50)	(1 650)
Other Production	(2 000)	(200)	(50)	(2 250)
Accounting	(500)	(200)	(50)	(750)
Other)	(1 500)	(150)	(50)	(1 650)
Clerical/Secretarial	2 500	1 500	2 000	6 000
Supervisory/Foremen[3]	4 000	2 000	6 500	12 500
(Including: Large Agriculture	(1 000)	(1 000)	(3 500)	(5 500)
Other)	(3 000)	(1 000)	(3 000)	(7 000)
Skilled–Non-Supervisory[4]	3 000	1 000	1 000	5 000
Semi-skilled[5]	2 500	7 500	40 000	50 000
(Including: Large Agriculture	(–)	(3 500)	(15 000)	(18 500)
Other)	(2 500)	(4 000)	(25 000)	(31 500)
'Unskilled'[6]	2 000	8 000	80 000	90 000
(Including: Large Agriculture	(500)	(2 000)	(25 000)	(27 000)
Other)	(1 500)	(6 000)	(55 000)	(62 500)
Domestic[7]	–	12 500	62 000	75 000
Small-scale non-agricultural self-employment[8]	2 500	3 500	6 500	12 500
Small agricultural[9]	–	10 000	230 000	240 000
Total (Totals are rounded)	36 500	48 500	433 000	518 000

[1] Includes proprietors of large and middle-sized businesses, middle and senior managers and civil servants.

[2] Broadly defined. At para-professional and para-technical level division between this category and skilled or semi-skilled labour is a matter of choice.

[3] Includes skilled and semi-skilled (but not professional or technical) who have significant supervisory or foreman duties.

[4] Basically skilled artisans requiring over 18 months' specialized formal training or in-service equivalent, e.g. linotype operators, senior mechanics.

[5] Includes workers with specialized on-the-job acquired skills if inexperienced workers would be unable to perform job adequately with six months' normal job experience, e.g. junior mechanics, herdsmen with responsibility for moving herds and/or lambing and calving.

[6] Posts not requiring prior experience and satisfactorily performed with six or less months' normal job experience, e.g. sweepers, messengers, pick and shovel road workers.

[7] Some workers highly skilled but not in general possessing skills transferable to other activities.

[8] Small shops or service establishment not requiring specialized skills readily transferable to other activities, but requiring significant skills or experience not possessed by unskilled worker.

[9] Some workers are highly skilled but the skills are not transferable to other activities.

Note: Estimates are built up from fragmentary data of different dates, sources, methods, reliability. As a result they are highly approximate. They are broadly consistent with Thomas's parallel estimates produced by a similar method but with more access to unpublished official data.

TABLE 8
Sectoral Personpower Requirement at Independence Estimates
(High and Middle Level Qualification Personnel)[1]

Sector	Present	Redundant[2]	New Needs[3]	New Total	Present Europeans[4]	New Expats.	Namibians Total[5]	New to Post
Agriculture[6]	10 000	1 000	1 500	10 500	750	1 250	8 500	4 500
Fishing	1 000	NB[7]	–	1 000	100	250	650	150
Mining	5 000	–	100	5 100	2 500	500	2 100	1 000
Manufacturing	3 000	750	250	2 500	1 000	500	1 000	500
Water & Power	1 000	–	400	1 400	200	500	700	400
Construction	2 500	250	750	3 000	250	500	2 250	750
Transport	1 500	–	1 000	2 500	100	200	2 200	1 200
Communications	750	–	250	1 000	50	450	500	350
Commerce	5 000	2 250	250	3 000	650	250	2 100	600
Finance	500	–	250	750	150	200	400	300
Other services	1 750	250	250	1 750	500	–	1 250	250
Government[8]	18 000	8 000	12 500	22 500[10]	1 250	2 700	18 550	12 000
Including Admin.[9]	(4 500)	(4 000)	(250)	(750)	(–)	(250)	(500)	(500)
Education	(6 500)	(1 500)	(6 250)	(11 250)	(500)	(1 250)	(9 500)	(6 000)
Health	(3 500)	(1 000)	(3 500)	(6 000)	(500)	(500)	(5 000)	(3 000)
Agriculture	(1 500)	(500)	(1 000)	(2 000)	(100)	(400)	(1 500)	(1 000)
Other[10]	(2 000)	(1 000)	(1 500)	(2 500)	(150)	(300)	(2 050)	(1 500)
Total	50 000	12 500	17 500	55 000	7 500	7 500	40 000	22 000

[1] Includes all managerial/administrative (10 000), professional/technical/para-professional (16 800), 2/3 supervisory/foreman 2/3 (8 250), skilled (4 750) plus 1/2 clerical/secretarial (3 250) and 1/7 semi-skilled (7 000). Cross-estimated against sectoral data. (See Tables 4, 6).

[2] Posts either inappropriate, unnecessary or non-priority in an independent Namibia.

[3] Posts reiating to priority programme and institution requirements – see Sectoral Notes below for somewhat more detail.

[4] Includes personnel replaced by their employers (e.g. mining companies), by voluntary agencies (e.g. churches) and by new management contractors (e.g. for nationalized enterprises).

[5] Present total 20 000 of whom 10% 2 000 assumed unavailable or unacceptable after independence. 22 000 promotions and new entries with, when possible, brief 'upgrading' and gap-filling courses.

[6] Excludes government agricultural services.

[7] Special case. Immediate post-independence data assure loss of present Fishing Fleet and substitution foreign 'contract' fleet with partially Namibian crews. See Sectoral Notes.

[8] Includes government agricultural services. Excludes police, prison, armed forces.

[9] Categories not comparable. Present post figure includes 'Bantu Administration', 'Coloured Administration', 'Security' Forces other than army (i.e. police, prisons).

[10] Excludes army, policy, prisons.

Note: These estimates are constructed from Sectoral Data, Table 7 and Table 6. They are, therefore, subject to considerable inaccuracy or wrong 'guestimation' of independent government programme priorities. Work is continuing on reducing the technical errors and inaccuracies by more detailed sector data collection, analysis and estimation.

TABLE 9
Occupational Category Projections to '1985–1986'
A *Magnitude by category*

Category[2]	'1980/81'[1] High–Middle Qualification[3]	'1980/81'[1] Other	'1980/81'[1] Total	'1985/86'[5] High–Middle Qualification[3]	'1985/86'[5] Other	'1985/86'[5] Total
Managers/Admin.[4]	6 000	–	6 000	7 500	–	7 500
Professionals/ Para-professionals	25 000	–	25 000	32 500	–	32 500
Clerical/Secretarial	3 500	5 000	8 500	4 000	7 000	11 000
Supervisory/Foreman	10 500	10 000	20 500	17 500	10 000	27 500
(Large Agri.)	(6 500)	(4 000)	(10 500)	(12 500)	–	(12 500)
(Other)	(4 000)	(6 000)	(10 000)	(5 000)	(10 000)	(15 000)
Skilled	5 000	–	5 000	6 500	–	6 500
Semi-skilled	5 000	70 000	75 000	10 000	87 500	97 500
(Large Agri.)	(–)	(25 000)	(25 000)	(–)	(37 500)	(37 500)
(Other)[6]	(5 000)	(45 000)	(50 000)	(10 000)	(50 000)	(60 000)
Unskilled	–	130 000	130 000	–	155 000	155 000
(Large Agri.)	(–)	(75 000)	(75 000)	(–)	(90 000)	(90 000)
(Other)[6]	(–)	(55 000)	(55 000)	(–)	(65 000)	(65 000)
Domestic	–	30 000	30 000	–	30 000	30 000
Small Scale Non-Agri. Self-employed[6]	–	10 000	10 000	–	20 000	20 000
Small Agriculture	–	200 000	200 000	–	175 000	175 000
Total employed	55 000	455 000	510 000	78 000	484 000	562 500
(Small Agriculture)	(–)	(200 000)	(200 000)	(–)	(175 000)	(175 000)
(Large Agriculture)[7]	(8 500)	(103 500)	(112 000)	(14 500)	(127 500)	(142 000)
(Non-Agriculture)	(46 500)	(151 500)	(198 000)	(63 500)	(182 000)	(245 500)
European/Expatriates			15 000			16 000
Namibians			495 000			546 500
Namibian Labour Force			510 000			560 000
Unemployed/Security Forces[8]			15 000			13 500
Unemployed/Total Labour Force			2%			2%
Unemployed/Urban Labour Force			5%			4%

B *Target Urban Employment Changes*

1977–'80/81'		
1977 Urban employment (excluding unemployed)[9]		204 000
Less:		
Domestic Service Decline	–45 000	
Other Structural changes[10]	–30 000	
		–75 000
Added:		
High-Middle Qualification[11]	17 500	
Other Government Service	17 500	
Programmes Special[12]	25 000	
Other to be identified[13]	9 000	
		+69 000
'1980/81' Urban employment target		198 000
'1980/81'–'85/86'		
'1980/81' Urban employment target[13]		198 000
Added:		
High–Middle Qualification[14]	23 000	
Other 'Normal' Growth[15]	7 000	
Construction Sector Target[16]	7 500	
Self-employed – Small Service Units Target[17]	7 500	
Other to be identified[13]	2 500	
		47 500
'1985/86' Urban employment target		245 500

[1] See Notes 1–3, Table 3.

[2] Categorisation parallel to Table 7. Number for 1977 adjusted as at final note to Table 7.

[3] See Table 7, Note 1. Apparent change in ratios and rapid expansion over period relates to necessary use personnel with skills below medium-term acceptable level (and of vacancies which by definition possess no skills) in '1980/81'.

[4] Old category included proprietors and therefore 5 000-odd large farm owners/managers. In this table these are assumed to be largely gone (see Table 7) and replaced by 'Supervisor/Foreman' leaders on each unit plus supporting teams.

[5] '1980/81' assumes use some large agricultural unit foreman upgraded without additional training but trained by '1985/86'.

[6] See section B this table.

[7] From population projections (Table 3) and labour force projections (Table 5).

[8] No estimate of army/police/prisons has been included. Therefore this residual figure includes both security service employees and urban unemployed. For the unemployed % computations unemployed set at 10 000 and 8 500.

respectively, therefore assuming a pro forma security force employment of 5 000. The exclusion is justified partly on general security grounds but more particularly on the basis that the Liberation Movement has more technical expertise than UNIN in this field and will use some members of the Liberation Forces as the core for independent Namibian Security Forces.

[9] Table 6.

[10] Loss of employment consequential on closure of businesses previously serving European community only and of departure of European employers in other non-critical sectors. Includes 12 500 per Table 7 and 17 500 unskilled and semi-skilled.

[11] See Table 8.

[12] Special para-professional and small production unit for displaced domestic employees and women moving from rural areas.

[13] Target to be sought.

[14] From Part A this table.

[15] Assumes 15% overall growth of non-agricultural employment growth for 5 years, i.e. slightly under 3% a year.

[16] This is not in fact a major programme; if labour-intensive methods are used a moderate-sized dam and irrigation channels would require this order of work force.

[17] Includes cooperative urban ventures joint owner/operators as self-employed.

Note: These projections represent possible targets to be sought, not predictions nor the 'natural course of events'. They are subject to wide margins of error. The underlying population and labour force projections are too weak for the 'unemployment' figure to be taken seriously except as a broad indication of approximate balance if the estimates are broadly right and the target basically achieved.

TABLE 10
Education/Training Pattern Estimates (1977)
(for economically active population in Namibia[1])

Level[2]	European	'Coloured'	African	Total
University or equivalent	5 000	25	10	5 000
Other tertiary[3]	5 000	25	10	5 000
Secondary or equivalent[4]	10 000	3 000	2 000	15 000
Other post primary[5]	7 500	3 000	2 000	12 000
Complete primary	9 000	24 000	19 000	52 000
Substantial primary[6]	negl.	9 500	110 000	119 500
Negligible or nil[7]	negl.	9 000	300 000	309 000
	36 500	48 500	433 000	518 000[8]

[1] All Namibians outside Namibia are excluded.

[2] The university and other tertiary may be overestimated for present post holders if older ones have markedly less formal education and more experience and quasi-formal in-service training than new entrants.

[3] Significant post-secondary education or training (including in-service and part-time) – say minimum 12–18 months full-time equivalent.

[4] Form 6 and Form 4 completions grouped. (Largely Form 4 as Form 6 completion normally leads into further education or training.) Also includes 30 months or longer post-primary courses, eg. teacher and nurses training of that level and duration.

[5] Incomplete secondary and post-primary courses or training programmes of less than 30 months.

[6] Enough to retain ability to read, write, do simple arithmetic. Say over four years (including sub-standards).

[7] No education or partial primary education followed by relapse to functional illiteracy.

[8] For African and 'Coloured' persons who are not economically active in Namibia an approximate breakdown is:

Students	160 000
Substantial Primary	80 000
Negligible or Nil	420 000
Other	10 000

The other (i.e. complete primary or above) category is mainly Namibians outside Namibia including members of liberation struggle, refugees, overseas students. Probably 150–200 University or equivalent, 100–150 other tertiary or equivalent and 600–700 secondary or equivalent.

Note: All estimates highly approximate.

TABLE 11
'Bantu' Education/Health

A *Education*

	1973	1974	1975
Pupil enrolment in Primary Classes			
lower Primary (SSA – Std. 2)	86 980	93 006	98 926
higher Primary (Std. 3 – Std. 6)	26 254	29 432	31 001
total	113 234	122 438	129 927
Pupil enrolment in Secondary Classes			
Junior Secondary (Form I–III)	2 042	2 427	3 475
Senior Secondary (Form IV–V)	212	205	179
total	2 254	2 632	3 654
Student enrolment in			
teacher training	463	492	576
advanced technical training	–	–	354
trade and vocational training	354	297	–
universities in the RSA	31	approx. 37	approx. 40
total	848	826	970
Total pupils and students	116 336	125 596	134 551
Total teachers	2 662	2 901	3 142
Total schools, training institutions	493	525	571
Number of pupils /students[2] per teacher	43.7	43.3	42.6
Number of pupils/teachers per school	236.0	240.0	235.6

[1] Data from *Bantu Education Journal*, 1975/76.

[2] Not counting students enrolled at universities in the Republic of South Africa.

B *Health and Demography*

Life Expectancy at Birth	41
Infant Mortality (per 1 000 live births)	177[1]
Birth Rate	45
Death Rate	16

Source: USAID, *Development Needs and Opportunities For Cooperation in South Africa*, Washington, 1974, p. 66.

[1] 1975 Municipal data for Windhoek cited by W. H. Thomas are 163 for Africans, 145 for 'Coloureds', 21 for Europeans.

TABLE 12
Education/Training Sector: '1985–1986' Target

A *Formal, full-time institutions with enrolment directly related to high–middle qualification needs*

Programme	Years Length[2]	Total Jobs[3]	Annual Course Completions: For Jobs[4]	For further Education[5]	Total[6]	In Namibia	Abroad	Total Enrolment: In Namibia[14]	Abroad[14]	Teaching staff[15]
Quarternary[7]	1 to 5	1 000	110	–	110	50	60	100	140	(20)[16]
University[8]	3 to 5	5 000	550	125	660	550	110	2 375	475	325
Other Tertiary	2 to 4	5 000	550	–	550	500	50	1 625	175	90
Secondary '6'[9]										
Technical	2	5 000	550	700	1 100	1 100	–	2 600	–	175
Other	2	5 000	550	700	1 100	1 100	–	2 350	–	150
Secondary '1/5'[9]	5	10 000	900	2 550	3 100	3 100	–	17 500	–	850
Agricultural Post-Primary[10]	2 to 3	8 500	765	–	765	765	–	2 500	–	150
Other Technical Post-Primary[11]	2 to 3	12 500	900	–	900	900	–	2 500	–	125
Teacher Train.[12]	5	10 000	600	–	600	600	–	3 500	–	150
Other Post-primary[13]	2 to 4	12 500	900	–	900	900	–	2 500	–	125
Total	–	74 500	6 375	4 075	9 785	9 565	220	37 550	790	2 250
Primary Graduate				7 650	40 000					

TABLE 12 (continued)

B *Training programmes at workplaces, part time, short course*

Programme	**Students**	**Teaching Staff**
Correspondence[17]	25 000	250[18]
Other formal institutions		
Full time	(In A)	(In A)
Short Course[19]	5 000	(In A)
Part time	25 000	(In A)
Workplace – entry refresher, upgrading[20]	100 000	1 000[21]
Total	155 000	1 000

C *Basic primary and continuing education*

Programme	**Students**		**Teaching Staff**
Primary school (6 years)	260 000	8 500	(500)[22]
Continuing education	260 000	500	(15 000)[23]
Basic skills[24]	(100 000)	–	
Applied skills[25]	(100 000)	–	
Other[26]	(60 000)	–	
Total		9 000	(15 000)

D *Total education target*

	Students		**Teaching Staff**
Group A	37 500	2 250	
Group B	155 000	1 250	
Group C	520 000	24 500	(9 000)[27]
Total	712 500	28 000	(12 500)

Population age 7 and over: 1 050 000
Enrolment ratio: 68% (712 500)
Population age 13 and over: 750 000
Enrolment ratio: 60% (452 500)

[1] Targets beyond Secondary '6' and above cannot literally be met in 1985–86 because of time lags and the need to deploy some of present secondary-school students directly to work on completion of secondary '1 to 5' or Secondary '6'.

[2] Ranges indicate different probable lengths for different courses, e.g. social sciences (including management) might be three years, natural sciences (including agriculture) four, engineering and medicine five in university programme.

[3] The working assumption is that about 70 000 out of the 78 000 high- and middle-level qualification posts and about 5 000 others (e.g. some foremen and secretarial) would require formal post-primary programmes of one year or longer.

[4] These output targets assume:
a 1% of year death and retirement of citizen job holders at tertiary, 2%

at secondary and post-primary levels (the ratios would move toward 2½–3% at all levels as age structure of senior Namibian personnel became more balanced);
b 3–4% a year typical expansion of jobs;
c phasing out of expatriates over 15–20 years with virtually all non-tertiary qualified and 50% of tertiary qualified phased out by 1990 reducing the expatriate personnel at that point to – say – 5 000–6 000;
d some upgrading and retraining of present serving personnel with weak qualifications;
e very gradual expansion (say 3% a year parallel to population growth) of the educational system to 1990–91, with a basic reassessment of long-term capacity requirements at that date.

[5] Required number of students completing given programme in order to enter another. A – in this column does not mean a 'dead end' but that direct continuation to another programme would be unusual.

[6] The previous two columns do not equal the total column. The 'for further education' column includes an allowance for students failing to complete the next programme. However, such students would become available for posts relating to the completed programme so literal addition of the columns would double count.

[7] Post-first (university) degree programmes.

[8] The distinction between University and other tertiary is somewhat doubtful. It does not characterize the USA, Japan, China or the USSR to same degree as UK, continental Europe and – as a result – Africa. The basic division here is that a programme totally concentrated on a fairly specific set of directly applicable skills, e.g. some of institutes cited in Sectoral Notes to Chapter IV, is termed 'Other Tertiary'. It does not logically follow that these programmes would necessarily be in different institutions from university programmes.

[9] Division between first five forms and sixth form here on British/anglophonic West African basis. This is an analytical division not necessarily an institutional one.

[10] For para-professionals (including field-level extension staff), supervisors.

[11] Some para-technical, skilled, semi-skilled posts.

[12] For primary-school and training-programme teachers. Other posts in secondary and tertiary programmes.

[13] For example, nursing, health education and other para-medical posts, also some chemical/secretarial jobs.

[14] The assumed failure to complete programme rate is 15% except for secondary '1/5' and seconday '6' technical for which it is 20%.

[15] Includes research personnel. The basis for this is that research and teaching will be combined in each tertiary academic staff member's responsibilities. The figures given do not include educational administrators nor 'hotel management' (i.e. dormitory, catering service, transport, estates) administrators. The ratios of students to teachers are possible but at secondary and tertiary level require care in avoiding duplicative programmes leading to very small classes. In secondary and tertiary schools part-time tutorial and teaching-assistant work should be a normal part of the curriculum for final-year students.

[16] Equivalent time. These are included in University/Other Tertiary Staff.

[17] A correspondence unit (whether separate or part of a broader Continuing Education Institute) is envisaged.

[18] Full-time core staff only. Assumes the part-time use of staff of other institutions.

[19] Annual total enrolment. Perhaps 500 at any one time. Particular emphasis on needs of post holders with inadequate previous skill acquisition opportunities, e.g. senior liberation movement personnel who are necessarily engaged in armed struggle until independence.

[20] Includes only organized programmes of three weeks (full-time equivalent) and above. Annual enrolment given; perhaps 12 500 would be in courses at any one time.

[21] Includes full-time training/personnel development staff proportion of time to training.

[22] Bracketed figure is for trainee teachers (from post-primary programme, spending half time in practice teaching during fourth and fifth years).

[23] Bracketed figure is total part-time personnel including teachers and other holders of appropriate skills.

[24] For example, basic reading, writing, arithmetic, English.

[25] For example, agriculture, simple bookkeeping, basic construction skills. Includes Farm Training Institutes.

[26] For example, political education, drama, dancing.

[27] Bracketed figures are for full-time teachers.

TABLE 13
Gross Domestic Product Estimates 1920–1979
(R000 000 current prices)

Year	Sources[1]	GDP	Primary Sector	Agriculture/ Fishing	Mining	Secondary Sector	Manufacturing	Construction	Public Utilities[2]	Tertiary Sector	Transport, communications	Trade, Housing	Financial Services	Other Services	General Government
1920	A	13.0	9.2	1.7	7.6	0.4	0.3	0.1	–	3.2	(0.8)[3]	(0.8)	–	0.8	0.8
1925	A	10.6	6.4	1.3	5.1	0.6	0.5	0.1	–	3.6	(0.8)	(0.8)	–	1.2	0.8
1929	A	13.0	7.2	1.9	5.3	1.0	0.6	0.3	–	5.0	(1.1)	(1.1)	–	1.8	1.0
1930	A	9.8	4.8	0.5	4.3	0.8	0.6	0.2	–	4.2	(0.8)	(0.8)	–	1.5	1.1
1933	A	3.8	0.6	0.7	(Negl.)[4]	0.6	0.5	0.1	–	2.6	(0.4)	(0.4)	–	1.2	0.6
1935	A	8.4	4.8	3.9	1.0	0.6	0.4	0.1	–	2.8	(0.5)	(0.5)	–	1.1	0.7
1940	A	10.4	5.4	5.1	0.4	0.6	0.5	0.1	–	4.4	(0.8)	(0.9)	–	1.7	1.0
1945	A	19.8	11.6	9.0	2.6	1.2	0.8	0.5	–	6.8	(1.6)	(1.7)	–	2.1	1.5
1946	B	22.2	(12.2)	6.4	5.8	(1.6)	1.6	5	6	(8.4)	1.6	2.4	–	2.3	2.1
1950	B	61.0	(40.9)	20.8	20.1	(3.4)	3.4	5	6	(16.7)	3.7	4.6	–	4.4	4.0
1954	B	107.2	(68.0)	32.2	35.8	(7.5)	7.5	5	6	(31.7)	5.4	10.0	–	8.7	7.6
1956	B	141.6	(93.5)	33.5	60.0	(8.7)	8.7	5	6	(39.4)	6.7	12.6	–	10.8	9.3
1958	B	121.3	(66.2)	23.3	42.9	(14.1)	14.1	5	6	(41.0)	6.1	11.0	–	12.4	11.5
1960a	B	122.0	(62.6)	13.2	49.4	(14.9)	14.9	5	6	(44.5)	8.5	8.5	–	13.8	13.7
1960b	D	141.6	69.0	21.1	47.9	18.4	12.7	4	1.4	54.2	12.2	15.8	11.5	6.1	8.8
1962	B	146.7	(82.5)	35.2	47.3	(14.2)	14.2	5	6	(50.0)	10.7	9.7	–	14.5	15.1
1965	C	213.9	142.5	42.8	99.7	(17.0)	–	–	–	(54.4)	–	–	–	–	–
1970a	D	379.4	175.8	60.7	115.1	54.5	35.8	14.8	3.9	149.1	26.7	45.5	30.9	15.9	30.1
1970b	E	373.1	–	–	–	–	–	–	–	–	–	–	–	–	–
1972	D	455.5	–	–	–	–	–	–	–	–	–	–	–	–	–
1973	E	615.6	492.0	123.0	369.0	(30.9)	–	–	–	(92.7)	–	–	–	–	–
1974	D	592	–	–	–	–	–	–	–	–	–	–	–	–	–
1976	F	741	–	–	–	–	–	–	–	–	–	–	–	–	–
1977	G	1 135	575	210[7]	365	160	85	60	15	400	60	135	85	50	70
1979	H	1 425	850	195[7]	655	150	80	52.5	17.5	425	65	140	90	55	75

[1] The procedures, coverage, categories of the different sources vary. Neither totals nor sectoral components are fully comparable.

[2] Water, electricity.

[3] Bracketed ( ) figures are interpolated, not direct from source.

[4] Negative value added.

[5] Included in manufacturing.

[6] Included in other services.

[7] Includes forestry.

Sources:
A D. C. Krogh: The National Income and Expenditure of South West Africa (1920–1950), *South African Journal of Economics*, Vol. 28.
B Odendaal Report, Pretoria, 1964, Table CVIII.
C R. Murray 'The Namibian Economy' in R. Murray *et al.*, *The Role of Foreign Firms in Namibia*, London, 1974.
D W. H. Thomas, '*The Economy of South West Africa: An Overall Perspective*', mimeo.
E United Nations, *Report of Special Committee on Granting of Independence to Colonial Countries and Peoples*, A/10023, September 1975.
F RSA Official Estimate Reported to 'SWA Legislative Assembly' by D. Mudge. 1975 Official Estimate R644 million. Alternative 1975 figures Thomas R755 million and W. S. Barthold R826.4 million (*Namibia's Economic Potential*, Berlin, 1977) estimated from fragmentary RSA and unofficial data.
G Table 15.
H Table 17.

TABLE 14
GDP/GNP Gap Estimates

Year	GDP	GNP	GNP % of GDP
1946	22.2	20.4	92
1950	61.0	46.4	76
1954	107.2	74.4	70
1956	141.6	85.1	60
1958	121.3	83.2	69
1962	146.7	104.1	71
1969	368.9	278.0	75
1977	1 135.0	710.0	63
1979	1 425.0	950.0	67

Sources: Odendaal Report, Pretoria, 1964. *Financial Mail,* 'Desert Deadlock', 2 March 1973; Tables 13, 15, 17.

TABLE 15
1977 Territorial Accounts

A *Namibian Gross Domestic Product, 1977* **(R000 000)**

Sector		Value added			%	
Agriculture		157½	(177½)[3]		13.9	(15.2)[3]
Peasant Household Use[1]	20		(40)[3]	1.9		(3.4)[3]
Commercial[2]	137½			12.1		
Forestry		2			0.2	
Fishing		40½	(41)		3.5	
Household Use	½		(1)	0.1		(0.1)[3]
Commercial	40			3.4		
Mining[4]		375			33.2	
Primary Sector		575	(595½)		50.7	(51.0)[3]
Manufacturing		85			7.5	
Food Processing	50			4.4		
Other Large Scale	25			2.2		
Small Scale[5]	10		(12½)	0.9		(1.0)[3]
Construction[6]		60			5.3	
Electricity/Water		15			1.3	
Secondary Sector		160	(162½)		14.1	(14.0)[3]
Transport/Communication/ Storage		60			5.3	
Trade		110			9.7	
Accommodation[7]		25	(32½)		2.2	(2.8)[3]
Financial Services		85			7.5	
Social and Personal Services		50			4.4	
Domestic Service	15			1.3		
Other	35			3.1		
General Government[8]		70			6.2	
Tertiary Sector		400	(407½)		35.2	(35.0)[3]
Gross Domestic Product		1 135	(1 165)		100.0	(100.0)[3]

[1] Food produced and consumed in the same household unit. Estimated at R100 times 200 000 households with some food production. Implies physical output per 'subsistence sector' household about one-half Tanzanian level.

[2] Estimated make-up of sales in R000 000:

Beef	70–75
Milk/butter	7½
Small stock/eggs/hides	12½
Karakul pelts	50–55
Wool	2½
Cereals	5–7½
Other crops	5–7½
Total	152½–167½
Less Inputs purchased	20–25
Value Added	132½–142½

[3] All bracketed figures re-estimate household consumed output at urban price equivalent (household import parity) instead of farm-gate prices (household export parity) or nominal cost of materials.

[4] Computed as slightly over 80% of export value. Earlier years data shows up to 89% ratios. Downward adjustment is for fuel cost increase and higher import content in uranium.

[5] Includes R2.5 million (R5.0 million per note 3) African household produced/consumed handicraft and related value added.

[6] Approximately 2/3 government construction equivalent to 33 1/3% of capital budget.

[7] 17 500 European houses rental average R1 000: hotels and lodging houses R5 million. African rural houses R2½ million on material cost or R10 million on rental value basis.

[8] Excludes public enterprises and value added in government construction. Basically Recurrent Budget wages and salaries (R55–65 million).

TABLE 15

B *Distribution of Gross Domestic Product* (R000 000)

Household Own-Use Production		25		2.2
Wages and Salaries				
European[1]	210	(18.5%)		
African/'Coloured'[2]	105	(9.3%)	315	27.8%
Taxes on Proprietors[3]			175	15.4%
Surpluses of Production Units[4]	15	(1.3%)	620	54.6%
Small European[5]	105	(9.3%)		
Large European[6]	500	(44.1%)	—	—
			1 135	100.0%

[1] Estimated at 30 000 times R7 000 average. Includes pensions, social security, fringe benefits.

[2] Estimated at R200 per employee in Domestic Service: R250 large

Agriculture: R400 Construction; R500 Fishing and other; R600 Government, Transport and Communication, Commerce, Finance; R1 000 Mining, Manufacturing, Water and Electricity. Includes payments in kind and provident Funds.

[3] Minerals taxes, company tax, income tax on business undertakings but not income tax on wages/salaries or consumption taxes.

[4] Net of taxes is listed at Note 3. Gross of depreciation.

[5] Cash sales related surpluses e.g. livestock, milk, petty commerce.

[6] Estimated 10 500 business at average surplus of R10 000. Includes individual proprietors, normal partnerships, companies with surplus of R50 000 or less.

TABLE 15

C *Distribution of Personal Income* (R000 000)

Personal Income[1]	**Total (R000 000)**		***Per Capita* (Rand)**	
African/'Coloured'				
'Subsistence'	25		22	
Wages (including 'in kind')	105		91	
Other	15	145	13	126
European				
Wages/Salaries	210		1 983	
Production Unit Surpluses (excluding corporate profits)	105	315	992	2 975

[1] Derived from Tables 1 and 13B.

TABLE 15

D *Gross National Product* (Remittance Basis) (R000 000)

GDP		1 135
Remittances[5]		
European Wages/Salaries (25%)	−52.5	
Small Enterprise Surplus (25%)	−32.5	
Large Enterprise	−300.0	
State–Recurrent Account[2]	−60.0	
State Enterprises[3]	20.0	−425
Gross National Product		710

[1] Strictly foreign-owned surpluses retained in a territory constitute a deduction from GDP (and a net inflow of foreign investment). Practically, most computations work from estimates of remitted foreign earnings.

[2] The 'state' in question is South Africa and thus *not* a Namibian body. On recurrent account there is a surplus of about R60 million. This is *not* properly offset by government capital expenditure which in the case of Namibia constitutes 'foreign investment'. 1976/77 Budget Year surplus on this basis was of the order of R46 million. 1977/78 presumptively was higher given enhanced diamond tax revenue.

[3] Operating losses of Posts, Telecommunications, Railways.

Notes: As with exports, South Africa has gone to considerable effort to prevent estimation of GDP. These estimates are made from incomplete data of varying dates and degrees of consistency and reliability. The estimates should be treated as approximations. South African military expenditure in Namibia (except a portion of road and communication spending) *excluded*. Walvis Bay *included*.

TABLE 16
Possible Reconciliation 1976–1977 GDP Estimates

A *SWA Estimate*	
1 1976 RSA Estimate for 'SWA'	R741 million
2 1976–77 Growth.	
General (1%)	7½
Uranium[1]	6½
3 1976–77 Price Increase (12%)[2]	90
4 Probable 1977 RSA Estimate	R905 million
5 Differences in Coverage RSA Estimate and Table 15.	
'Subsistence' Agriculture	17½
Commercial Agriculture	17½–15
Housing/Other Small-Scale Activity	20–25
SWA Account and Parastatal Spending[3]	50–55
	R115 million
6 Probable Differences Due to Transfer Prices of Exports[4]	
Agricultural Products	13
Fish Products	10
Minerals	22
	R45 million
7 Total After Adjustments	R1 065 million
8 Table 15 1977 Estimate	R1 135 million
9 Unexplained Divergence RSA/Table 15 Estimates	R70 million
B *Barthold Estimate*	
1 1976 Estimates	826.4
2 Output Increase	68.6
3 Price Increase	107.5
4 Pro Forma 1977	1 002.5 million
5 Coverage Adjustments[5]	50
6 Transfer Pricing Adjustments	45
7 Comparable Total	1 097.5 million
8 Unexplained Divergence Barthold/Table 15 Estimates	37.5 million

[1] Rössing output 1976 under 750 tonnes, 1977 in 2 500–3 000 tonne range.

[2] 1976 price deflator increase over 1975 was 14%.

[3] Wages, salaries and value added in construction related to 'SWA' Account and some Parastatal Account spending are apparently treated as RSA, not 'SWA' value.

[4] Artificial export prices by RSA or overseas companies shifting value added from 'SWA' to RSA, UK or USA. Estimated pro forma at 10% for agricultural exports, 15% for fish products.

[5] Barthold's estimate is adjusted upward by about R85 million on the official estimate cited. The exact items covered are unclear but are not identical to those listed in 'A'.

TABLE 17
Territorial Accounts Projections

A Namibian Gross Domestic Product Projections: 1979–'1985/86' (R000 000)[1]

Sector[2]	**1979 Value Added**	**%**	**'1985/86' Value Added**	**%**
Agriculture	162½	11	140[3]	8
Forestry	2½	–	2½	–
Fishing	30	2	42½[4]	2½
Mining	655	47	850[5]	50
Primary Sector	850	60	1 035	61
Manufacturing	80	6	105	6
Food Processing	(40)		(45)[6]	
Other	(40)		(60)[7]	
Construction	52½	4	90[8]	5
Electricity/Water	17½	1	20	1
Secondary Sector	150	11	215	13
Transport/Communication/ Storage	65	4	75	4½
Trade	110	8	90[9]	5
Accommodation	30	2	25	1
Financial Services	90	6	75[9]	4½
Social and Personal Services	55	4	35[9]	2
General Government	75	5	150[10]	9
Tertiary Sector	425	29	450	27
Gross Domestic Product	1 425	100	1 700	100

[1] 1978 Prices

[2] See Notes Table 16.

[3] Livestock–50, Dairying + 10, Crops + 17½

[4] Recovery to 1976–77 levels.

[5] Increase in uranium oxide, reactivation base metal capacity closed in 1979.

[6] Additional meat packing, milling.

[7] Including a cement plant but largely small scale.

[8] Includes small-scale housing, water, urban works. Assumes at least one major rail or irrigation project.

[9] Sectors sharply affected by decline in resident European population.

[10] General expansion services plus (pro forma) security force salaries.

TABLE 17

B *Distribution of Gross Product* (R000 000)[1]

	1979	%	'1985–86'	%
Household Production For Own Use	25	2	50	3
Wages and Salaries	390	28	750	44
African/'Coloured'	(130)	(9)	(500)	(29)
European	(260)	(18)	(250)	(14)
Surpluses of Production Units	810	56	500	29
African– Private	(20)	(1)	(40)	(2)
African – State	(NA)	(–)	(225)	(13)
Small European	(90)	(6)	(25)	(1)
Large European	(700)	(49)	(210)	(12)
Taxes on Proprietors	200	14	400	24
	1 425	100	1 700	100

[1] See Notes Table 16B.

TABLE 17

C *Personal Income*

	1979		'1985–86'		
Personal Income[1] (R000 000)		**Total**		**Total**	***Per Capita* (Rand)**
African/'Coloured'		195		590	407
Household Production	25		50		34
Wages	130		500		345
Other	20		40		28
European		350		275	5 500
Wages/Salaries	260		250		5 000
Production Unit Surpluses (excluding corporate profits)	90		25		500

[1] Derived From Tables 6, 7, 16B.

TABLE 17 (Concluded)

D *Gross National Product*

	(Remittance Basis)[1] 1979		(R000 000) '1985–86'	
GDP	1 425	(100%)	1 700	(100%)
Remittances[1]	–475	(33%)	–125	(7%)
European Wages/Salaries	(–57½)		(–50)	
Small Enterprise Surplus	(–22½)		(–10)	
Large Enterprise	(–320)		(–65)	
State–Recurrent Account	(–100)		(Negl.)	
State Enterprises	(+25)		(–)	
Gross National Product	950	(67%)	1 575	(93%)

[1] See Notes Table 16B.

TABLE 18
Namibian Visible Exports 1966–1977 (R000 000)
(Current Prices)

	1966	%	1970	%	1973	%	1977	%
Agricultural Products	32.6	15.6	49	20.9	93	26.6	130	20/18
Karakul Pelts	15.9	7.6	25	10.7	50	13.6	60–65	10
Wool	( )		( )		( )		2–3	0.3
Meat & Products	(16.6)	7.9	(24)	10.2	(48)	13.0	60–65	10
Other	( )		( )		( )		2–3	0.3
Fishery Products	48.9	23.4	56	23.8	80[4]	21.7	65	10/9
Fish-Meal	22.4	10.7	28	11.9	40	10.8	30–35	5
Tinned Fish	14.0	6.7	16	6.8	25	6.5	20–25	3
Other[1]	12.5	6.0	12	5.1	15	4.4	10–15	2
Mineral Products	127.8	61.1	130	56.3	190[4]	51.7	465–515	70/74
Diamonds	85.0	40.6	70	29.8	100[3]	27.8	250–300[5]	36/40
Uranium	–	–	–	–	–	–	80–105[6]	14
Copper	19.2	9.2	25	10.6	40	10.9	50–60	9
Lead	12.3	5.9	18	7.7	28	7.5	37½–47½	6
Zinc and Other[2]	11.3	5.4	17	7.2	22	5.6	25–30	4
Total Visible Exports	209.3	100.0	234	100.0	368[4]	100.0	660–710	100
Exports as % of GDP	67%		62%		62½		58/62%[7]	

[1] Fish, Oil, Lobster, Seal Products, Frozen Fish.

[2] Tin, Vanadium, Cadmium, Lithium, Manganese, Silver.

[3] Alternative estimates R127m to R147m appears likely to be more nearly accurate.

[4] Alternative estimate by Barthold, R380m–£230m minerals, 60m fish and products, 90m agricultural products.

[5] Estimated from 1976–77 volume and price increases and alternatively from calendar 1977 tax estimates and normal ratio of tax to exports.

[6] Assumes 2 000–2 250 tonnes concentrate exports of 3 000 produced.

[7] Coverage of 1977 GDP estimate is broader than earlier ones. On the 1973 GDP comparable basis the ratio would be 65–69%.

Sources:
1966 – *South West Africa Survey 1967*
1970 – 1973/74 – W. H. Thomas, *The Economy of South West Africa*, mimeo.
1977 – Various sources.

Note:
a All post-1966 estimates are based on calculations from fragmentary data of different dates, coverage and accuracy. The Republic of South Africa has gone to considerable effort to make it impossible to compile Namibian external trade data. All estimates are, therefore, at best approximate.

b All estimates include products of and exports through Walvis Bay.

c All estimates include trade to and through the RSA.

TABLE 19
Namibian Export Projections 1979–'1985/1986' (R000 000)[1]

	1979	%	'1985–86'	%
Agricultural Products	130	13	70[2]	6
Karakul Pelts	65	6.5	40	3
Wool	2½	–	2½	–
Meat and Products	60	6	25	2
Other	2½	–	2½	–
Fishery Products[3]	30	3	40[2]	3
Fish	10	1	12½	1
Tinned Fish	10	1	17½	1.5
Other	10	1	10	1
Mineral Products	850	85	1 140	91
Diamonds[4]	475	47	475	38
Uranium[5]	275	27	550	44
Copper[6]	30	3	50	4
Lead[6]	40	4	32½	3
Zinc and Other[6]	30	3	32½	3
Total Visible Exports	1 010		1 250	
Exports as % of GDP	71%		74%	

[1] In 1978 Prices.

[2] Assumes significant transitional damage to sector not fully made good by '1985–86'.

[3] Sector badly damaged by overfishing.

[4] Assumes static output post-1977.

[5] Assumes 4 000^{+} tonnes 1979; 8 000 tonnes 1985–86.

[6] Some capacity closed in 1979; assumed to be reactivated by '1985–86'.

TABLE 20
Balance of Payments Estimates[1] **(R000 000)**

Visible Trade	1977	1979	'1985–86'[12]
Visible Exports	700	1 000	1 250
Visible Imports	450	700	1 150
	+ 250	+ 300	+ 100
Invisible Trade[2]			
Services Exports	15	15	5
Services Imports	65	90	125
Services Balance	–50	–75	–100

Remittances (– means outflow)			
a Individuals from Income	–52.5	–57½	–50[13]
b Small Proprietors from Income	–32.5	–22½	–10
c Large Firms from Income	–300	–320	–65[14]
d Government Recurrent Account[3]	–60	–100	Negl.
e Railways, Telecoms. Recurrent Account	+20	+25	NA
Remittances Balance	–425	–475	–125
Long-Term Capital[4] (– means outflow)			
a Individuals	–50	–75	–5
b Small-Term Proprietors	–50	–75	–5
c Large Firms[5]	+60	+50	Negl.
d Government Capital Account[6]	+115	+125	+50[15]
e Parastatals Capital Account[7]	+30	+30	+110
f Reduction Financial Institution Claims on South Africa	+100	+150	NA
Long-Term Capital Balance	+205	+205	+150
Short-Term Capital[8]	+ ?	+ ?	+25
Central Bank[9]	?	?	–50[16]
Errors and Omissions[10]	+20	+45	?

[1] See Tables 15, 17, 18, 19. Estimates are all approximate. No official data are made public. Since there is no RSA/Namibia exchange control barrier invisible, remittance, banking system and commercial credit data probably do not exist in any systematic form.

[2] Excludes interest, dividends – these are included in remittances.

[3] Recurrent revenue exceeds recurrent expenditure in Namibia.

[4] Items a and b represent capital flight. Very crude estimates. These appear to have been financed largely by running down deposits with financial institutions (or increasing borrowing from them). As these institutions have held net investment/deposit balances in the Republic as part of the counterpart to Namibian deposits, f (reducing claims on South Africa) should offset a, b. Errors in f and a, b guestimates should, therefore, be largely cross-cancelling.

[5] Basically mineral prospecting plus Langer Heinrich development.

[6] Derived from 76–77 Estimates.

[7] Derived from 76–77 Estimates. Railways and Harbours, Post and Telecommunications (R18 million) and rough guess as to other parastatal (e.g. electricity, water) capital spending not financed through government budget or from territorial operating surplus.

[8] Probably a net inflow because of decline of outstanding fish processing unit end of year claims from 1976 because of low 1977 catch. No data available.

[9] Pro forma. Given that there is neither a territorial central bank nor a separate currency this item would be the net change of currency (South African) in circulation in Namibia. Some remittances and capital flight have taken the form of notes thus reducing circulation in Namibia. However, inflation has presumptively had the opposite effect so the net movement of currency circulation is unclear. No data exist and no official estimates are available.

[10] Balancing item.

[11] 1979 and '1985–86' in 1978 prices.

[12] High speculative.

[13] Assumes exchange control but relatively liberal remittances for resident expatriates.

[14] Assumes dividend control but allows some dividends abroad.

[15] Includes grant technical assistance.

[16] i.e. R50 million addition to Central Bank external reserves. (Assumed target level R250–350 million. Initial level by conversion of rand, R50 million; additions year 1–4 of independence R100–150 million.)

TABLE 21
Land use patterns 1976 (000 hectares)[1]

	Total	European Ranches	African Areas
Total Area	82 400	37 700	32 600
Arable	700	100	600
Of which irrigated[2]	(0.07)	(0.07)	(–)
Permanent Pastures	52 900	36 800	16 100
Forest, Woodland[3]	10 400	400	6 000
Waste and Other[4]	18 300	370	9 850
Permanent Water[5]	100	30	50

[1] All estimates except total area highly approximate. Permanent pasture in African areas is particularly suspect and includes, at best, a high proportion of sub-marginal quality. The 'missing' 12 100 000 hectares are largely natural parks and closed areas made up primarily of desert salt pan, swamp and sparse savannah 'woodland'.

[2] Approximately 1 500 ha Hardap Scheme and 5 500 spot irrigation.

[3] Includes a high proportion of very sparse savannah woodland.

[4] Desert, bare rock, swamp and urban.

[5] Small lakes, excluding salt pans and areas of temporary seasonal inundation.

Sources:
FAO, *Production Yearbook*, 1977.
Namibia, Food and Agriculture Sector, 1975.
Southern African Development Coordination Conference, *Agriculture, Forestry and Fisheries*, London, 1979.
A. M. Mbamba, 'Possibilities for the Future Development of Livestock Ranching in an Independent Namibia', MA thesis, University of Sussex, 1977.

TABLE 22
Commercial Agriculture: Estimated Sectoral Accounts 1977–1978 (R000)

European Cash Sales	162.5
European Production Used to Pay Labour	1.5
African Cash Sales	10.0
	174.0

Beef	85.0	European Wages	4.0
Dairy	7.5	African Wages	15.0
Smallstock, Eggs, Hides	12.5	Cash (7.5)	
Karakul	55.0	Kind (7.5)	
Wool	2.5	Implements	20.0
Cereals	5	Operating Inputs	25.0
Other	6.5	Gross Fixed Investment	15.0
	174.0	Financial Charges	10.0
		Net Operating Surplus	85.0
			174.0

Note: A tentative estimation from scattered data of different dates.

Sources: Estimated from data in:
C. Nixon, 'Land Use and Development in Namibia – a Report Prepared for UNIN', 1978.
A. M. Mbamba, 'Possibilities For the Future Development of Livestock Ranching in an Independent Namibia', MA thesis, University of Sussex, 1977.
G. Max, 'Wage Survey', 1976 (unpublished).
Windhoek Observer, various issues, 1978–1979.

TABLE 23
Livestock Patterns 1913–1976 (000)

Animal	Year	Total	European owned	African owned
Cattle	1913[1]	206	183	23
	1958	3 222	2 078	1 150
	1960	2 440	1 832	608
	1965	2 347	1 543	805
	1970	2 500[2]	2 130	370[2]
	1971	2 810	1 940	870
	1976	2 875	2 000	875
Sheep	1960	3 131[3]	2 654	477[3]
	1965	3 839	3 641	199
	1970	4 000	3 750	250
	1971	4 100	3 825	275
	1976	5 085[4]	4 750[4]	335

Goats	1960	1 359	525	834
	1965	1 541	625	916
	1970	1 700	650	1 050
	1971	1 750	675	1 075
	1976	2 026	800	1 226
Sheep & Goats	1913[1]	1 034	738	316
Pigs	1965	20	20	–
	1970	24	24	–
	1971	26	26	–
	1976	30	30	–
Poultry	1965	339	–	–
	1970	400	–	–
	1971	410	–	–
	1976	500	–	–
Horses, Asses, Mules	1976	111[5]	–	–

[1] Police Zone only – excludes Kaokoveld, Ovambo, Okavango, Caprivi.

[2] Underestimate. More likely total 3 000 and African 870.

[3] Rehoboth figure of 344 (versus 49 in 1965) incredible. Probably correct figure was 34 in which case African 167, Total 2 821.

[4] Probably overestimated. 4 335 total and 4 000 European appears more likely.

[5] Excludes Turnhalle members.

Sources: Compiled from
FAO, *Namibia Prospects for Future Development*, Rome, 1977. *Production Yearbook*, 1977.
Republic of South Africa, Bureau of Statistics, Report No. 3, 1964. *South West African Survey, 1967.*
A. F. Calvert, *South West Africa Under The German Occupation*, T. W. Laurie, London, 1916.
A. M. Mbamba, 'Possibilities for the Future Development of Livestock Ranching in an Independent Namibia', MA thesis, University of Sussex, 1977.

TABLE 24
European Cattle Herds, Offtake (000)

Year	Number of Head of Cattle kept by Europeans	Offtake (Culling-rate)	
		Total[1]	on the hoof exports to the RSA
1968	1 500	317	259
1969	1 980	312	241
1970	2 130	417	306
1971	1 940	502	353
1972	1 950	583	435
1973	1 500	507	n.a.
1974	1 880	276	n.a.
1975	n.a.	n.a.	n.a.
1976	n.a.	n.a.	328[2]
1977	2 000	400	320

[1] In recent years, some 33 000 head of cattle have been slaughtered annually in Namibia to supply the Namibian public with fresh meat.

[2] Estimate.

Sources: *South African Financial Gazette*, Supplement on South West Africa, 30 August 1974, p. 9. ECA, *Summaries of Economic Data*, Namibia 1973, 6th Year, No. 2.
South West Africa Survey 1974, Department of Foreign Affairs of the Republic of South Africa, 1975, p. 34.

TABLE 25
Karakul Pelt Exports 1960–1976

	Export of South African and Namibian Karakul Pelts[1]	Average Price per Karakul Pelt[1]	Number of Namibian Karakul Pelts Exported[2]	Value of Namibian Karakul Pelts Exports
Year	Number	Rand	Number	million Rand
1960	2 747 659	4.38	1 648 595	7.2
1970	5 148 396	5.78	3 089 037	17.9
1971	5 388 182	8.09	3 232 909	26.2
1972	5 514 011	9.96	3 308 406	33.0
1973	5 009 443	9.21	3 005 665	27.7
1974	4 692 500	9.33	2 815 500	26.3
1975	4 841 995	11.90	2 905 197	34.6
1976	4 809 802	17.82[3]	2 885 881	51.4

[1] Source provides this column.

[2] Calculated on the basis of column 2 on estimate that 2/5 of total production originates in the Republic of South Africa and 3/5 originates in Namibia.

[3] The price rise is partly due to the devaluation of the Rand by 15%.

Sources: Karakul Board, *Annual Report for the Finance Year Ended 30 June 1974*, Windhoek; information by Mr Manning of the Karakul Board, 31 January 1977, Windhoek.

TABLE 26
Crop Production Estimates 1971–1976 (hectares, tonnes)

Crop[1]	1971	1972	1973	1974	1975	1976
Wheat						
Area	600	600	700	700	700	700
Production	600	600	700	700	700	700
Maize						
Area[2]	30 000	32 000	32 000	32 000	32 000	32 000
Production	10 000	12 000	12 000	12 000	12 000	14 000
Millet						
Area[2]	48 000	49 000	50 000	51 000	52 000	53 000
Production	17 000	17 500	18 000	18 500	19 000	19 500
Sorghum						
Area[2]	6 000	7 000	7 000	7 000	7 000	9 500
Production	2 000	2 300	2 300	2 300	2 300	2 300
Total Grain						
Area	84 600	88 600	89 700	90 700	91 700	93 200
Production	29 600	32 400	33 000	33 500	34 000	36 500
Roots and Tubers						
Area	12 500	12 500	13 000	13 500	14 500	14 500
Production	105 000	105 000	110 000	115 000	120 000	125 000
Pulses						
Area	3 300	3 300	3 300	3 400	3 400	3 400
Production	5 900	6 000	6 200	6 300	6 400	6 600
Fresh Vegetables						
Production[3]	16 500	17 000	17 500	18 000	18 500	19 000
Total						
Area[4]	104 500	108 600	109 400	112 100	114 200	115 900
Production	157 000	160 400	166 700	172 800	178 900	187 100

[1] All data are highly approximate trend estimates. They do not take account of weather and, therefore, actual annual output fluctuations.

[2] Probably grossly underestimated. Outputs may be closer to correct as yields, per hectare appear to be grossly overestimated.

[3] Production and implicit hectar probably seriously underestimated.

[4] Apparent gross underestimate. 1960 South African Agricultural Census Data (Report No. 1 of 1963) show about 640 000 hectares under cultivation – 66 000 European and 574 000 African.

Sources: Data from FAO, *Namibia: Prospects for Future Development*, Rome, 1977.

TABLE 27
Coastal Fishery Catch 1966–1977
(000 tonne)

	Catch of South African Fishing Boats				Catch Quotas	Fish Products Manufactured in Namibia			
Year	Pilchard	Anchovey	Others[1]	Total	Pilchard	Total	Fish-meal	Fish body oil	Canned Pilchard
1966	–	–	–	–	–	730.0	–	–	–
1967[2]	915.1	10.7	0.1	925.9	–	–	172.5	38.5	83.7
1968[2]	1 331.1	142.1	0.2	1 473.4	–	–	238.4	68.3	80.3
1969[2]	1 109.1	179.8	2.4	1 291.3	–	–	202.7	45.2	79.1
1970	509.7	197.1	0.8	707.6	–	–	156.3	43.9	90.1
1971	309.8	266.7	83.3	659.8	498.7	1 038.7	135.4	27.2	57.1
1972	363.7	144.6	16.6	524.9	–	–	112.3	28.1	110.5
1973	396.0	301.7	9.2	706.9	–	–	143.1	46.8	135.0
1974	554.7	252.8	26.1	833.6	568.3	940.5	161.2	28.3	186.6
1975	545.4	194.4	19.4	795.2	568.3	940.5	146.6	28.3	194.0
1976	447.3	94.1	31.1	572.5	475.3	940.5	106.1	19.1	172.8
1977	–	–	–	–	250.0	940.5	–	–	–

[1] Red-eye, mackerel, maasbanker.

[2] From 1967–1969, two South African fish-meal factory ships caught and processed considerable quantities of pilchard off the Namibian coast.

Sources: *South African Fishing Industry Handbook and Buyer's Guide*, 13th Edition 1976/77, Capetown (undated), p. 43.
The South African Shipping News and Fishing Industry Review, September, 1976, p. 42.
Africa Research Bulletin, Vol. 14, No. 2., 31 March, 1977, p. 4208C.

TABLE 28
Offshore Catch Estimates 1975
(000 tonne)[1,2]

Country	tonnes	%
USSR	209 320	42.6
Spain	169 885	34.6
Poland	37 122	7.6
Cuba	28 652	5.8
Republic of South Africa	19 715	4.0
Bulgaria	8 750	1.8
Italy	6 780	1.4
Israel	6 000	1.2
Japan	5 103	1.0
Total	419 327[3]	100.0

[1] Groundfish including hake, redfish, bass and congers.

[2] Between latitude 150° S and latitude 30° S, i.e. within an area somewhat longer than the Namibian coastline.

[3] Incomplete.

Source: International Commission for the South East Atlantic Fisheries (ICSEAF).

TABLE 29
Mines, Minerals, Mining Companies

Mining Company and Mine	*Type of Mineral*	*Parent Companies*
1 Diamonds		
CDM of SWA Limited Oranjemund, Diamond Area No. 1	Gemstones	De Beers Consolidated Mines Limited (100%)
Marine Diamond Corporation (Pty) Ltd., Foreshore and sea concessions off DA No. 1	Gemstones	De Beers
2 Base Minerals		
Tsumeb Corporation Ltd., TCL Tsumeb, Kombat, Matchless, Asis Ost.	Cadmium, blister copper refined lead, smelter silver, zinc concentrates; by-products, arsenic trioxide, germanium	AMAX Inc (29.6%), Newmont Mining Corporation (29.6%), Selection Trust (14.2%), O'Kiep Copper Company (9.5%), Union Corporation (9.4%), SWACO (2.4%).
South West Africa Company Limited (SWACO) Berg Aukas, Brandberg West, Asis Ost	Lead vanadium concs., lead and zinc sulphides, zinc silicates, tin/tungsten concs.	Anglo American (44%) Consolidated Goldfields CGF (43%), Charter Consolidated (2%), 11% other until 1976. Then Kiln Products Ltd. (100%).
Kiln Products Limited Berg Aukas	Waelz kiln production zinc oxide concs.	Goldfields of South Africa GFSA (55%) unlisted subsidiary.
Oamites Mining Company (Pty) Limited Oamites	Copper concs., Silver ores.	Falconbridge Nickel Mines (74.9%), Industrial Development Corporation of SA, IDC (25.1%).
Otjihase Mining Company (Pty) Limited Otjihase	Copper concs., pyrite concs., precious metals.	Johannesburg Consolidated Investments (67%), Minerts.
Klein Aub Koper Maatskappy Beperk Klein Aub	Copper concs.	General Mining/Federale Mynbou (100%).
Imcor Zinc (Pty) Limited Rosh Pinah	Lead and zinc concs.	ISCOR (100%).
Uis Tin Mining Company Ltd Uis	Tin concs.	ISCOR (100%).
Onganja mine Seeis	Copper concs.	Zapata Corporation via 93%-owned Granby Mining Corporation.
Nordex Joint Venture Ltd., Krantzberg	Tungsten concs.	Nord Resources Corporation (40%), Ebco Mining Company (Bethlehem Steel) (60%).
S.W.A. Lithium Mines (Pty) Ltd., Karibib	Lithium ores, ambligonite, lepidolite, petalite.	Metallgesellschaft AG (100%).
Dr Bergers Mines (Pty) Ltd., Karibib	Marble, wollostonite.	Dr Bergers Mines
Bantu Mining Corporation Oshakati	Sodalite	SA Government
Tantalite Valley Minerals (Pty) Limited Karasburg	Tantalite	Tantalite Valley
3 Uranium		
Rössing Uranium Limited Rössing/Arandis	Uranium Oxide	Rio Tinto Zinc Corp. (45.5%), IDC (13.2%), Rio Algom (RTZ) (10%), Minatomes SA (10%), General Mining (6.8%), Other (14.5%).
Langer Heinrich Uranium (Pty) Limited (Under Development)	Uranium Oxide	General Mining/Federale Mynbou (100%)

[1] Anglo American, De Beers, Johannesburg Consolidated and Charter Consolidated are jointly controlled. South African.

[2] General Mining, Federale Minbou, Minerts and Union are South African controlled.

[3] ISCOR and IDC are South African state corporations.

[4] Newmont and AMAX are US controlled. O'Kiep is controlled by them jointly; Selection Trust by AMAX.

[5] Bethlehem Steel is US controlled.

[6] Falconbridge is Canadian and Zapata joint Canadian–US controlled.

[7] RTZ and Consolidated Gold Fields are British controlled. Kiln is controlled by Consolidated.

[8] Metalgesellschaft is German controlled.

TABLE 30
Mineral, Metal Production 1972–1976
(tonnes unless otherwise specified)

Commodity	1972	1973	1974	1975	1976
Diamonds[1]	1 500 000	1 600 000	1 500 000	1 747 739	1 693 994
Silver[2]	1 373 000	1 563 000	1 556 000	1 600 000	n.a.
Copper	–	–	–	–	43 000
blister	26 200	22 000	46 775	36 500	
concentrates	22 000	66 000	60 000	66 000	
Lead	–	–	–	–	40 000
refined	68 200	59 000	64 600	44 400	
concentrates	700	20 000	26 000	22 000	
lead/vanadium concentrates	4 500	9 000	6 000	5 000	
Cadmium	100	100	100	100	
Zinc	–	–	–	–	30 000
Silicate concentrates	29 000	28 000	24 000	20 000	
Sulphide concentrates	43 400	43 000	40 000	40 000	
Zinc Oxides	23 900	28 000	32 000		
Lithium ores	–	–	–	–	n.a.
amblygonite	n.a.	51	60	n.a.	
lepidolite	n.a.	3 500	4 500	n.a.	
petalite	n.a.	3 500	1 500	n.a.	
Tin	–	–	–	–	
metal	660	–	–	–	–
concentrate	–	1 060	1 100	1 117	800
Wolfram	–	120	230	n.a.	
Uranium	–	–	–	–	1 500

[1] Carats

[2] Ounces

Source: *World Mining*, Catalog, Survey and Directory Number, June 1973, June 1977, New York.

(The figures are prepared by *World Mining* editors from 'a variety of individual sources'. As such their accuracy cannot be guaranteed and there are some discrepancies with those of other non-official sources in the field, particularly with respect to copper and lead production; however these have been found to be the most generally reliable.)

TABLE 31
Recurrent Budget Summary 1976–1977

Revenue	**Item**		**%**
Income Tax	26.5		14
Company Tax	83.7		45
Value Added Tax	7.4		4
Duty	36.0		19
Repayment of loans, interest	7.0		4
Other income	26.2		14
Total Revenue	186.8		100
Expenditure			
White:	74.0		53
General administration		12.2	
Education		15.0	
Health		14.2	
Other social expenditure		8.3	
Economic services		24.3	
African:	53.6		38
Bantu administration		49.5	
Bantu education		3.5	
'Coloured':	13.0		9
Administration		12.0	
Education		1.0	
Total Expenditure	140.0[1]		100
Security Police	4.5[1]		
Military expenditure	250.0[2]		

[1] Excludes Security Police which is in SWA Budget.

[2] In RSA not SWA Budget; rough estimates of portion relating to Namibia.

Source: Data derived from Tables 32, 33, *Economic Development in Namibia.*

TABLE 32
Government Revenue and Expenditure
(R000 000)

	1978/79[1] (Estimated Actuals)		**'1985/86'[4] (Projected Estimates)**	
Revenue				
Diamonds		190		200
Company Tax	125		135	
Profits Tax	30		30	
Export Duty	35		35	
Other Company Tax		16½		200
Uranium	–		125	
Other Mining	–		25	
Other	16½		50	
Income Tax		37½		65
Loan Levy		25		–
Customs and Excise		45½		50
Sales Tax		8		50
Licences		2		2½
Departmental Revenue[3]		13		15
Proceeds on Investments[4]		3		50
Loan Recoveries		7½		5
Miscellaneous		8		12½
		356		650
Expenditure[5]				
Recurrent		215[6]		350–400[7]
Capital		140[6]		350–400[8]
		355		700–750
Domestic Borrowing		–		25
External Grants/Borrowing		–		50

[1] 1978/79 Consolidation of South West Africa Account, Consolidated Revenue Fund (RSA) and Territorial Estimates of Revenue and Expenditure (SWA). Diamond revenue adjusted for probable outcome above estimates.

[2] '1985–86' assumes higher excess profits and company taxes, somewhat more progressive personal income tax, about the same rates of indirect tax.

[3] 1978/79 excludes an item appearing as expenditure in RSA and revenue in SWA Accounts in respect of 'Coloured – Rehoboth – Nama' expenditure.

[4] '1985/86' assumes profit from Central Bank and a few other state bodies paid into general revenue but R175 million retained for parastatal investment.

[5] The sectoral breakdown of existing accounts is not very revealing. Further, it is based on colour divided services in a manner making reconstruction of the figures along lines comparable to a '1985/86' budget almost impossible.

[6] 'Security' expenditure not included.

[7] Assumes basic service provision approaching universal coverage. Includes some security expenditure.

[8] Assumed public sector investment budget:

Government (R000 000)	
Recurrent Revenue	300
Domestic Borrowing	25
Foreign Grants/Borrowing	50
Total Revenue	375
Government Projects	325
Investment in Parastatals	50
Total Expenditure	375
Public Enterprises (Parastatals)	
Retained Surplus	175
Local Borrowing (Net)	30
Foreign Borrowing (Net)	100
State Investment	50
Total Resources	355
Investment	350
State Loan Repayment	5
Total Uses	355
Consolidated Public Sector Investment	675

General Note to Tables

Tables 1–10, 12–13, 15–16, 18, 20 derived from *Toward Manpower Development For Namibia*, United Nations Institute for Namibia, Lusaka, and Tables 21, 23, 24, 26 largely constructed from FAO sources.

Tables 11, 24–25, 27–28 derived from W. S. Barthold, *Namibia's Economic Potential and Existing Economic Ties with the Republic of South Africa,* German Development Institute, Berlin, 1977.

Tables 29 and 30 derived from Commonwealth Secretariat, *The Mineral Industry of Namibia: Perspectives for Independence*, London, 1978.

Tables 31 and 32 derived from RSA and SWA Estimates and W. H. Thomas, *Economic Development In Namibia*, Kaiser, Grünewald, Munich, 1978.

In the absence of either complete or reliable official statistics, most tables constructed in large measure from a wide array of newspapers, journal, company and observer reports and estimations.

Bibliography

Official Publications

Republic of Botswana, *National Policy For Rural Development*, Paper No. 2 of 1973, Government Printer, Gaborone, 1973.

Republic of Botswana, *National Policy on Tribal Grazing Land*, Government Paper No. 2 of 1965, Government Printer, Gaborone, 1975.

Republic of Botswana, *The Rural Income Distribution Survey in Botswana 1974/75*, Government Printer, Gaborone, 1976.

Republic of Botswana, Ministry of Local Development and Lands, *Preliminary Report on the Public Consultation on the National Policy on Tribal Grazing Land*, Gaborone, 1976.

Republic of Kenya, *Report of the Mission on the Land Settlement in Kenya* (Van Arkadie Report), Nairobi, 1966.

Republic of South Africa, Bantu Investment Corporation, *Homelands, The Role of the Corporations in the Republic of South Africa*, Chris van Rensburg Publications, Johannesburg (n.d.).

Republic of South Africa, *Decision by the Government on the Recommendation of the Commission of Enquiry into South West Africa Affairs,* Memorandum, 1964.

Republic of South Africa, *Decisions by the Government on the financial and economic relations between the Republic and South West Africa*, Memorandum, 1968.

Republic of South Africa, *Department of Finance, Estimates, South West Africa Account of the Consolidated Revenue Fund*, 1973/74–1978/79, Government Printer, Pretoria, 1973–78.

Republic of South Africa, Department of Foreign Affairs, *Owambo,* Government Printer, 1971.

Republic of South Africa, Department of Foreign Affairs, *South West Africa Survey*, Pretoria, 1967 and 1974.

Republic of South Africa, *Development of Self-government for Native Nations in South West Africa Bill*, Pretoria, 1968.

Republic of South Africa, *Explanatory Memorandum explaining the background and objects of the development of self-government for native nations in the South West Africa Bill*, Pretoria, 1968.

Republic of South Africa, *Government Gazette*, No. 1 033, Pretoria, 1968 (Proclamations of the State President of the Republic of South Africa).

Republic of South Africa, *Report of the Commission of Enquiry into South West Africa Affairs 1962–1963* (Odendaal Commission), Pretoria, 1964.

Union of South Africa, *Report of the South West Africa Commission*, U.G.26, Government Printer, Pretoria, 1936.

Estimates (Expenditure, Revenue), South West Africa Administration, 1973/74–1978/79, Government Printer, Windhoek, 1973–1978.

FAO, *Namibia, A Preliminary Note Towards a Country Development Brief*, Rome, 1975.

FAO, *Namibia, Prospects for Future Development*, W/K9407, Rome, 1977.

International Commission of Jurists, *Apartheid in South Africa and South West Africa*, Geneva, 1967.

International Court of Justice, Reports of Judgements, Advisory Opinion and Orders, Leyden, 1962, 1966, 1971.

International Labour Office, *Labour and Discrimination In Namibia* (Consultant N. Rubin), Geneva, 1977.

League of Nations, Permanent Mandates Commission, *Reports 1921–39*, Geneva, 1921–39.

United Nations, *Apartheid in Practice*, Office of Public Information, New York, 1976.

United Nations, *Decolonization*, 1, 3, 1974 (Issue on Namibia), Department of Political Affairs, Trusteeship and Decolonization.

United Nations, Economic and Social Council, *The Activities of Transnational Corporations in the Industrial, Mining and Military Sectors of Southern Africa*, Commission on Transnational Corporations, E/C 10/51, March 1979.

United Nations, *Infringements of Trade Union Rights in Southern Africa*, New York, 1970.

United Nations, *International Conference in Support of the Peoples of Zimbabwe and Namibia*, May 1977, Report.

United Nations, Notes and Documents, *World Conference for Action against Apartheid, Lagos, Nigeria, August 1977*, Conference 1/part II, Centre Against Apartheid, Department of Political and Security Council Affairs, New York, 1977.

UN Monthly Chronicle, United Nations Publications, New York, 1975–1978.

United Nations, *A Principle in Torment, The United Nations and Namibia*, New York, 1971.

United Nations, *A Trust Betrayed: Namibia*, Office of Public Information, New York, 1974.

United Nations, *The United Nations and Decolonization*, Office of Public Information, New York, 1977.

United Nations, *Reports* of the United Nations Council for Namibia.

United Nations, *Yearbook of the United Nations*, New York, 1946.

United Nations, *Namibia: A Unique UN Responsibility*, Department of Public Information, New York.

United Nations, Institute for Namibia, *Manpower Estimates and Implications for Namibia*, Namibia Studies Series No. 1 (R. H. Green, consultant, W. K. Duggal, ed.), Lusaka, 1978.

United Nations, Institute for Namibia, *Constitutional Options for Namibia: A Historical Perspective*, Namibia Studies Series No. 2 (M. D. Bomani and C. Ushewokuuze, consultants, N. K. Duggal, ed.), Lusaka, 1979.

UNESCO, *Racism and Apartheid in Southern Africa*, Paris, 1974.

League of Nations, Permanent Mandates Commission, *Reports 1921–39*, Geneva, 1921–39.

USAID, *Development Needs and Opportunities for Cooperation in Southern Africa*, Annex A, Namibia, Washington, 1979.

US Congress, House of Representatives, Committee on Foreign Affairs, Subcommittee on Africa, *Critical Developments in Namibia*, Hearings, 1974.

Books and Articles

AFRICA BUREAU, *The Great White Hoax: South Africa's International Propaganda Machine*, London, 1977

AFRICAN NATIONAL CONGRESS, *Guerrilla Warfare*, South African Studies 1, London, 1970.

AFRO-ASIAN PEOPLE'S SOLIDARITY ORGANISATION, *Namibia Struggles for Freedom*, Cairo, 1972.

AHLSEN, B., *Namibia (Sydvästafrika)*, Nordiska Afrikainstitutet, Uppsala, 1970.

AL-NAGAR, U., 'African Initiative in Namibia in the Pre-Colonial Period', Paper presented at International Conference on Southern African History, Rome, August 1977.

AMERICAN LUTHERAN CHURCH, Division of Life and Mission in the Congregation of the American Lutheran Church, Minneapolis, *Event*, Vol. 14, No. 2, 1974.

AMIN, S., *The Class Struggle in Africa*, Africa Research Group, Cambridge, n.d.

AYDELOTTE, W. O., *Bismarck and British Colonial Policy: The Problem of South West Africa 1883–85*, Philadelphia, 1935.

BARTHOLD, W. S., *Namibia's Economic Potential and Existing Economic Ties with the Republic of South Africa*, German Development Institute, Berlin, 1977.

BERG, E. J., 'Namibia: Economic Growth, Structure and Prospects', Centre for Research on Economic Development, University of Michigan, Ann Arbor (for African American Scholars Council), 1976.

BLAUSTEN, R., 'Foreign Investment in the Black Homelands of South Africa', *African Affairs*, 229, 1976.

BLEY, H., *South West Africa Under German Rule 1894–1914*, Heinemann, London, 1971.

BRUWER, J. P. von S., *South West Africa: The Disputed Land*, Nasionale Boekhandel, Capetown, 1966.

CABRAL, A., *Revolution in Guinea: An African People's Struggle*, Imprimerie Joseph Adam, Brussels, 1974.

CALLINICOS, A., and ROGERS, J., *Southern Africa after Soweto*, Pluto Press, London, 1977.

CARLSON, J., *No Neutral Ground*, New York, 1973.

CARROLL, F., *South West Africa and the United Nations*, University of Kentucky Press, Lexington, 1967.

CHRISTIAN CENTRE IN NAMIBIA, *Report on the Registration and Election Campaigning in Namibia 1978*, Windhoek, 1978.

CHRISTODOULOU, D., 'Land Settlement: Some Oft-Neglected Basic Issues', *Monthly Bulletin of Agricultural Economic Statistics*, 14, 10, FAO, Rome, 1961.

CHRISTIE, R., 'Who Benefits by the Kunene Hydro-electric Schemes?' *Social Dynamics*, 2, 1, 1976.

CHAMBERS, R., *Settlement Schemes in Tropical Africa: a Study of Organisations and Development*, Routledge and Kegan Paul, London, 1969.

'Administrators: A Neglected Factor in Pastoral Development', *Journal of Administration Overseas*, XVIII, 2, Ministry of Overseas Development, HMSO, London, April 1979.

CHAMBERS, R., FELDMAN, R., and FELDMAN, D., *Report on Rural Development*, Ministry of Finance and Development Planning, Government Printer, Gaborone, Botswana, 1973.

CLARENCE-SMITH, W. G., and MOORSOM, R., 'Underdevelopment and Class formation in Ovamboland 1845–1915', *Journal of African History*, 16, 3, 1975.

COHEN, B., and EL-KHAWES, M. (eds.), *The Kissinger Study of Southern Africa*, Spokesman Books, Nottingham, 1975.

COMMITTEE FOR FREEDOM IN MOZAMBIQUE, ANGOLA AND GUINEA, *White Power: the Kunene River Scheme*, London, n.d. (1970).

COMMONWEALTH SECRETARIAT (R. Murray, consultant), *The Mineral Industry of Namibia: Perspectives for Independence*, London, 1978.

COUNTER INFORMATION SERVICES, *The Rio Tinto Zinc Corporation Ltd.*, London, 1974.

COURTNEY W., and DAVIS, J., *Namibia: U.S. Corporate Involvement*, The Africa Fund, New York, 1972.

CRONJE, G. and S., *The Workers of Namibia*, International Defence and Aid Fund, London, 1979.

DAVIDSON, B., *Which Way Africa? The Search for a New Society*, Penguin Books, 1971.

Africa in History, Paladin, 1974.

DAVIDSON, B., SLOVO, J., and WILKINSON, A. R., *Southern Africa: The New Politics of Revolution*, Penguin Books, 1976.

DRESCHLER, H., *Südwestafrika unter deutscher Kolonialherrschaft*, Berlin, 1966.

DUGARD, J. (ed.), *The South West Africa/Namibia Dispute*, Documents and scholarly writings on the controversy between South Africa and the United Nations, University of California Press, Berkeley, 1973.

ELLIS, J., *Elections in Nambia?*, British Council of Churches/Catholic Institute for International Relations, London, 1979.

FANON, F., *The Wretched of the Earth*, Macgibbon and Kee, London, 1965.

FERREIRA, E. de S., 'International Capital in Namibia', Paper presented at International Namibia Conference, Brussels, May 1972 (mimeo).

Portuguese Colonialism from South Africa to Europe, Economic and Political Studies on the Portuguese Colonies, South Africa and Namibia, Göttingen, 1972.

FIRST, R., 'The Bantustans: The implementation of the Odendaal Report', Paper presented at International Namibia Conference, Brussels, May 1972.

South West Africa, Penguin African Library, London, 1963.

FIRST, R., STEELE, J., and GURNEY, C., *The South African Connection: Western Investment in Apartheid*, Temple Smith, London, 1972.

FOREIGN AND COMMONWEALTH OFFICE, London, 'Namibia (South West Africa): Independence Proposals, Background and Chronology', London, 1979 (mimeo).

FRAENKEL, P., *The Namibians of South West Africa*, Minority Rights Group, London, 1974.

FREISCHLICH, R., *The Last Tribal War: A History of the Bondelswart Uprising which Took Place in South West Africa in 1922*, Capetown, 1964.

GEBHARDT, F. B., 'The Socio-economic Status of Farm Labourers in Namibia', *South African Labour Bulletin*, Vol. 4, 1 and 2, January–February 1978.

GIBSON, R., *African Liberation Movements, Contemporary Struggles against White Minority Rule*, Institute of Race Relations, London, 1972.

GOLDBLATT, J., *History of South West Africa from the Beginning of the Nineteenth Century*, Juta, Johannesburg, 1971.

The Mandated Territory of South West Africa in Relation to the United Nations, Struik, Capetown, 1961.

GORDON, R., 'A Note on the History of Labour Action in Namibia', *South African Labour Bulletin*, April 1975.

GORDON, R. J., *Mines, Masters and Migrants: Life in a Namibian Compound*, Ravan Press, Johannesburg, 1977.

GOTTSCHALK, K., 'South African Labour Policy in Namibia 1915–1975', *South African Labour Bulletin*, January–February 1978.

GREEN, R. H., 'Constellation, Association, Liberation: the Struggle for Southern African Development Coordination', *African Contemporary Record 1979–80*, Oceana, London.

'Christianity and Political Economy in Africa', *Ecumenical Review*, 30/(1) 1978.

'Law, Laws and Public Enterprise Planning in Africa', in Y. Ghai, *Law in the Political Economy of Public Enterprise*, African Perspectives, Scandinavian Institute of African Studies, Uppsala, 1977.

Namibia: A Political Economic Survey, Institute of Development Studies (Sussex), Discussion Paper 144, 1979.

'Economic Coordination, Liberation and Development: Botswana/Namibia Perspectives', in C. Harvey (ed.), *The Political Economy of Botswana*, Heinemann, London, 1981.

Toward Socialism and Self-Reliance: Tanzania's Striving for Sustained Transition Projected, Scandinavian Institute of African Studies, Uppsala. 1977.

GREEN, J., and SEIDMAN, A., *Unity or Poverty: The Economics of Pan-Africanism*, Penguin Books, 1967.

HAHN, C. H. L., VEDDER, H., and FOURIE, L., *The Native Tribes of South West Africa*, Frank Cass and Co., London, 1966.

HARVEY, C., WALLERSTEIN, I., LEGUM, C., *et al., The Policy Debate: Study Project on External Investment in South Africa and Namibia (S.W. Africa)*, Africa Publications Trust, 1975.

HEPPLE, A., *Workers under Apartheid*, International Defence and Aid Fund, London, 1971.

HITCHCOCK, R. K., *Kalahari Cattle Posts: a Regional Study of Hunter-gatherers, Pastoralists and Agriculturalists in the Western Sandveld Region, Central District, Botswana*, Volume I and Volume II – Appendices, Government Printer, Gaborone, October 1978.

'Meeting Communal Needs in Commercial Areas: Integrated Land Use Planning and the Communal Service Center Concept', Consultancy Report No. 5, Ministry of Local Government and Lands, Gaborone, 1978.

HORRELL, M., *South-West Africa*, South African Institute of Race Relations, Johannesburg, 1967.

HOUGHTON, H. D., *The South African Economy*, Oxford University Press, 1973.

HUBRICH, H-G., and MELBER, H., *Namibia–Geschichte und Degenwart zur Frage der Dekolonisation einer Siedlerkolonie*, Informationsstelle südliches Afrika e.v., Wissenschaffliche Reihe 7, Bonn, 1977.

HUNKE, J., and ELLIS, J., *Torture–a Cancer in Our Society*, Catholic Institute for International Relations/British Council of Churches, London, 1978.

IDOC, documentation project, *Namibia Now, the Future of the Missionary Enterprise*, Rome, 1973.

IMISHUE, R. W., *South West Africa: an International Problem*, London, 1965.

INNES, D., 'Imperialism and the National Struggle in Namibia', *Review of African Political Economy*, 9, 1978.

Our Country, Our Responsibility, The Africa Bureau, London.

INNES, D., and BIENEFELD, M., 'Capital Accumulation and South Africa', *Review of African Political Economy*, 7, 1976.

INTERNATIONAL COMMISSION OF JURISTS, *Apartheid in South Africa and South West Africa*, Geneva, 1967.

KANE-BERMAN, J., *Contract Labour in South West Africa*, South African Institute of Race Relations, Johannesburg, 1972.

KATJAVIVI, P., 'They fight to free a nation', *Anti-Apartheid News*, September 1970.

KILJUNEN, K., *Alikehityksen Maailma* (The Underdeveloped World), Tammi, Helsinki, 1976.

KILJUNEN, K. (ed.), *Rotusorron kahleissa, Perustietoja eteläisen Afrikan tilanteesta* (In the chains of racial discrimination), Joensuu, 1975.

KILJUNEN, K. and INNES, D., *Namibia*, Sadankomitearihkot no. 2, Vaasa, 1980.

KILJUNEN, K. and M–L. (eds.), *Namibia – Viimeinen Sirtomaa* (Namibia – the Last Colony), Tammi, Helsinki, 1980.

KILJUNEN, K. and M–L., *Report on Visit to Namibia*, 1978 (mimeo).

KILJUNEN, M–L., 'South African Colonialism in Namibia: from Segregation to Ethnic Democracy', MA Thesis, University of Sussex, 1977.

KOOY, M., 'The Contract Labour System and the Ovambo Crisis of 1971 in South West Africa', *African Studies Review*, 1973.

KRAMER, R., and HULTMAN, T., *Tsumeb: A profile of US contribution to underdevelopment in Namibia*, Corporate Information Center, National Council of Churches, New York, 1973.

LANDIS, E., 'Namibia: The Beginnings of Disengagement', *Studies in Race and Nations*, Denver University, 2, No. 1, 1970.

LAZAR, L., *Namibia*, The Africa Bureau, London, 1972.

LEGUM, C., *Vorster's Gamble for Africa: How the Search for Peace Failed*, Rex Collings, London, 1976.

LEGUM, C., and HODGES, T., *After Angola: The war over Southern Africa*, Rex Collings, London, 1976.

LEYS, C., *Underdevelopment in Kenya: The Political Economy of Neo-Colonialism*, Heinemann, London, 1975.

LIBERATION SUPPORT MOVEMENT INFORMATION CENTER, *Interviews in Depth, Namibia, SWAPO*, Richmond, Canada, 1973.

Breaking Contract: The Story of Vinnia Ndadi, Life Histories from the Revolution, Namibia, SWAPO 1, Richmond, Canada, 1974.

LSM News, Special Issue on Namibia, No. 11–12, Richmond, Canada, 1976.

LISSNER, J. (ed.), *Namibia 1975: Hope, Fear and Ambiguity*, Lutheran World Federation, Geneva, 1976.

MANCHESTER NONVIOLENT ACTION GROUP, *Namibia, A Call to be Answered*, London, 1972.

MBAMBA, A. M., 'Namibia, Traditional and Modern Economic Sectors Development Strategies', MA Thesis, University of Gothenburg, 1975.

'Possibilities for the Future Development of Livestock Ranching in an Independent Namibia', MA Thesis, University of Sussex, 1977.

MINTY, A. S., *South Africa's Defence Strategy*, Anti-Apartheid Movement, London, 1969.

MOLTENO, R., *Africa and South Africa: the implications of South Africa's 'outward looking' policy*, The Africa Bureau, London, 1971.

MOORSOM, R., 'Colonization and Proletarianization: An Exploratory Investigation of the Formation of the Working Class in Namibia under

German and South African rule to 1945', MA Thesis, University of Sussex, 1973.

'Agriculture in Namibia', *Ideas and Action*, FAO Bulletin 126, No. 7/8, 1978.

'Underdevelopment and Class Formation: the Origin of Migrant Labour in Namibia, 1850–1915', paper delivered to the Workshop on Southern Africa, Oxford University, 1974.

'Underdevelopment, Contract Labour and Worker Consciousness in Namibia 1915–1972', *Journal of Southern African Studies*, October 1977.

'Labour Consciousness and the 1971–72 Contract Workers' Strike in Namibia', *Development and Change*, Vol. 10, 1979.

MSHONGA, S., 'Agrarian Reform Options for an Independent Namibia', discussion draft, Division of Agriculture and Land Resources, United Nations Institute for Namibia, Lusaka, 1979.

MURRAY, R., MORRIS, J., DUGARD, J., and RUBIN, N., *The Role of Foreign Firms in Namibia*, Study project on external investments in South Africa and Namibia, Africa Publications Trust, London, 1974.

NAMIBIA SUPPORT COMMITTEE, *Turnhalle: South Africa's Neo-colonial Solution for Namibia*, London, 1977.

South Africa's Sham Elections in Namibia, London, 1979.

NIXON, C., 'Land Use and Development in Namibia – A Report Prepared for UNIN', 1978.

O'CALLAGHAN, M., *Namibia: the Effects of Apartheid on Culture and Education*, UNESCO, Paris, 1977.

ODELL, M. L., *Village Area Development Programme, a Review and Evaluation of an Experiment in Integrated Rural Development*, Government Printer, Gaborone, Botswana, October 1978.

PEARSELL, C. W., 'Some Aspects of the Development of Secondary Industry in the Union of South Africa', *South African Journal of Economics*, 1937.

PENDLETON, W. C., *Katutura: A Place Where We Do Not Stay*, San Diego, University Press, 1974.

ROGERS, B., *Divide and Rule: South Africa's Bantustans*, International Defence and Aid Fund, London, 1976.

White Wealth and Black Poverty: American Investments in Southern Africa, University of Denver, Studies in Race Relations 2, Westport, Connecticut, 1976.

RUDEBECK, L., *Guinea-Bissau: A Study of Political Mobilization*, Scandinavian Institute of African Studies, Uppsala, 1974.

SCANDINAVIAN INSTITUTE OF AFRICAN STUDIES, *Nordic Statements on Apartheid*, Uppsala, 1977.

SEGAL, R., and FIRST, R. (eds.), *South West Africa: Travesty of Trust*, Deutsch, London, 1967.

SERFONTEIN, J. H. P., *Namibia?* Fokus Suid Publishers, Pretoria, 1976.

SHAMUYARIRA, N. M., *Essays on the Liberation of Southern Africa*, University of Dar es Salaam, 1975.

SIK, E., *The History of Black Africa*, Vols. I–II, Akadémiai Kiadó, Budapest, 1972.

SILVEIRA, O., *Africa South of the Sahara: Party Systems and Ideologies of Socialism*, Scandinavian Institute of African Studies, Uppsala, 1976.

SIMONS, H. J. and R. E., *Class and Colour in South Africa 1850–1950*, Penguin Books, 1969.

SIMONS, R., 'The Namibian Challenge', Paper presented at International Namibia Conference, Brussels, May 1972 (mimeo).

SIPRI, Stockholm International Peace Research Institute, *Southern Africa: The Escalation of a Conflict*, Uppsala, 1976.

SLONIM, S., *South West Africa and the United Nations: An International Mandate in Dispute*, Johns Hopkins University Press, Baltimore, 1973.

SOUTH AFRICAN CONGRESS OF TRADE UNIONS, *Apartheid in South African Industry*, London, 1971.

SOUTH AFRICAN DEPARTMENT OF INFORMATION, *Progress through Separate Development*, 1973.

SOUTHERN AFRICA DEVELOPMENT COORDINATION CONFERENCE,

'Southern Africa: Toward Economic Liberation', Arusha, 1979.

'First Steps Toward Economic Integration', London, 1979.

'Namibia', London, 1979.

SPENCE, J. E., *The Political and Military Framework*, Study Project on External Investment in South Africa and Namibia (S. W. Africa), Africa Publications Trust, 1975.

STOKKE, O., and WIDSTRAND, C. (eds.), *Southern Africa: The UN–OAU Conference, Oslo 1973*, Vols. I–II, Scandinavian Institute of African Studies, Uppsala, 1973.

SUCKLING, J., WEISS, R., and INNES, D., *The Economic Factor: Foreign Investments in South Africa*, Study Project on External Investment in South Africa and Namibia (S. W. Africa), Africa Publications Trust, 1975.

SWAPO, *Constitution of the South West Africa People's Organisation*, Lusaka, 1976.

Discussion Paper on the Constitution of Independent Namibia, Lusaka, 1975.

The Programme, Lusaka, 1960.

The Political Programme of the South West Africa People's Organisation, Lusaka, 1976.

Programme of Action, Lusaka, 1976.
Department of Information, *Massacre in Cassinga*, Lusaka, 1978.

Department of Information, *SWAPO Information: No. 1 SWAPO a Historical Profile; No. 2 The People's Resistance 1976–77; No. 3 Namibian Political Prisoners*, Lusaka, 1978.

UK and Western European Office, *Application of an 'Internationally Acceptable Solution'*, London, 1979.

THOMAS, W. H., *Economic Development in Namibia: Towards Acceptable*

Development Strategies for Independent Namibia, Kaiser, Grünewald, Munich, 1978.

THOMAS, W. H., MAREE, J., BEINART, W. *et al., The Conditions of the Black Worker*, Study Project on External Investment in South Africa and Namibia (S.W. Africa), Africa Publications Trust, 1975.

TÖTEMEYER, G., *South West Africa, Namibia*, Fokus Suid Publishers, Pretoria, 1977.

TROUP, F., *South Africa: an Historical Introduction*, Penguin Books, 1975.

UMOZURIKE, U. O., 'International Law and Self-Determination in Namibia', *Journal of Modern African Studies*, 8, 1970.

UNITED NATIONS YOUTH AND STUDENT ASSOCIATION OF THE UK, *Namibia File*, London, 1974.

VAITSOS, C. V., *Intercountry Income Distribution and Transnational Enterprises*, Oxford University Press, 1974.

VÄRYNEN, R., *Interdependence vs. Self-Reliance: Two approaches to International Economic Relations,* Research Reports No. 16, Tampere Peace Research Institute, 1978.

'South Africa: A coming nuclear weapon power?' *Current Research on Peace and Violence*, 1977.

VEDDER, H., *South West Africa in Early Times*, Oxford University Press, 1938.

VIGNE, R., *A Dwelling Place of Our Own: The Story of the Namibian Nation*, International Defence and Aid Fund, London, 1973.

WALSHE, P., *Black Nationalism in South Africa: a Short History*, Spro-Cas Publications, Ravan Press, Johannesburg, 1973.

WELLINGTON, J., *South West Africa and its Human Issues*, Oxford University Press, 1967.

Southern Africa – A Geographical Study, 2 vols., Cambridge, 1955.

WILSON, M., and THOMPSON, L. (eds.), *The Oxford History of South Africa*, Vols. I and II, Oxford University Press, 1969.

WILY, L., 'Settlement as a Strategy of Securing Land for Nomads: an examination of the Botswana Government's current programme for settling the Kalahari San', *Pastoral Network Paper* 7c, Agricultural Administration Unit, Overseas Development Institute, London, 1979.

WOLPE, H., 'Capitalism and cheap labour power in South Africa: from segregation to apartheid', *Economy and Society*, 1, 4, 1972.

WORLD COUNCIL OF CHURCHES, *Kunene Dam Scheme*, Geneva, 1971.

'Second List (revised) of corporations investing in Southern Africa', Geneva, 1973.

Namibia – the Struggle for Liberation, Geneva, 1972.

Newspapers and Periodicals

Africa, London.

Africa Contemporary Record, London.

African Business, London.

Africa South of the Sahara, London.

The African Communist, London.

African Development, London.

Anti-Apartheid News, London.

African Studies Review, Johannesburg.

Current Events in Namibia, SWAPO, Dar es Salaam.

Current Research on Peace and Violence, Tampere, Finland.

Fact Paper on Southern Africa, International Defence and Aid Fund, London.

Financial Mail, Johannesburg.

Financial Times, London.

Focus (on political repression in Southern Africa), International Defence and Aid Fund, London.

Guardian, London.

Information Comments, SWAPO of Namibia, Stockholm.

Journal of African History, London.

Journal of Southern African Studies, Oxford.

Kommunikee, Anti-apartheids beweging, Amsterdam.

Namibia (formerly *Namibia News*), SWAPO, Lusaka.

Namibia Bulletin, United Nations, New York.

Namibia News, Fortnightly summary of news reports, SWAPO, London.

The Namibian Review, A journal of Contemporary South West African Affairs, Stockholm.

Namibia Today, SWAPO, Lusaka.

New African Yearbook, London.

Notes and Documents, Centre Against Apartheid, Department of Political and Security Council Affairs, New York.

Objective: Justice, United Nations Office of Public Information, New York.

Rand Daily Mail, Johannesburg.

Reports, Toronto Committee for the Liberation of Southern Africa, Toronto.

Review of African Political Economy, London.

South African Labour Bulletin, Durban.

The Star, Johannesburg.

Survey of Race Relations in South Africa, South African Institute of Race Relations, Johannesburg.

Windhoek Advertiser, Windhoek.

Windhoek Observer, Windhoek.

Workers Unity, Organ of the South African Congress of Trade Unions, London.

X-Ray on Southern Africa, Africa Trust, London.

Index

3

2